Summary of Contents

1. Introducing Dreamweaver MX
2. The Dreamweaver Interface
3. Begining Layout
4. Layout with Templates
5. Cascading Style Sheets
6. Creating Content for our Site
7. The Code Window
8. Introducing Dynamic Content
9. Using PHP and Apache
10. Further PHP
11. PHP/MySQL: The Real Dynamic Duo
12. Secure Login and Registration
13. Case Study : Dynamic Image Viewer
    Appendix : Dreamweaver Extensions

Foundation Dreamweaver MX

Craig Grannell
Todd Marks
George McLachlan
Matt Stephens
Jerome Turner

Foundation Dreamweaver MX

© 2002 Apress

Originally published by friends of ED in 2002

All rights reserved. No part of this book may be reproduced, stored in a retrieval system or transmitted in any form or by any means, without the prior written permission of the publisher, except in the case of brief quotations embodied in critical articles or reviews.

The authors and publisher have made every effort in the preparation of this book to ensure the accuracy of the information. However, the information contained in this book is sold without warranty, either express or implied. Neither the authors, friends of ED nor its dealers or distributors will be held liable for any damages caused or alleged to be caused either directly or indirectly by this book.

First Printed October 2002

Trademark Acknowledgements

friends of ED has endeavored to provide trademark information about all the companies and products mentioned in this book by the appropriate use of capitals. However, friends of ED cannot guarantee the accuracy of this information.

Published by friends of ED

ISBN 978-1-59059-197-0   ISBN 978-1-4302-5213-9 (eBook)
DOI 10.1007/978-1-4302-5213-9

Foundation Dreamweaver MX

Credits

Authors
Craig Grannell
Todd Marks
George McLachlan
Matt Stephens
Jerome Turner

Additional Material
Kristian Besley
Vibha Roy

Technical Reviewers
Alexandra Blackburn
Vibha Roy
Jan Badger
Jake Smith
Ben Hyland
Steve McCormick
Kevin Stacey
Phil Sherry

Index
Fiona Murray

Proof Readers
Victoria Blackburn
Cathy Succamore

Commissioning Editors
Luke Harvey
Matthew Knight

Editors
Alan McCann
Paul Thewlis
Matthew Knight

Author Agents
Chris Matterface

Project Managers
Vicky Idiens
Simon Brand

Managing Editor
Chris Hindley

Graphic Editors
Matt Clark
Chantal Hepworth

Cover Design
Katy Freer

ABOUT THE AUTHORS

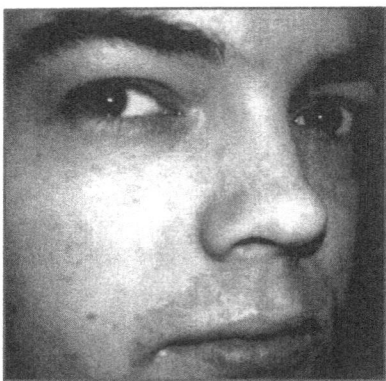

Craig Grannell
www.snubcommunications.com.

Craig was trained in the fine arts, but later became immersed in the world of digital media, showing videos and multimedia pieces at leading European media festivals. The web caught his attention in 1995, and he's been working with it ever since; along with writing for several web and design-related magazines, he finds time to create web sites for the likes of 2000 AD, work on his eclectic Veer Musikal Unit project, and occasionally delve back into the world of video. Project links, downloads, rants, movies and dancing trees can be found at his web site, Snub Communications.

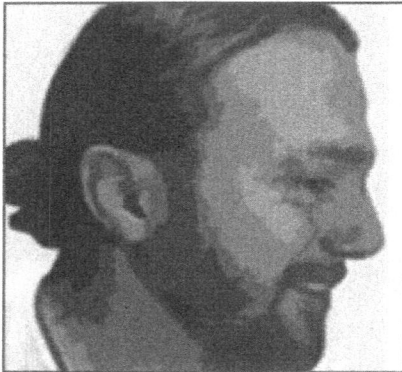

Todd Marks
www.mindgrub.com

Todd is currently a freelance developer, instructor, and author. In 2000 Todd moved from teaching Mathematics and Computer Science in the public sector to become VP of Research and Development at digitalorganism (www.digitalorganism.com). Since then Todd has worked extensively with ActionScript, PHP, Lingo, and numerous other development languages, placing cutting edge code in several projects (including digitalorganism's showcase site.) Todd's contributions have earned three Flash Film Festival nominations, Macromedia Site of the Day, two Addy Awards, and several educational partnerships. Todd is a Macromedia Certified Developer, Designer, and Subject Matter Expert, and has contributed to several books about Flash.

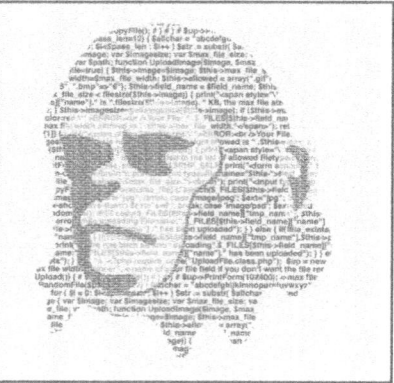

George McLachlan

George lives in Glasgow, Scotland and is a freelance PHP developer. He was one of the beta testers for Dreamweaver MX, and also one of the developers for a third party extension called PHPMXDB, which aims to provide additional database support for PHP within MX. He is a member of Team Macromedia and is a regular contributor in the Macromedia newsgroups. George is a strong supporter of Open Source and, when time permits, he tries to provide feedback to the PHP QA team.

Matt Stephens

www.deviantart.com

Born in 1982 and raised in Dallas, Matt Stephens is currently attending the University of Texas at Austin, studying "Convergent Medias". In high school, Matt started wastedyouth.org to teach people how to use Photoshop, Dreamweaver, Flash, and other programs. Later, he started DeviantArt.com, which has grown into the largest digital art community in the world. He continues to help artists and programmers on a daily basis, and enjoys getting e-mails from fans and friends.

Jerome Turner

Jerome comes from Leighton Buzzard where his first cinematic experience was watching Tom and Jerry beat the hell out of each other on his parents' wood chip wallpaper. He studied Art at Bedford College where he learnt that photography was cool because you could visit the Fine Art department whilst your films were drying. Following this, he traveled to Exeter, where he wouldn't touch the cider but did wander off with a degree in Media Arts/Visual Arts.

Since then, he's moved to Poole with his long-suffering partner Claire and worked on a number of film and video productions as a production assistant, camera operator, script writer, boom operator, 1st AD, runner, producer, and director. When he's very bored he goes to the boating lake to film Canada geese.

Table of Contents

Welcome　　　　1

　　The aim of this book 1
　　What you'll need 3
　　Macs and PCs 3
　　Server technologies: PHP and MySQL 4
　　Conventions 4
　　Download files 5
　　Support – we're here to help 6

Introducing Dreamweaver MX　　　　9

　　What is Dreamweaver? 10
　　　　Dreamweaver settings 10
　　The case study 20
　　　　Brainstorming 21
　　　　Visual inspiration 23
　　　　Design 25
　　　　Structure 26
　　　　Content 29
　　　　The case study – final designs 31

The Dreamweaver Interface　　　　39

　　　　Organizing site assets 40
　　　　　　The Site panel 45
　　　　The Dreamweaver interface 47

Beginning Layout　　　　63

　　　　Splash pages 64
　　　　　　GIFs and JPEGs 69
　　　　The splash page 71
　　　　Finishing design touches 84
　　　　Adding functionality to our splash page 88

Layout with Templates　　　　95

　　　　Layout types 96
　　　　　　Plain text 97
　　　　　　Frames 98
　　　　　　Layers 104
　　　　　　Tables 107
　　　　　　Cascading Style Sheets 112
　　　　The case study 129
　　　　　　Page defaults 132
　　　　　　Planning the layout 135

Cascading Style Sheets — 133

 Checking our visual ...134
 The main table ...134
 The navigation ...136
 The gray bars ...144

Creating Content for our Site — 151

 Using Form Objects ...170
 When to start using other file formats ...175
  Flash Files ...175
  QuickTime files ...184

The Code Window — 189

 Code preferences ...190
  Code coloring ...190
  Formatting ...192
  Code hints ...193
  Code rewriting ...194
  Internal preferences ...195
 Working with code ...196
  Adding tags ...197
  The tag editor ...202
 Our case study site ...218
  The contact page ...218
  Dogs in Cars ...222
  Further validation ...229
  Loose ends ...230

Introducing Dynamic Content — 235

 How do dynamic sites work? ...236
 Installation ...239
 Installing PHP and Apache on a PC ...239
  Troubleshooting tips ...243
 Switching on PHP in Mac OS X ...246
 Using PHP in Dreamweaver ...256
  Troubleshooting ...260

Using PHP and Apache — 263

 An introduction to PHP ...269
  Variables ...270
  Forms and PHP ...276
  Conditional Statements ...279
  Logical operators ...282
 Guest books ...287

Processing the form 288

Further PHP **297**

Looping 298
Arrays 300
Cookies 304

PHP/MySQL: The Real Dynamic Duo **313**

Installing, configuring and running MySQL on Win32 314
    The MySQL daemon 315
    MySQL monitor 317
    Testing, testing 318
Installing and setting up MySQL for Mac OS X 319
    Instructions for Mac OS 10.1.x and 10.2.x 321
    MySQL security 322
Preparing MySQL 322
Downloading phpMyAdmin 326
Configuring phpMyAdmin 327
Building a PHP application 330
    Planning our database table 331
Testing our form by retrieving information 339

Secure Login and Registration **347**

    PHP coding conventions used in this chapter 348
Working with PHP sessions 349
Building our Registration / Login application 356
Validation 359
    Security issues 364
Testing our application 373

Case Study: Dynamic Image Viewer **377**

Making things modular 379
Creating the three main PHP files 382
iFrames 390
Databases 402
imageViewer.php 405

Dreamweaver Extensions **417**

Where to find Extensions 421

Welcome

Macromedia Dreamweaver stands at the apogee of web design software. Once dismissed as a simple HTML editor, Dreamweaver has evolved into a complex powerhouse of web creation tools that no one serious about web design can do without.

As well as offering the visual design tools for which it became famous, Dreamweaver now offers an unrivalled package of web development tools. This began with the release of Dreamweaver UltraDev, which gave designers the opportunity to combine their visual talents with cutting edge dynamic content technologies.

With the release of the MX family, Macromedia have combined Dreamweaver and Dreamweaver UltraDev into one product, recognizing a seismic shift in web design trends. Where once static pages ruled the world, dynamic web applications – sites that interact with users and return changing information from a database – have taken over. People are fully aware of what the web is capable of, and static content is no longer good enough.

If you're scared by that thought, don't be. Firstly, dynamic sites give you far more potential for creative design. Secondly, Dreamweaver MX makes integrating database elements with sites incredibly easy.

Dreamweaver MX is the perfect choice for designers who want to create great looking dynamic web sites. It's a fantastic visual design tool, with support for powerful server-side technologies. Now you *can* have it all: and this book will show you how.

The aim of this book

This book aims to give you a thorough foundation in the use of all of Dreamweaver's features, starting at simple layout tasks and ending with a fully dynamic database-driven site example.

We'll start by introducing you to the case study that we'll be using in the first seven chapters of the book, and the planning process that needs to take place before you open Dreamweaver. We'll go on to introduce you to layout techniques and the different options that Dreamweaver provides, the creation and use of templates and cascading style sheets, and the use of code in Dreamweaver.

Then, in the second half of the book (**Chapter 8** onwards), we'll move on to look at the database side of Dreamweaver. We'll show you how to install the Apache web server, PHP, and a MySQL database. We'll then teach you how to combine these technologies with Dreamweaver to develop some exciting database-driven dynamic applications that will take your web design skills to another level.

Introduction

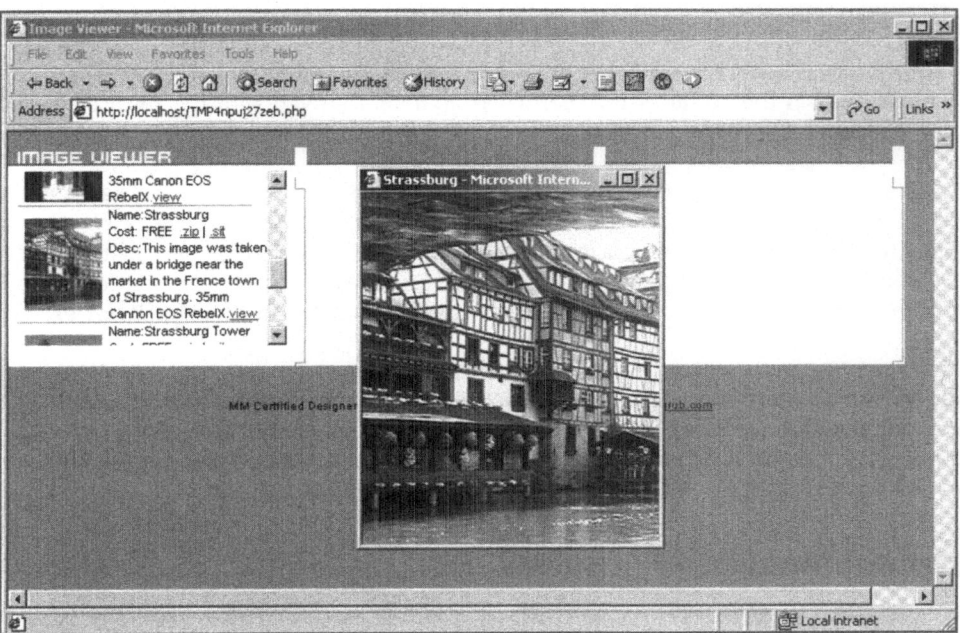

The final chapter brings together everything you've learned with the creation of a complex dynamic e-commerce application. You'll be amazed at how well developed your Dreamweaver skills have become by the time you reach the end of the book. By then, you won't need instructions from us any more, you'll be able to confidently set about building dynamic web sites on your own!

We don't believe in books that show principles using theoretical examples that would never hack it in the real world, so both case studies are real-world projects that demonstrate professional techniques.

What you'll need

We do expect you to know your way around your operating system and be comfortable with creating folders, renaming files, and so on. For the exercises, you'll either need a PC with a Windows 95 or newer operating system or a Mac with an OS X or newer operating system. You'll also need an Internet connection if you want to download some of the source files.

Apart from that, you don't need a great deal - this is a book that makes no assumptions. We'll be starting at the beginning, and giving you full instructions at every step of the way. If things do go wrong, then friends of ED offers free and comprehensive technical support for all of our books, so help is just an e-mail away (see the support section of this introduction for contact details).

Macs and PCs

It has been an accusation frequently thrown at Macs that they just can't handle database-driven web design. The last nail in the coffin of that particular argument arrived with the release of OS X, which makes using dynamic content ... (whisper it) no more difficult than on a PC.

There may be no difference in the difficulty levels, but there is a difference in the way you have to set up a few things, due to the rather different structure of OS X and Windows. We've provided full instructions for everything that we do in this book, and that includes full sets of both Mac and PC instructions in the places where things differ, so you're catered for whichever platform you're using. (Go and take a look at the two sets of instructions for installing PHP in **Chapter 8**, for example.)

When friends of ED produced Foundation Dreamweaver UltraDev 4, we caused a few howls of anguish from devoted Mac-owners by using ASP code for the examples throughout the book. Whilst ASP is still an incredibly popular and powerful technology, it's limited to one platform, and we do try to respond to feedback from readers. As you'll see from the next section, Dreamweaver MX allows a true cross-platform alternative that we're only too happy to take.

Server technologies: PHP and MySQL

As we've just said, Dreamweaver MX has become the first version of Dreamweaver to incorporate support for the PHP scripting language and MySQL, the popular database solution. More details on these later on in the book (starting in **Chapter 8**), but a couple of important points to put your mind at rest:

- Both of these products, and the utilities we'll be using with them, are available for personal and commercial use entirely free of charge.

- We will be providing exhaustive guides to the installation and setting up of these on your machines.

Even if you plan to use **ColdFusion** or **ASP** with Dreamweaver eventually, don't abandon ship here. The concepts behind creating dynamic pages are exactly the same no matter what technology you're using, as are the processes for setting up a connection between Dreamweaver MX and a database, so you'll still learn a lot. ASP and ColdFusion also have some very useful reference material included as part of your Dreamweaver installation.

We chose PHP/MySQL because:

- PHP, MySQL, and the third party applications we use are 100% **free**.

- PHP, MySQL, and the third party applications we use are 100% **cross-platform**.

- PHP and MySQL are widely used technologies that perform well in comparison with competitors, and have a thriving community of users.

Introduction

Conventions

We've tried to keep this book as clear and easy to follow as possible, so we've only used a few layout styles:

- When you come across an important word or phrase, it will be in **bold** type.

- We'll use a different font to emphasize phrases that appear on the screen, code, filenames, what to hit on the KEYBOARD, and hyperlinks (e.g. www.friendsofed.com)

- Menu commands are written in the form Menu > Sub-menu > Sub-menu.

- When there's some information we think is really important, we'll highlight it like this:

  > *This is very important stuff – make sure you're paying attention!*

- Worked exercises are laid out like this:

  1. Open up Dreamweaver

  2. Save your file as form.php

  3. and so on

- When the code we're showing you is too long to fit onto one line, we've used a code continuation character like this ➥ to show you that the code is still on the same line in Dreamweaver. If you see a ➥, don't go hitting that ENTER key just yet.

Download files

We've provided all the source files and finished versions for the exercises that you'll work through in the book for download at www.friendsofed.com. Do whatever you like with them, but when things go wrong with your version, take advantage of the ability to compare your file with the finished file before giving up – it often helps. The Print Code option in the File menu in Dreamweaver can be especially useful here – print out your version and the download version, then sit down with a cup of coffee and mark up any differences with a big red pen.

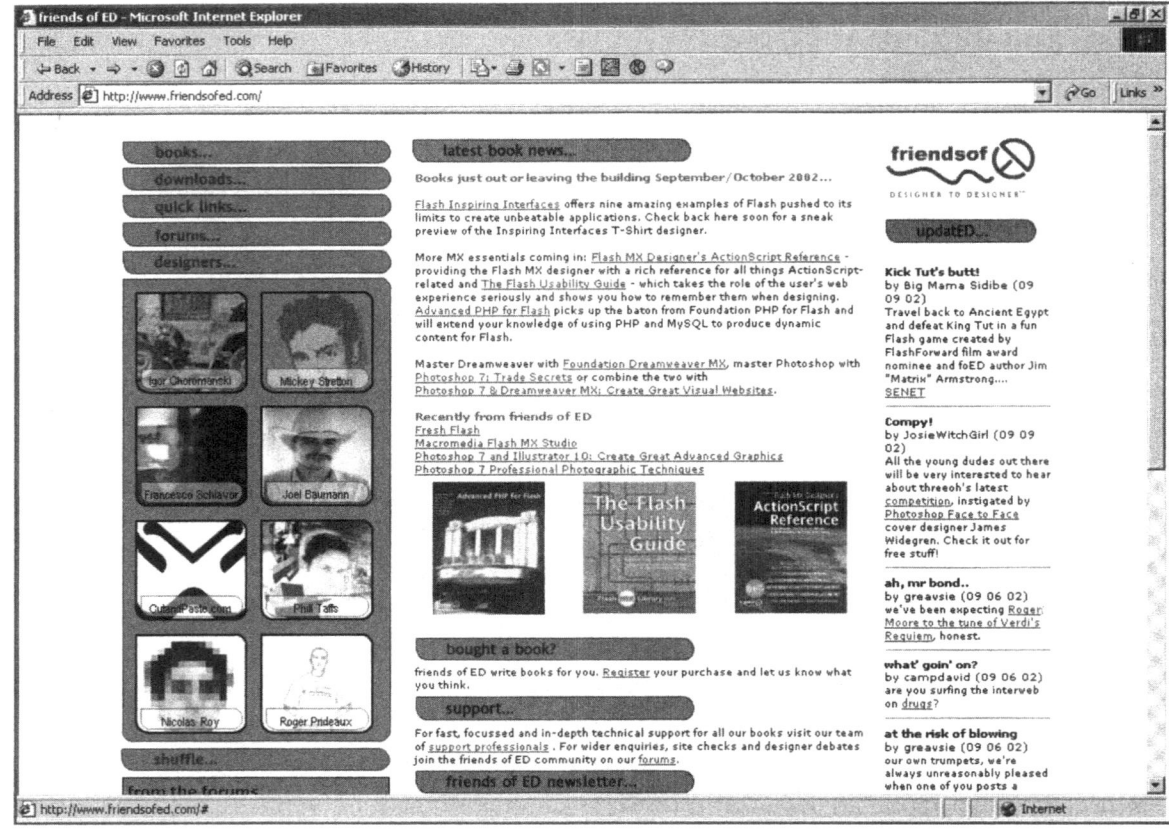

Support – we're here to help

All books from friends of ED aim to be easy to follow and error-free. However, if you do run into problems, don't hesitate to get in touch – our support is fast, friendly, and free.

You can reach us at support@friendsofED.com, quoting the last for digits of the ISBN in the subject of the e-mail (that's 4054 for those of you too lazy to turn over to the back cover). If you're having technical problems with a specific file that you've created from an exercise, it can sometimes help to include a copy of that file with your mail.

Even if our dedicated support team are unable to solve your problem immediately, your queries will be passed onto the people who put the book together – the editors and authors – to solve. All foED authors help with the support on their books, and will either directly mail people with answers, or (more usually) send their response to an editor to pass on.

We'd love to hear from you, whether it's to request future books, ask about friends of ED, or tell us about the sites you went on to create after you read this book.

Introduction

> *To tell us a bit about yourself and make comments about the book, why not fill out the reply card at the back and send it to us! Or register online at* www.friendsofed.com/replycard.asp

If your enquiry concerns an issue not directly related to any book content, then the best place for these types of questions is our message board at:

http://friendsofed.infopop.net/2/OpenTopic

Here, you'll find a variety of designers talking about what they do and how they do it. They should be able to provide some ideas and suggestions.

Alternatively, for news, more books, sample chapters, downloads, author interviews and more, just send your browser to www.friendsofED.com.

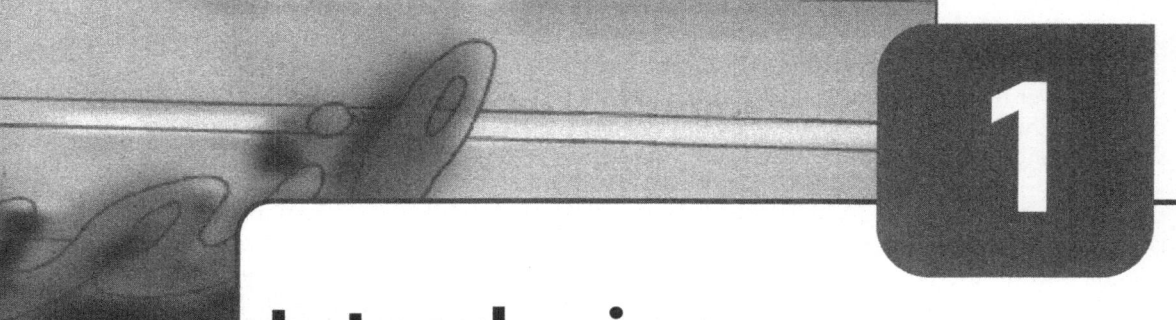

Introducing Dreamweaver MX

What we'll cover in this chapter

- *Introducing Dreamweaver MX*
- *Creating our first Dreamweaver web page*
- *Planning our case study*

Foundation Dreamweaver MX

What is Dreamweaver?

Dreamweaver is a tool for creating web pages, but then you already knew that. What's less well known is how far this particular application has come; there's a lot more to Dreamweaver than a few HTML shortcuts, and this book aims to take you to the depths of this versatile program.

Dreamweaver has always featured high on the list of essential web design software skills, but Dreamweaver MX has made itself even more desirable for two reasons. Firstly, it now offers unrivalled integration with the other members of Macromedia's MX Studio, which groups together ColdFusion, Fireworks, Flash, and Freehand. Secondly, and for the first time, Macromedia have merged the functionality of Dreamweaver 4's companion product Dreamweaver UltraDev with Dreamweaver. This gives access to an unprecedented variety of dynamic options, where information and content can change. The web is increasingly dependent on dynamic content, and it's no longer good enough to restrict dynamic options to just one set of users; everyone needs the functionality.

We'll be starting from scratch and assuming nothing. Those of you used to an older version of Dreamweaver, don't worry – we'll cover all of the changes from earlier versions.

> *If you look at the start-up dialog, Dreamweaver MX is labeled as 'Dreamweaver 6'. You'll spend rather a long time looking for Dreamweaver 5, though – the last version was 4, and Macromedia have simply brought Dreamweaver (and Fireworks) forward two versions to standardize version numbers across the MX family.*

Dreamweaver settings

You've probably already sneaked in for a quick look before you purchased this book, but if you're opening Dreamweaver MX for the first time, you'll be presented with a couple of choices. If you're on a PC, then the first choice is this window (it doesn't appear if you're using a Mac):

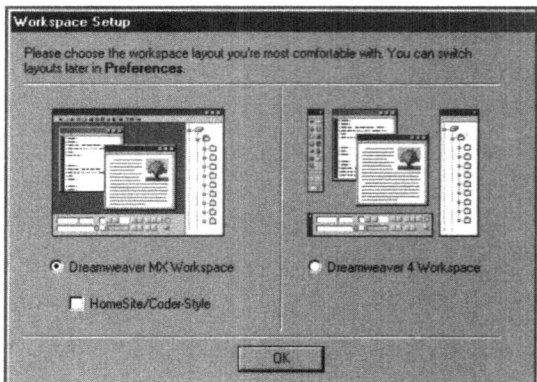

Here, you want to keep the default options as shown (Dreamweaver MX Workspace, with HomeSite/Coder-Style unchecked). If you think that you set Dreamweaver up differently originally, wait

Introducing Dreamweaver MX

until you're in Dreamweaver, go to Edit > Preferences, and select Change Workspace, as shown in the screenshot below, to get the same dialog box up.

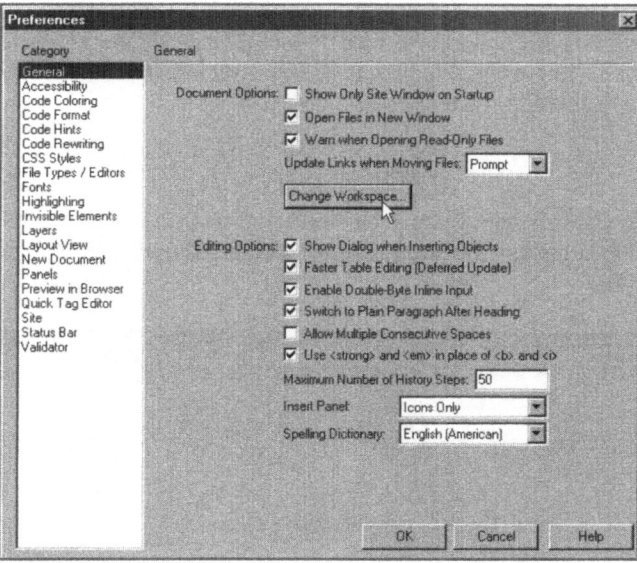

You may also see a dialog box like the one pictured below. Feel free to go off and read some of the Macromedia information, but close the window when you're ready to come back to this exercise. (You can bring this dialog back up any time you want with Help > Welcome.)

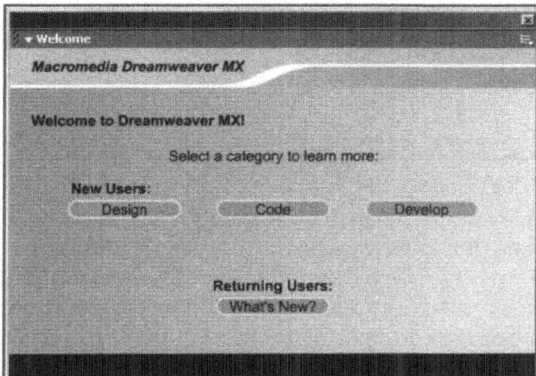

Your first Dreamweaver MX web page

As this is the first chapter, it seems only right to give you a taste of the power that Dreamweaver MX offers. This is just to give you an idea of what's possible, so don't worry if we don't go into exhaustive detail about all of the features we're using – that'll come in the following chapters.

Foundation Dreamweaver MX

There are four very small images that we use in this exercise, available for download from the friends of ED website. Place them on your hard drive before you begin (check the introduction for more details if you're not sure).

1. With the application open you'll see a large Document window in the center of the screen, titled 'Untitled Document'. To start with, make sure that the Show Design View button at the top left of your screen is selected, as shown:

   You can also maximize the Document window (the one that's called Untitled Document (Untitled 1)) by clicking on the maximize button. This should give you a clear white space to work with, like this:

   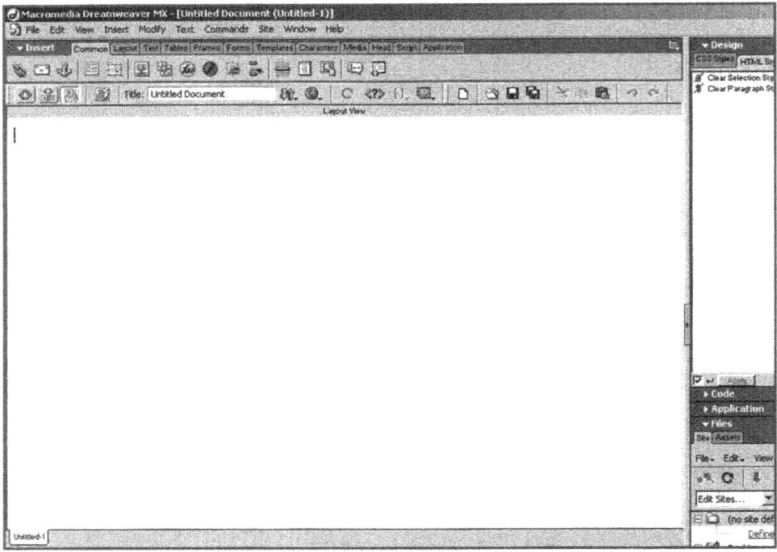

2. Select Site > New Site from the menus. What we're going to do here is simply set up a directory for Dreamweaver to keep our files in, just as if we were setting up a directory to keep all our word processor documents in. There are some pretty involved options in the following process, but don't worry – we'll come back to them later. If the dialog box doesn't appear as shown, then make sure that you've selected the Basic tab at the top left of the box.

Introducing Dreamweaver MX

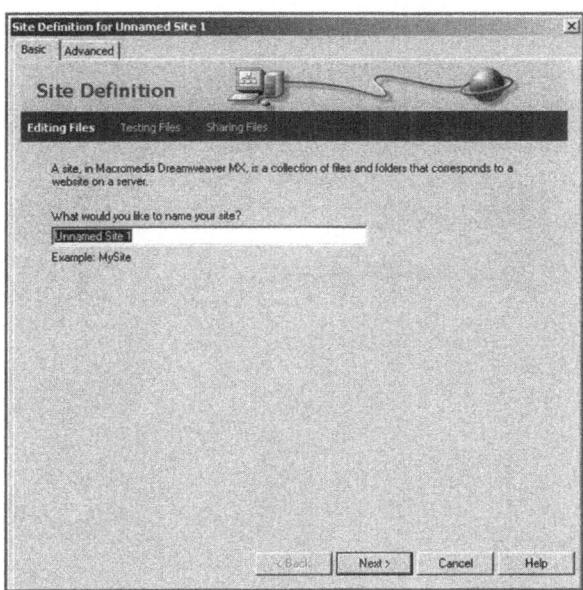

3. Give the site a suitable name (for example, first dw site), and hit Next. The next page will ask whether you want to work with a server technology such as ColdFusion, ASP.NET, ASP, JSP, or PHP. We'll be doing this in the second half of the book, but for the moment select No, and move onto the next screen.

4. At the next screen, select the first bulleted option, Edit local copies on my machine, then upload to server when ready, and enter a directory on your hard drive to store your files in:

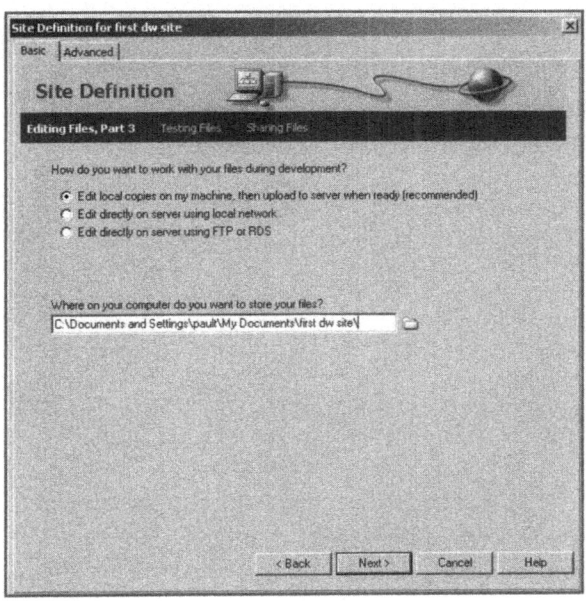

Foundation Dreamweaver MX

5. The next page asks you how you connect to your remote server. Select None from the first drop-down menu, and move onto the next page.

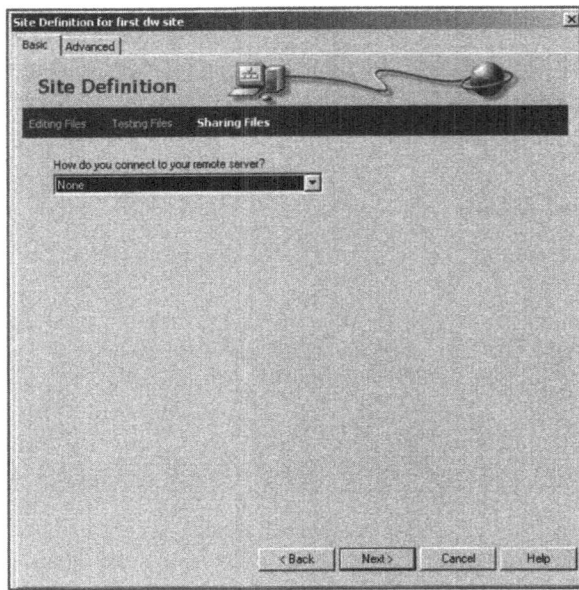

This will give you a quick summary of your choices, which you can OK and move on. You should be back to the white screen, but with the name and the directory you chose displayed under the Site tab in the Files panel on the right of your screen, as shown in the screenshot below

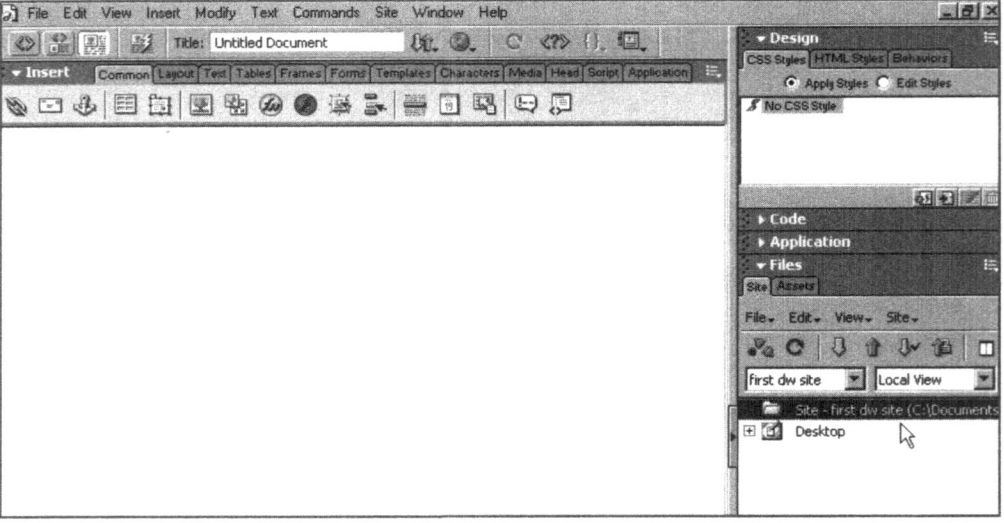

Having set up the site's Root directory, let's set up a quick page to illustrate how the basic web design process works in Dreamweaver. Don't worry that this doesn't relate to your own ideas about your site or our case study (beginning later in this chapter), we just want to get a look and feel for the application.

Introducing Dreamweaver MX

6. Choose File > New. Select Page Designs (Accessible) from the General tab on the left, and select Text: Journal Entry under the Page Designs menu that appears on the right. Click Create.

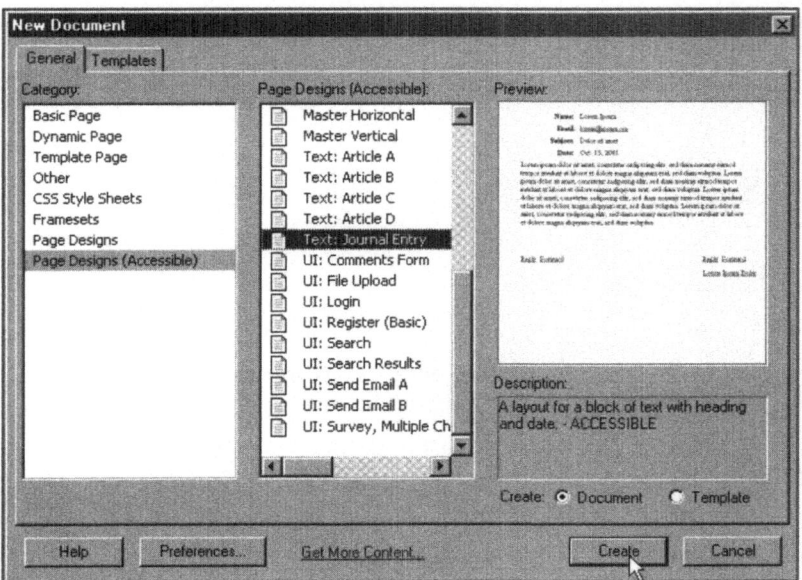

You'll see a load of Latin appear on your screen, as someone at Macromedia obviously thought this would be a great way to provide 'placeholding' text for you to replace with your own. What you've done is load up one of the many standard layouts (you saw how long the list was!) that Macromedia have thoughtfully provided with Dreamweaver. In this case, it's a journal layout, so let's customize this a little.

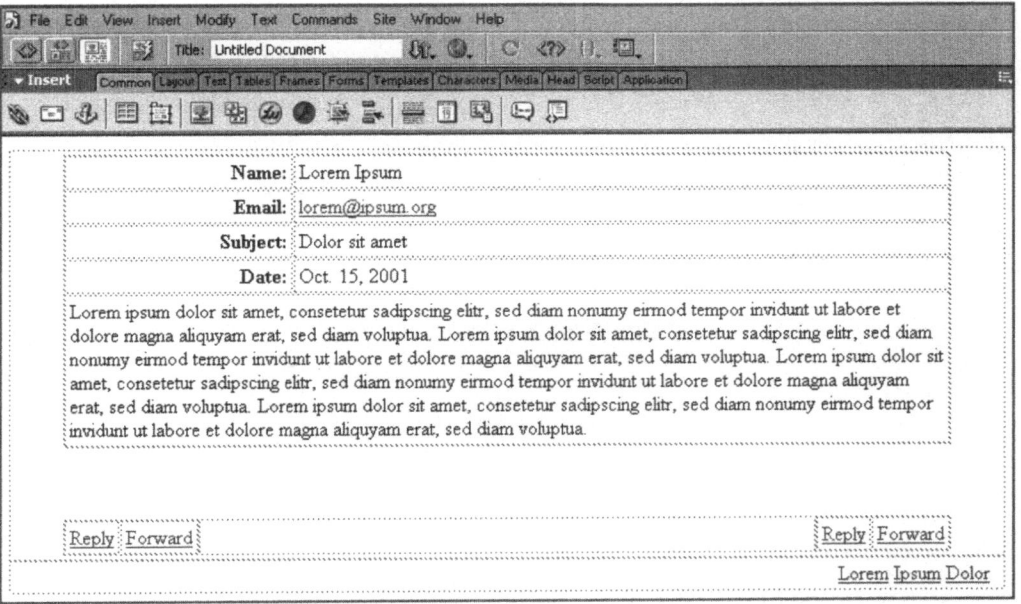

7. Go to View > Table View and select Standard View (if it isn't already checked). With your mouse, highlight Name at the top left, and press DELETE. You'll find that you can now type in replacement text where Name used to be. We're going for a journal feel here, so I've decided that my first field will be Location:. You can do the same as me, or come up with something more imaginative.

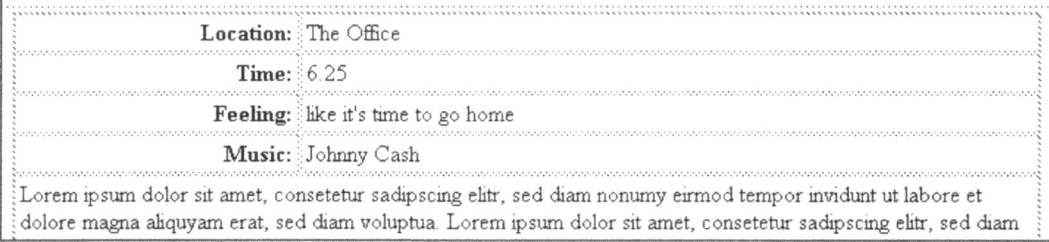

8. Do the same for the other boxes, and enter some appropriate text. You can tab through the boxes just as you would cells in a database if you get tired of using the mouse.

> Make sure that you delete the lorem@ipsum.org text before entering new text. If you just type over it, Dreamweaver will continue to think that it's an e-mail address and underline it accordingly.

9. Use the same technique to add some appropriate journal text in the big area underneath. Click outside the box, and it will shrink to fit the text you've just entered. When you're finished, use File > Save to save this as `journal1.html`.

10. In the little boxes underneath the text, carefully highlight all the underlined words (Reply, Forward, Reply, Forward, Lorem, Ipsum, and Dolor) one by one with your mouse, and press DELETE each time to remove them.

11. Now carefully place your mouse cursor in the gray box furthest to the left. Go to Insert > Image, and select `write.jpg` - the first of the four small image files that are available for download for this chapter from the friends of ED website.

12. Dreamweaver will ask you if you wish to copy the image to your root directory now. Select Yes.

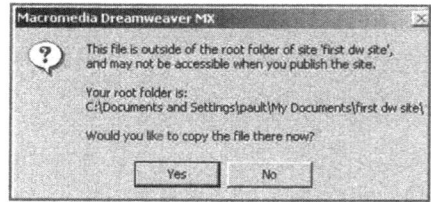

Introducing Dreamweaver MX 1

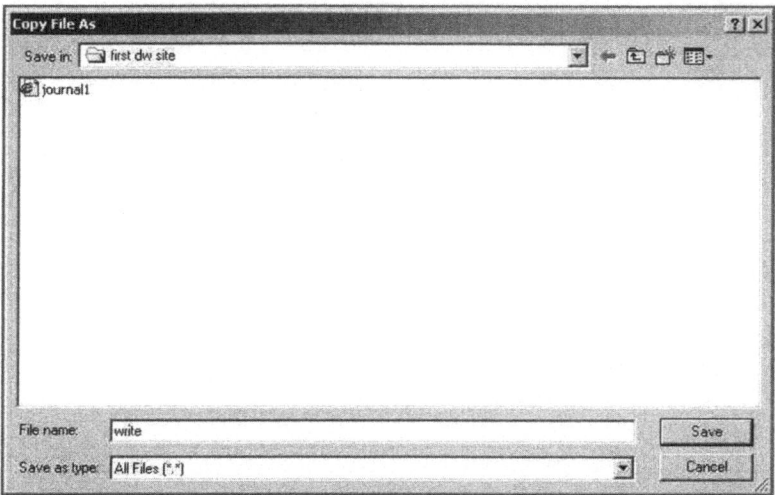

13. In the box just next to this, insert home.jpg, and in the box on the far right-hand side, insert rightarrow.jpg. Copy both images to your Root directory, as you did with write.jpg. If you check the Files panel you'll notice that the image files have been added to your root folder in the list of site files under the Site tab (this might take a moment, so be patient).

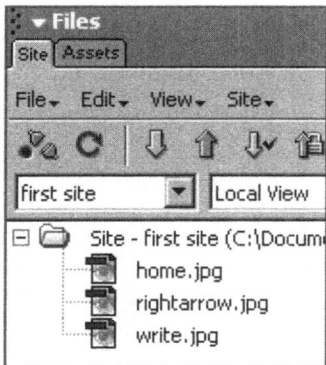

14. Select write.jpg by clicking on the image and take a look in the Properties bar at the bottom of your screen. If you can't see this, pick Properties from the Window menu, making sure the bar is fully opened.

15. In the Link box, enter mailto:youremailaddress@wherever.com. This will mean that a visitor to your page can e-mail you when they click on the write.jpg image.

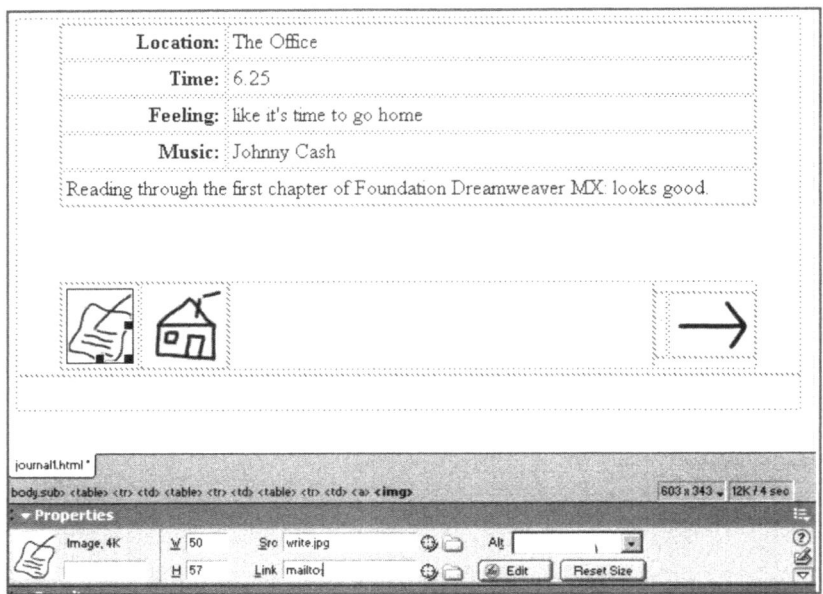

16. Select the Home icon by clicking on the image, and, in the Link box, enter the URL of your home page, if you have one – if not, enter any other web address that you feel a particular affinity for (make sure you include the **http://** prefix). This will allow visitors to navigate to your home page by clicking on the home.jpg graphic.

17. Select File > Save, and save your file again. Now, alter the text on screen to reflect another journal entry, and save it as journal2.html.

18. Open journal1.html again by double-clicking on it in the Site tab on the right-hand side of your screen.

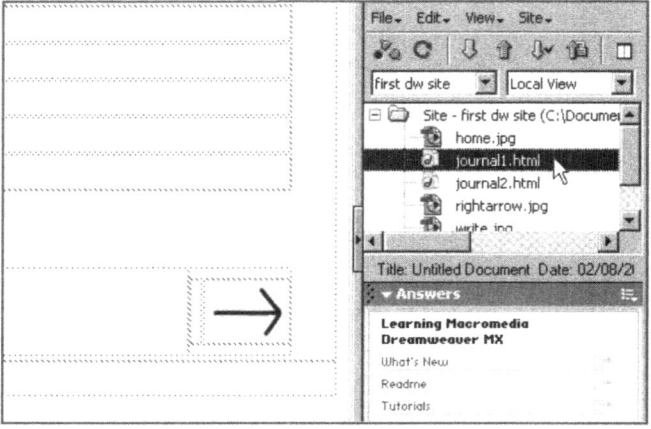

19. Select the right arrow graphic, and enter `journal2.html` into the Link box, as we did with your home page URL.

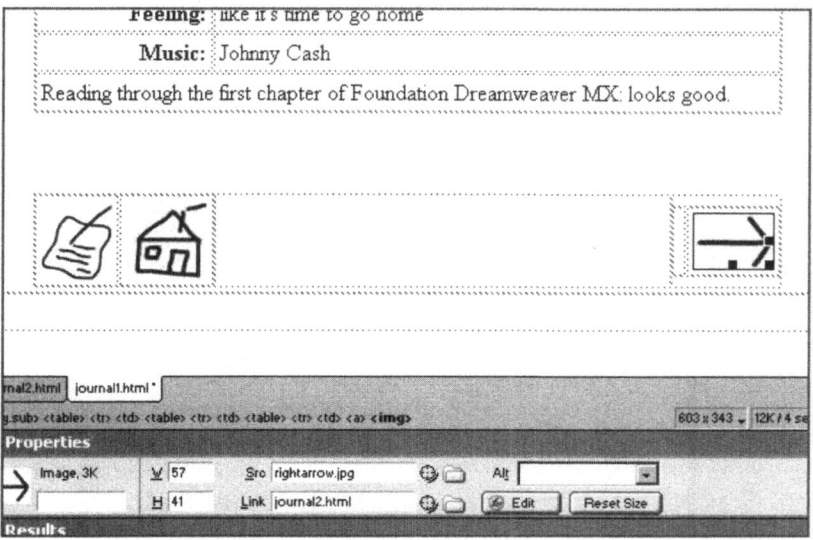

20. At the bottom left of your screen, you should see that there's a tag for both of the files you have open: `journal1.html`, and `journal2.html`. Select `journal2.html` using either this, or the Window menu.

21. In journal2.htm, select the empty box on the right-hand side, and import the leftarrow.jpg picture into it. In the Link box, enter `journal1.html`.

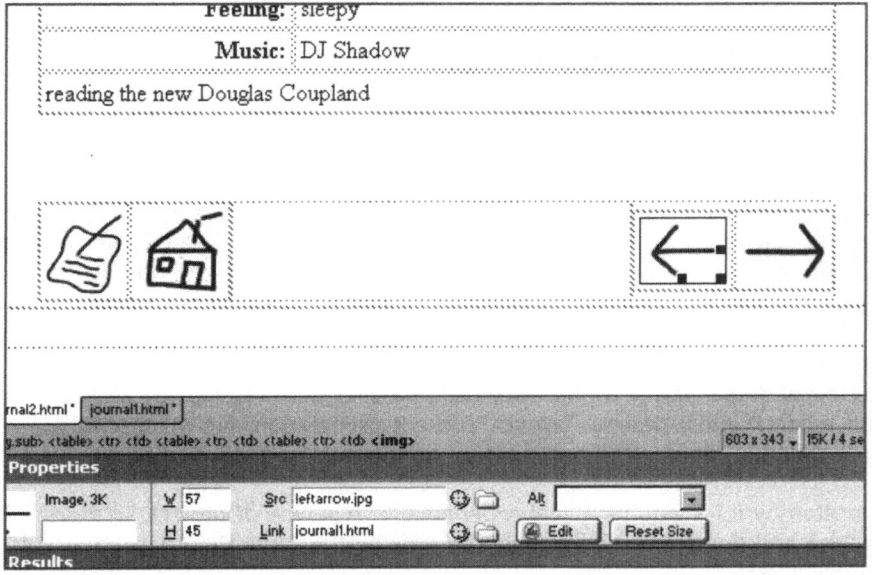

22. Save both pages (this is a very important step, so don't miss it out!).

That's it! In a short space of time, you've just created a fully usable set of Dreamweaver web pages.

Press F12 to test the pages in your browser. You should be able to navigate from page 1 to 2 and back again with ease.

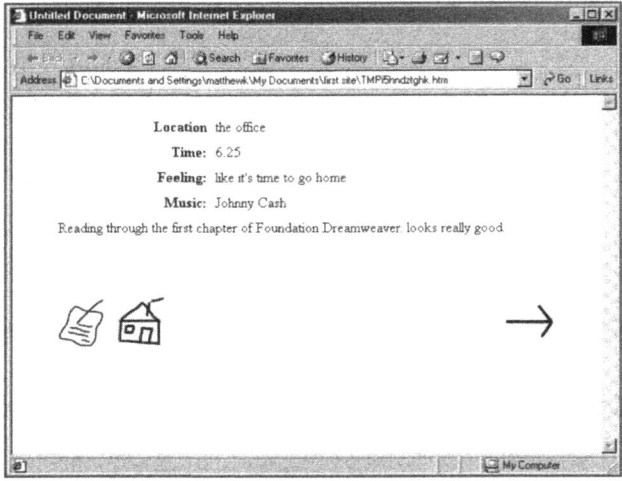

If you don't see anything when you press F12, it's because Dreamweaver hasn't automatically detected your browser. This doesn't happen very often, but to fix it, go to File > Preview in Browser > Edit Browser List, *and use the + icon to locate the executable file that opens your browser. We'll be looking at this in greater detail in the next chapter.*

The case study

So now we've had a bit of a play, what's the best way to show you the capabilities of a tool like Dreamweaver MX? We're not going to throw around a lot of unrelated exercises, or bombard you with science and then run away when it comes to the practical bits. Foundation books are all about working with everyday practices that will be useful to you in the real world of web design.

We'll be taking you through the case study of a professional photographer's promotional web site. This is a project created specifically to illustrate the power at the fingertips of a Dreamweaver designer, covering all aspects: initial designs, layouts, content preparation, file management, testing - before adding some dynamic content and putting it up on the web for the world to see.

This is all written by folks who have real experience of this type of project, so there will be plenty of practical advice and tips 'from the field'. By the time you've turned that last page, you'll be up there with the rest of the web gurus.

Now that we've seen a quick exercise to get us acquainted with Dreamweaver MX, we're going to spend some time planning the case study so that we've got a strong basis to start with as we work through the project. Web site construction gives us a lot to be thinking about before we even get anywhere near the computer, so let's sit down and work through the process logically.

Brainstorming

Whether it be a web site, an animation, or a video edit, there are a few common questions I need to ask myself whenever I start a new project. These take a somewhat roundabout form, and obviously change depending on the type of work, but we're really looking at a simple brainstorming exercise.

For our project, as with any other, we need to go through the questions below and try to come up with some answers.

- What is the purpose of my web site?
- Who will see the site?
- How does this target audience affect my approach?
- Am I working for a client and what are their needs?
- How large will my site be?
- How long do I have to spend on the site?
- What do I want my site to look like?
- What extra materials and files do I need for the site?

People often get very wound up about the many different approaches to web site design, but as soon as you sit back and think clearly about your aims, everything will start to slot into place. There's no science to it, but these questions should help consolidate your ideas.

Let's take a look at some answers for the case study site.

What is the purpose of my web site?
I want to design a site that shows off my photographic skills. Maybe this will develop into a sales site but for now, it's quite simple – put my work up on the web so that people can see it.

Who should see the site?
Firstly, the general web-viewing public – there's no reason why they shouldn't. The work isn't confidential and should be accessible to everyone.

In addition, if anyone wanted to commission work, I'd like to think they could contact me, having seen my prints beautifully displayed on the web. If this does turn out to be a sales site, I also need to aim this towards people who are likely to buy existing work.

So I want people to look, to buy work that's already there, and also to commission new work. The people I'm most interested in will be those in the last two groups, and these will probably range from 18-60 years old, depending on the type of photo.

How does this target audience alter my approach?
I need to remember that the design of the site will sell the product just as much as the merit of the photos themselves. If the site does a bad job of presenting my product, then no one will be interested. You wouldn't stand for eating great five-star food in a restaurant if they brought it out to you in a bucket, would you?

However, I don't want to be limited by the conventions of other 'sales' sites, as users of the site might find this off-putting. Giving users something fresh and innovative means that they probably won't notice the well-integrated 'selling' part, and are less likely to treat you like one more person after their cash.

Finally, in this instance, I'm not only selling the product, but the **idea** of the product and the ownership that it entails. Don't forget that the web is an experience. It can represent a lot of things to different people, but, when approached in the right way, that experience can be something special. If you can make this idea concrete and sell it on, then the user will feel like they've bought into the site.

Am I working for a client and what are their needs?
If you're not working for a client at the moment, don't be led into thinking that this only applies to 'web professionals'. Another form of this question could be, "Who am I making this site for and what do they expect of it?" So, even if it's just a site to show off photos from your last vacation, you have an 'audience': your friends and family. They will expect to see good quality images to illustrate just how fantastically sunny it was. There will *always* be an audience, because any web site is made for a reason.

Often, ideas will need to be changed or tweaked because of other factors, and it helps to keep the idea of a client in mind here. You might like the site in blue and red, but the client wants their corporate colors of green and purple. In situations like these, be flexible. If you're working with a client remember that just because they're not the artist, it doesn't mean that they don't know what they're talking about.

How large will my site be?
Or, how many pages and how much content will there be? You will definitely have a home page - that much is certain. From there, it's up to the needs of your project. Most sites would probably include a **home** page, an **about** page describing the site, a **contact** page so the users can get in touch, and any amount of pages containing the majority of your site content.

As far as my site is concerned, I'll have the above and the content areas will naturally display my photos, maybe in some sort of categorization. If I do decide to try and sell through this site, I'll need a number of pages to do that as well, but for the moment I'm thinking:

- HOME PAGE – with navigation and a short intro.
- ABOUT – with more details about the site, what the user can hope to find, and me as a photographer.

Introducing Dreamweaver MX

- CONTENT – pages containing photos .
- SALES – details about how to buy the photos or commission others.
- CONTACT – e-mail details as well as my address and cell phone number.

How long do I have to spend on the site?

A beautiful masterpiece covered in animations won't be much use to the client if you've only had time to create one of ten pages when it comes to your submission date. If you feel that the deadline is a little tight for what the client has asked of you, tell them and don't sit on the information feeling it's too big a problem to approach them with. They'll be happy to discuss the problem with you and come up with a more reasonable compromise.

No matter who is in charge of the deadline, try to be realistic and make estimates based on previous jobs. If in doubt, deal with the content first, and then the structure, and finally the design. You can spend all day fiddling with how it all fits together on the page, but if there's nothing to go there in the first place, your fiddling is pretty academic.

Visual inspiration

This will develop as we progress through the book, but we've got a pretty solid idea of how the site is going to work. You may have noticed that I've left two questions unanswered:

- What do I want my site to look like?
- What extra materials and files do I need for the site?

This is because I want to start getting some ideas down on paper. You might feel comfortable brainstorming like we have just done for some time, but eventually you'll have reached a point where you actually need to start working on visuals. However much I enjoy making notes and theorizing on how my site will work, the next stage is the springboard that launches you into the world of web design, Dreamweaver style.

Don't touch that computer!

As we're now starting to think quite clearly about our site, let's prepare a few materials. It may surprise you to find that many web designers use quite a traditional method to plan and design their sites.

It's called *drawing*.

That's right; with a pencil, on paper.

I know we've been thinking quite clearly about what we're working towards but you may still find, as I often do, that you're finding it a little hard to actually picture the site. You know what's necessary but not exactly how it's all going to fit together visually. My suggestion is this:

Draw.

Draw anything, however useless it might seem. Go with gut instincts and don't be worried about keeping it neat because when you start making visual connections and the creative urge grips you, who knows where you'll end up? Notice I'm not telling you what to draw, because at this stage I want to leave it as open as possible.

1 Foundation Dreamweaver MX

These are my initial doodlings...

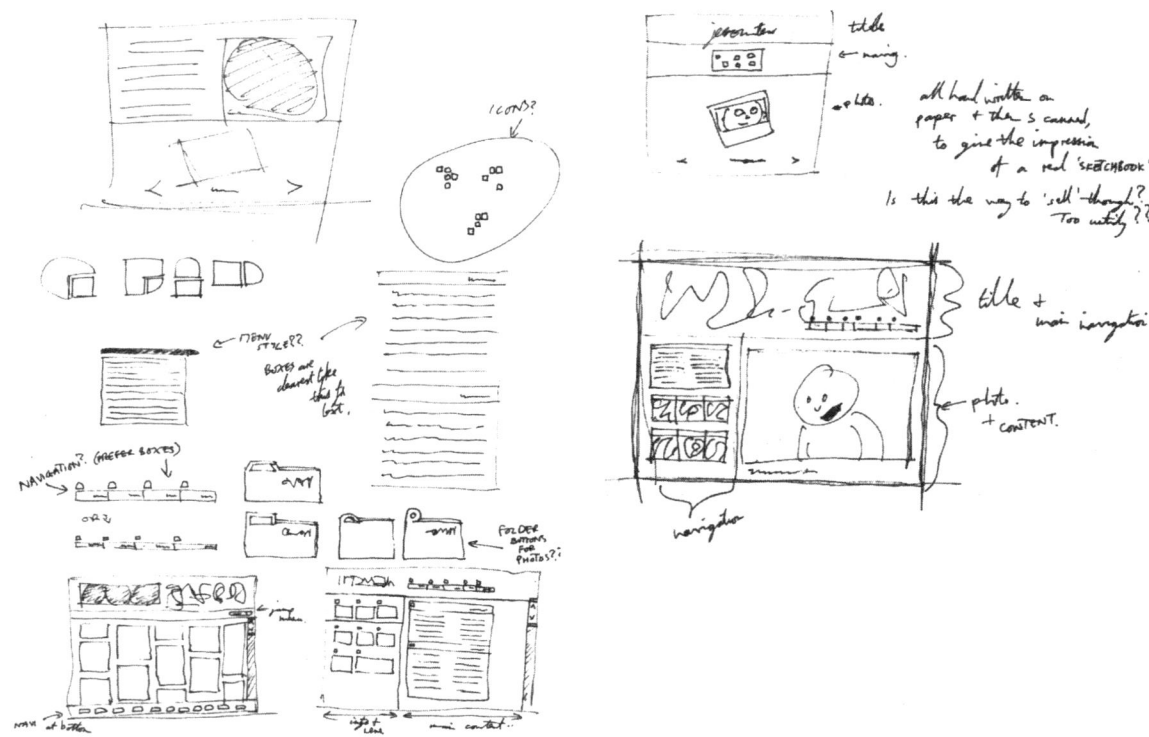

Also feel free to add key words, and phrases to remind you, and note any content ideas or instructions on how the site might work.

I know these aren't great, but they're not meant to be fine art for a gallery. What's important is that with just a few seconds of scribbling, I've started producing ideas. Try it yourself – even if you think that you haven't got an idea in your head. In the above two sheets I've tackled logos, navigation layouts, whole page layouts, some random symbols... just put anything you think of on that white space.

We're going to carry on with our site in a moment, but if this is for your own site, I'd suggest not returning to this book until you've covered at least five sheets of paper. After that, you'll have something to work from, with enough elements for you to draw a rough layout for at least the first page of your site.

Web research

To start with, the temptation will be to design simple-looking sites whilst you get to grips with Dreamweaver. At this point, I often turn to another source of inspiration: the Web. Visit sites randomly, and keep notes when you see something that interests you. I use a few favorite sites to link to other locations and sources of inspiration.

Try to keep the research specific to the type of site you're looking to create – mine is basically an art portfolio, so I'm trying to base my surfing around similar themed sites. If you're making something for a gardening service, for example, run a search through www.google.com for other gardening web sites and see:

- How other people have approached the subject.
- What the competition is like (or how you can improve what has been done before).

You could find that you hate the navigation on a particular site, so should steer clear of using anything like that, or maybe a nicely shaped logo could provide inspiration for your intro page. Look out for interesting colour combinations and novel uses of shapes. I usually bookmark pages I really like to make sure I can find them again, and take screenshots (use the PRINT SCREEN key on a PC or APPLE-SHIFT-F3 on a Mac, and then paste). Of course, you should never copy anything directly but gathering ideas like this for inspiration doesn't hurt anyone.

We've now got three elements to work from:

- Brainstorming notes
- Sketches
- Web research

These can be combined to form a strong picture of your site. If we break down the process we can identify three major concerns in the overall design of the web-presence we're planning to build: **Design**, **Structure**, and **Content**. We'll spend the rest of the chapter looking at these.

Design

Single out the graphic elements you're happiest with from the initial sketching stage. Try some more drawings, setting them against each other in a frame to see how they might be laid out. Do those circles really make sense laid out with the vertical lines splitting up the page like that? Does the title of the site need to run across the *top* of the page? In fact, do you even need the title there at all? Is there enough room for the main content to be displayed when you've covered everything else in fancy graphics? Is there too much text in your plan that will put the user off? Does the color code work and if not, why not?

At this point, we come across another concern; people will need to be able to use the site. Obviously, that stands to reason… but it's surprising how often it seems to slip the minds of web designers that electro-pink text on a lime green background might just be a strain on the eyes, or that not everyone has a 1024 by 768 resolution monitor.

The design will be one of the main factors causing users to close the window and move onto something less painful, as overly flashy and gaudy sites don't fool most people who are usually there for content. Heavy use of graphics and animations will mean a high file size and a slow download, which is very off-putting. If you can draw them into the site with a tasteful design in order to see your lovely content, then the balance is just right.

These are my sketches for the first few pages of the case study site. These are still open to interpretation – Dreamweaver MX will allow me to update and alter my designs right up until the last minute, so there's really no need to worry about getting things absolutely rock certain for the moment. What's important is that we've got something to work with.

Foundation Dreamweaver MX

← HOME or MAYBE 'ABOUT'

PORTFOLIO

EACH BOX is a button + description to a more detailed gallery.

NEWS page

Structure

Now that we roughly know what the site will look like, let's think more clearly about the structure. You've probably already been considering this anyway – I came up with a few early sketches for my navigation system:

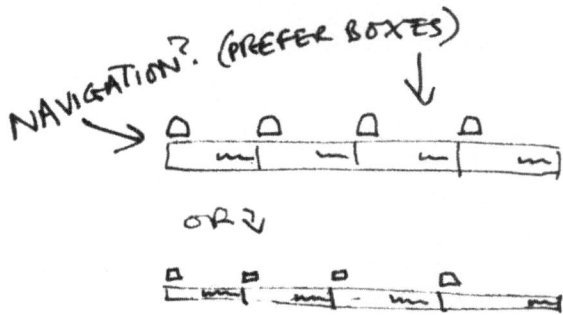

This simple row of boxes would probably be used in the top half of the page to navigate to any other page (or at least other sections) in the case study web site. I also started thinking about how this would relate to the page's layout, and you can see the row of buttons in the top of the following sketch:

Let's assume we're in the home page of a site, with a navigation bar of buttons across the top. Don't worry about how it's made – we'll come to all this later. For now, think about the bigger picture of how you want your site to work.

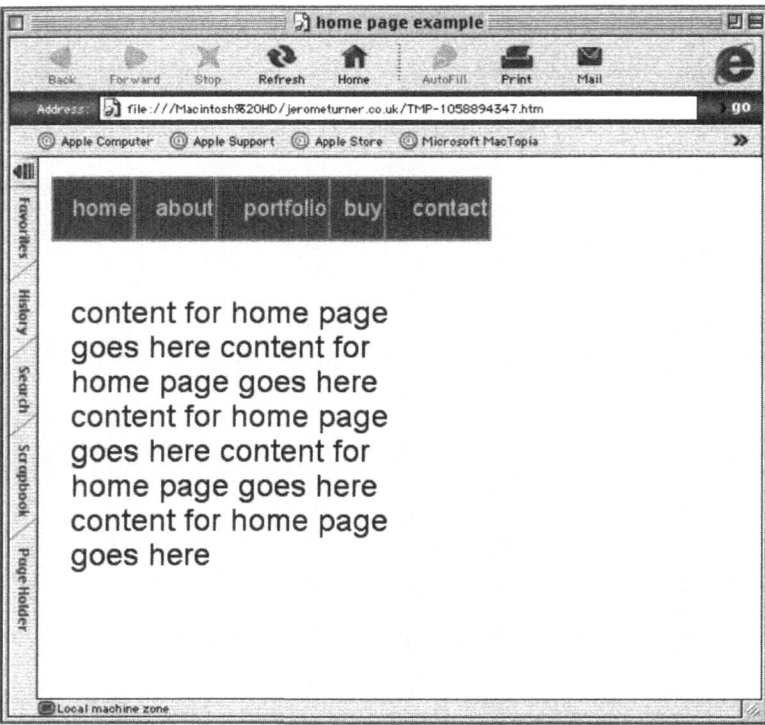

From this page it's clear that clicking any of the buttons in the navigation bar will send an instruction to load a different page into the browser, replacing the home page with whatever you choose, whether it's the home, about, folio, buy, or contact page.

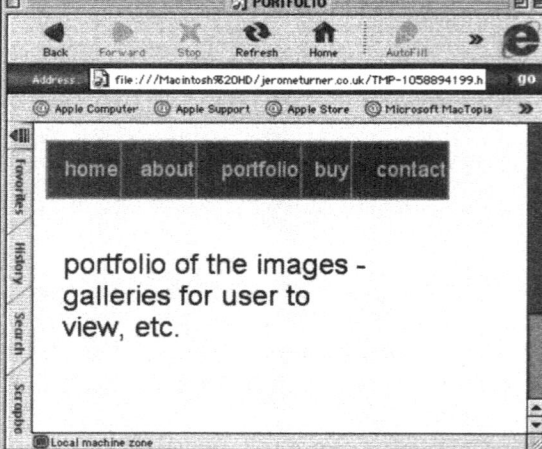

We're not just limited to navigation with the bar. In the following example, we can use the navigation bar as before but we also have the option of clicking on the word principle to jump to a new relevant page, or we can click on any of the images to jump to a page showing them at their full size.

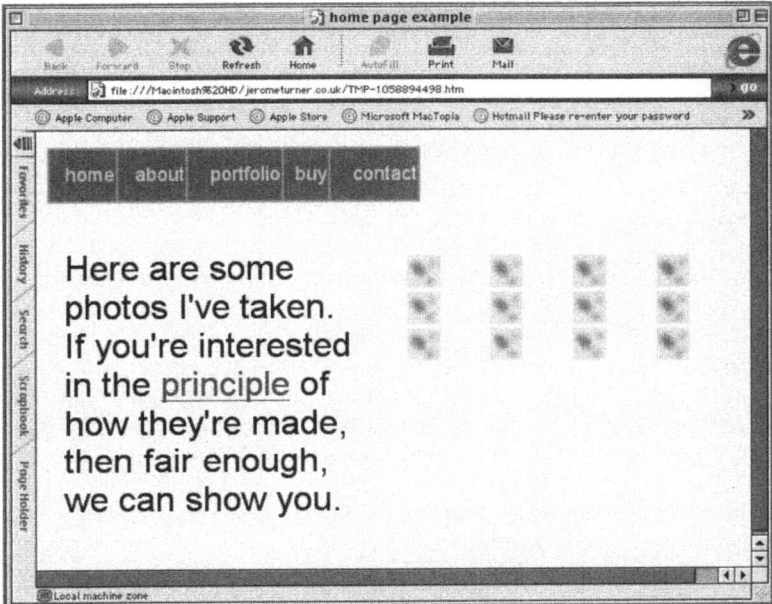

Adding extra links like this means that your user isn't limited in the way they delve deeper into the site. It's a good idea to try and anticipate where your user will want to know more. Give them too many options, and they'll get confused; give too few, and they'll be frustrated. Never forget that a user doesn't have your knowledge about what's on all the pages and what the core content is.

If you keep the structure clear in your own mind, then it's likely that the site will reflect this. It sometimes helps to think of your site pages in terms of a tree with top levels containing the most important pages that then lead down to lower levels of detail as the user progresses.

It can also be useful to build a site map using sticky notes for each individual page – you can change the whole arrangement just by moving sticky notes around.

Content

We're going to round-up some ideas here, before going on to look at our final design thoughts. These ideas will be put into action in the following chapters, and we shouldn't be too concerned about content before moving on, so we'll keep this brief and to the point.

Typically, content comes in two forms: text and graphics. Long gone are the days of 'text-only' sites, throwing huge blocks of tiny scrawl at the user, but people still use the written form in everyday life – it's quite simply the best way to make yourself clearly understood.

In the case study, I know that I want the following text:

Home page intro
This should grab the attention of the user, and has to be pretty arresting not only in what it says, but also in how it's laid out. Remember: you're leading the user round the site. If you want them to read one area of a page first, you need to make sure they see it first by highlighting it, placing it in a box, or making it a different color.

About page
This text will remain constant during the life of the site. As it's probably going to be something along the lines of an informal résumé, it could almost be laid out in table form with a list of skills, education, interests, previous exhibitions, and so on. We don't need to be as concerned about the 'punchiness' here, because having entered the site and seen the home page introduction, the user has made a decision to move on. The 'sell' part has worked and the user is drawn in to read the small print.

Portfolio pages
Text here should be minimal, simply instructing the user how to navigate round the photos within their various categories and maybe a short description of how each photographic style works or is 'made'. That description would probably be no more than 25 words, possibly with a link to a page that goes into more detail about photographic processes and some tutorial 'how to' videos.

The photos themselves will be labeled by title, medium, and year of completion – as you'd see in a gallery. There will also be an option to show a larger 'full size' version of each image.

Whilst a picture can speak a thousand words, it doesn't necessarily follow that one thousand pictures will speak a million words. It's more likely they'll just put your user off using the site whilst they wait for them all to download, so it's best to try to keep the use of images and animation down to a minimum. Everything in our site should have some kind of function - even if that function is to provide eye candy that draws the user in.

Most of my graphic content will be in the shape of the photos themselves. As I don't want to draw too much away from that content, it'll be best to keep the background designs simple. Similarly, it makes sense that icons and buttons are based around a few simple shapes. In the case of making a 'back' button I want the image to follow the rest of the design and describe its function as well:

Given that we've identified the two main areas of content, we need to consider how these balance out. Does the text inform the reading of the images, and does it need to? If a picture will better describe what you're typing, stop typing and get drawing. Think back to the design process again and consider where text and images need to be placed if they relate to each other. The obvious choice is to 'underline' an image with the caption but that doesn't mean it's the *best* way to do it.

The case study – final designs

By this stage, you'll have been thinking about and visualizing your site for quite some time. Whilst it probably seems like a headache to spend so much time planning this on paper and balancing the design, structure and content, it will prove helpful in the long run. Dreamweaver gives us plenty of scope for adjusting and developing the web pages but if we've got a solid base to work from, then we're on to a winner.

At this stage, I started making some mock-ups of the web pages in a graphics package (you can use any program you feel comfortable with: Photoshop, Paint Shop Pro, Flash, or whatever) in order to get a neater idea of the final product. Whilst sketches are fine for generating ideas and layouts, there's always a point where I want to see it on the screen. You might also find that it's got to the stage where it will be helpful to show the client something. If you can show them a layout with a color scheme, home page, or whatever they're most interested in, it will increase their confidence in the project.

From my initial sketches, I came up with the first few pages, drawn in Flash. When I looked at them, there seemed to be something missing. The design itself seemed a little barren, as if it was only half finished. So I went back to some of my original sources of inspiration from the web to compare my ideas with theirs. Whilst pacing around my apartment trying to work it out, something caught my attention.

I opened a magazine and there it was.

What better interface design is there than that of a magazine? Magazine design is simple and uncluttered without looking lazy and uninspiring. It's informative, with punchy tag lines to draw you in. Magazine photographs – both in content and style – let you know that you're probably in for something a bit different. In short, it would make the perfect professional-looking home page.

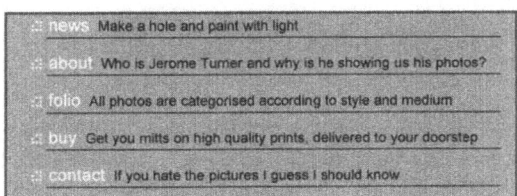

Having seen this, I made a decision to move on from what I'd started with and change the site to one based loosely on the layout of a Sunday supplement magazine. This made even more sense when I started flicking through these publications and saw how they presented photography, which is especially relevant to this site. I went back to Flash and came up with the four mock-ups that follow in the rest of this chapter.

More to the point, *you're allowed to do this*. No one said there were any rules to follow. I only suggested researching on the web because it can be a useful kick-start to get you thinking like a web designer. Feel free to take inspiration from wherever you like. Be motivated by anything you see in your daily life, however mundane it might seem. When applied to the layout and navigation of a web site, it puts a whole new twist on the subject. If you free yourself up like this you'll be amazed at how much has been sitting there right in front of you waiting to be discovered. A few examples could be:

- Road signs made into buttons.
- Jars of food lined up in a cupboard, where each one is a button.
- A site based on 'pieces of paper' – you go to the next web page, it shows the sheet flipped over. The text is 'hand written'.
- An apartment building showing a person in each window, where each person works as a button.
- A site based on scraps from your pocket: sales dockets, keys, loose change…

These are just a few ideas to be getting on with. All of the above could be drawn from scratch or made up from scanned images.

With this new spurt of enthusiasm, I came up with these new designs. I find them more stylish. Empty spaces aren't a concern; they work as part of the design and layout. Notice that whilst the design is inspired by the magazine layout, certain elements have been altered so that it works properly as a web site.

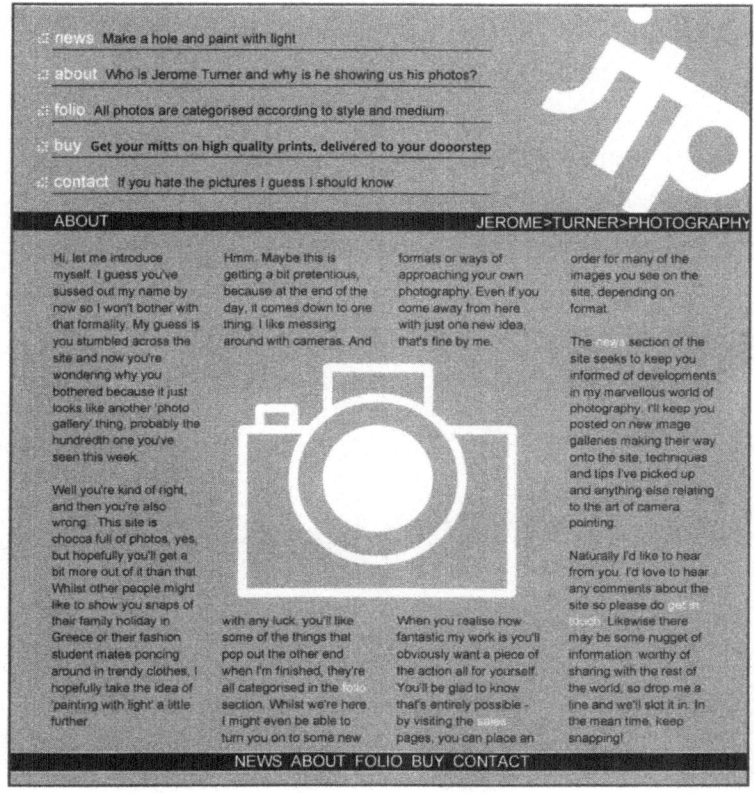

Foundation Dreamweaver MX

::: news Make a hole and paint with light
::: about Who is Jerome Turner and why is he showing us his photos?
::: folio All photos are categorised according to style and medium
::: buy Get you mitts on high quality prints, delivered to your doorstep
::: contact If you hate the pictures I guess I should know

NEWS   JEROME>TURNER>PHOTOGRAPHY

17/07/02

Experiments start with new 'light projection' techniques. Ever since starting pinhole photography a few years ago, I've been really into working straight onto paper, at least it's something you can do from home. As soon as I've got something more to show you, I will.

14/07/02

I know, I know. There was a promise that I'd never put up my holiday photos but hey, some of these snaps of Frankfurt were just so fantastic I couldn't resist!

25/06/02

The 'dogs in cars' project goes from strength to strength with now 15 mutt mug shots. You can find them in the Projects section of the folio. Remember a dog is for snapping, not just for Christmas.

14/06/02

There's a new 'joiner' landscape taken on the grounds of Alnwich Castle, Northumbria. The green-fingered amongst you may be interested to know this was the work of famous landscape gardener Capability Brown.

10/06/02

I've been playing with Photoshop again and some of the results are up in the Altered Images part of the folio. It's a bit of a mish-mash also using 3D graphics made up in Strata Studio Pro Blitz - see what you think. The whole 3D thing is going off in interesting directions too but that's a different story, to be discovered at www.jerometurner.co.uk

NEWS ABOUT FOLIO BUY CONTACT

Introducing Dreamweaver MX

I'm not really too concerned about it 'looking' like a web site - as long as the user can clearly and easily find their way around I'm happy. To make sure of that, I've even added a menu at the bottom that parallels the main list, so that if the user has to scroll down and loses the top of the page, they are able to navigate from this end too.

Summary

This chapter has given you an introduction to what Dreamweaver is. You've had the chance to open the application and make your first rudimentary web pages. This should have given you a brief taste of how Dreamweaver looks and works, and what you can do with it.

In our case study we've got a firm idea of where we're going and what our site should look like. If you feel it's not all quite there yet, don't worry too much. The main thing is that we want to keep the work process flowing – it's all too easy to get bogged down in details when they can actually be fine tuned in later stages.

We've got a grasp on the fundamentals of the inspiration behind our site and what we're trying to achieve, so it's time to move on to making this a reality with Dreamweaver. In the next chapter, we're going to get comfortable with Dreamweaver's interface so that we're ready to start creating our case study site in **Chapter 3.**

Introducing Dreamweaver MX

The Dreamweaver Interface

What we'll cover in this chapter

- *Learning how Dreamweaver organizes site assets*
- *Defining the site for our case study*
- *Taking a tour around Dreamweaver's interface*
- *Setting Dreamweaver's Preferences*

In the last chapter, we decided what we were expecting of our web site, and started thinking about how we wanted it to look. To continue to build the solid foundation for our project, we need to set up Dreamweaver so that everything is in place for us to create our site seamlessly.

First we need to introduce you to Dreamweaver, and make you feel at home with the basic operating layout. This chapter will introduce you to the Dreamweaver interface, and then we'll go on to create the settings for our case study site.

Let's get started right away. Open up Dreamweaver – you should see something like this screenshot:

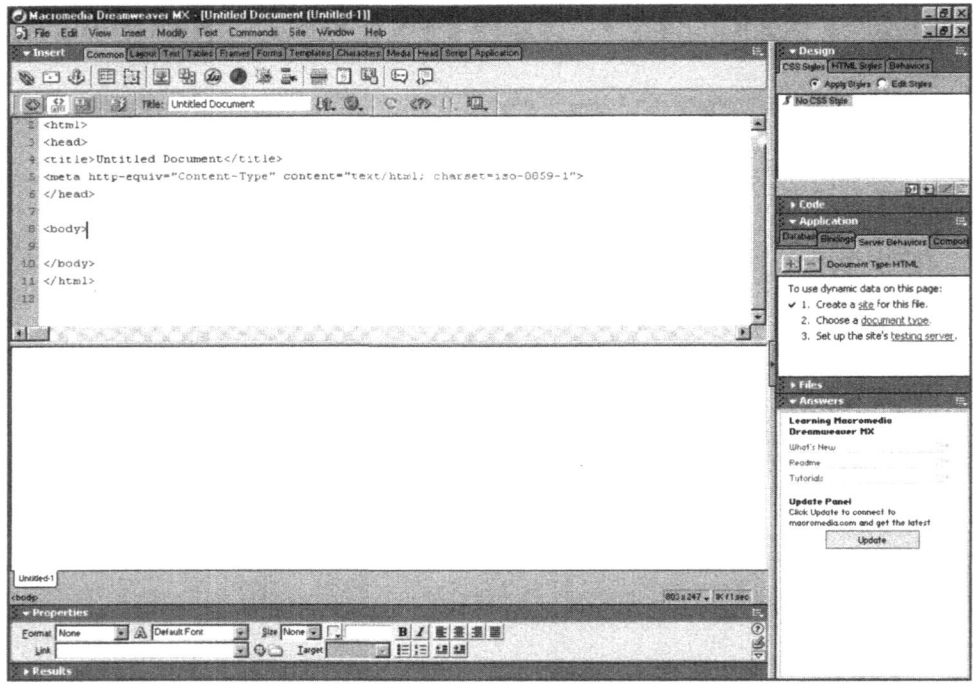

As you can see, it might be an idea to have a paper bag handy for some breathing exercises – an interface like that can cause panic in even the most hardened designer. If you step back for a minute though, you'll realize that all those little boxes and icons mean that Dreamweaver can do an awful lot for you.

We're not going to try and blind you by immediately telling you what every single part of this interface does – that would be like showing you round a party of fifty people and expecting you to remember all their names. And we all know how embarrassing it can be when you start forgetting them!

There's only so much you need to know to get started with Dreamweaver web design, and that's what we'll cover in this chapter. If you start looking at all of the menus you'll see a lot of bewildering stuff there. Ignore it for the moment. We'll introduce you to each bit as and when the need arises. By the end of the book, you'll know everything you need to, and be best friends with the interface.

The Dreamweaver Interface 2

Organizing site assets

One of the common misconceptions about web pages is that they're made up of one piece of information – the HTML page made up in Dreamweaver. This is true for a simple layout using text and tables solely originated in Dreamweaver like this:

But as soon as we start dropping in **assets** that have been made up in Photoshop, Flash, or other design tools, it's a different story. These pictures, animations, and so on make up the page – but when the viewer types in the URL, they'll have to wait for each asset to load. Whilst the HTML page knows where the images are supposed to go, they still need to be collected from your web space for the viewer to see.

In cases where there are a lot of external files, web pages often show symbols like this in the first few seconds:

...only to end up with all the pieces slotted together to make the final design once it's finished loading.

When you put work on the web, all the relevant information (HTML pages, images, etc.) is held on a **server**, which basically provides 'space' for your files to reside and be downloaded from when users want to access your site.

Foundation Dreamweaver MX

You're probably used to seeing your files in folders like this on your hard disk (HD)

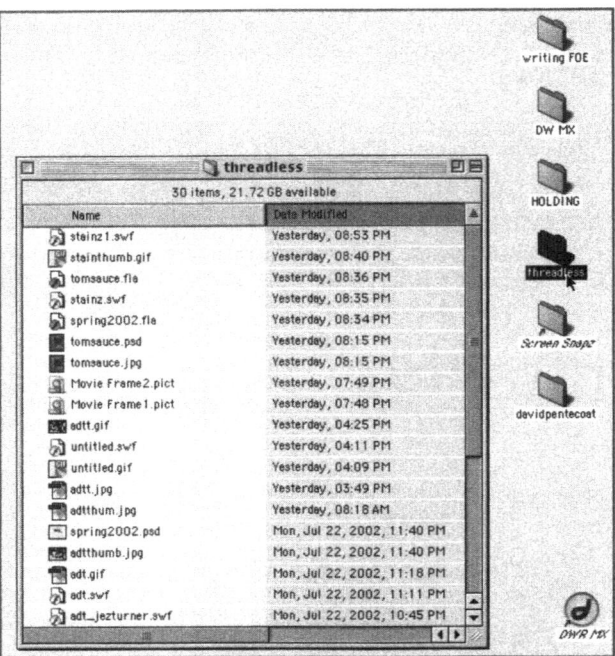

Files on your server can be arranged in a similar way. Users won't be aware of how you do this, because as far as they're concerned, they hit a button and it just takes them to the next page. However, from your point of view as a web designer, it's crucial to keep tabs on your files, otherwise you'll end up with someone clicking a button and getting nowhere, because you put the new page in the wrong place.

So you might have a folder called 'portfolio content' and within that a number of files and maybe more folders...

It makes sense that the way we organize files for a site on our hard drives (and that means *all* the content) should parallel the way it will one day be stored on your server. Let's take a look at how Dreamweaver allows us to do this, and set things up for our case study.

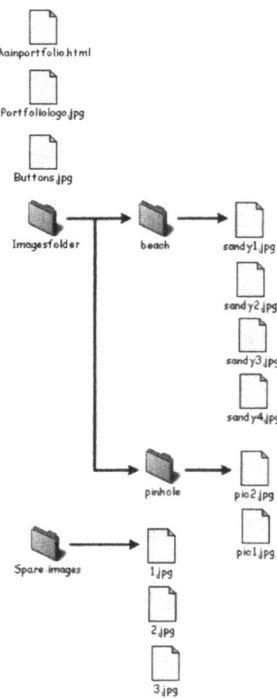

The Dreamweaver Interface 2

Defining a site

1. Go to the Site menu and click on Site > New Site. You'll see the Site Definition window appear, just as it did in **Chapter 1**.

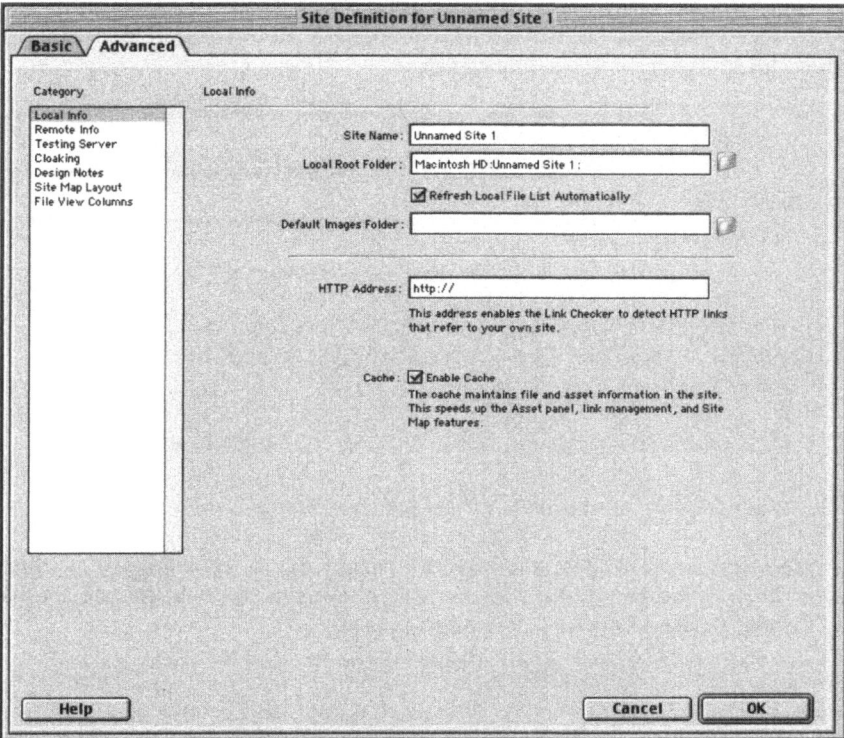

2. This time though, click on the Advanced tab at the top. As we'll be using the Advanced tab more often than the Basic one, it makes sense to get used to seeing it.

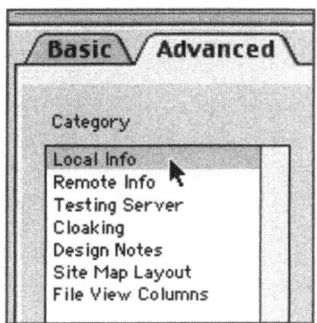

43

3. Select Local Info. This deals with everything based on your HD, as opposed to Remote Info, which deals with the set-up of the files on your server.

4. Enter a Site Name. As you may be working on more than one site at a time, Dreamweaver names sites so you can easily switch between projects.

5. In the same window, create a Local Root Folder. You can either browse to a folder, or enter a name for a new folder, which will be automatically created for you. This will be the folder where all of the files relating to your site are kept.

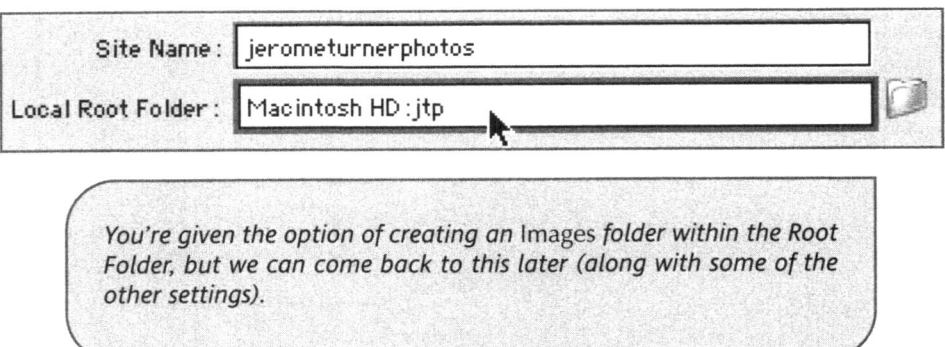

You're given the option of creating an Images folder within the Root Folder, but we can come back to this later (along with some of the other settings).

6. Choose Testing Server from the list in the Category window on the left.

7. Click on the Access drop-down and choose Local/Network. This means that when you want to test your site with working links, your Root Folder in the HD will simulate the web experience in your default browser (mine is Internet Explorer).

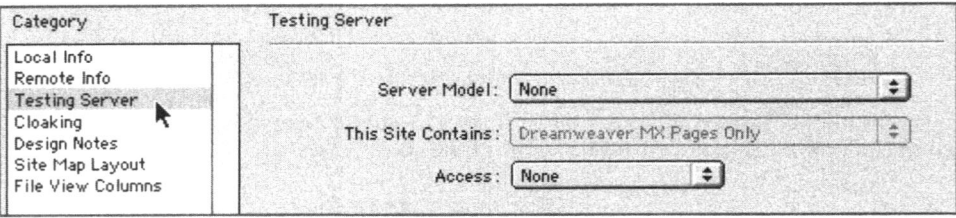

The other option here is FTP. This stands for File Transfer Protocol and is the standard way of putting files up on the web. If you were to choose FTP here you'd actually be using an FTP application to put your files up on the web for each test, meaning you'd need to be online whilst working.

The Dreamweaver Interface 2

8. Dreamweaver will automatically fill in the Testing Server Folder and URL Prefix fields with the details that we gave it in step 5, so click OK to finish.

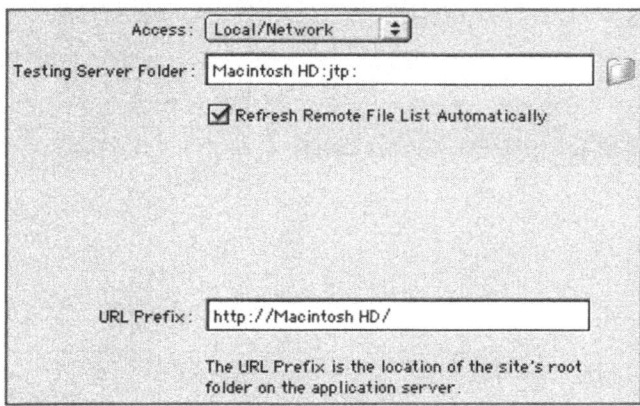

If you're on a Mac, the next panel you'll see is the **Site panel**. If you're on a PC, you're probably going to be returned to the screen we started with at the beginning of this chapter, with the Site panel sitting politely amongst the other panels on the right of your screen. Either way, this panel is well worth learning about, as we'll be referring to it a lot throughout this book, so let's take a look.

The Site panel

If you can't see this already, then bring it into view using Window > Site. This panel shows the files behind your site. If you're on a PC, then you probably want to undock this from the panels on the right of your screen by clicking on the black dots at the top left of the window (as shown), and dragging it out into the middle of the screen.

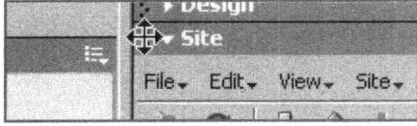

If you don't see a two-column layout, then click on the Expand button in the right-hand side of the row of icons at the top of the Site panel.

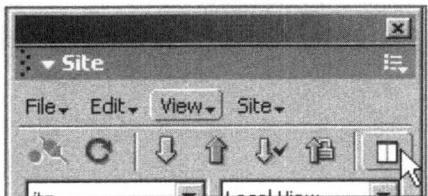

45

You should now see something like this, with the files in the root folder we set up earlier listed on the right-hand side of the window.

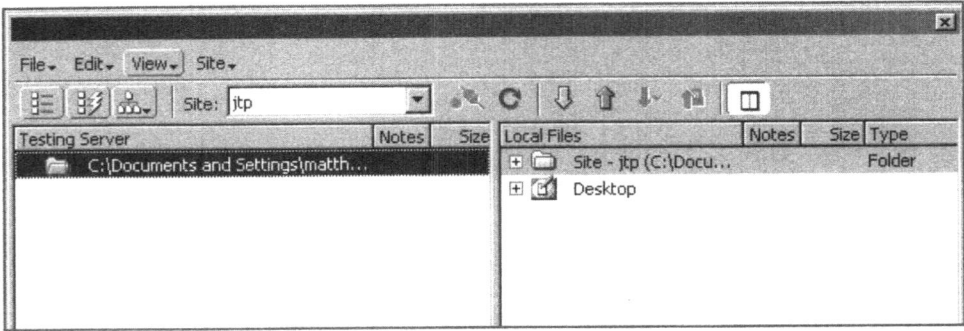

Dreamweaver may create an `index.html` *page automatically for you in your root directory. This is because* `index.html` *is the first page a browser will load when visiting a site. Try typing www.jerometurner.co.uk into your browser for example, and you'll end up seeing the page www.jerometurner.co.uk/index.html.*

The **right-hand column** is what will be shown by default when you collapse the window back to one column (PC users only!). As you can see, Dreamweaver lists the contents of your entire HD as well as what's in your root folder. This means you can easily track down files anywhere on your computer from within Dreamweaver. Don't forget, all files that you use for your web site must be stored in your root folder – so if you find a file you want to use, simply copy it by dragging and dropping between the directories in this window. Otherwise, you may find that Dreamweaver prompts you to do this anyway – it's friendly like that.

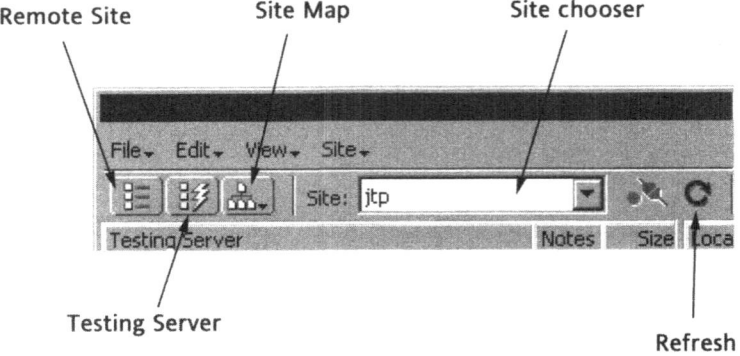

The **left-hand side** of the Site window can show three different things: the Remote Site, the Testing Server, and a Site Map.

The Dreamweaver Interface 2

- The **Remote Site** list will give you information about what is currently stored on your online server. We're working offline and testing our site locally on our machine at the moment, so don't worry too much about this.
- You'll remember that Dreamweaver automatically filled in the **Testing Server** folder with our local folder details, and the Testing Server will simply show these. (It's also possible to set up an online testing server to allow you to test the site before, say, uploading it to a client's permanent server.)
- The **Site Map** option gives you a drop-down option to view just the Map, or the Map and Files. Select the Map and Files option to see a family tree of the HTML links you've created to navigate from one page to another. Once you've created a few pages, this can be very useful.

Also in the top bar, you'll find a selection of buttons mainly used for online testing, but the first two might prove useful to us:

- The **Site chooser** lets you select the site that you want to work on.
- The **Refresh** button updates the files and links listed in the window to accommodate changes that may have been made to your site. If it looks like something's missing when it shouldn't be, try hitting this.

We're finished with the Site window for the moment, so close it. It's a good idea to get used to using the Site window as a reference point (comfort blanket) when you're not sure where your files might have got to (Testing Server view) or how they're connected (Site Map). If you're using a PC and want to re-dock it with the panels on the right of your screen, you'll need to collapse it back to a one column format **first**, before clicking on the black dots at the top left corner and dragging back across to the other panels. Mac users can simply reduce the window to a bar and let it sit in the background.

The Dreamweaver interface

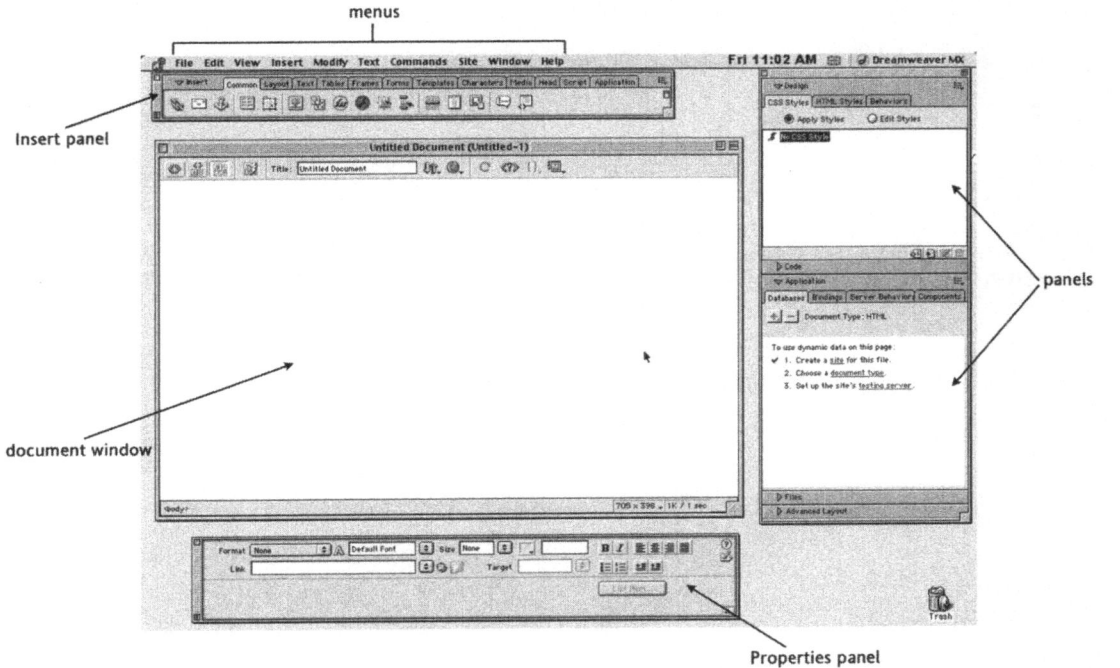

47

Foundation Dreamweaver MX

As you can see labeled, there are five major parts to the Dreamweaver interface. We're going to take a look at each of them now, so you know what's what. We'll start with the most important – the Document window.

The Document window

This is where all the designing goes on, the blank canvas ready for your work. Dreamweaver offers us a number of ways of displaying our pages on the canvas, so let's take a look.

1. To start with, open the ch2.html file (available from the friends of ED site in the usual way) in Dreamweaver using File > Open. You'll see it's a simple page containing an image.

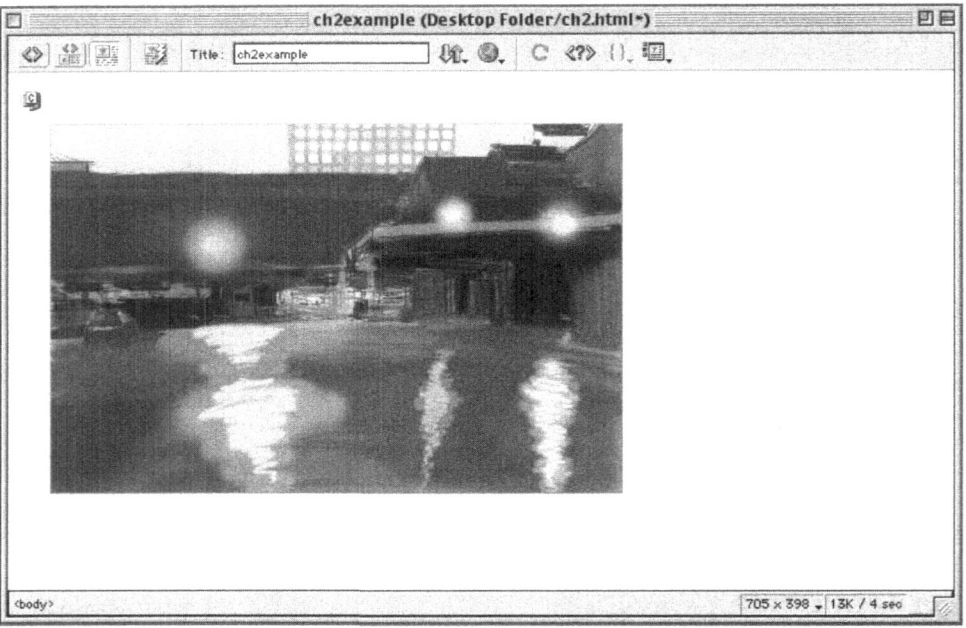

2. There are three choices about how you view this window, accessed through the icons at the top left-hand corner. Click on the Design View button on the right of the three, as shown.

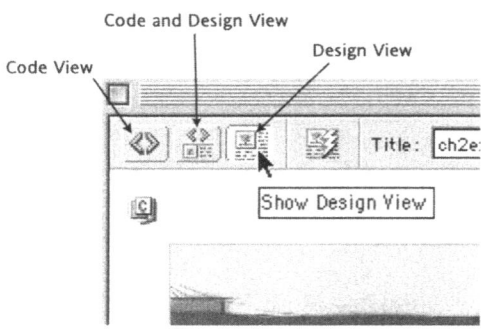

The Dreamweaver Interface 2

3. The Design View layout shows a visual representation of a page as it will appear to the user of your site. If you're a Windows user, you probably have the Document window maximized, but if you're a Mac user, or you have resized the Document window, you can re-size the window by dragging the corner. (Note that you can't zoom in, as the layout is always shown to scale.)

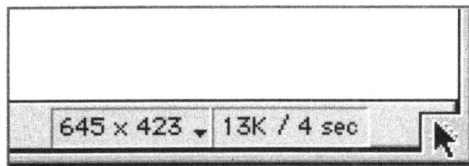

In the same corner, we can also see the size of the page as we're looking at it - in this case, 645 pixels by 423 pixels. We're also shown the size of the file (13K), and, more importantly, the time that it will take for the user to download (four seconds).

4. Click on the little downward facing arrow next to the size of the page. You'll see a handy menu displayed that allows you to see how your page will look to users using different monitor sizes.

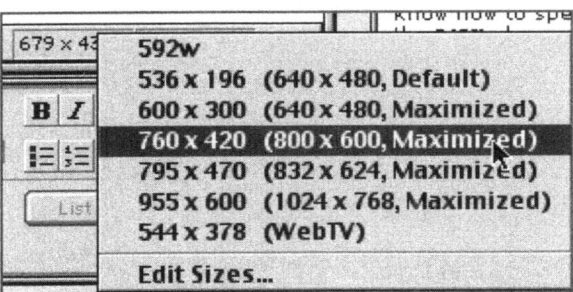

5. As your users' monitors will vary, this allows you to take into account the varying sizes so that everyone can experience your page without having to scroll all over the place just to find the edge of the page. Pick a few different sizes to see how the window changes. You won't be able to select any of the sizes in the list if the Document window is maximized. If this is the case, select Window > Tile Horizontally to restore the Document window.

The dimensions in the brackets show the width and height of the browser window once the HTML page has been opened inside it and the numbers on the left show the amount of space within that browser that you have to work with.

For example, in the above selection, I can see that the Dreamweaver page I'm creating is 760 pixels by 420. If I then put this on the Web, the user's browser will need a resolution of at least 800 by 600 to view it without scrolling. In everyday terms though, this menu allows you to view for the two most common resolutions: 800 by 600 and 1024 by 768.

6. However pretty your content might be, it's all held in place by (mainly HTML) code. Back at the top of the screen where we selected Design View in step 2, click the button on the left to view the code behind our page.

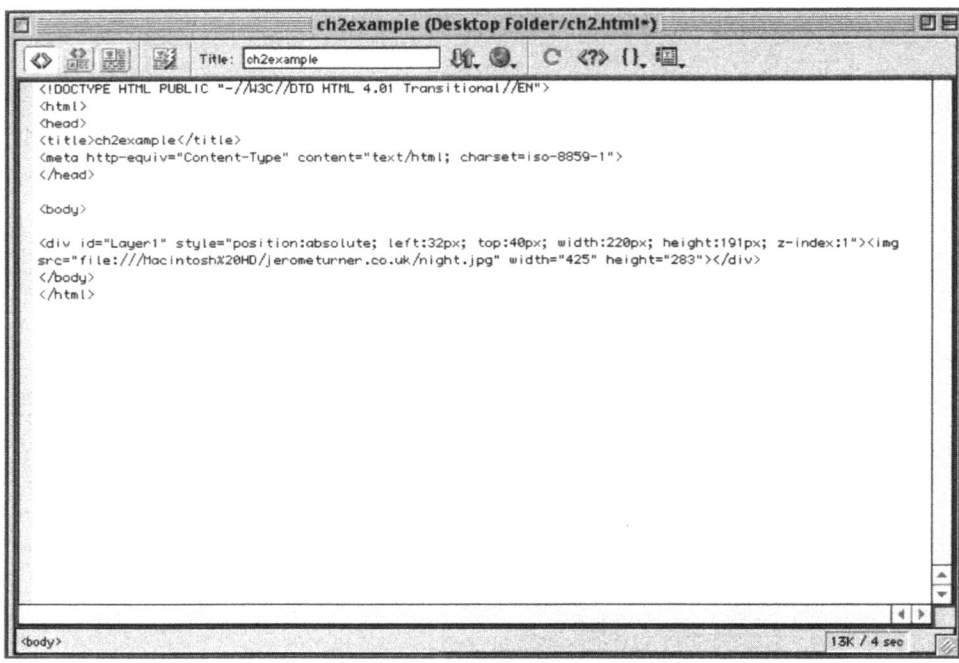

You should see something like this. We'll return to this in future chapters, so don't worry if it looks confusing for the moment – just relax in the grateful knowledge that Dreamweaver creates a lot of this for you, rather than leaving you to type it all in by hand.

7. The third way of viewing your Dreamweaver file is as a mix of the two we've just looked at. Click on the middle button to see the Code and Design View.

8. This is actually more useful than you might think. Click on the image that we have in our sample file, and you'll see the HTML code relating to this picture highlighted in the code section:

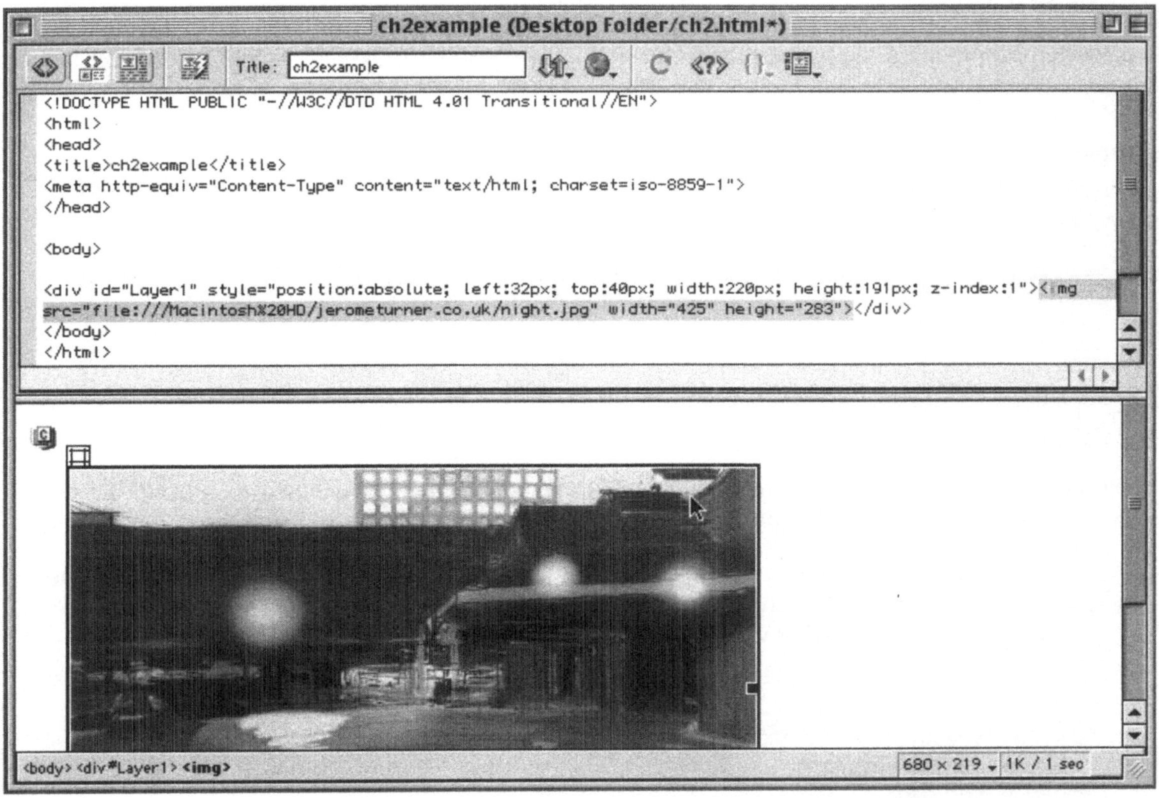

[Screenshot of Dreamweaver document window showing ch2example with HTML code view on top and design view below displaying a night image]

9. You might find that you have to scroll across in the Code window to find the highlighted code. To fix that, go to View > Code View Options, and make sure that Word Wrap is checked.

   Generally, clicking on anything in the Design view will bring up the associated code in the Code view, and allow you to alter it as necessary. Again, this is a topic that we shall return to at greater length in subsequent chapters, but the three view options will all prove very useful to you at different points in your Dreamweaver use.

The Insert panel

We've seen how we look at them, but how do we actually build up the pages? Just above the Document window, you'll see the Insert panel. If you can't see it there, use Window > Insert or click on the arrow. The most commonly used options appear on the left, the Common and Layout tabs.

The **Common** tab is used to insert files such as JPEGs and SWFs. It also allows you to create tables and layers in which to display text and other elements. The **Layout** tab also lets you create tables and layers, but with more control over how the spaces are made for the work.

We could go through the rest of the tabs now, but it'll be easier to grasp if we leave this until we actually start laying out in the next chapter. For now, all we need to remember is that the Insert panel does exactly what is says on the tin: it inserts stuff.

The Properties panel

Next up is the Properties panel, which you'll find nestling at the bottom of the page. If it's not visible, use Window > Properties to display it.

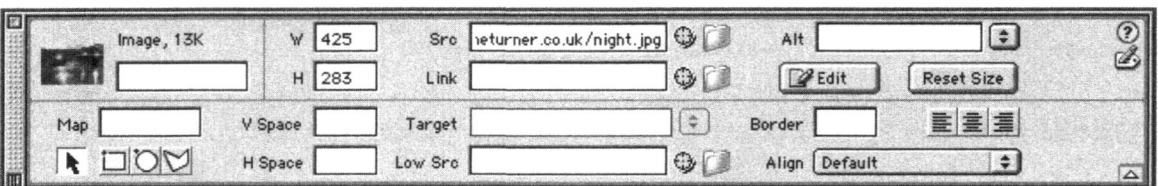

The Properties panel allows us to view and edit any of the material in the Document window (JPGs, text, SWFs, movies, and so on). Like the Insert panel, this is something we'll be using in the next chapter.

In ch2.html, select the image in the Document window, and you should see something like the screenshot above – with the size and source of the image displayed, along with several other links (including the hyperlink option that we used fleetingly in the last chapter).

> *If you only get a half-size version of the Properties panel, try clicking on the little arrow in the bottom right of the panel to expand it to full size.*

The Properties panel is context-specific, so if you select outside the picture, you'll get some options for dealing with text, as shown:

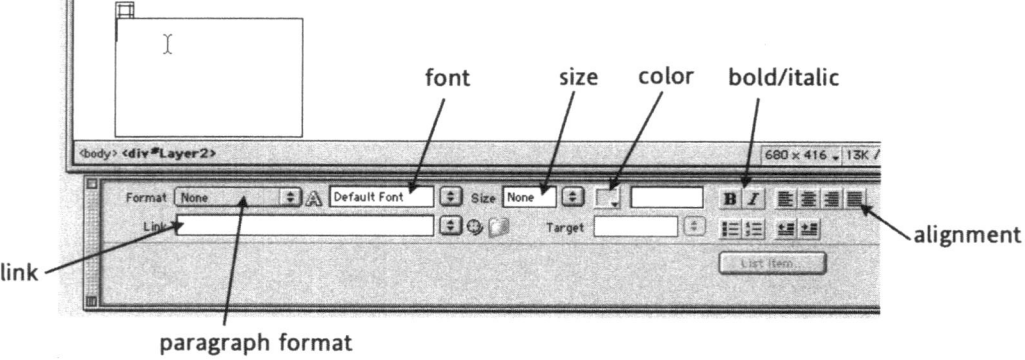

These include setting the text type to a pre-determined format, choosing a font, selecting a size and color for the text, making the text bold or italicised, and even making the text link to another page.

Panels

The last set of controllers and viewers are the **Panels**. I know we've been referring to other windows as panels but I'm specifically talking about the vertical column on the right of the screen, which should by default look something like this:
(As we've covered already, Windows users will probably have the Site panel stored here.)

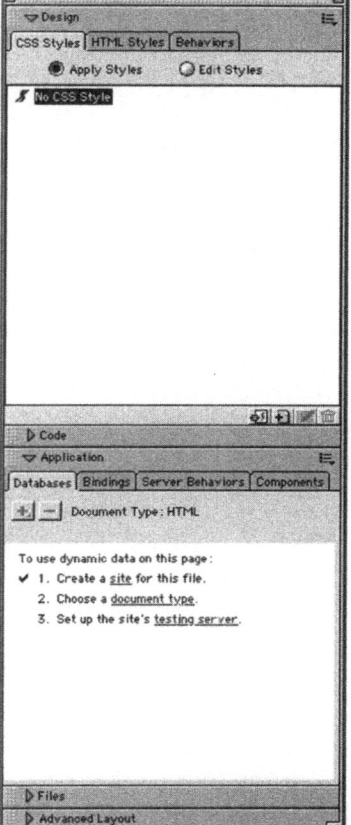

Each one of the titles - Design, Code, Application - describes a different panel. The arrows in the bar of each title are used to expand and fold away each panel at your convenience. Try it now.

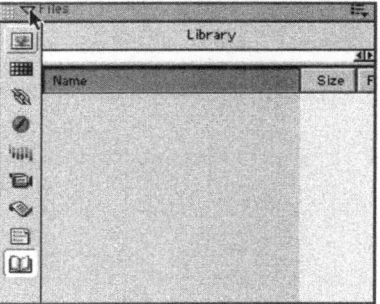

Dreamweaver stacks the panels, giving priority to any that are opened so that you can see the contents and get to the controls. There will be times during your Dreamweaver work when certain panels are more useful than others, and this allows you to switch easily between these without necessitating a second monitor.

To close a Panel altogether, hover over the top left area of the relevant bar until the hand icon appears on a Mac, or the four-arrowed icon we saw earlier appears on a PC.

Click and drag the panel away from the stack and close it.

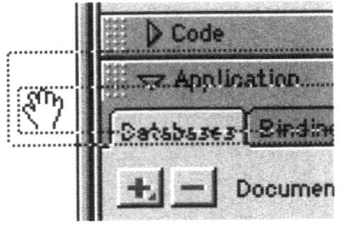 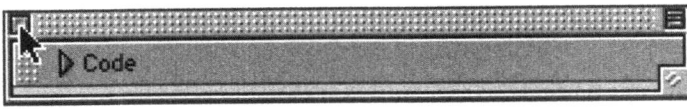

You can view and use panels if they're not part of the stack but this can get a bit messy and encroach on the rest of the viewing space. Once we've closed a panel, we can also open it again from the Window menu.

One problem: it's not always entirely clear which panel relates to the name on the list. For example, if I decide to remove and close the Files panel from the stack...

...I then can't find it when I look in the Window menu. This is because it's referred to as Assets in the list, which might seem a bit illogical.

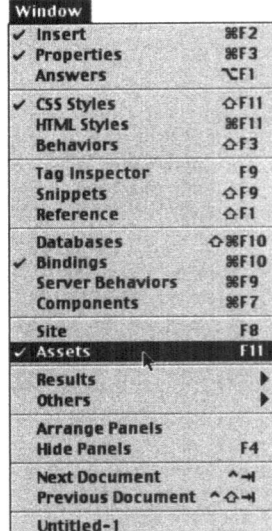

Some knowledge that should help you in such circumstances is that the Window menu is split into sections, grouping controls and panels that have similar functions together. **CSS Styles**, **HTML Styles**, and **Behaviors** can all be found in the **Design** panel. They deal with simple HTML and text control with CSS (more on this in **Chapter 4**).

 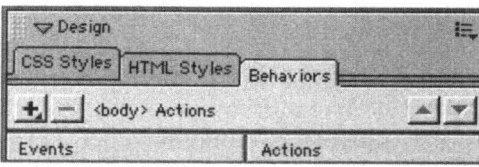

Tag Inspector, **Snippets**, and **Reference** relate to the **Code** panel, dealing with the coding and drag-and-drop elements provided by Dreamweaver. **Databases**, **Bindings**, **Server Behaviors**, and **Components** can all be found in the **Applications** tab, used in conjunction with database sites and those using large amounts of data from other sources. There is more on both of these panels in the second half of this book.

In the **Others** part of the menu, the **History** panel is worth looking at. This works like an undo, allowing you to take steps backwards through the 'history' of your changes to the site – very useful when you make the inevitable mistakes involved in web design...

Finally, **Arrange Panels** cleans up if you've been having a bit of a fiddle with your layout, and **Hide/Show Panels** hides all the panels so you can concentrate on the Document window.

If all that's given you a bit of a headache and the use of each panel doesn't mean a lot right now, that's fine. Just have a go at moving the panels around and getting used to accessing different ones from the menu. Once you've started working on a few projects it will come more easily.

The menus

We're going to take a quick look at the menus across the top of the screen, and then our tour of Dreamweaver should pretty much be over. To start us off, open each of the menus and see if there's anything that you recognize.

The chances are that you'll find it a little scary, apart from the first menus where we're familiar with commands such as Save, Cut, Paste, and so on. It's not as bad as it looks because a) Dreamweaver designers can go years before using all of the menu options, b) all the wonderful Dreamweaver features have been well categorized according to their use, and c) many of the menu items can be found elsewhere in Dreamweaver.

File deals with everything relating to how the HTML files are saved, opened, closed, and tested in the browser. The **Edit** menu allows us to make changes to our work. **View** is used to select different ways of viewing the HTML files in Dreamweaver, and **Insert** doubles up the functions and tools of the Insert panel.

Modify works on a similar theme to the Edit menu. If you expect something to be found in one and it isn't, try the other! The **Text** menu allows you the same formatting control that we saw in the Properties panel, and we've just looked at **Window**.

The **Site** menu features some additional extras that complement the Site panel, looking at the broader picture of the site and related files. **Commands** deals with a few remaining options such as extensions, HTML cleaning, and a couple of other functions.

Out of the whole lot, I probably only ever use File, Edit, Modify, Insert, Site, and Window on a regular basis, and even then I only use three or four items from each list. Many of these menu items also crop up elsewhere in Dreamweaver, either as keyboard short cuts or through panels, so don't worry about learning about all of these menus. Just remember that if you're looking for something, the titles of the menus should make things fairly logical.

We've had a pretty thorough look at the layout of Dreamweaver now. What might have seemed like an amazing display of boxes and figures at the beginning of the chapter should now be starting to make sense.

Setting preferences for our case study

In the next chapter we'll start laying out for the first page of the case study, so there are a few things we need to do to prepare for this before finishing here.

1. Make sure that the site we defined earlier on is open (in my case it's the one called `jerometurnerphotos`), and open the Site panel if it isn't already open. PC users don't really need to expand this to its full two-column layout here.

The Dreamweaver Interface 2

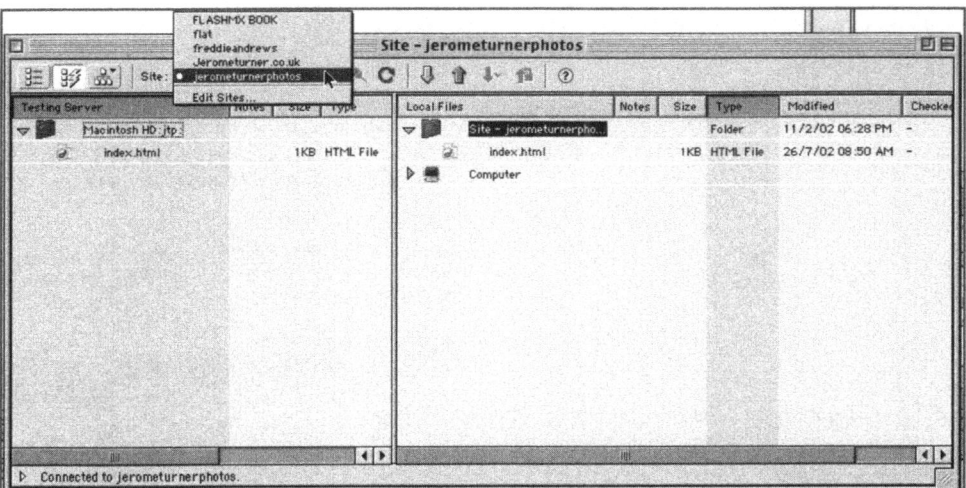

2. Close any documents that are open.

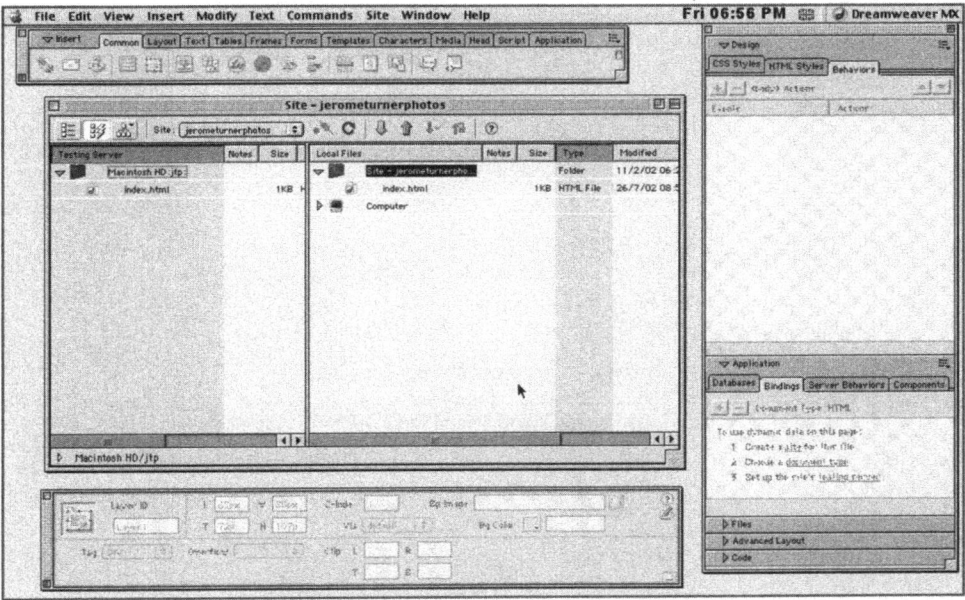

When you're designing, you'll probably find that it helps to have the Document and Site windows open at the same time. On a Mac, one usually lays under the other quite comfortably, whilst PC users can just dock it with the other panels on the right.

Foundation Dreamweaver MX

3. We need to make sure that when we come round to testing our pages, we've chosen a browser to do so in. Go to File > Preview in Browser and you should see the options shown in the screenshot.

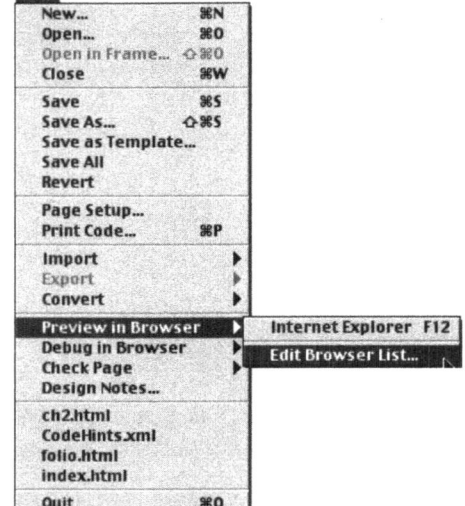

4. Even if you're happy with what you see listed, select Edit Browser List. Mine is set up to test in Internet Explorer at the moment, as you can see, but I also want to add Netscape Navigator to the list to see how users of the browser would see each page.

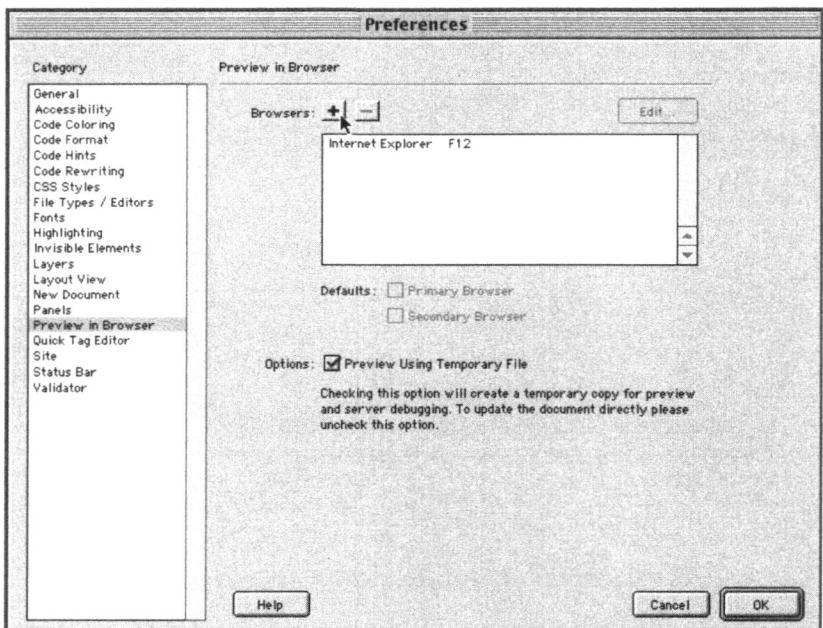

*If you highlight Internet Explorer in the list, you will notice that the **Primary Browser** box is ticked. This means that you can use the keyboard shortcut of F12 to quickly test pages in Internet Explorer. You can test pages in your secondary browser with **Cmd + F12** on a Mac, or **Ctrl + F12** on a PC.*

The Dreamweaver Interface 2

5. To add another browser to the list, click + as shown, and then browse to the location of your browser application file. On a Mac this will probably be in a folder called Internet or something similar, and on a PC, try looking in Program Files. Once that's OK'd, you should find that your browser has been added to the Preview In Browser list.

> As we shall see, it's always best to test your page in as many different browsers as possible before putting it on the web, so if you don't have at least a version of Internet Explorer and a version of Netscape, it might be a good idea to get one now.

6. We just saw the Preferences settings, so let's take another visit there to see what's on offer. Go to the Edit menu and you'll find Preferences right at the bottom. Click on it to open the window.

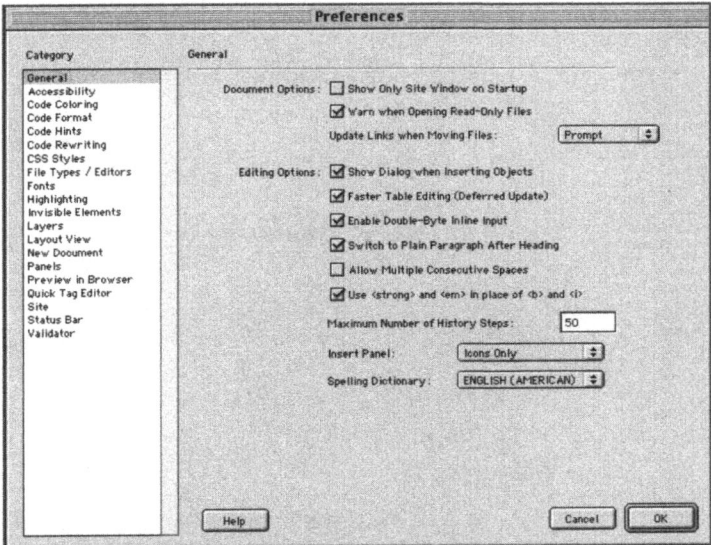

7. Select General in the left-hand pane. If you look in the right-hand pane towards the bottom, you'll see that you can set the number of History Steps, or the number of actions you can undo. Here we see that if we deleted 50 blocks of text for example and then decided we didn't want to, we could jump back 50 History Steps to recover them.

2   Foundation Dreamweaver MX

> *Dreamweaver has to store these steps, so think carefully before you increase the number, as this places additional demands on your system. The default of 50 is probably fair and gives enough room for error to account for even the most inept designers.*

8. You can also set how you'd like to view the Insert panel – as you get tool tips on mouse over anyway, I'd recommend leaving it at the default of Icons Only, though you can try the other options to see if they help. Finally, the Spelling Dictionary sets the Dictionary that will be used when you use the Check Spelling option in the text menu, so select your region of preference.

9. Select Status Bar in the left pane.

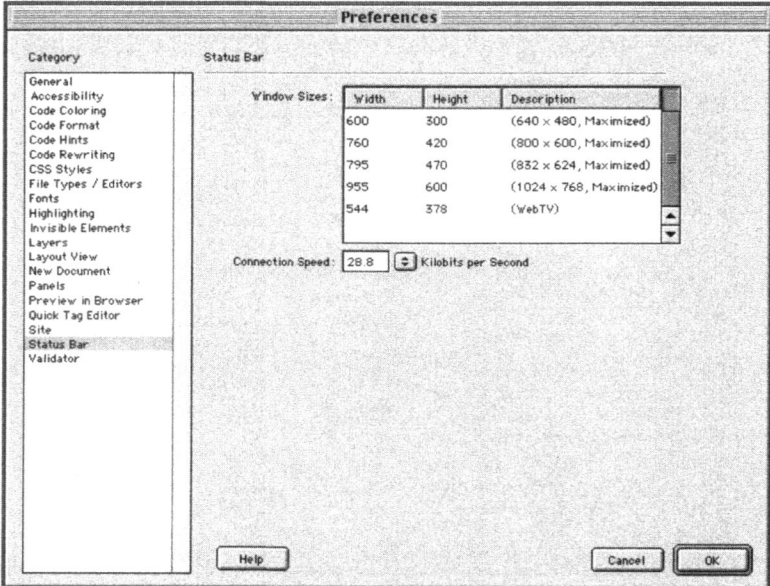

See anything familiar there? Well, the figures relate to the Status Bar that we found running along the bottom of the Document window. Remember all the different settings we picked for the window size to 'jump' to? Well each set can be altered, and there's even room to add your own fresh dimensions at the bottom.

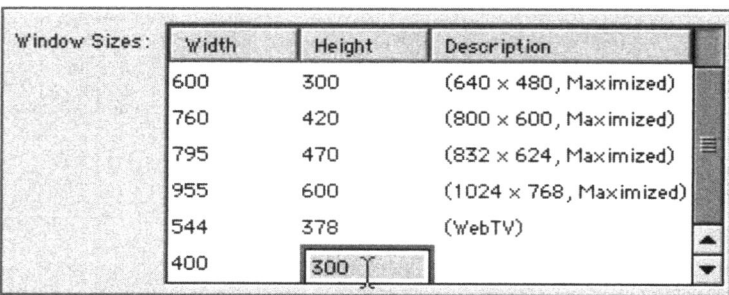

10. Below this, there's another setting that also affects the info on the Status Bar: the connection speed. Earlier, we saw that our ch2.html file was 13k and would take four seconds to load. These loading times obviously depend on the connection speed of your users, so choose this setting according to your target audience. Most people use a 56k modem from home, so that's what I'm using as a basis to display the download times.

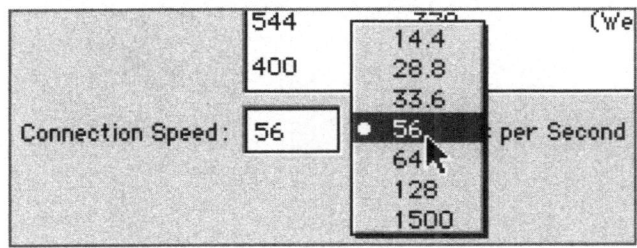

11. Finally we'll set some of the accessibility preferences. Select Accessibility from the list on the left of the Preferences window. Place a check in the box for Images and click OK. This will allow us to add certain attributes to images when we insert them into our web page designs. This is an important part of the design process. By giving textual descriptions of our images we are allowing visitors to our site who use a screenreader, because they are visually impaired, to have access to our images. It also helps users of non-graphical browsers and those people who prefer to set their browsers not to download images to see what's going on on the page.

Summary

Well, it wasn't so scary, was it? As well as setting up Dreamweaver so that we can carry on with the (far more fun) process of creating our web site in the next chapter, we've got ourselves acquainted with all those windows, menus, and options that looked so bewildering at the beginning of the chapter.

Dreamweaver is an easy to use yet incredibly rich and sophisticated tool with a wide range of uses. This means that it has to provide a way to access a huge number of options quickly, and Macromedia have put a lot of hard work in over five versions to make sure that this works well. At some point, you'll probably forget how to find and apply some aspect of Dreamweaver's functionality. You should now know where to go looking for it.

Feel free to come back and visit this chapter to check up on aspects of the interface as you work through the book, but now it's time to move on to the really exciting bit where we start to put our web site plans into practice.

Beginning Layout

What we'll cover in this chapter

- Preparing some images for use in our site
- Designing and creating a 'splash' page
- Adding hyperlinks and buttons to our page

In the previous two chapters, we've sorted out what we want to do with our site, and made ourselves at home with Dreamweaver. Now it's time to start working on our site for real. This chapter is going to involve a lot of practical work, so make sure that your computer is switched on and ready to go before proceeding any further.

In this chapter, we'll be making our first page in Dreamweaver, using the Design View option we saw in the last chapter. This will give us a chance to concentrate on the basics such as text, image insertion, and links for navigation before we look at some of the more advanced options in the next chapter.

Splash pages

The `index.html` page in a site is the first one a browser will load. This page is often treated as the home page – that is, the central stopping off point from which all your other pages branch off. However, that's not always the case. As many sites contain very specific content or file types and are best viewed in certain ways, site developers will often make their `index.html` into a splash page.

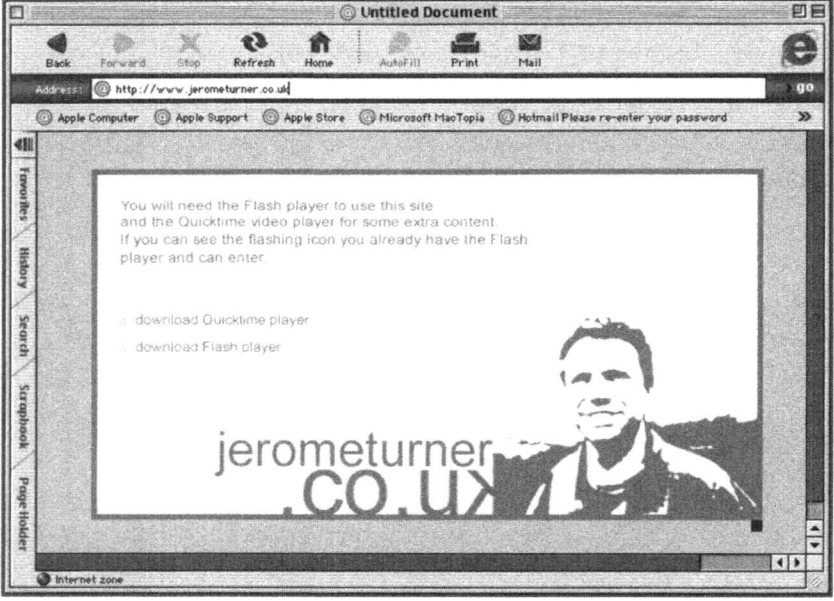

This kind of page prepares the user for the site in case they need any extra downloads or plug-ins to view the site content. Some might say that the best sites are those that can be viewed without plug-ins, but progress on the web is increasingly dependent on technologies like this. Equally, the size of the downloads for the plug-ins is decreasing, making it quicker and easier to download them (the Macromedia Flash MX plug-in will only take 2 - 3 minutes to download on a 56k modem, for example).

Beginning Layout

> *As we'll see in later chapters, we're going to include both some Flash content and some QuickTime movie content in the site, so we need to make sure that our users can view these.*

A splash page can also help by concisely describing your site in a few words, so that a user knows what to expect. Once the user has sorted themselves out with any plug-ins that they need, and decided that they're interested in our site, we also need to provide them with an Enter button to allow them to proceed to our main site. If you take a look at the screenshot of the splash page for my site, you'll see an example of what we're looking for.

Based on this, I created a quick 'drawing' to show what I wanted for the 'JEROME>TURNER>PHOTOGRAPHY' splash page. The sketch represents quite a small layout, maybe taking up a third of the page – it isn't meant to fit completely in the browser.

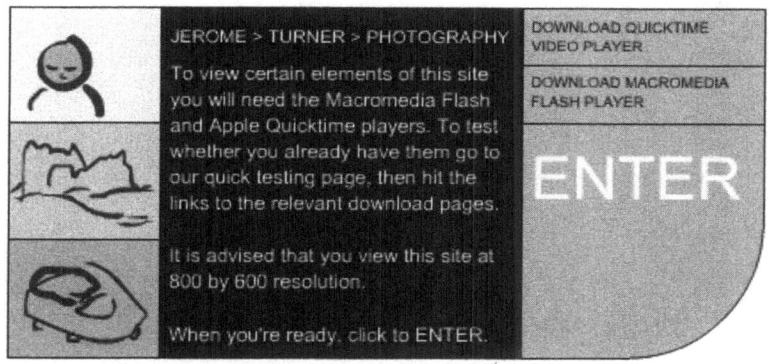

Preparing images for layout

In my sketch for the splash page, I have a column of three images down the left-hand side. These will be 'teaser' images, photos from the site that will hopefully draw the viewer inside. The idea of spending a little time on checking plug-ins shouldn't be a problem to the viewer tempted by such visual delights.

However, I want to make sure these little thumbnail images load up quickly – the splash page must work efficiently from the outset, acting as the ambassador for the rest of the site. If the user can't even see the first page, what does that suggest about the rest of the content? We need to **optimize** our images.

> *An **optimized** image is one that has been saved with the intention of getting the best (or optimum) image quality alongside the smallest file size.*

My sketch was only drawn as a rough idea, so I'll guess that the dimensions are at a ratio of 2:1. Given this, I'll make each image 4cm long and 2cm wide and see how that works out.

1. First, open the images in Photoshop, or in Fireworks. You could just as easily use any other tool that allows you to re-size, crop, and export as a JPEG file – the menu commands will be a little different to the ones we use here, but the functionality will work in exactly the same way.

2. Use the Marquee tool to select the region you want to use. Conveniently, this option is at the top left of the toolbar in both Photoshop and Fireworks.

3. When you've got the region you want, select the crop option – Image > Crop in Photoshop, or Edit > Crop Document in Fireworks.

4. When you've got your cropped image, select the image re-sizing option (Image > Image Size in Photoshop, Modify > Canvas > Image Size in Fireworks). As you can see from the two screenshots, Fireworks and Photoshop users will end up with almost exactly the same dialog box.

5. You'll see that there's a Constrain Proportions option in the bottom left-hand corner, and you'll probably need to un-check this to get the exact sizes you want for the image. Generally, the less you have to stretch pixels in one direction only, the better – so it helps if your original cropping in step 3 was in roughly the correct ratio.

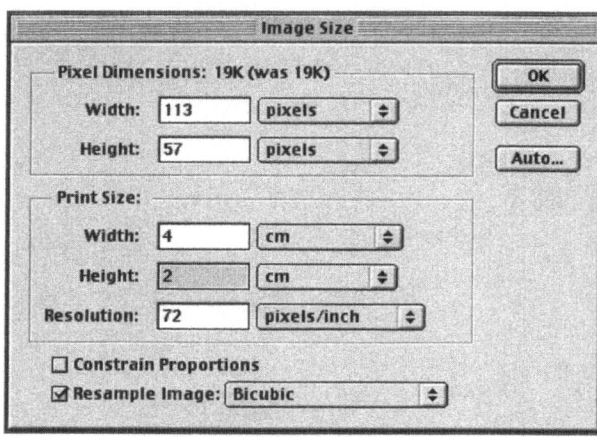 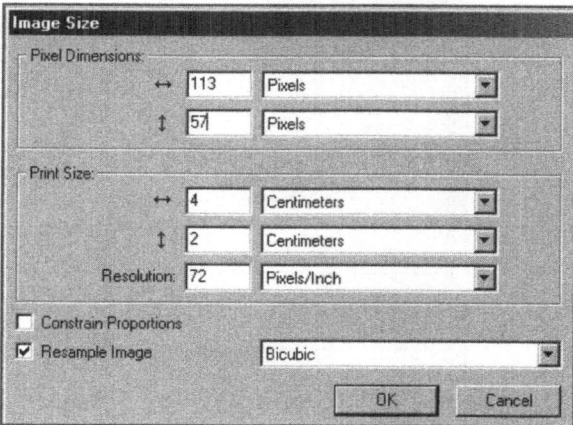

6. Before you click OK, select 72 dots per inch in the Resolution option towards the bottom. Now click OK, and you'll be returned to your image.

7. Finally, we need to export the image as a file suitable for the web. Fireworks allows us to click on the tabs along the top of our image to see different options:

In Photoshop, you'll have to go to File > Save for Web to have the same options.

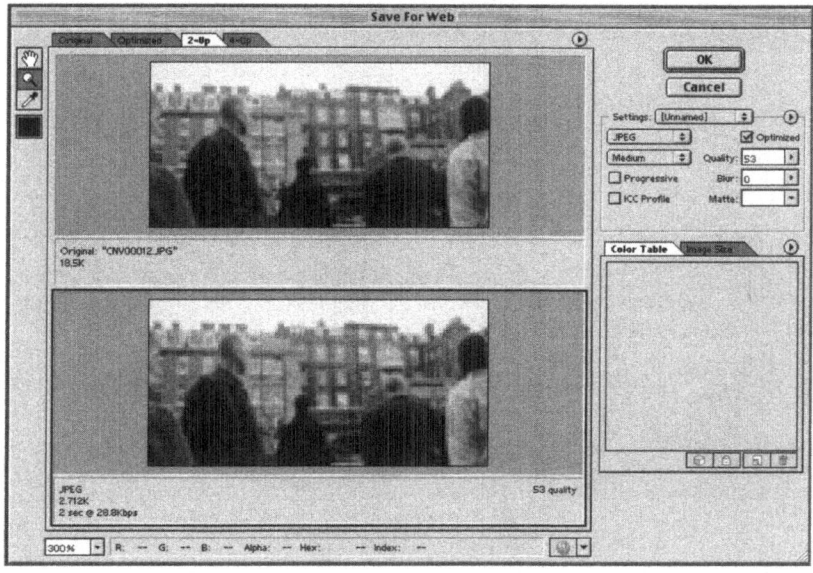

8. In both programs, you'll see that you're presented with what the program thinks is the best option, and some settings for you to play around with in the panel on the right (to see this in Fireworks, you might need to expand the Optimize panel just as you would a panel in Dreamweaver).

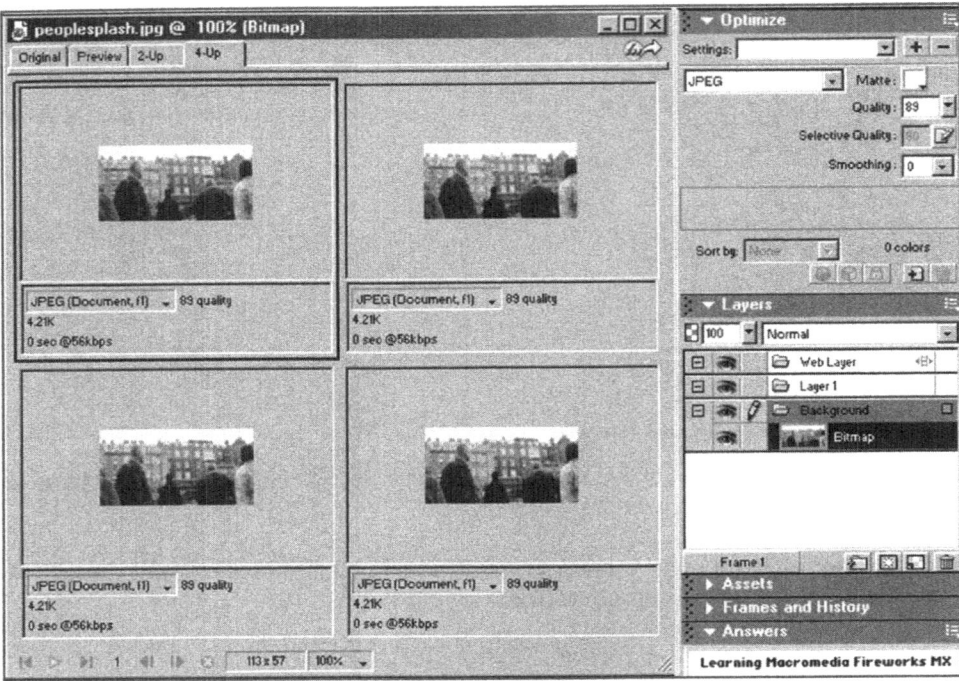

9. Alter the settings until you're convinced that the file size is small enough without affecting the image quality. Both programs will give you file sizes and estimated download times. In this case, I wanted to get each image down to a size where it would take less than two seconds to load.

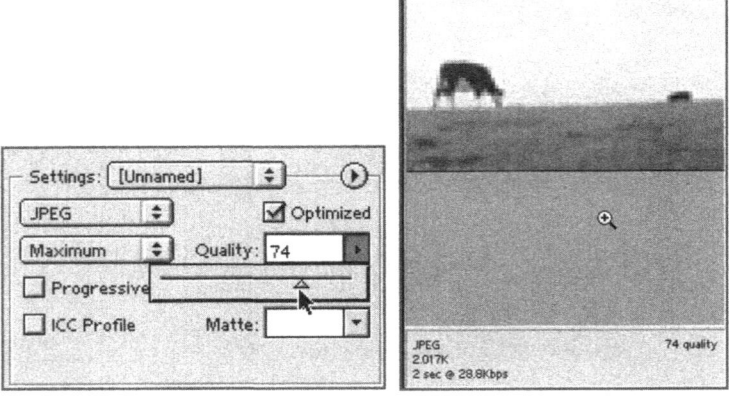

10. If you're using different software, and don't have the option of viewing your export in a layout like that shown in the screenshots, don't worry. Just experiment with the Save as JPEG options in whatever program you're using until you get a reasonable file size.

> *Of course, you may decide that you want to try out Fireworks or Photoshop, in which case, trial versions of Fireworks MX, and Photoshop 7 are available at these URLs:*
> http://www.macromedia.com/software/fireworks/download/
> http://www.adobe.co.uk/support/downloads/main.html

GIFs and JPEGs

Once we've optimized our three pictures, we need to think about other graphics for our splash page. In particular, there's our bottom right-hand corner to consider. Here's where we discover that JPEGs aren't the answer to everything.

Even if we draw our curved shape on a transparent background, the export preview will show a white backing, as you can see from the picture on the right in the screenshot.

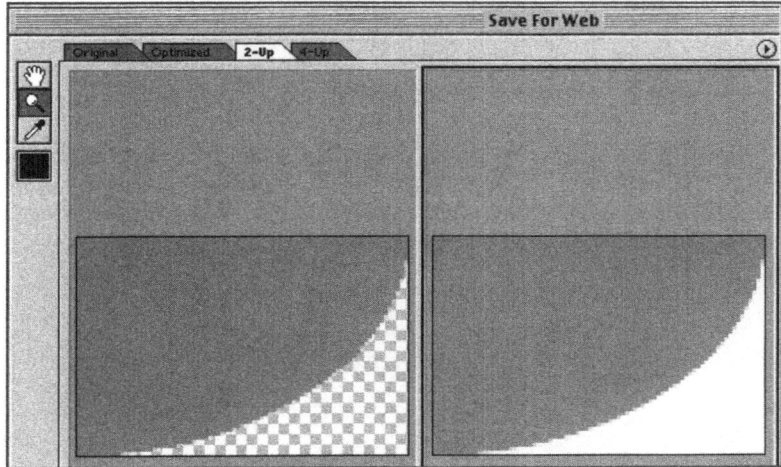

This is fine if you know your Dreamweaver document will also have a white background. As we haven't decided this yet, it would be nice to make the image background transparent, so that we can place it on any color background without a big white block showing up. In other words, we want something like the top image rather than the bottom image in the screenshot over the page.

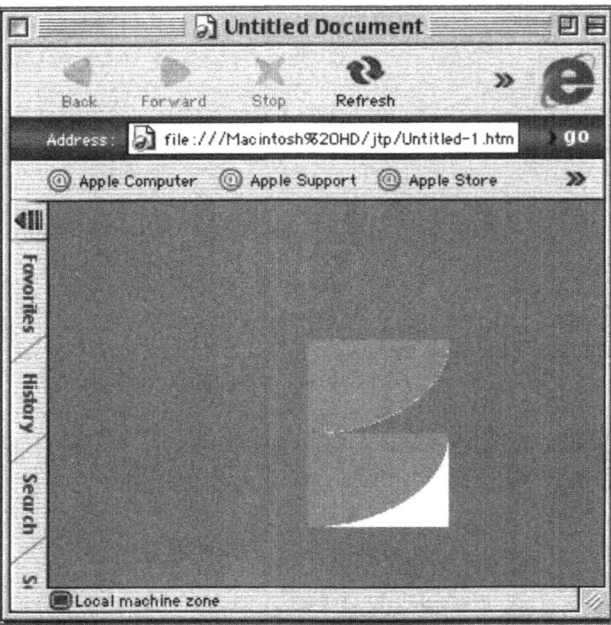

Unfortunately, if you're exporting as a JPEG, you won't find such an option. Instead, we need to make a GIF file instead, and tick the Transparency box in the setting options we get when we save it. Of course, if you decide to go with a JPEG anyway, then make sure that the color matches your Dreamweaver background (the easiest way of doing this is simply to use the same hex color for both).

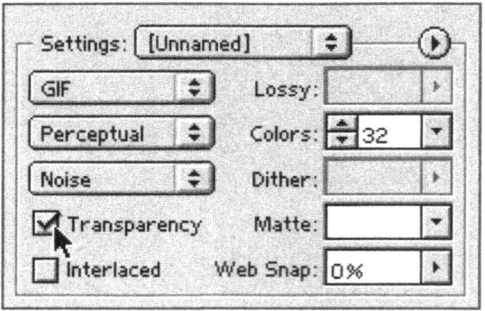

Always hold onto any material in editable form for as long as you're still working on the site. So, in this case, I have a corner.psd *file saved elsewhere that I can return to in Photoshop to tweak later if necessary (in Fireworks this would be* corner.png*) If you do accidentally start deleting these files, you'll be kicking yourself at later stages when you need to alter them.*

Beginning Layout

If you're creating this yourself rather than using the source files – and there's no reason why you shouldn't – you'll need to use the color #99CCFF to create a curve like the one pictured (hint: create an ellipse, and cut the bottom-right hand quarter out). Use your image size options to make it 83x56 pixels in size. As a final step, add the text 'enter' in a bold Arial font to the curve.

We've finished with our images – but if you remember one thing, it should be this: the key is always the file size. Image shape and size can be altered in Dreamweaver but once the file has been dropped into the page, the file size is constant.

The splash page

Now that we have our three pictures, and corner file, we can get started with our splash page. We need to lay the ground for our page by doing three things: moving our image files into our site folder, setting the background color, and creating some cells to hold our content.

Setting up our splash page

First, our image files. If you haven't been able to create these in the previous exercise, you can download the ready-optimized versions from the usual source. We already know that the file will need to be saved in the Local Root Folder (called `jtp` in my case) because it makes up part of the site, but we can also start organizing a bit further.

1. Open up Dreamweaver, and make sure you've opened the correct site from the Site menu. If you've only defined one site, Dreamweaver will probably show you that as the default anyway.

2. Once you've got your site open in the Site window, we want to make a new folder to hold all the external files we'll use in our Dreamweaver pages – images, video, animations, and so on. Do this by right / CTRL-clicking on the root folder, and selecting New Folder (as shown). Give it the name `Assets`.

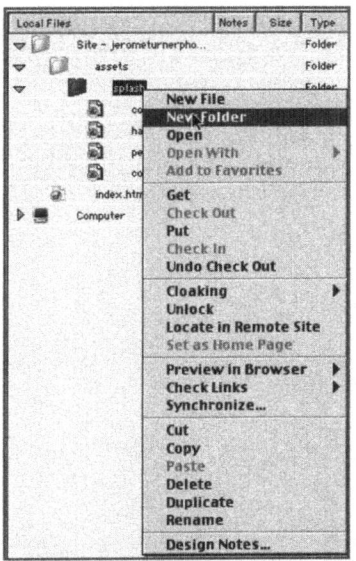
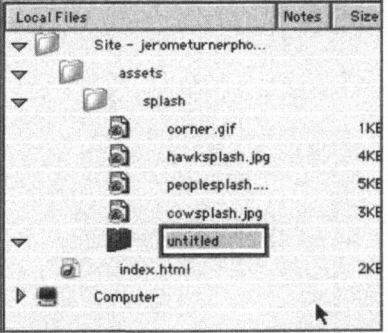

3. Within your new folder, create another folder called splash for our splash page assets.

4. Save our three splash thumbnail images and corner.gif to the splash folder.

> In **Chapter 2,** we discussed the relationship between your Local Root Folder and the FTP server. As Dreamweaver recognizes the location of files by the way you organize them on your HD, it's worth remembering that you must keep the same folder arrangement when you upload the files to the server.

5. As discussed earlier, we're going to make our splash page from the index.html file. As we said in the last chapter, Dreamweaver may well have created one of these for you. If there is one in your folder, double-click on it to open it. If there isn't, go to File > New and create a Basic Page > HTML (in other words, a blank one), and save it into your root folder as index.html.

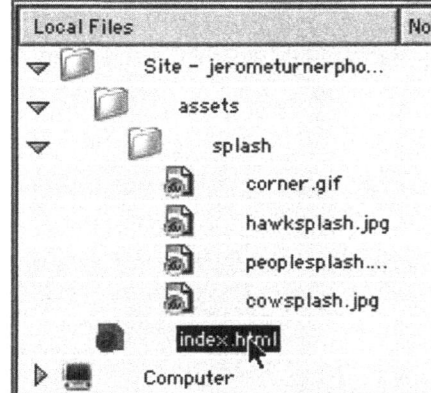

6. Let's take a look at a few of the properties for our index.html page. Go to the Modify menu and select Page Properties.

7. It's pretty clear that we should set the title first, as it's already highlighted. This will appear as the heading in the browser when people view the site, so enter something fairly descriptive. I've gone for JEROME>TURNER>PHOTOGRAPHY>WELCOME.

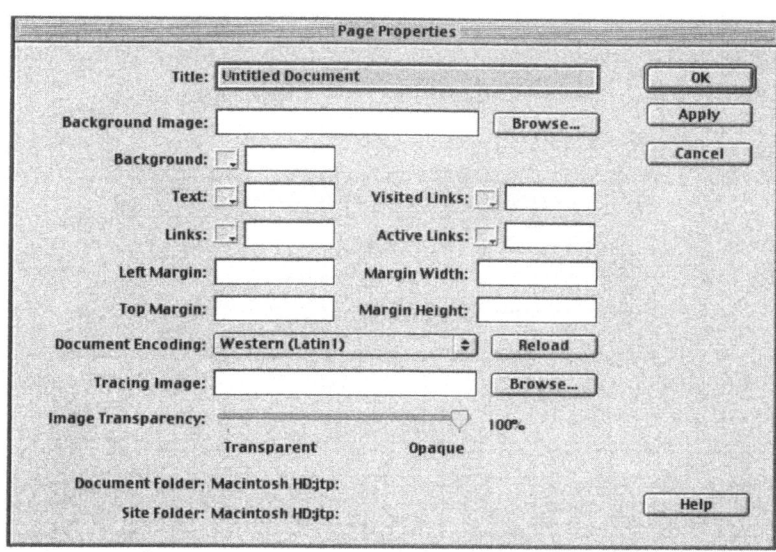

8. We're not going to set every option here, but I'd suggest setting the Background color to something quite neutral and not too imposing, such as a light gray.

9. Give your Text and Links options a color – I've chosen black for text, and a brown color for links. You could also set colors for Visited Links (where the user has already been), and Active Links (what the user is currently looking at), but these aren't so crucial. Click Apply and OK when you've got the colors sorted out to your satisfaction.

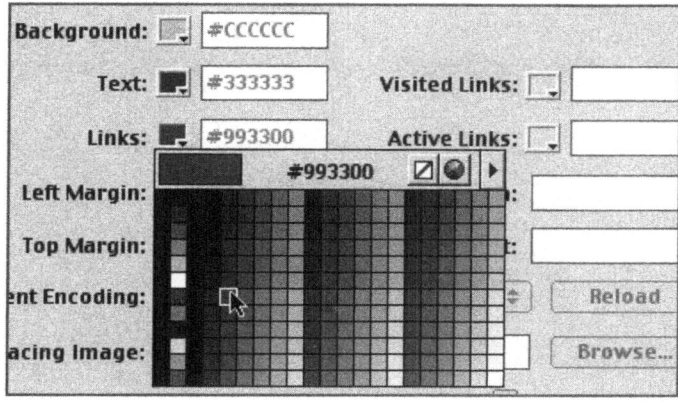

10. Having set up our file to start work, let's get designing. We need to start by drawing some cells to hold our content. Select Layout View so that we can concentrate on what we're doing.

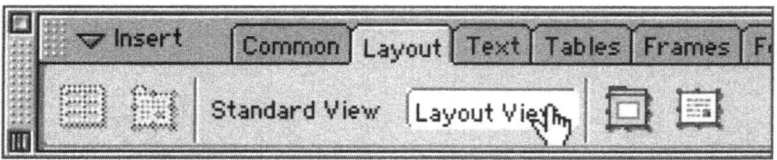

As we've mentioned before, you can select Standard View or Layout View from the Layout tab when laying out content in Dreamweaver. We've Selected Layout View here, as it will allow us to draw tables and spaces right *into* the document.

11. In the Layout tab click on Draw Layout Cell.

Notice the description at the bottom of the Document window, giving hints as to how the tool should be used.

Draw a cell in an empty area. Command draws multiple cells, Option disables snapping.

12. Now, we need to draw a Layout Cell for the first of our images. After selecting the Draw Layout Cell icon, you'll notice that your mouse turns into a crosshair when you move it across the stage. Click and drag to create a cell. Don't worry too much about the size of the cell – we'll fix that in a moment – and don't be confused by the fact that the appearance of the whole page changes on releasing the mouse (as shown below).

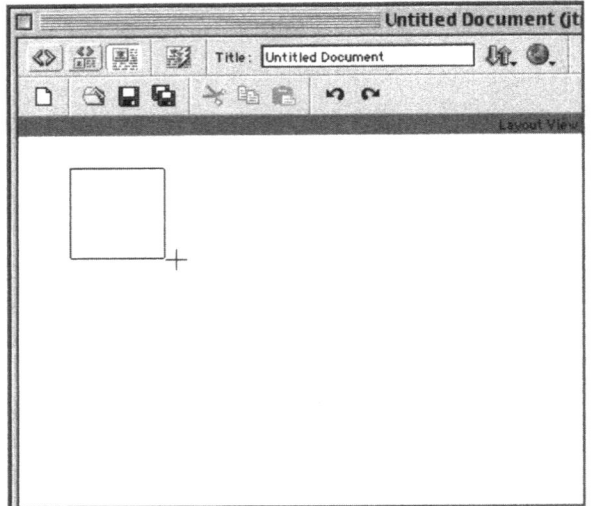
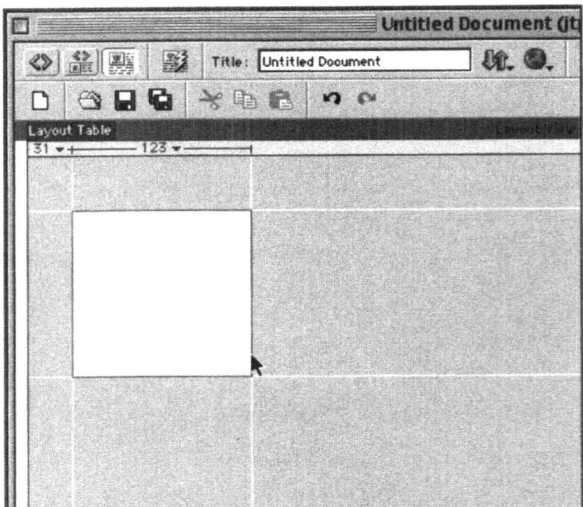

13. There are various ways of placing the image in your newly made space. You could use the Insert > Common tab or the Insert menu, but both methods require you to Browse for your image and find it in the relevant folder. There's a quicker way – select Window > Assets, and click on the Images icon in the top left (as shown).

Beginning Layout

14. This will list all images stored in the Root Folder (regardless of any sub folders). To place the image in your new space, simply drag and drop your file into the document. I started off with the cow image.

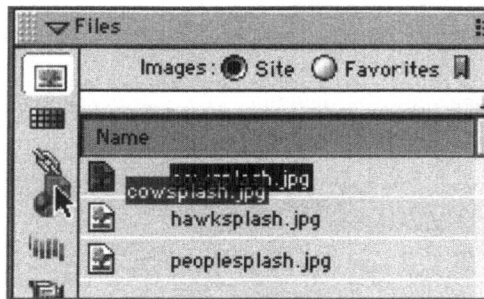
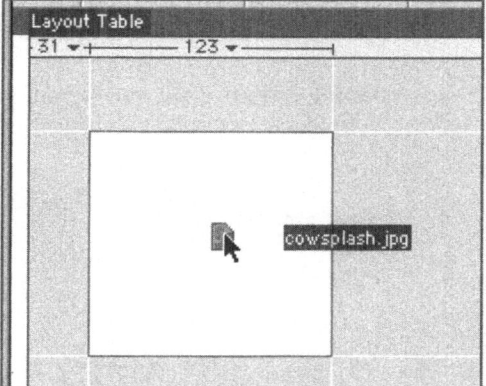

15. A pop-up window will ask you to add a short or long description of the image here for users who either can't or choose not to view the images on your site. Enter a quick description, and we can move on.

Working with cells

We have our page nicely set up, and we have our first photo in our cell. We can see that the photo doesn't quite fit in our cell, though, so let's fix this.

1. Click once on the center of the image to select it (as shown).

2. Hover over the bottom right corner of the image until the diagonal arrows appear, then click and drag the image out. On releasing you'll see the new size/shape.

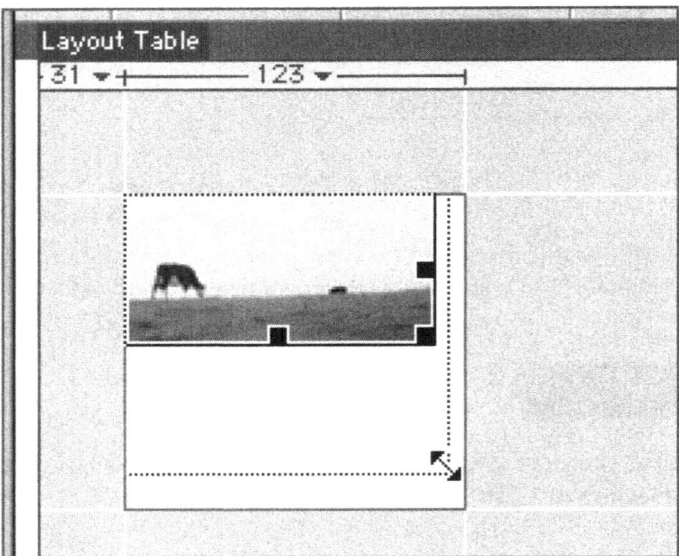

To stretch in a horizontal or vertical direction, use either of the other two handles on the image. To enlarge to scale, hold down the SHIFT *key whilst dragging the handles.*

3. You'll notice a loss in picture quality as the pixels have been stretched to accommodate the new dimensions. After all, Dreamweaver only has the original image to work with – if it's enlarged, there's nowhere for it to get any extra detail from. This isn't going to look great, so return our picture to its original dimensions by clicking Reset Size in the Properties panel.

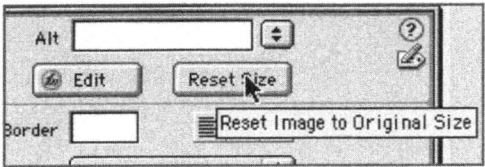

4. Our other option is to resize the cell that holds the image. Select the cell by clicking on its outline (as opposed to the image itself). Hover over a corner until you see the diagonal arrows and drag and drop the Cell outline around the image. To make sure it will fit snugly around the image, release the mouse when it's over the center, and the cell will align itself to the edges of the image.

3   Foundation Dreamweaver MX

You could have also re-sized the cell by selecting the cell outline and then matching the cell dimensions in the Properties panel to those of the image.

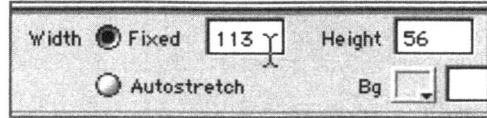

5. So, we've got our first picture sorted. Time to make two more cells for our other pictures. Select the Draw Layout Cell button again, and draw another cell underneath the first one. You should find that it snaps easily into line with the previous cell.

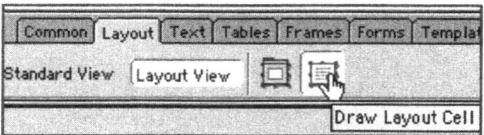

To avoid having to keep returning to the Draw Layout Cell *button for each cell, keep the* CTRL/APPLE *key held down whilst drawing.*

If you look at the image above you'll see that my bottom Cell is shorter than the others. Won't this cause a problem given that all the images are the same size? No, because if a Cell is too small for an Asset, it automatically resizes to be big enough to accommodate the image.

6. Import the other two pictures into you two new cells. You'll probably now get something like the picture shown, with extra cells underneath both pictures where you've re-sized the cells. Click on the outside of the bottom picture, and drag the top of that cell up to meet the picture above it, and then resize the cell around the picture.

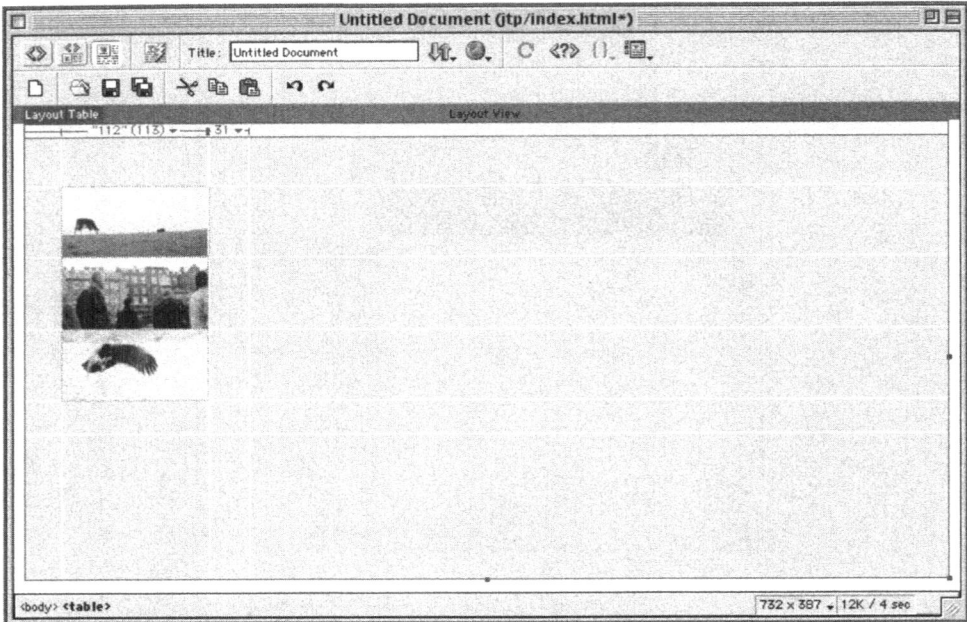

7. So far, our design should look like the shot above. We now want to add the text in the middle, so we need to add some new cells for the text to fit into. Add two cells (as shown) to the right of your pictures. Make sure the new cells finish flush with the photos.

8. To add the text, click inside the top cell and take a look at the Properties panel. As this is the title, choose the Arial font, size 3.

Beginning Layout 3

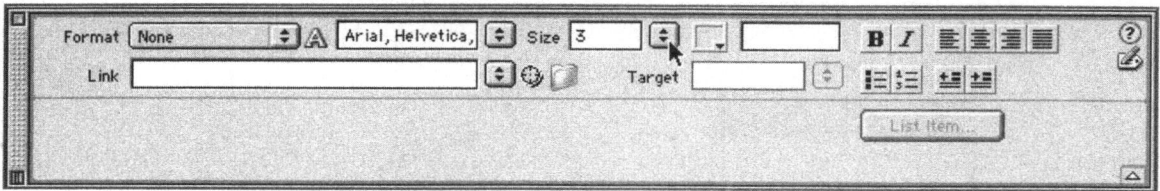

Please note: this way of choosing fonts is not always considered the best option for web pages. It's fine for our purposes, as we're keeping things simple in this chapter, but the next chapter will be showing us a different way of dealing with fonts and styles in our main site.

9. Back in the Document window, type the title. As the cell is quite small, it scrolls onto the next line and resizes the cell when I reach the edge, leaving a horrible white space underneath the first photo.

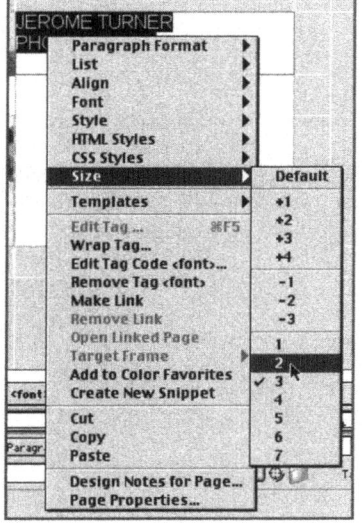

10. To fix this, make the text a bit smaller by selecting it and reducing the size to 2 (either in the Properties panel, or – as shown – by right/CTRL-clicking). If it still takes up more than one line, then click on the text cell outline, and use the handle to drag the cell until it's wide enough for the text.

11. Reduce the size of the picture cell until it sits flush with the pictures below it again in the same way.

12. Drag the handles on the other image cells until the images are all realigned as before. Don't forget to move the empty text cell underneath up to meet the title cell.

13. The gap on the left is still too small, as I want my design to appear a couple of centimeters from the top left corner. Standard View allows you to manipulate whole columns and is better suited to the job of enlarging the space (now seen as a column) on the left, so select that now.

Beginning Layout

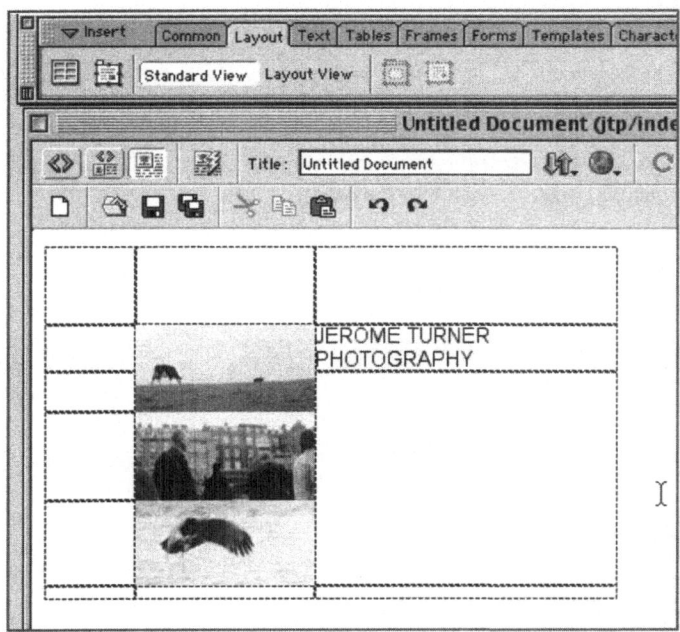

As soon as you switch over you should notice that the layout you've just been working on is now seen as a table. There is no physical transformation – if you go back to Layout View it's all there as before.

14. Hover your mouse over the right edge of the second column until the 'dragging arrows' icon appears, as shown. Drag right to stretch the column and watch all the cells in the column move as one (in Layout View, you'll remember, each cell is independent of the others). Now hover over the right edge of the first column and drag right until Dreamweaver won't let you drag any further. You should notice that the gap opening up to the right of each image is fixed as you re-size the first column.

> As you resize the column, you might find it hits a point where you can't drag it any more. In this case, select the table as a whole, by clicking on the very edge, and pull this out. This gives more room to stretch out that troublesome column, as the column is after all something contained within the table.

16. Return to Layout View to see the design we've created.

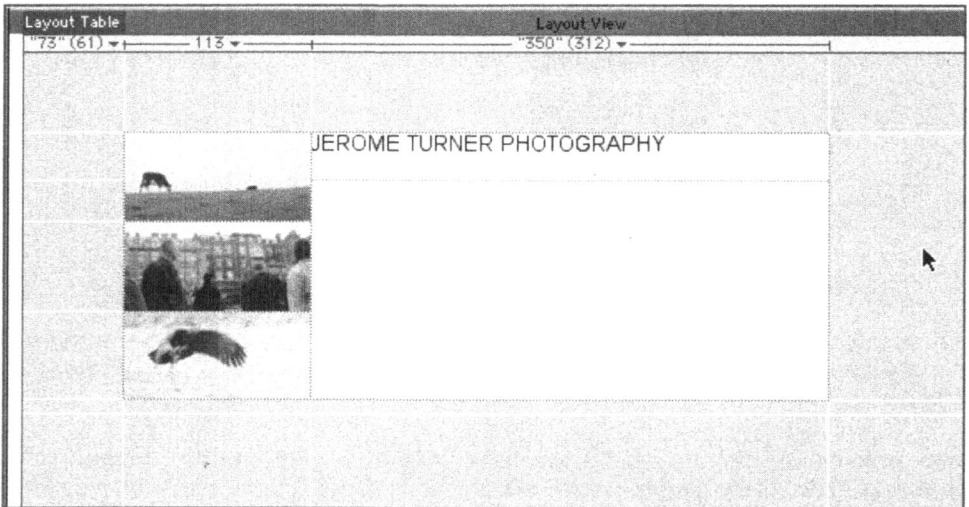

Finishing design touches

So now it's only left for me to make three new cells in the column to the right of the main text column, enter some more text and an image. We spoke earlier about transparent GIF files that can be used when the image isn't a rectangle and needs to be laid over a colored background. The `corner.gif` image is an example of this, and we're going to see how useful it is now.

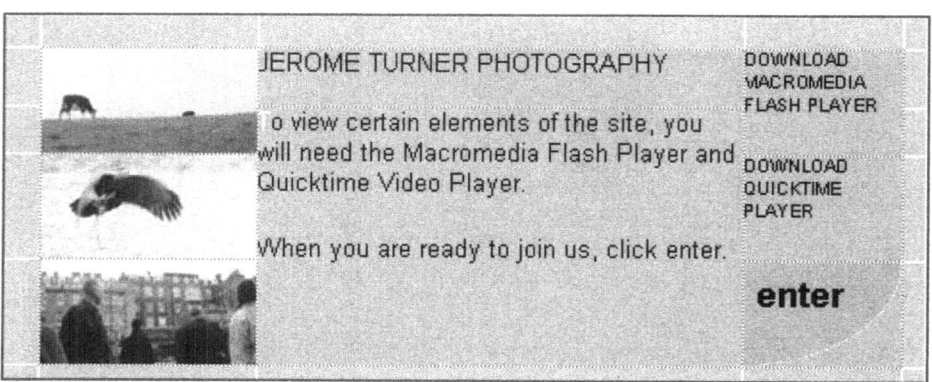

Beginning Layout 3

Finishing off the design

Everything's in place but we're still not quite there. The color of the two download areas needs to match the blue corner piece for starters.

1. Make sure Layout View is still selected, and add the three cells to the right of our main text column. You should remember how to do this by now – if not, go and check out the previous exercises!

2. Add the `corner.gif` graphic to the bottom cell. Remember that the right hand side of the graphic starts at the far right corner of the blue corner. If you can see white between the top right-hand corner of the corner and the side of the frame, then you need to resize the frame by clicking on the frame border and dragging it out.

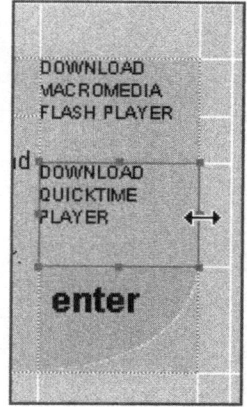

3. Resize the cells so that they all match the size of the corner cell, and add the text you can see in the screenshot (I used the same Arial font, size 1). If you use different text, make sure that your text is no longer than that shown, as this will cause the text to be bigger than our corner graphic.

4. Select the cell above the corner graphic by clicking on the outline, and take a look at the Properties panel. Click on the Bg option to select a background color – I've used #99CCFF, the same blue that appears in the rest of the site and the corner graphic.

> *You'll appreciate that the more you work with different colors, it might help to keep a note of those you're using. If you want to find out what color an element on your page is, simply click on the color with the eyedropper tool that comes up as soon as you open the color palette.*

5. Do the same with the next cell up, to form a column of blue.

I'd like to do something different with the middle text column, but if you remember the original designs, I'm working with a pretty limited palette of colors – blue, black, and white. So, let's make the middle section black and the text white.

6. Hold on, didn't we set the text color to black in the Document Properties? Well yes, but we can override that by selecting the text and choosing a new color in the Properties panel. The predefined color works more like a 'default' color that's used if nothing else is specified. So, select the text, and select white from the Properties panel.

> *When we start adding links to our text, the color will always be as defined in the Page Properties.*

7. Next, set the background color of the cells to black in the same way that we've just made our cells on the right blue.

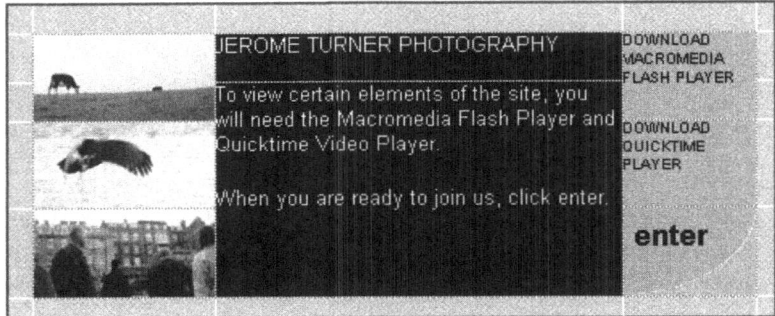

8. Finally, I don't really like the way the text appears in the right column in the screenshot. Justify the text to the right by selecting the text, and clicking on Align Right from the Paragraph settings in the Properties panel. Repeat this for the other cell.

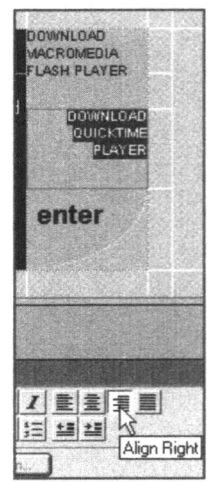

9. Test this in your browser. If it looks great, then that just goes to show that you *always* need to test things on a variety of browsers and platforms. If you test it on Internet Explorer for the PC, for example, you'll get something like the shot pictured overleaf:

Oops. We've got a few more things to sort out before we finish, then. We'll make things a little simpler – never a bad idea in web design. We'll also fix the issue with the alignment of our curved graphic that you can see in the screenshot – which happens because different browsers have different default settings for line/word spacing.

10. First, the tidying. switch to Standard View, click on the first cell, and SHIFT-click on the other two cells to select them all.

11. Now click on the Merge cells button, as pictured.

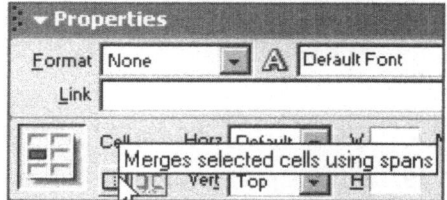

12. This will leave you with all three pictures strung out along the top of your screen. Place the cursor before the second and third pictures (if you have difficulty placing it, place it at the end of the cell, and use your cursor keys). Insert a carriage return before each picture by pressing SHIFT+RETURN.

13. Select the pictures, and set their alignment to Top. If this results in a little white space at the bottom, shift back to Layout View, and drag the cell up so that the bottom line fits the pictures snugly. Align the bottom of the other cells to this.

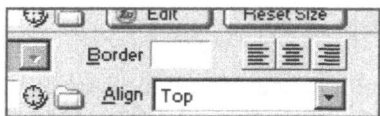

14. Now that we've had some practice merging and inserting carriage returns, we're going to merge the two cells in the middle. In Standard View, select and merge them in the same way as before.

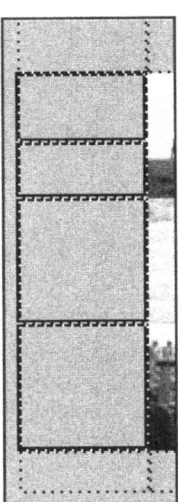

15. Do the same to the empty 'spacer' cells on the left and right (as shown).

16. As you can see, all those cells helped when we were laying stuff out, but taking a moment to simplify things before proceeding is well worth it. Merge the two cells with the Flash and QuickTime links in them and we're done with merging cells.

17. Add carriage returns (as before, with SHIFT+RETURN) to the end of each line of text. This will make sure that your browser doesn't try and scroll the text onto one line when different browsers give the text slightly different qualities.

18. If you test in your browser now, you'll notice a white gap between the right-hand cells. This means we need to set the height for the top cell so that it doesn't get things wrong. If you click on the images to see the values, you'll see that the height of the pictures of the left (169) minus the height of the corner graphic (56) is 113. Select the cell with the links in, and enter 113 into the height box in the Properties panel.

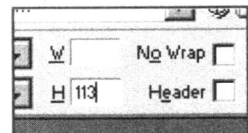

19. Test the page in your browser, and everything should be looking great. If you're not convinced by the background color you set earlier, go to Modify > Page Properties, and choose a color from the Background palette until you're happy with the results.

Adding functionality to our splash page

To finish off our splash page, we need to add functionality to our nicely designed elements. In other words, we need to add an Enter sign to take the user to the main site, and we need to create the links to the download sites for the two plug-ins.

Creating web links

1. The best way to find the URLs for our plug-in downloads is by going to the appropriate sites, finding the correct page, and copying the URL out of your browser address bar with Edit > Copy. Make sure the page that you've selected allows your viewer to make any choices they need to – for example, make sure they can choose between PC and Mac downloads.

2. Back in Dreamweaver, highlight the piece of text that we want to make 'clickable' as the link to the page, and use Edit > Paste to paste the URL into the Link field in the Properties panel, as shown.

Beginning Layout

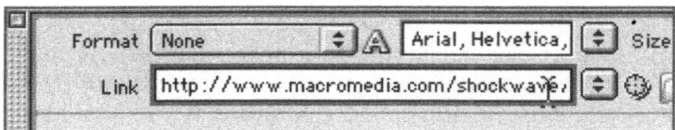

3. Do the same for the Quicktime download. You should notice that both 'download' pieces of text are now underlined in the color you specified in the Page properties earlier. The beauty of this method of linking from one page to the next is that you can do it anywhere in your text.

4. Once you've used a link once, you can apply the same URL link to other objects very easily. Select the 'Macromedia Flash Player' text in the middle cell, and bring up the Files panel (Window > Assets).

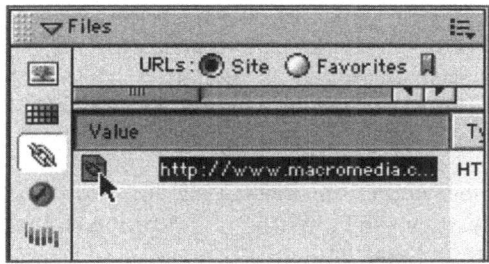

5. Click on the chain icon in the set of icons on the left-hand side of the box. Drag the URL link from here, and drop it on the text. Repeat this for the 'QuickTime Video Player' text.

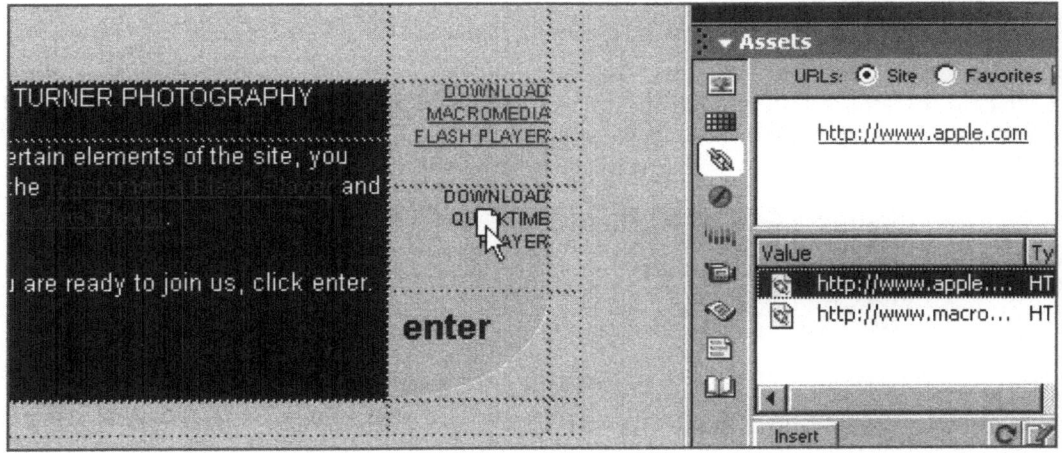

You create links using images in exactly the same way as we just have for the text, by selecting the image and either typing the URL into the Properties panel or dragging the URL over from the Files panel.

Creating internal links

The friendly usability of Dreamweaver extends as far as linking between our own pages. To do this, we simply highlight the text or image as before, and enter the address. The difference is that, this time, we don't need to put all the http:// information because the file we're working on is on the same level in the server.

So, for a link to mainpage.html I could just type mainpage.html into the Link field. If that file was in a folder called pages within the Root folder, then the link would need to read pages/mainpage.html.

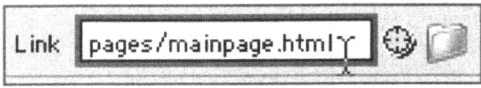

If you feel like a rest from typing, then you might notice two icons to the right of the Link field in the Properties panel. The folder icon will let you browse to the HTML file you want to link to, while the circular target icon is a bit more interesting. This allows you to 'point' to the file you wish to link to.

To test it, create a blank Dreamweaver document, and save it with a name. Then, make sure the Site window is open and at least partly visible, even if it's just sitting in the background. Highlight an image, and click and hold down on the target icon.

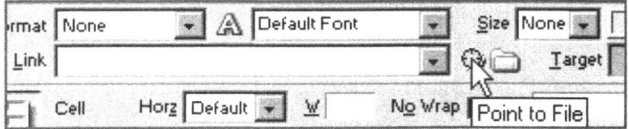

An arrow will appear, and this can be dragged to the Site window, where you can choose a file to link to. Release the mouse button, and the correct link will appear in the Link field. We're going to do something a little more sophisticated for our enter button, but this method will prove very useful to you in your Dreamweaver journeys – so don't forget about it!

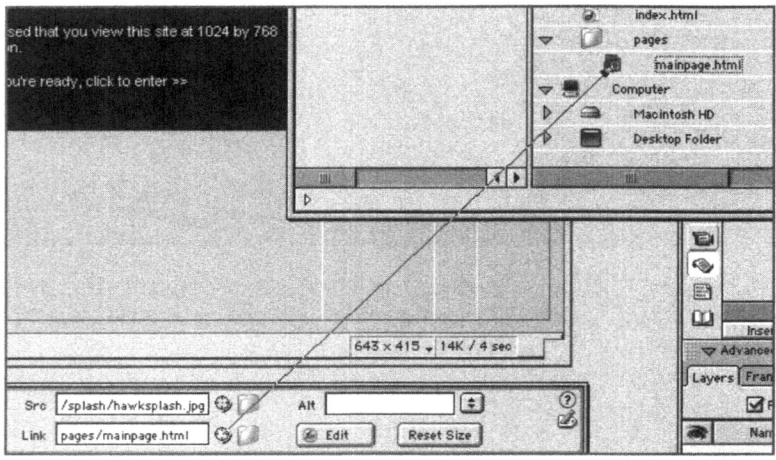

Linking with hotspots

Often, a site will contain large or odd shaped graphics that are used as links. In the case of my `corner.gif` I'd like the graphic to provide a link to enter the site. The problem is that if I simply select the image, the 'clickable' area will be the entire (square) image, and not just the blue area.

To fix this we can draw what's called a **hotspot** over the image. This will specify that only certain areas of the image are clickable.

1. Select our blue corner, as shown above.

2. In the Properties panel, you will find three buttons for creating hotspot areas, as shown below. (These are only visible if you have the Properties panel extended to its full size, so click on the arrow in the bottom right-hand corner if you can only see the top half of the screenshot.) As we want the area to cover an odd shape, pick the Polygon Hotspot Tool on the right of the three icons.

3. Create the hotspot by clicking on the image. Then click where you want the hotspot to start, move the mouse to a new point, click again, and so on until you come back round to complete the shape as shown.

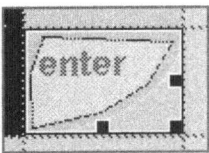

4. Once the hotspot is complete, select it, and add the Link in the Properties panel as usual. This will link straight into the site so we'll make it navigate to the `about.html` page.

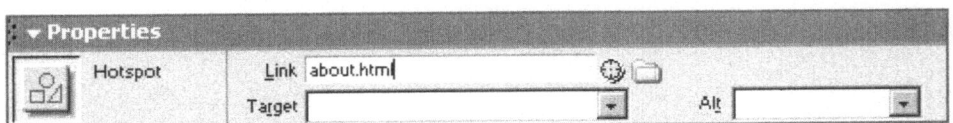

Summary

Congratulations! Three chapters in, and we've got our first real Dreamweaver page up and running.

This chapter has given us an opportunity to cover some of the key features of Dreamweaver layout using the Design view. We'll be continuing to look at some more layout options in future chapters, but don't ever be afraid to experiment with the various settings Dreamweaver offers; that's exactly how I learned a lot of this information! Just remember to keep hitting F12 as often as possible to preview the page in your browser – it will help you to keep perspective on what you're doing.

In the next chapter, we'll be looking at a slightly different way of dealing with some of what we've done in this chapter. When we come to our main site, we're going to want to be consistent in design across all the pages, and we're also going to want to save ourselves as much work as possible. We'll be doing this by using a CSS file to provide formatting and styling for our pages, and a template to provide the layout elements that remain consistent across all the pages.

Layout with Templates

What we'll cover in this chapter

- *The basics of page layout in Dreamweaver MX*
- *Using frames to arrange content*
- *Introducing layers as a dynamic layout alternative*
- *Using Cascading Style Sheets to standardize and coordinate colors, fonts and other visual elements*

People often forget that the web is fairly young. In fact, it was 'invented' in the early 1990s and only became popular several years later. Despite this, it's moved swiftly in terms of what you can do with regards to page layout – to the extent that both web browsers and design tools have struggled to keep up with designers' needs and ever-evolving web standards.

This chapter will show you how Dreamweaver MX can cope with anything from the basic pages of old to cutting-edge design ideas. We'll cover concepts like **frames**, **layers**, and **tables** before starting to set up a template for our case study with a page that uses tables and a **Cascading Style Sheet (CSS)**.

> *Cascading Style Sheets are documents external to your HTML pages that enable you to define how aspects such as the size and font used in your text is handled across the entirety of your site – more on these later in the chapter.*

Layout types

Each of the various methods that you can use to lay out your web pages has its own strengths and weaknesses, and each can be useful in particular circumstances. Later in the chapter, we'll be going over what's best for our case study. Before we do that though, let's take a look at the options that Dreamweaver offers you.

Plain text

Since the web was originally used as a repository for technical documents, no real flamboyance was needed. Documents were marked up simply, and the only formatting that took place was the ability to create headers, lists, and paragraphs in text, along with the odd table.

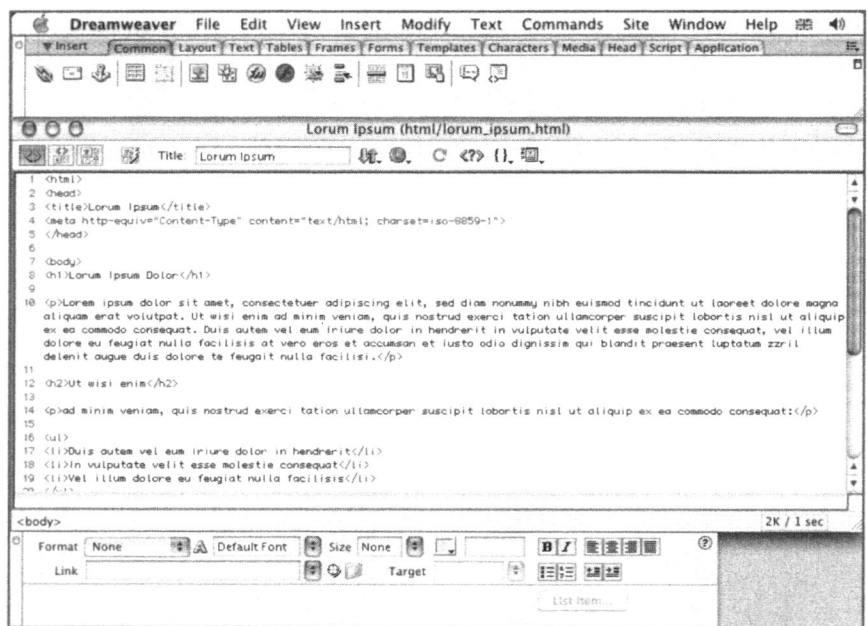

Most of us have seen HTML like that shown on the previous page, and the idea of making some text bold by putting <b> and </b> either side of it isn't too hard to grasp for those of us who haven't.

The obvious advantage of using such a method is that the pages will display on *any* browser and download very quickly. As you can see from the second screenshot, though, it's not terribly visually appealing. Plain text is useful for part of our site, but if we want our page to have some impact, it's time to go and look at some alternatives.

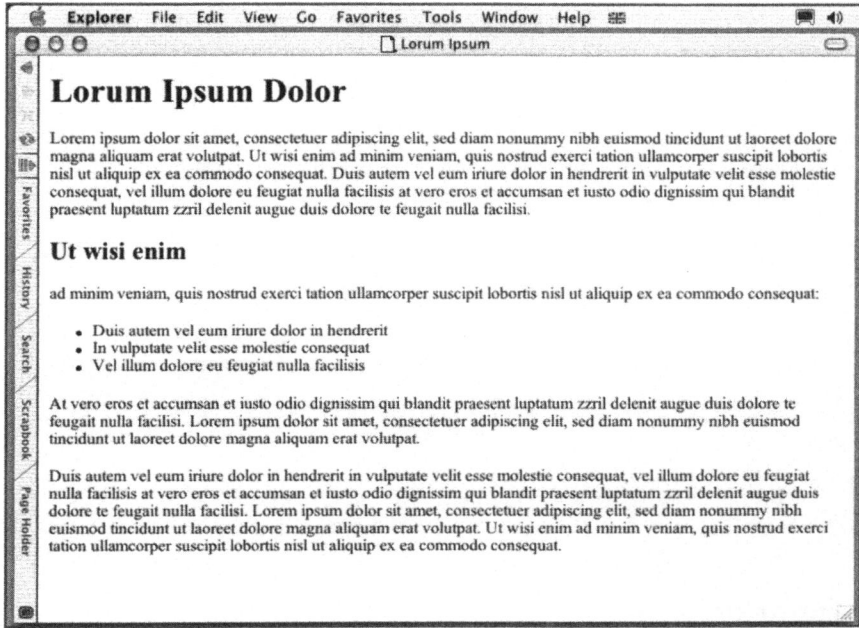

Frames

Despite their massive popularity around four years ago, frames are in decline on the web, and for good reason. While they do offer benefits – such as enabling a site's navigation area to always remain static and on-screen in a specific location – using frames can cause all sorts of issues for web designers. There are three main problems with frames:

- Unless you use some fairly hefty scripting, you cannot bookmark individual pages; your browser will simply bookmark the frameset and the pages you see when you first arrive at the site. This is something that confuses and annoys a fair amount of people who use the web.

- Frames can also be awkward to update when dealing with a template-based site; in fact, you'll notice how few of the biggest online brands make use of frames for this very reason.

- Frames-based sites don't work particularly well with search engines. Typically, the frameset and all its pages will each be spidered individually. This means that web users will often end up clicking on links to 'orphaned' pages, which only show part of the page you want to see, and therefore lack navigation, footers, and so on.

> 'Spidering' is the term given to a search engine working its way through a web site and saving all the page details to its database.

You can get around the search engine problem by using JavaScript to force the entire frameset to load, but this causes further problems as it chokes certain browsers. As you can already see, this is merely trying to get around a problem with a clunky workaround – never a great start for a site.

Enough of the negative; surely there are some reasons to use frames? Well, perhaps. Some news/community sites make good use of them, such as designers' Mecca www.newstoday.com. On this site, the frames enable a large amount of news content to be immediately accessible, along with providing a way of updating forum posts without reloading the entire site (or, for that matter, perhaps losing something you were reading elsewhere on the page).

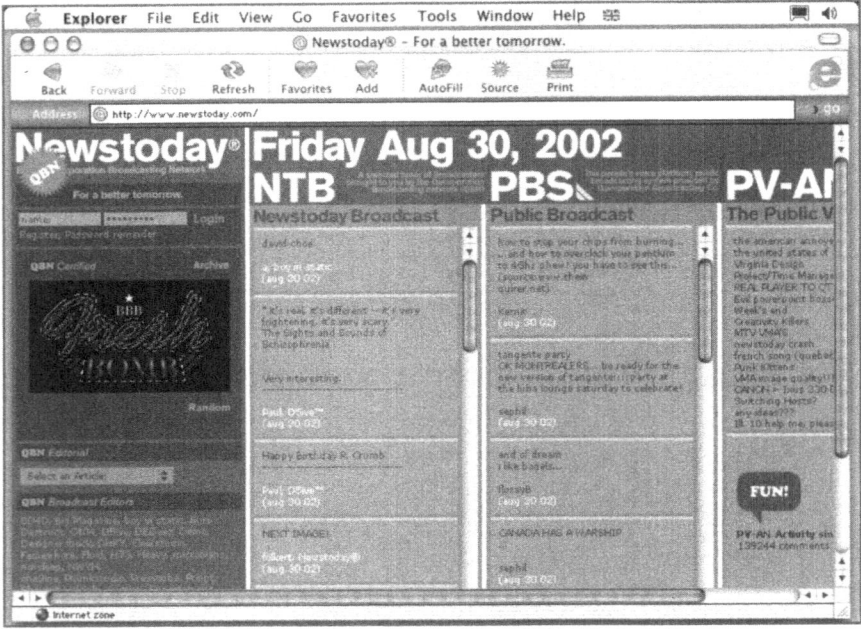

Many sites also make use of frames so that they can have a static navigation and corporate identity on-screen at all times. This can be an advantage, although you often end up with a jarring design 'split' in the page where the frame with the navigation bar meets the frame with the rest of the content – something we're aiming to avoid with our design-led site.

Creating frames in Dreamweaver

In most cases it's better to follow the path that we'll take later in this chapter: have a version of your navigation at the top *and* foot of the page, and avoid frames entirely. That doesn't change the fact that

Layout with Templates 4

they can be useful in certain circumstances, and if you decide that frames are for you then Dreamweaver MX can handle them with little fuss.

1. Make sure that you're in the site that we've set up and used in the last few chapters, and go to File > New Document. Select Framesets from the left-hand column, as pictured.

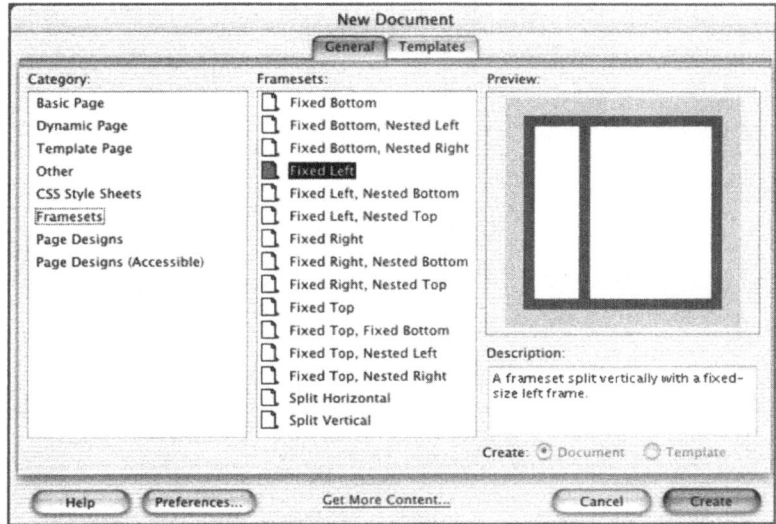

2. In the right-hand column, you'll be presented with a number of options, along with a visual preview and short description of the frameset. It's best to stick with two-frame set-ups, as nesting – creating framesets within framesets – can become complicated extremely quickly, so choose any of the two frame layouts from this column. You'll see from the screenshot that we've gone for the Fixed Left option.

> *Any frames referred to as 'fixed' in the descriptions in the bottom right remain static, while the content in the others will be 'liquid' in terms of their design (in other words, they'll stretch to take up any remaining screen space). 'Fixed Left' means that our left-hand frame has a set width, and the right-hand frame will simply fill the rest of the page.*

3. Click on Create once you've selected your frameset, and you'll see it displayed on your screen. You can then use the Frames panel to select a frame to work on in order to add content, and the Properties panel to edit various details about each individual frame.

Foundation Dreamweaver MX

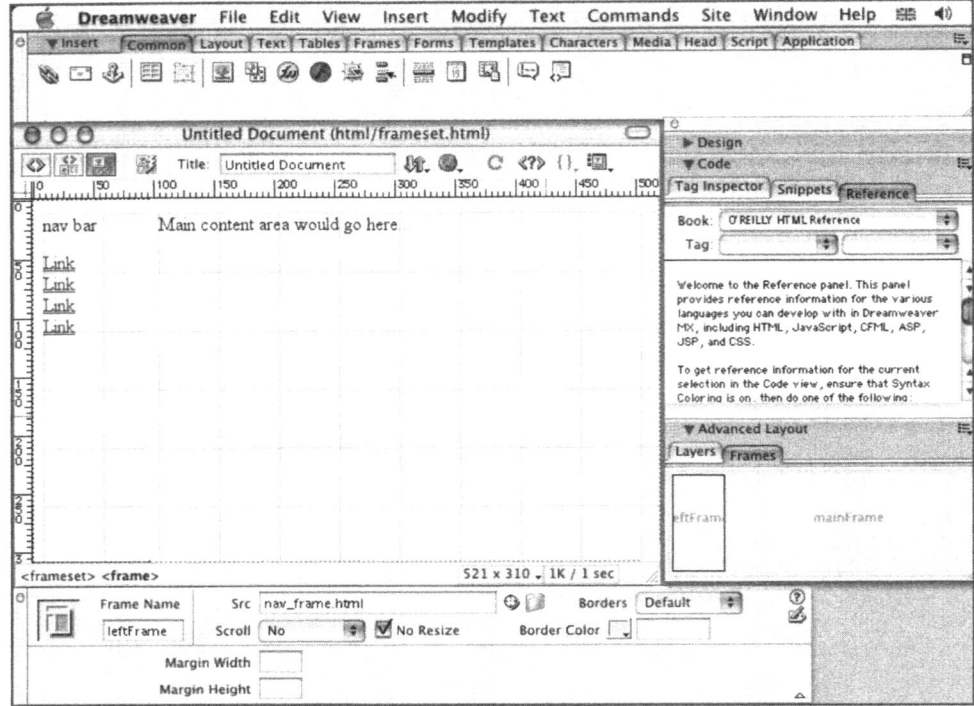

It's important that you give each frame a name, because when you open a link in a frame, the HTML will look something like this:

```
<a href="page.html" target="mainFrame">Link to page</a>
```

The value of target is the name of the frame that the file page.html will open in.

> This can be very important as by default links will open in the frame that contains the link. Imagine a page where we have a navigation bar in a frame down the left and we need to open the links in the 'main' frame on the right. If we didn't specify a frame name in our links, our pages would try to open within our navigation frame!

4. You can change the dimensions of the frames by first selecting the entire frameset in the Frames panel (click its edge, so a thick black line surrounds it), then by clicking one of the gray columns in the Properties panel.

Layout with Templates 4

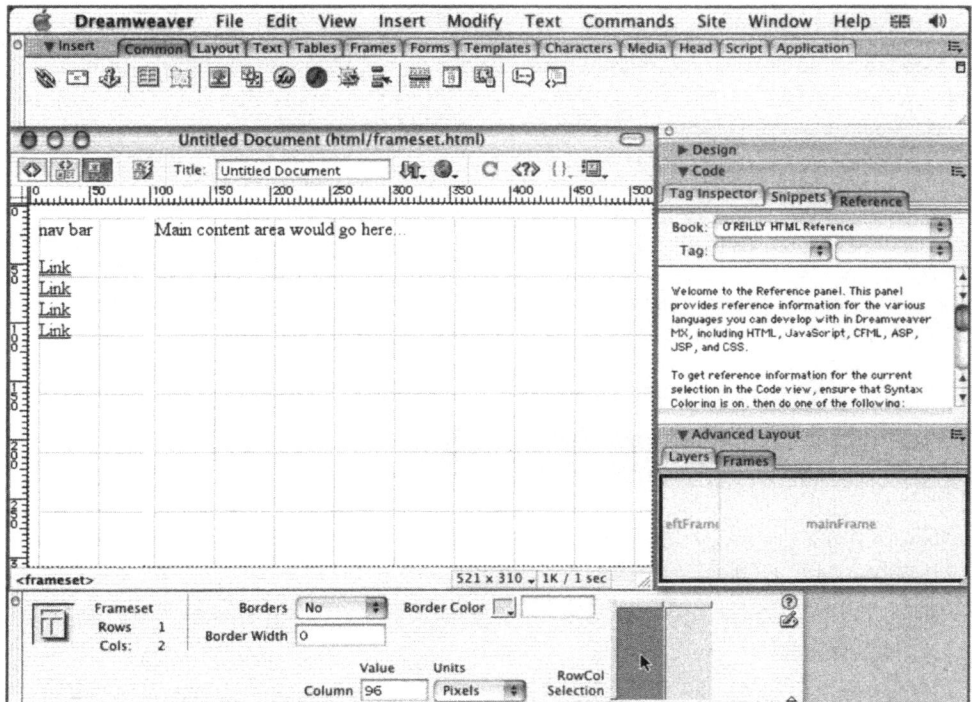

5. Go to Modify > Frameset > Edit NoFrames Content. This lets you enter text for the `<noframes>` tag, which will display a message on browsers that don't support frames. The usual thing to enter here is a brief explanation about the site and the fact that it usually requires a frames-compatible browser, along with a set of links to the site's main pages.

6. It's important to remember that, although Dreamweaver will often display all the frames at once, each frame is a separate HTML document, as is the frameset itself. This means that you have to save each individual document **within the frameset**, and then the frameset itself; so, for a site with two frames, such as the one pictured, you'll have three HTML documents.

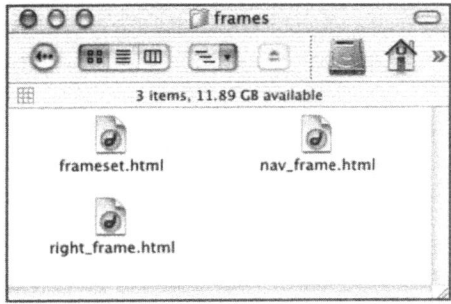

101

Layers

Anyone who's worked with image manipulation packages will understand the principle behind layers. Essentially, you work as you might do with a number of clear sheets, each of which sits on top of the others, and each of which can be moved independently of the others.

While graphic designers out there will no doubt be licking their lips in anticipation, imagining this to be the web equivalent of working with Quark XPress or Photoshop, there are a number of things to take into account. Layers can cause problems when getting sites to work across platforms, and can be tricky to maintain. There can also be problems with regards to screen resolution. Although a layered site might look great to you in your screen resolution, it will sometimes vary for different resolutions, perhaps causing the site to look bad, and even potentially be unreadable.

This said, they can still be useful, particularly when used sparingly, so let's take a quick look.

Creating layers in Dreamweaver

1. Either in a new page, or in one of the frames that you have left over from the last exercise, select the Layout tab on the Insert panel.

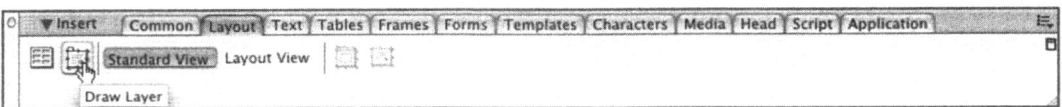

2. Click on the Draw Layer icon. You won't notice any immediate change, but as soon as you move your mouse into the Design view area, it'll change to a crosshair. Click at the top left of the area you want to make into a layer, and drag out a box just as you would draw a rectangle in a graphics package.

> After creating one layer, the mouse goes back to its default properties, so you'll need to click on the icon for each layer that you want to create.

3. Import the night.jpg picture that we used in **Chapter 2** into your new layer. You can move the layer by dragging the tab on the top-left corner.

Layout with Templates 4

4. Create another layer, just as before, and enter some text. Layers are just as simple as that.

5. If you click on the little tab that you've just dragged the layer with, you'll see that the Properties panel will display the settings for that layer. (You must click on the tab, and not just anywhere in the window.) Included in these settings is the Z-index, which sets where the layer will rest in the stack – the higher the number, the closer to the top the layer will be.

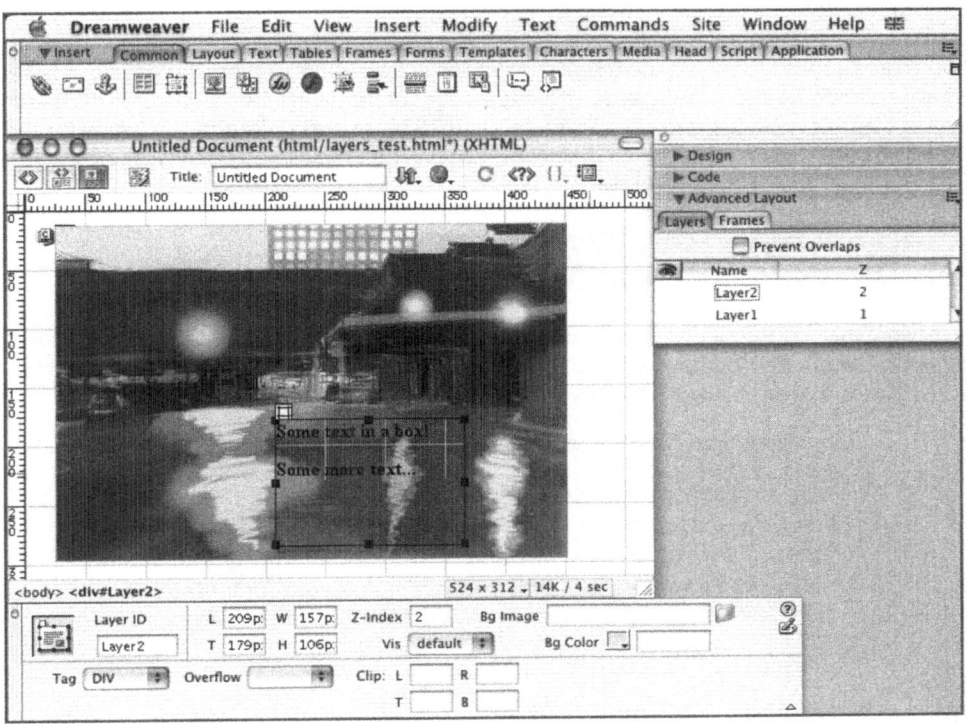

103

6. The bad news is that the more z-settings there are, the more likely you are to crash a browser. This is particularly the case with overlapping layers, and you can select Modify > Arrange > Prevent Layer Overlaps to make sure this doesn't happen (this will only prevent overlaps for layers that you create after checking it).

One thing you can do is use layers to work out your basic layout, and then use Dreamweaver MX's extremely handy conversion function to turn them into tables (Modify > Convert > Layers to Table). Results can be erratic though, so you're probably better off starting with tables in the first place. Speaking of which...

Tables

Cutting-edge web designers will probably give you a dirty look for relying on tables for all your layout purposes, arguing that you should be using Style Sheets for all 'design' things. To a certain extent, they're right; tables should ideally only be used for tabular data rather than graphical layout and can cause messy HTML if you're not careful. While this may not seem like a big problem, anyone trying to access such a site with a screen reader will have major problems, as the content will be in loads of cells, positioned arbitrarily within the HTML document, rather than logically if tables were avoided altogether. Furthermore, shifting things around with a tables-based layout can be time consuming, whereas working with Style Sheets only means editing a single document and potentially pixel-perfect precision without having to rely on invisible GIFs for spacing.

The thing is, tables are easy to get to grips with, and designers continue to use them as a hack for implanting visual layouts. They have the advantage of working accurately across almost all web browsers with identical results (unlike pure CSS layouts – the CSS standards aren't fully supported by some web browsers).

What you need to ensure is that you're extremely careful not to nest tables too heavily – that is, create tables within tables within tables. Not only does this cause havoc for the aforementioned screen readers, but also it's trickier for you to edit later, and web browsers often have to load a table's entire contents before displaying everything. Therefore, the more complex your tables, and the more nesting you use, the longer your pages will take to load.

Creating tables in Dreamweaver

Dreamweaver MX's table-editing tools are quite advanced and enable a great deal of flexibility. Dreamweaver even has built-in support for rudimentary accessibility by prompting for additional attribute values in order to help out screen readers when accessing web sites.

> Note that while these Preferences should always be turned on, as they do aid people using the site, they **won't** make your site fully accessible. In fact, if you are aiming to comply with US legislation for accessible web sites, you'll probably have to avoid tables altogether. Of course, this isn't so much of a problem with personal sites.

Layout with Templates 4

1. For some reason, these options aren't turned on by default, so go to Edit > Preferences, select Accessibility from the left-hand panel, and tick all the checkboxes now (as shown).

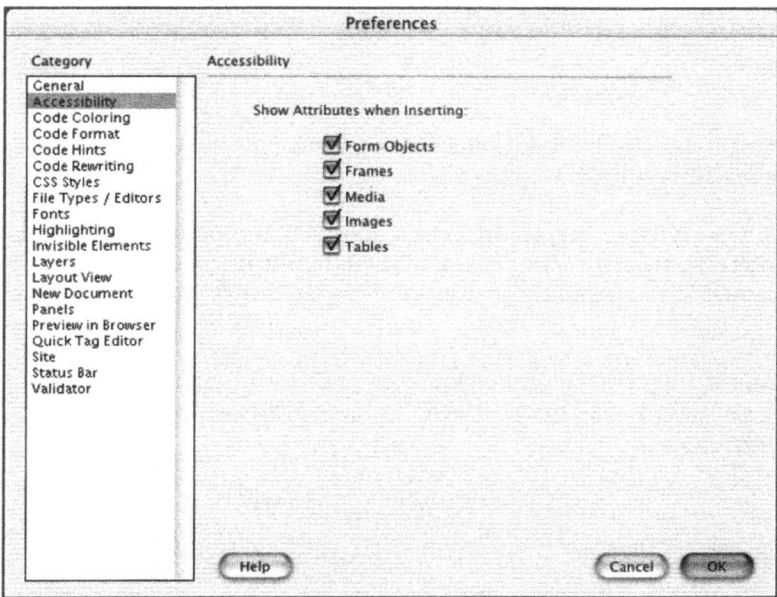

2. Now, open a new Dreamweaver file, and click the Insert table icon on the Insert panel under the Table tab.

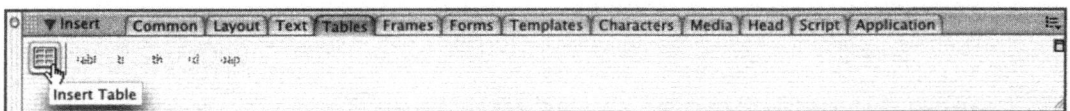

3. You'll be prompted for the number of rows and columns for your table, along with various other attributes.

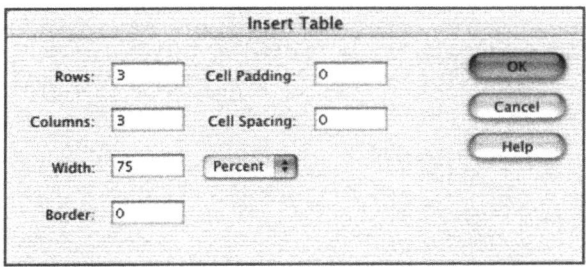

4. Cell Padding refers to the space between the content and the edge of each table cell. This is used when you don't want content to hug the sides of each cell. You'd typically set this to zero when positioning graphical elements of your page. However, padding is usually controlled more accurately via a Style Sheet (see the next section), so set this to 0.

PADDING **NO PADDING**

Cell Spacing refers to the space between each cell; note that, as you'd expect, measurements for padding and spacing are in pixels.

The final two attributes are Border, which adds a clunky border to your table (again, you can control these better via a Style Sheet) and Width, which is pretty obvious! This can be a fixed-pixel measurement, or a percentage of the browser window width, in order to create a flexible layout.

5. If you've turned on the Accessibility options, you'll be given a prompt to add further attributes, including an important Summary which includes an overview of the table's purpose for people using screen readers.

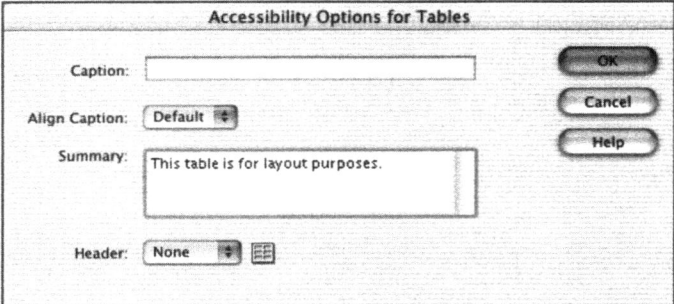

6. Click OK, and you'll find that selecting individual cells enables you to edit their contents.

7. Hovering near the border edges changes the cursor to a horizontal or vertical arrow, which enables you to edit properties for entire rows and columns. Dragging border edges stretches the cells, making them specific pixel sizes.

8. You can also merge cells quite simply: select the ones you want to merge by click-dragging, right/CTRL-click to bring up the contextual menu, and select Table > Merge Cells.

Layout with Templates 4

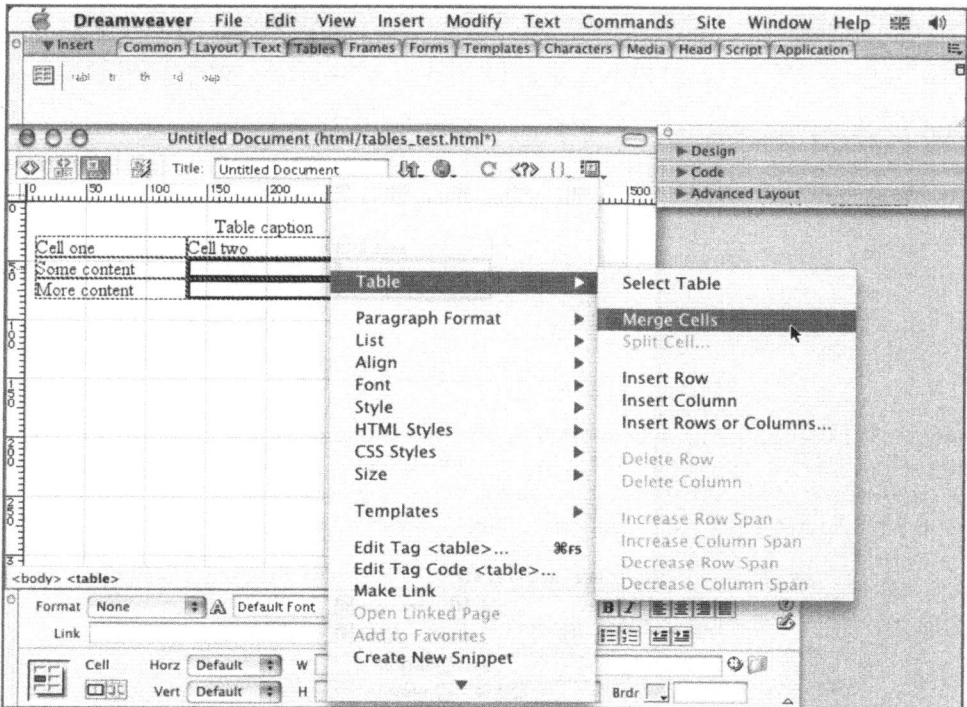

You can see that you can also insert/delete rows and columns using the same menu.

Cascading Style Sheets

HTML is supposed to be a mark-up language that only deals with the *structure* of information, and not one that deals with the *appearance* of that information. That might seem like a small difference, but it's an important one. Unfortunately, there are numerous HTML tags that pollute the mix between structure and appearance, often leading to bloated page sizes and cross-platform inconsistency.

Luckily, modern browsers all support at least some elements of the CSS (or Cascading Style Sheet) standard. A CSS document is separate to the HTML file, and enables you to move most of your design elements into it, leaving HTML to do what it was supposed to do.

> *While modern browsers support almost all of the CSS1 specification from the W3C and parts of the more advanced CSS2, there are still inconsistencies. For instance, Internet Explorer 5.x for Windows has incomplete or inaccurate support for what's known as the 'box model', which affects padding and borders on elements. However, this shouldn't affect our case study, as by and large we'll only be using the simpler aspects of CSS1. Note that pre-version 5 browsers such as Netscape 4, generally have poor support for CSS. However, these account for a small and rapidly declining percentage of the user base. Additionally, people using such browsers will still be able to view your site and its content, but some things may display slightly inaccurately.*

The advantage of using CSS instead of older (now deprecated) methods such as `<font>` tags is that you generally ensure much better cross-browser and platform compatibility, and also end up with smaller page weights. You can also amend things like fonts site-wide by editing a single document.

This means you can control site-wide settings like font usage with a single document, making updates and site-wide consistency a simple process. Your main HTML pages will also become smaller, meaning faster downloads for your visitors.

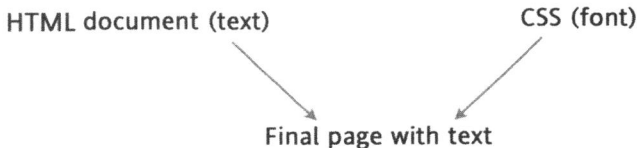

Many designers are used to using Style Sheets in place of the deprecated `<font>` tag, but you can use CSS for *all* of your layout. If you do this, then advanced layout possibilities, including 'skinning' your site, open up. However, this can be a complex process that is beyond visual web editing tools, and also requires code that sometimes doesn't work accurately in even modern browsers.

> Many well-known HTML tags are marked as 'deprecated' in the current specification laid down by W3C.org. This means that they are marked for removal in future versions of browsers, and shouldn't be used. Common examples include `<font>` and `<center>`. Mozilla/Netscape has already dropped support for several lesser-used tags. Opera is following suit, and Microsoft's Internet Explorer probably will at some point in the near future. Using CSS offers a viable alternative solution in such cases, which is also 'future-proof'.

As we've said, some modern browsers aren't yet ready for the more complex CSS attributes, but there's no need to worry about this – the more complex CSS attributes are beyond the scope of this book, and the parts that we'll be showing you should work fine.

Dreamweaver offers a number of ways to create and edit Style Sheet information, which we'll briefly run through now.

Creating and attaching a Style Sheet

1. Go to File > New to bring up the familiar dialog box. Choose CSS Style Sheets from the category and then Basic: Verdana from the selection given.

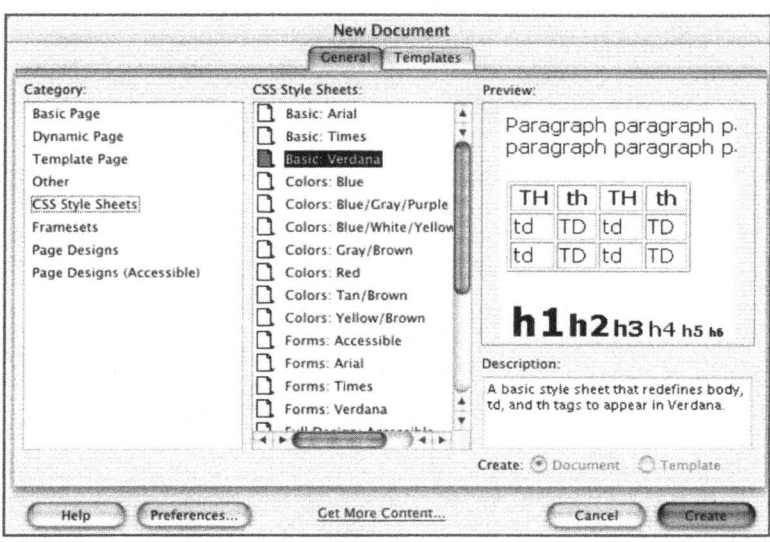

2. Click Create and you'll be presented with a basic Style Sheet. Note that this is in Code view, as Style Sheets simply contain design information to be read in tandem with your (X)HTML documents and interpreted by a web browser. Save your file as `css_test.css`.

3. Create a new HTML document, save it, and then type some dummy text within it.

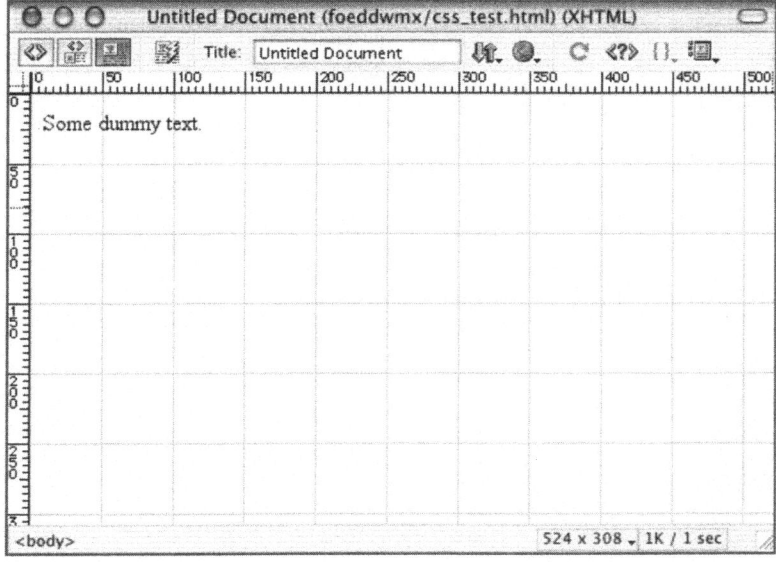

4. Preview this in a web browser, and you'll get something like the screen on the next page. The text is whatever is set in the browser's default, and won't be consistent across platforms and browsers.

4 **Foundation Dreamweaver MX**

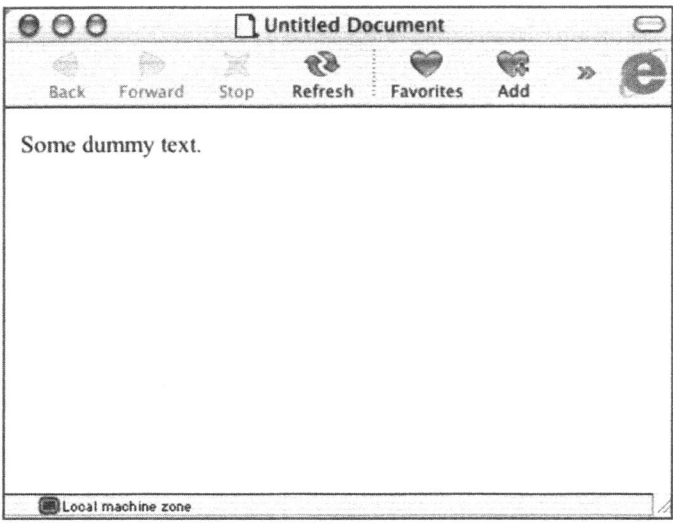

5. Go back to Dreamweaver MX, select the text you typed and use the Properties panel to format it (select Paragraph from the drop-down menu).

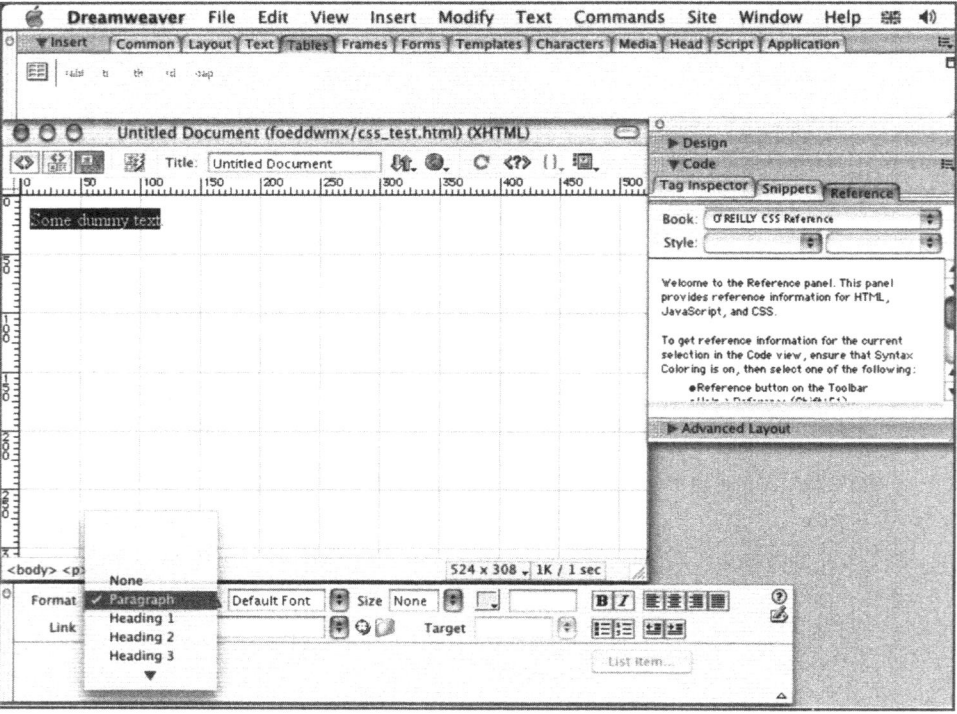

6. Next we need to attach our Style Sheet, but by default, Dreamweaver MX uses legacy tags in the Properties panel. You can set it to use CSS by clicking the icon next to the drop-down menu.

Layout with Templates 4

When it looks like the image below, it's in CSS mode. (You shouldn't have to toggle this back to HTML mode, as you should always be using CSS for text formatting.)

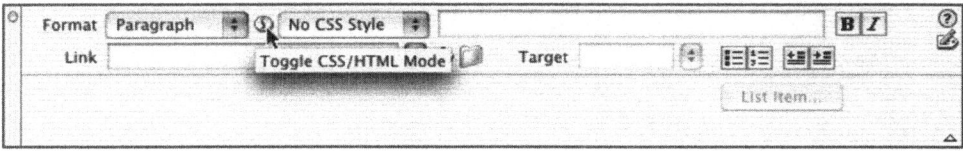

7. Use the drop-down menu to attach the Style Sheet you saved earlier. For now, use the Link method of attaching it when prompted in the dialog box.

8. You should immediately see your text change to Verdana in Dreamweaver MX's Design view. Save your HTML page and refresh it in your web browser and this will be confirmed.

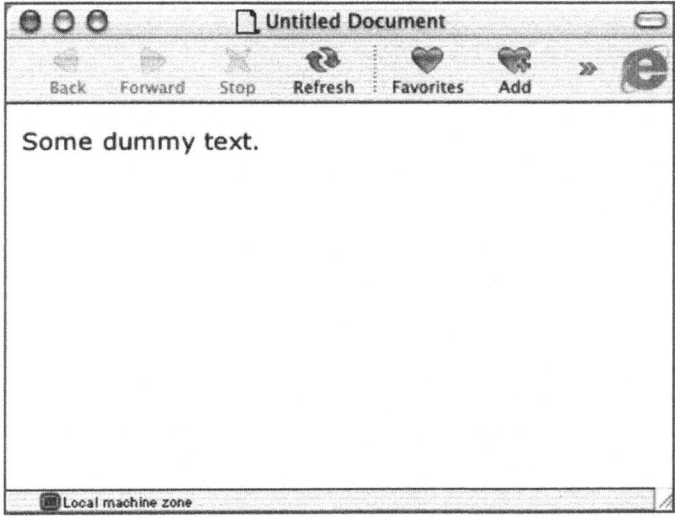

So, how does this work? After all, we've not added any font tags. Well, a quick look at the Style Sheet reveals the following:

```
<<CSS>> (css_test.css)
1  body {
2      font-family: Verdana, Geneva, Arial, helvetica, sans-serif;
3  }
4
5  td {
6      font-family: Verdana, Geneva, Arial, helvetica, sans-serif;
7  }
8
9  th {
10     font-family: Verdana, Geneva, Arial, helvetica, sans-serif;
11 }
```

This is the simple Style Sheet that's built in to Dreamweaver that you chose in the previous exercise. (The application has many more built in Style Sheets for you to experiment with.) While this may look complicated, all it's really doing is this:

```
element sector
        {
        attribute: value, value, value;
        attribute: value, value, value;
        }
```

In the case of fonts, a list is displayed in case people haven't got a specific one installed. Here, the browser looks for Verdana and then works through the list if it's missing, finally getting to 'sans-serif' which means any generic sans-serif font. The advantage over deprecated font tags is this: whatever you define in the body tag will be the default font for your *entire* site. Should you wish to change this later, all you have to do is edit one line in the CSS file.

However, you can also easily add variations to the defaults via the Style Sheet that can be used on various HTML elements. These are referred to as **classes**. In the following exercise, we're going to keep it simple and create a class that will turn any elements it's attached to blue.

Layout with Templates 4

Creating a class

1. Type a new line of text in your HTML document, and format it as a paragraph once again. Then select it and use the Properties CSS drop-down box to create a New CSS Style...

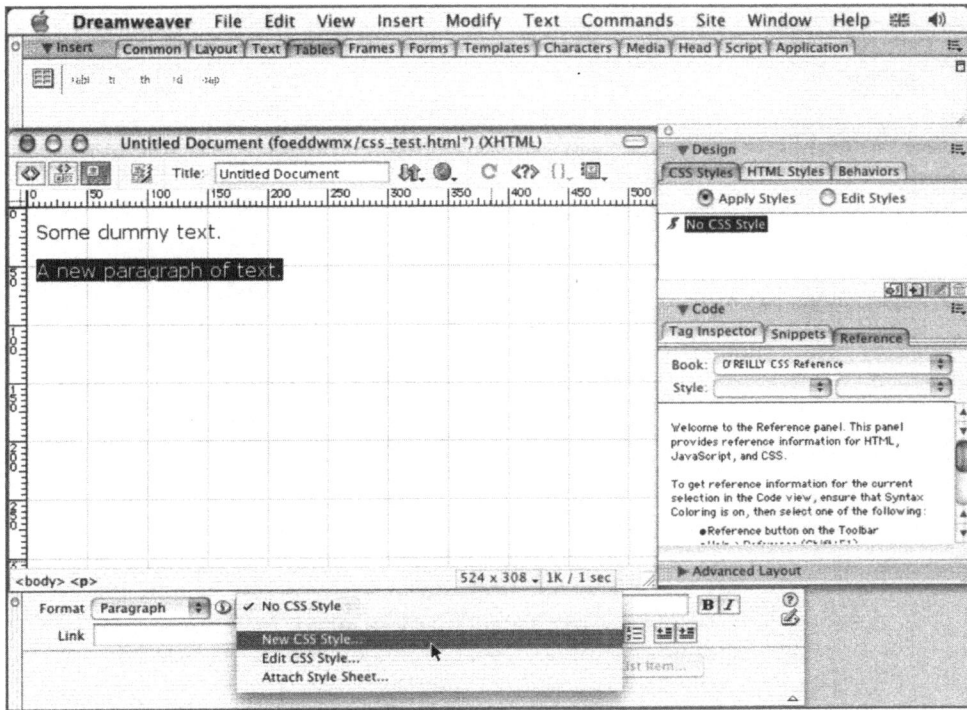

2. Give that class a name preceded by a period – .blue will do just fine. Leave the default options alone – we want to Make [a] Custom Style (class) and Define [it] In `css_test.css` – the CSS file we saved earlier. If you only plan to use a CSS class once, you can attach it to the current HTML file via This Document Only. However, it's usually best to define them in the global Style Sheet, as they take up very little download time, and you never know whether you'll use them later.

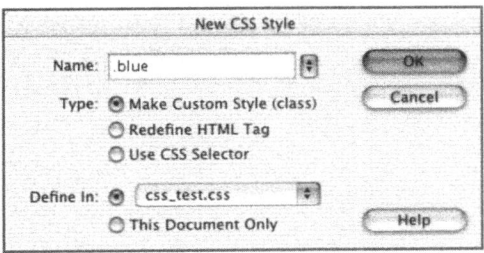

3. The complex dialog box that follows is the CSS Style Definition. We're currently only interested in defining the color as blue, so use the relevant drop-down menu under the Type category to select a blue color and click OK to continue.

113

Foundation Dreamweaver MX

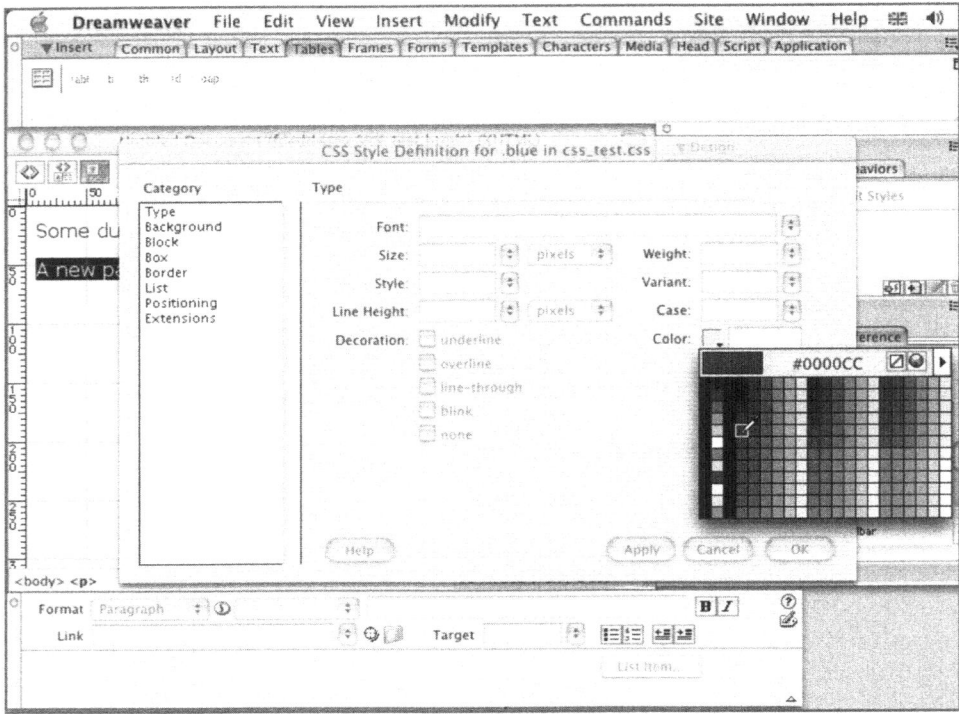

> If you get a warning from Dreamweaver MX about the Style Sheet being altered outside of the application, it's probably because it's been left open while editing it from the dialog in step 3 – just click OK to continue.

4. Save your HTML file and preview it again in a browser. The second paragraph should now be blue.

5. As we've said, this class can now be applied to any elements within your site. For instance, type another line of text and use the Properties panel to turn it into Heading 1.

Layout with Templates 4

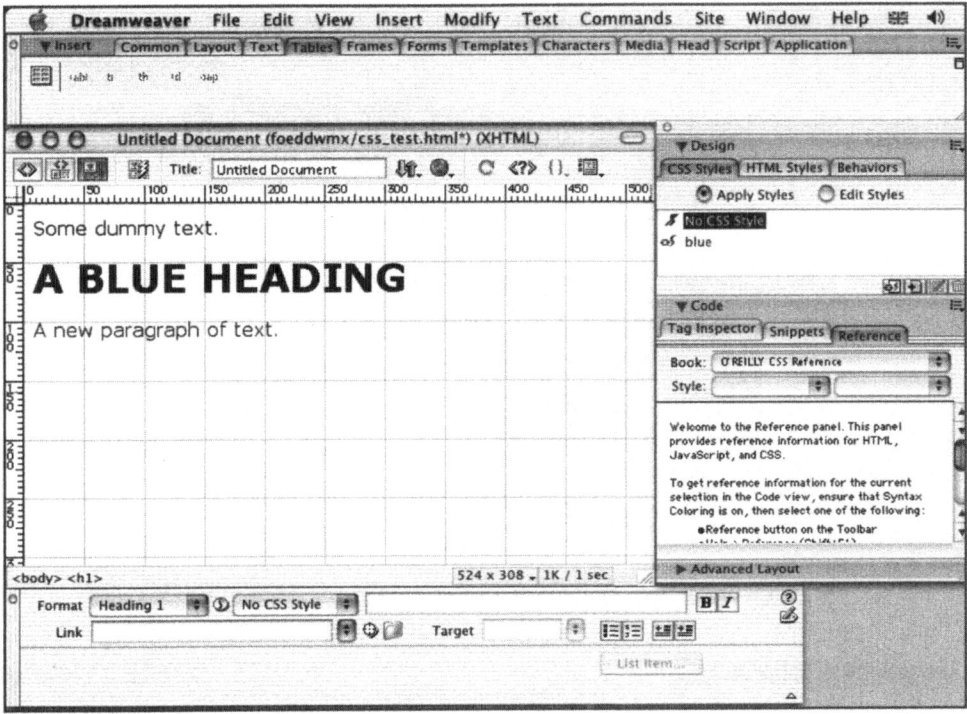

6. You can now apply the .blue class to this heading in two ways:

- Via the drop-down menu in the Properties panel.

- And via the CSS Styles panel, by clicking on the relevant class name.

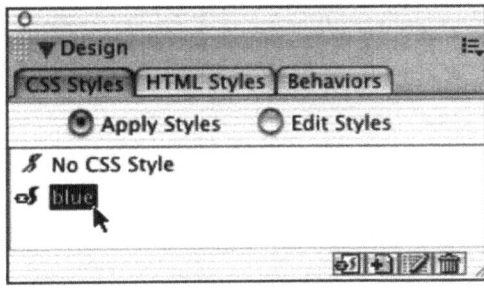

The CSS Styles panel is a useful organization tool. Using its own drop-down menu, you can Edit, Duplicate, Delete, and Apply styles, along with creating new ones.

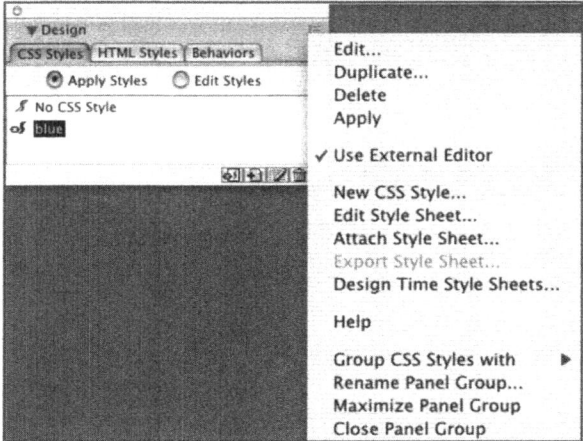

The drop-down list in the Properties panel also gives you rapid access to several of the more important options.

It's usually best to experiment with the interface and work out which method of achieving results is quicker and more comfortable for you. We typically make most use of the Properties panel, although the CSS Styles panel can be useful when you have dozens of classes to wade through.

The above examples styled entire paragraphs and headings, but you can also apply styles to specific characters. This is called a **span** and is achieved in exactly the same way as above, but you only select the characters you want to be affected by the class, as opposite.

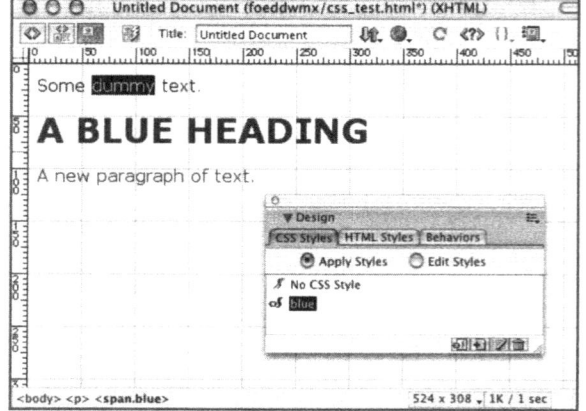

For the curious, the previous exercises have created the following HTML:

```
<p>Some <span class="blue">dummy</span> text.</p>
<h1 class="blue">A BLUE HEADING</h1>
<p class="blue">A new paragraph of text.</p>
```

Layout with Templates 4

This shouldn't faze anyone who's dabbled in HTML before – and even if you haven't, it's fairly easy to see what's going on. Anything with the .blue class applied has `class="blue"` appended to its opening tag. Anything applied to only a few characters rather than an entire paragraph or heading is wrapped in a `<span>` tag, also with the class applied.

To show how flexible the CSS approach is, if you wanted to change the blue color *and* make everything with that class bold, this would take mere seconds.

Editing a class

1. Select the class you wish to edit via the CSS Styles panel – in this case .blue – and click on the Edit Style Sheet icon (you could also use the panel's drop-down menu, or even access the following step via the Properties panel drop-down menu, such is Dreamweaver's flexibility).

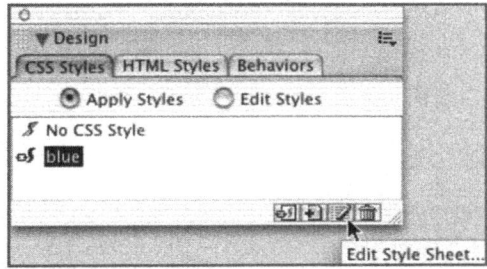

2. Use the color drop-down menu to select a new color – a lighter blue.

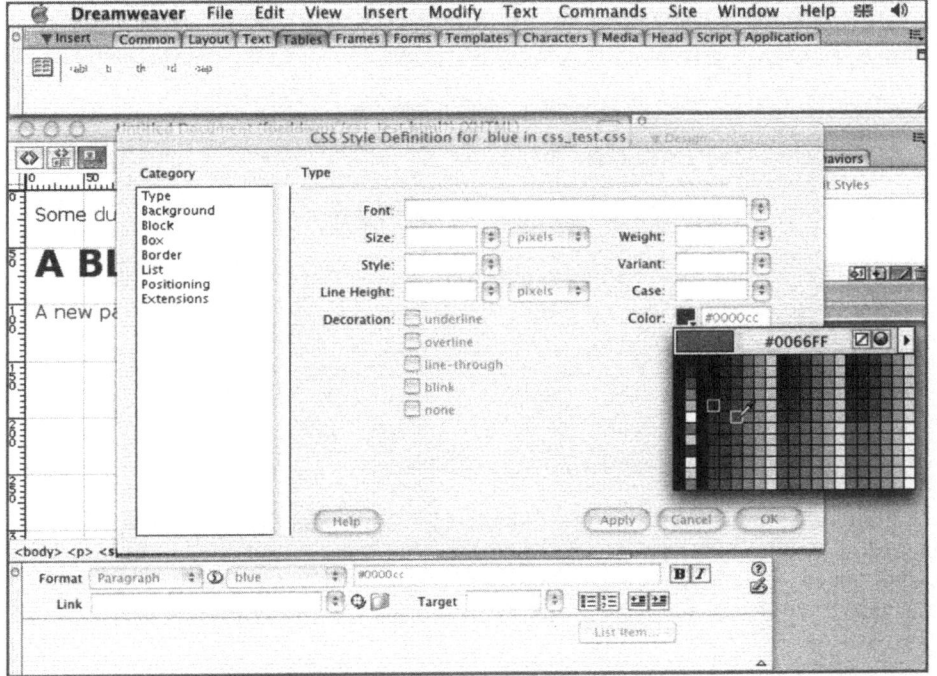

3. Then, under the Weight drop-down, select Bold.

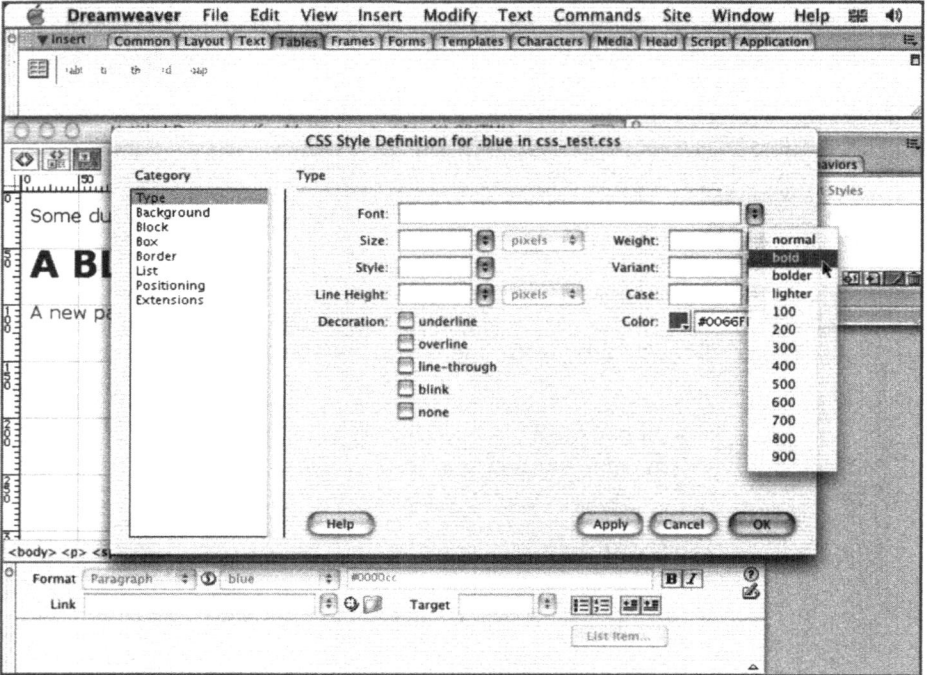

Here's what you should end up with:

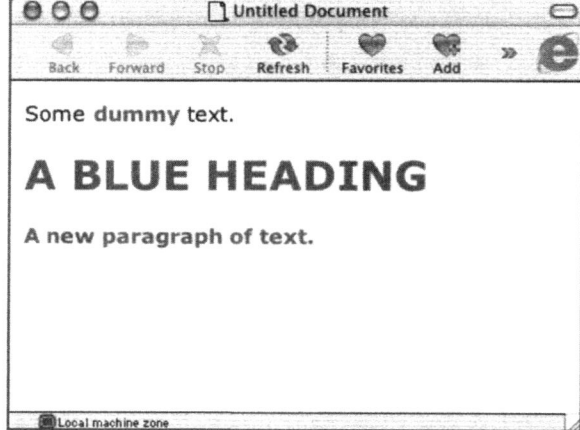

As you can see, everything with the .blue class is now lighter and bold. Imagine the time you would have saved if you had a 50-page site that used the blue style occasionally in various places on each page, having updated the Style Sheet rather than individual font tags. Now imagine how much time you'd save if you had to update 20 such styles.

However, one thing you may have noticed is that editing the CSS Styles could potentially be a time-consuming business. The dialog box has eight categories, each with a plethora of options:

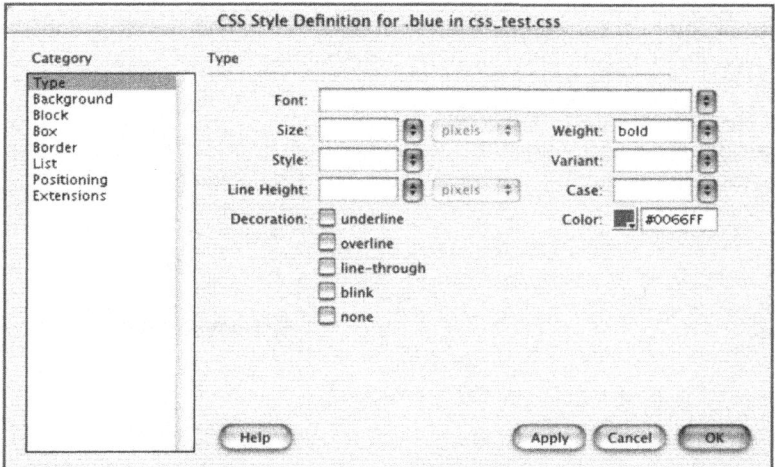

Type deals with font styling, while Background deals with backgrounds to any element the class is applied, such as table cells, but also text or lists.

Block mostly deals with text spacing and alignment, whereas Box looks after element size settings (width and height), padding, margins, and whether or not they 'float' so other elements can wrap around them. For example, an image might be 'floated' right, which would align it to the right of the page, allowing any body copy to flow around it, as you might see in a magazine.

Border enables you to define style, width, and color for borders, while List enables you to define (can you guess?) various things to do with lists.

Positioning mainly deals with pixel-perfect placement of layers, while Extensions contains a bunch of stuff that's supported in some – but not all – browsers, including various cursor types.

Of course, you don't have to define every option for every class, but it's often a lengthy process to get to what you want, so is there a quicker way? Well yes, you can type things in directly. Before you go into a huge panic and jump out of the window, let's take a quick look at the Style Sheet as it stands after the above exercise:

The .blue class is at the bottom and is simple enough to understand. The color value is displayed in hexadecimal format, but `font-weight: bold` is pretty self-explanatory. This is in fact the case with most CSS – once you get the hang of it, it's quicker just to type stuff directly into the Style Sheet, so that's what we'll be doing from this point on. However, it's always good to know the visual way of working in case you prefer that method or have code-phobia!

In either case, remember that Dreamweaver MX contains a useful guide on CSS within the Reference panel if you get stuck at any point.

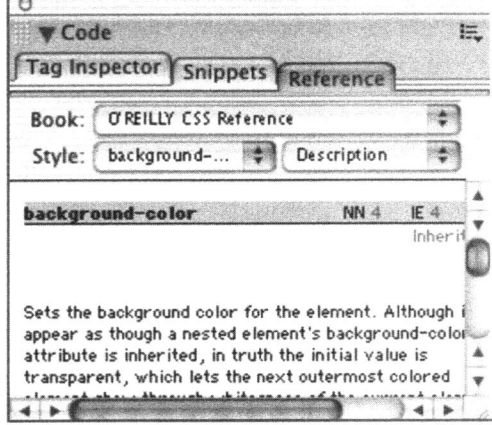

The case study

Now you've had a crash course in CSS, we're going to return to our case study, which makes use of that, along with a simple table-based layout. In this chapter, we'll concentrate on the general page layout, and in the following one, internal page content. The end of the following chapter will see us using our page template as the basis for several others, each of which can be used for specific types of pages.

As you're probably aware, Dreamweaver allows you to create **templates** for your site. A template is created just as you would usually create a page, but you add **Editable Regions** to it. When you (or anyone else) create a new page using the template, you'll be able to change and add content in the editable regions, but not in the other areas. So, if you had a navigation element that you wanted to appear across all of your pages, then you could make that into a template, and set up the remaining area as an editable region.

Layout with Templates 4

Your Site Banner Here

Link One

Link Two

Link Three

Link Four

Link Five

With the heading, navigation bar and footer being core page elements, we would put these in the TEMPLATE. We would be unable to edit these in each document, only from the TEMPLATE itself.

This section, which would change page by page, will be an EDITABLE REGION, meaning that each time we create a new page from our TEMPLATE, Dreamweaver allows us to put whatever we like in this special defined area.

You can have many EDITABLE REGIONS in a single TEMPLATE.

Footer Elements Here

What's really great about this is that, when you update the template, Dreamweaver MX updates all associated pages, and you can imagine how much time that can save on a big project. All you have to do is click on the relevant button when it prompts you to do so.

Create some new documents

Before we even begin the process of design within our page, we need to create two new documents – our template and our CSS file – and set up some basic defaults. As you're no doubt aware, the template and CSS file are dependent on each other, so we'll be editing them at the same time; you should keep both open while working on the site.

1. Go to File > New and choose Basic Page and HTML Template from the Category list. Check the box in the bottom right, to make the document XHTML-compliant.

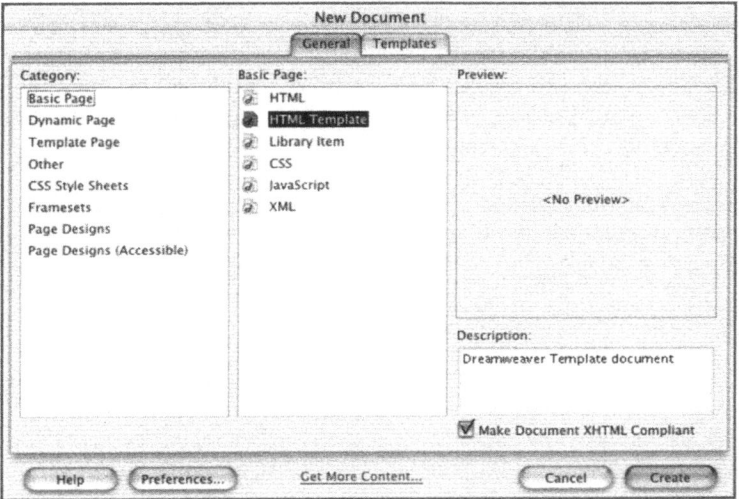

4 Foundation Dreamweaver MX

> XHTML is the reformulation of HTML 4 as an application of XML. If that makes no sense whatsoever to you, don't worry. All you need to know is that XHTML is more likely to create clean code, and also ensure your site is compatible with more of the current crop of web browsers.

2. Use File > Save as Template to save this document as MainTemplate. You will probably get an error message saying "This template doesn't include any editable regions: are you sure you want to continue?", but ignore this for the moment. We want to save our template so that Dreamweaver can create links to any associated documents accurately.

3. Go to File > New, and create a new CSS document by selecting Basic Page from the left panel and then CSS from the Basic Page selection.

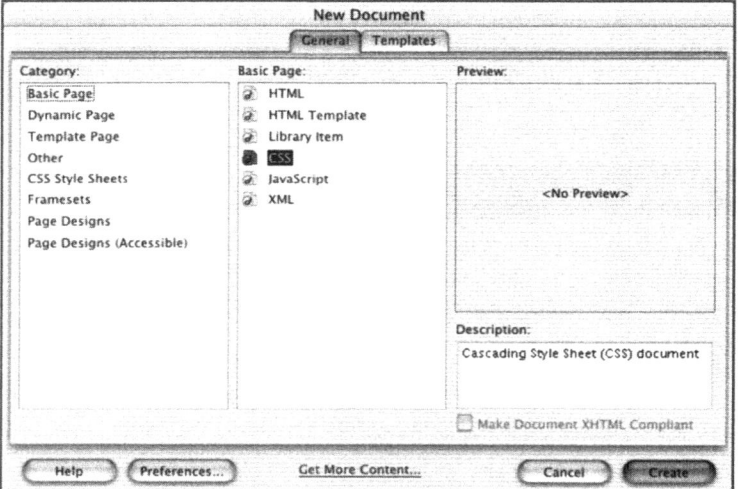

4. Save your CSS file as jtphotography.css. As we've mentioned before, there's no Design view for the Style Sheet; that's because you have to code things. Don't worry about this – it's simple to get the hang of, and we'll explain all the details as we work on the site.

5. Return to the template file. The first thing we need to do is set up some of the <head> elements within our HTML document. These are invisible to the site visitors, but useful to us in several ways. Start by bringing up Insert > Head Tags, which contains a sub-menu with most of the options.

Layout with Templates 4

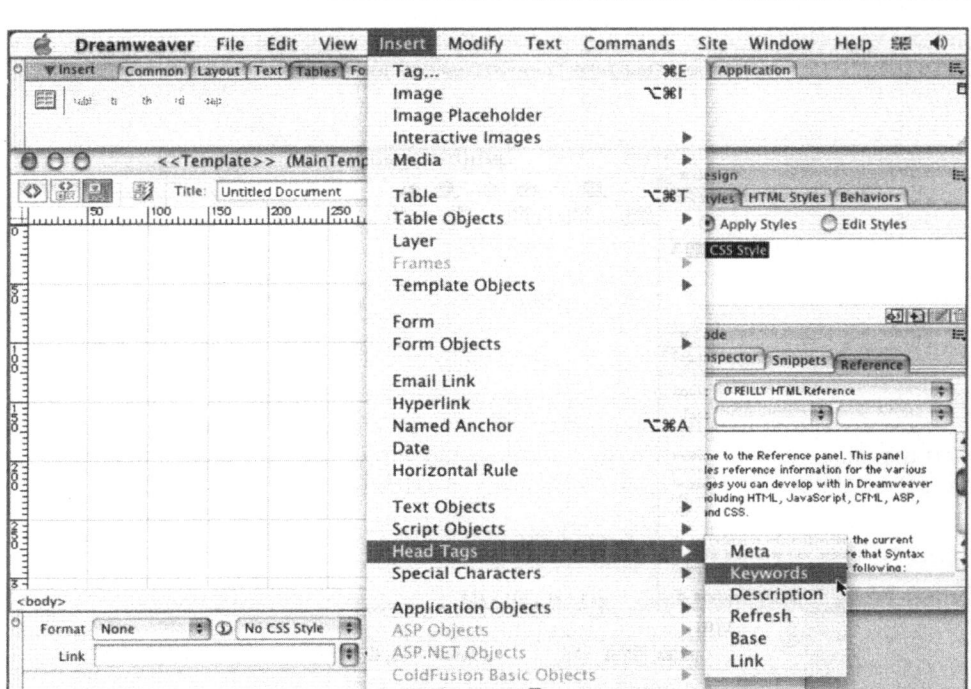

6. Add tags for Keywords and Description, which are used to provide search words and a short description of the site for search engines. It's best to restrict yourself to around 30 non-generic words or very short phrases, separated by commas here, as search engines don't like long descriptions. For this site, we could use something like Jez Turner, photography, dogs in cars, and so on for keywords. A description might read: "Jez Turner Photography – a site about painting with light; includes an online portfolio of work."

7. You'll see this text appear in the code window, if you have it open. If you're using Design view, then turn on View > Head Content, and you'll see some icons at the top of your screen. Click on these, and the Properties panel will allow you to view and change your head content.

8. Go to Text > CSS Styles > Attach Style Sheet, and browse to the jtphotography.css file we created earlier. Attach it via the Link method, as discussed earlier in this chapter, thus ensuring any browser can access the CSS file.

> *Why is it important to allow any browser to see the CSS file? This means that older browsers (such as Netscape 4) that cannot render the CSS can still see the content in your page – not ideal, but better than not being able to see anything.*

9. The last tag that I'm going to add is an optional personal preference. If you wish to follow suit, go to Insert > Head Tags > Meta and add the following:

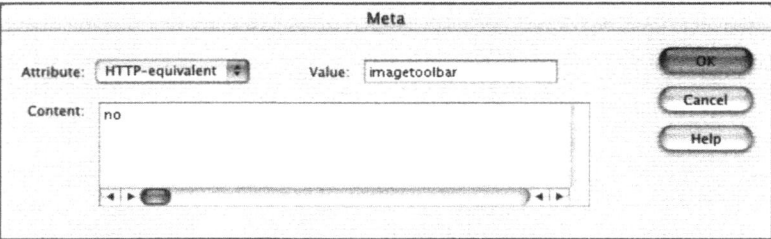

What this does is to remove the image toolbar in Internet Explorer 6 that appears when a mouse hovers over an image and allows the user to print/save that image. You can do this with menu commands anyway, but the image toolbar does make it a little easier for people to take copyrighted images off a site, and it gets in the way of the design by popping up everywhere.

Page defaults

Save your document and switch to the Style Sheet. We're now going to add a number of page defaults. Those of you who used HTML might have done this within the `<body>` tag before, with attributes such as `marginwidth="0"`, but this method has been deprecated. This is just as well, as it never worked in many browsers anyway.

```
/* Friends of Ed
   Foundation Dreamweaver MX
*/

body    {
        background: #ddd url(assets/shared/background_stripes.gif);
        margin: 0px;
        font-family: verdana, arial, helvetica, sans-serif;
        }
```

You'll see some code automatically placed in your CSS file by Dreamweaver. Select this, and delete it all – we're going to customize all of this to our own uses. Above, you can see our first two additions: a comment and the body tag defined.

Comments are easy to do in Style Sheets – just put whatever you want to say between slashes and asterisks arranged as follows:

```
/* This is a comment. */
```

These can also be done over multiple lines. However, always ensure you get the slashes and asterisks in the right order, otherwise your Style Sheet might fail to work properly, or even at all.

To set our page defaults, we have to lay out our code like this:

```
element sector
        {
        attribute: value;
        attribute: value, value, value;
        }
```

This looks really complex, until you look at what we're actually doing, and overcome the fear usually engendered in normal human beings when they start seeing brackets and funny indenting and start thinking they're back in school learning math.

Our element sector, or the section of our site that we want to affect with the settings that follow, is the <body> area of the template – anywhere with visible content. So, any settings placed between the { and } symbols here:

```
body
{
}
```

...will affect everything that we display in our site. We're going to set a gray background for the site, a default font, and margin sizes.

```
background: #ddd;
```

...sets the background to gray, and:

```
margin: 0px
```

...sets the margins to zero pixels, so that the content will align exactly with the sides of the browser window. Finally,

```
font-family: verdana, arial, helvetica, sans-serif;
```

...sets the default font to Verdana, falling back to Arial, Helvetica, and then any sans-serif font, if the user doesn't have our first choice font installed.

We now put these three lines between the {}, so that we have:

```
body
        {
        background: #ddd;
        margin: 0px;
        font-family: verdana, arial, helvetica, sans-serif;
        }
```

Not that difficult, was it?

> Although the tabbing of this code is optional, the colons, semi-colons, and curly brackets need to be entered exactly as shown for things to work as they should.

There's just one problem, though. If nothing else, this chapter has probably shown you why most web designers start breaking out in a cold sweat as soon as the words *cross-platform* are mentioned, and we've got another issue to sort out here.

Internet Explorer 5.5 for Windows – still in popular use – can't handle the global definition of `font-family` we've just added to our embryonic Style Sheet, so we also need to define fonts for the different text elements. Luckily, we can simply list these elements, and then the font list, rather than having to list the fonts for each element.

Instead of `body`, we want to affect the format of paragraphs (`p`), lists (`li`), and table cells (`td`) – so we start like this:

```
p, td, li       {
                }
```

...then we add the `font-family` as before, so that we have:

```
p, td, li       {
                font-family: verdana, arial, helvetica, sans-serif;
                }
```

We'll also set the font size, so that our final code looks like this:

```
p, td, li       {
                font-family: verdana, arial, helvetica, sans-serif;
                font-size: 11px;
                }
```

11px is a comfortable size for reading, but if you want to change it later site-wide all you have to do is change that value; ah, the beauty of Style Sheets!

You should now have the two blocks of code entered into your CSS file.

Planning the layout

We now need to start working out how we're going to lay out the site, based on a visual design. Note that the design is split into clearly defined rectangular areas. While not essential, this is good practice with web design, as it's less hassle to author pages quickly around this sort of design.

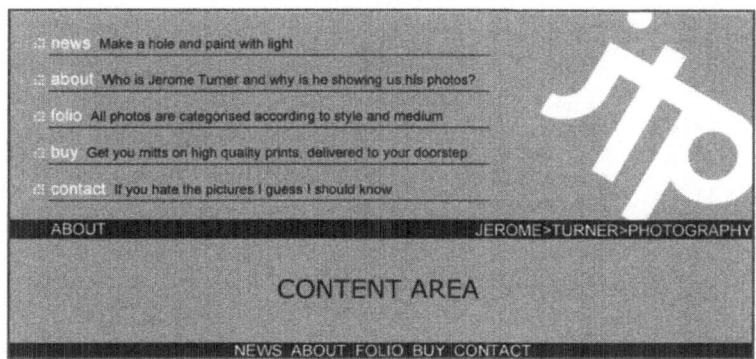

Different users have different monitor sizes, and these are getting bigger all the time. We don't want our content to be stuck in a corner of someone's new monitor, so we have two options. We can either make the design liquid so that it stretches with the web browser window, or we can make it remain a static width at all times, but remain centered.

Because this is a graphically oriented site and we don't want our pictures changing size, we're going to make it static, and center it on-screen. Therefore, our next step is to create a sort of 'container' area for all of our design to sit within. This is often referred to as a **wrapper**.

Wrapping up our site

We'll make this from an HTML table used as a grid to slot things into, an HTML division (an area of the page that you can give an identifier to and therefore assign design properties to via the Style Sheet). As we're going to be adding code, the Show Code and Design view split-screen option is probably the best to use here.

1. Return to our template file. The first thing we do is use an **ID selector** for our division, so we can refer to it from the Style Sheet. Select Insert > Tag, and the Tag Chooser window will appear.

4 Foundation Dreamweaver MX

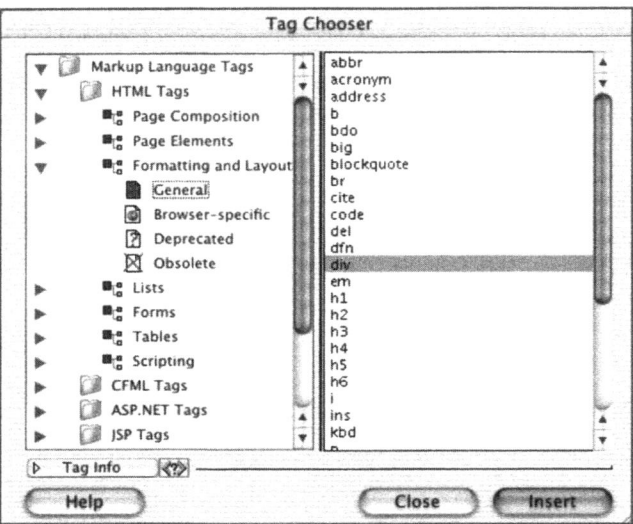

2. Select HTML Tags > Formatting and Layout > General. Select div from the right-hand pane, and click Insert.

3. You'll now be faced with another dialog window with four choices in the left-hand pane: General, Style Sheet/Accessibility, Language, and Events. Select Style Sheet/Accessibility and enter wrapper into the ID field.

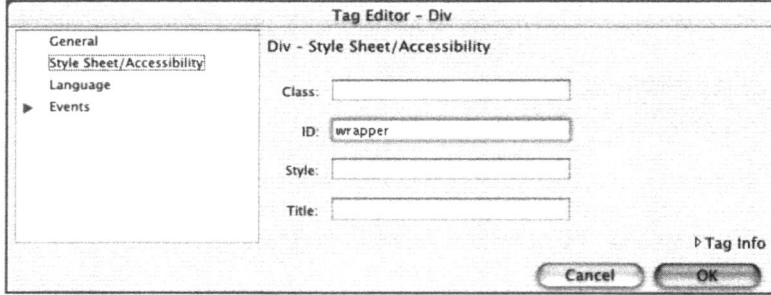

4. Click OK to continue, and close the Tag Chooser when you're done. Check out the Code view; you should see something like this:

```
<body>
<div id="wrapper"></div>
</body>
</html>
```

5. Switch to your CSS file and add this to set up a section where we can define some settings for our wrapper:

```
#wrapper     {
}
```

6. In between the curly brackets, we need to set a width for our content to fit in. 700 pixels is wide enough for this, and it fits comfortably in the 800 x 600 monitor resolution still used by almost half of web surfers, so add:

   ```
   width: 700px;
   ```

7. Next, we want to set a background color. We'll use a light-blue color that I took from the design mock-up, so add:

   ```
   background: #99ccff;
   ```

8. To make our content area stand out from the light gray background of the page as set in the `body` tag, we can add a border to our wrapper. We'll make this one pixel wide, solid, and a medium gray, so enter:

   ```
   border: 1px solid #888;
   ```

9. Lastly, the `margin` attribute is usually set with the values for top, right, bottom, and left (in that order). If you set just one, then it uses that value for all margins on the element. We're only going to use two here, which browsers will interpret as top *and* bottom, right *and* left. Add:

   ```
   margin: 20px auto;
   ```

   This translates as "set the top and bottom margins to 20 pixels, and the left and right to automatic", which should center the wrapper on-screen with a 20-pixel gap at the top and bottom.

   You should now have the following block of code in your CSS file:

   ```
   #wrapper
           {
           width: 700px;
           background: #99ccff;
           border: 1px solid #888;
           margin: 20px auto;
           }
   ```

   We have a little problem to deal with before finishing. While most browsers will render our margin settings accurately, Internet Explorer 5.5 for Windows does not. There are, as always, ways around this.

10. Firstly, the browser doesn't understand `auto` definitions within margins, so add the following line to your body selector to align all page content centrally:

    ```
    text-align: center;
    ```

11. Now add this line to the wrapper in order to align all content within that to the left:

    ```
    text-align: left;
    ```

That's the first problem fixed. The second problem is that Internet Explorer ignores the bottom margin, as there's no content underneath it.

12. To get around this, return to your template file, and follow steps 2 to 4 to add another `div` to your template, this time with an ID of `ie5fix`.

    In the Code view, don't add any de-facto content, but do add a comment tag (something like `<!--fix for IE Windows -->` in order to ensure that certain browsers don't ignore the entire division.

    ```
    <div id="ie5fix"><!-- fix for IE windows --></div>
    ```

13. Return to your Style Sheet, and add the following:

    ```
    #ie5fix
    {
            height: 1px;
            voice-family: "\"}\"";
            voice-family: inherit;
            display: none;
    }
    ```

    This provides some content – a one-pixel-high `div` – to make Explorer 5.5 happy and therefore make sure the 20px bottom margin on our wrapper shows. Explorer 5.5 doesn't understand the `voice-family` attribute, so it'll stop reading this element there, and display the `div`. Other browsers, however, will read the whole element and display nothing.

15. We're finished here for the moment, but so that you can check everything is present and correct before continuing, your template file should have a link to your CSS file, and also your two `div` tags (probably at the bottom). Don't worry about other code relating to your template – so long as these are there, you're fine. Your CSS file should look like this:

    ```
    body
            {
            background: #ddd;
            margin: 0px;
            font-family: verdana, arial, helvetica, sans-serif;
            text-align: center;
            }
    p, td, li
            {
            font-family: verdana, arial, helvetica, sans-serif;
            font-size: 11px;
            }
    #wrapper
            {
            width: 700px;
            margin: 20px auto;
            background: #99ccff;
    ```

```
              border: 1px solid #888;
              text-align: left;
              }
#ie5fix
              {
              height: 1px;
              voice-family: "\"}\"";
              voice-family: inherit;
              display: none;
              }
```

16. Once you're happy with everything, save both files. If you skip this step, you'll find that the template doesn't update and include the `div` that we've just included – which will make the next section challenging, to say the least.

Summary

So that's the general page defaults sorted, and hopefully you've now got an understanding of what Dreamweaver MX can offer with regards to page layouts. In the next chapter, we're going to continue working on our page layout, concentrating on internal page layout, some graphical elements, and finally building a template.

5

Cascading Style Sheets

What we'll cover in this chapter

- Building the template for our case study
- Adding to the design of our site with tables
- Creating Editable Regions in our template

In the previous chapter, you got some way towards creating the page layout for our case study. Backgrounds, colors and margins are sorted, as is the size of the area for the site content. Now we need to create the internal page layout, adding our site's logo and navigation, and then create some site templates in order to add content in the next chapter.

Checking our visual

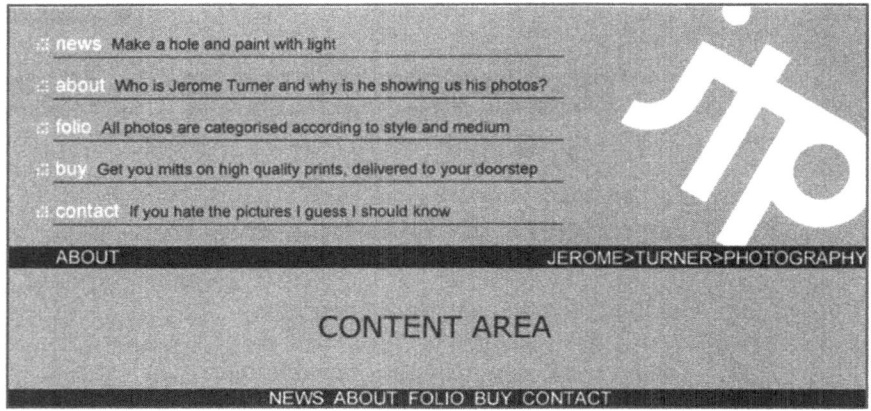

As you'll no doubt remember, this is what the visual mock-up of our site looks like. We need to work out how to arrive at this as a web page, and can split this into a number of tasks, each of which we'll work on in turn later in the chapter. It's also worth mentioning that this stage is where you need to work out what parts of the site need to be constructed from graphics, and which elements can be done with a combination of HTML and CSS.

Looking at the screen grab, there are actually only two purely graphical elements on the page: the logo in the top-right and the bullet-points on the navigation at the top-left of the page. Everything else is text-based, perhaps with varying colors and backgrounds, or underlines, but text all the same.

So here's what we need to do to arrive at our layout:

- Create the main table to hold all the page elements.
- Deal with the navigation area which is essentially a styled, bulleted list.
- Add the logo to the top-right corner.
- Create the gray bars and add their content—the right-aligned JEROME>TURNER>PHOTOGRAPHY title and the center-aligned navigation at the bottom of the page
- Turn the finished template into a number of embedded templates so we can have variations on pages, yet easily add content later *and* rapidly update our site if we need to.

Of course, as we work through the above tasks, other ideas are likely to crop up that may improve the site, so we'll cover any such eventualities, too!

The main table

Take the original visual layout and work out the simplest way of slicing it up. We don't want to nest tables, but this design can't be easily sliced into a table, as you'd end up with something like this:

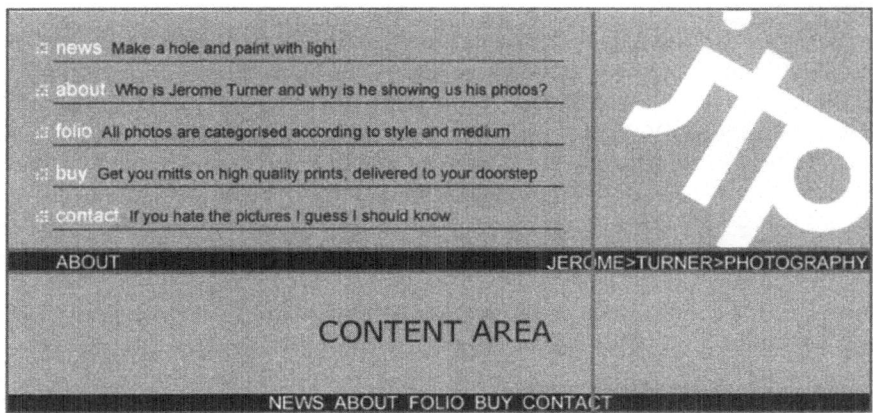

You could start merging cells for the content area and gray bars, and add a second table for the content of the first gray bar, but that's getting needlessly complex. There's a much better way of dealing with the positioning of the logo and JEROME>TURNER>PHOTOGRAPHY, and it will mean we can simplify our table; in fact, all we need is a table with four rows and one column.

The first row will contain the navigation and logo, the second, the name of the site, the third, the content area, and the fourth, the centered navigation at the foot of the page.

Creating the main table

1. Within your Design view you should currently have a blue rectangle (this is the div you defined earlier). Click inside this, because that's where we're going to add the table.

2. Add the table using the Layout tab, as we showed you in the previous chapter. Ensure that the page has 4 Rows, 1 Column and that cell padding, cell spacing and border are all set to 0. Set the width to 700 pixels, and add a simple summary such as this table is for the main page layout to the accessibility dialog box that follows. You should end up with something like this:

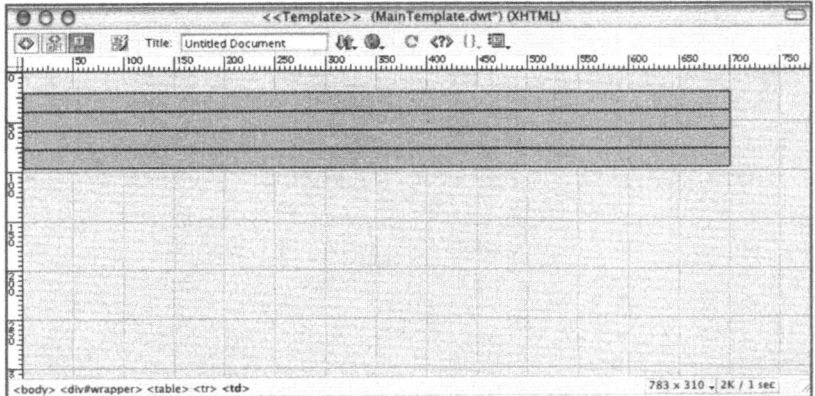

This is the basis for our site layout. It's pretty simple, but as we said, it's always best to create the simplest tables possible.

The navigation

Next, we're going to add the navigation area at the top of the page. While it's got styling in the form of graphical icons to the left of each section, and underlines beneath the section descriptions, it pretty much takes the form of a standard bulleted list, so that's what we'll use as the basis for the navigation. We'll then use CSS to style everything, including the addition of the icons in place of standard, circular bullet points. The only other method of doing this would be to create complex tables to house the graphical icons, links, description text and underlines, and this would needlessly complicate the code. Using CSS means that adding another link at a later date would be a fairly painless process, and as we'll see, it also gives far more flexibility with regards to controlling spacing.

Note that many of the concepts discussed here can be used in *any* list for a web page and that lists are often a suitable choice for a site's navigation area.

Adding the bulleted list

1. As we've mentioned, the first row of our table will contain the logo and the navigation. Let's start with the set of links. Click in the first row, and then the bullet symbol in the Properties panel – it actually displays unordered list on mouseover, and is just under the bold option.

2. Add this text, hitting ENTER to get a new bullet each time.

   - news Make a hole and paint with light
   - about Who is Jerome Turner and why is he showing us his photos?
   - folio All photos are categorized according to style and medium
   - buy Get your mitts on high-quality prints, delivered to your doorstep
   - contact If you hate the pictures, I guess I should know

   When I entered this in Dreamweaver, the table didn't seem too inclined to include the last bullet in the blue background for some reason. If the same happens to you, just quickly switch to Layout view and then back to Standard view (use the Layout tab).

3. Select the news text, and add a link to news.html in the Link section of the Properties panel. Now add links to about.html, folio.html, buy.html, and contact.html to the first words of the other lines.

Cascading Style Sheets

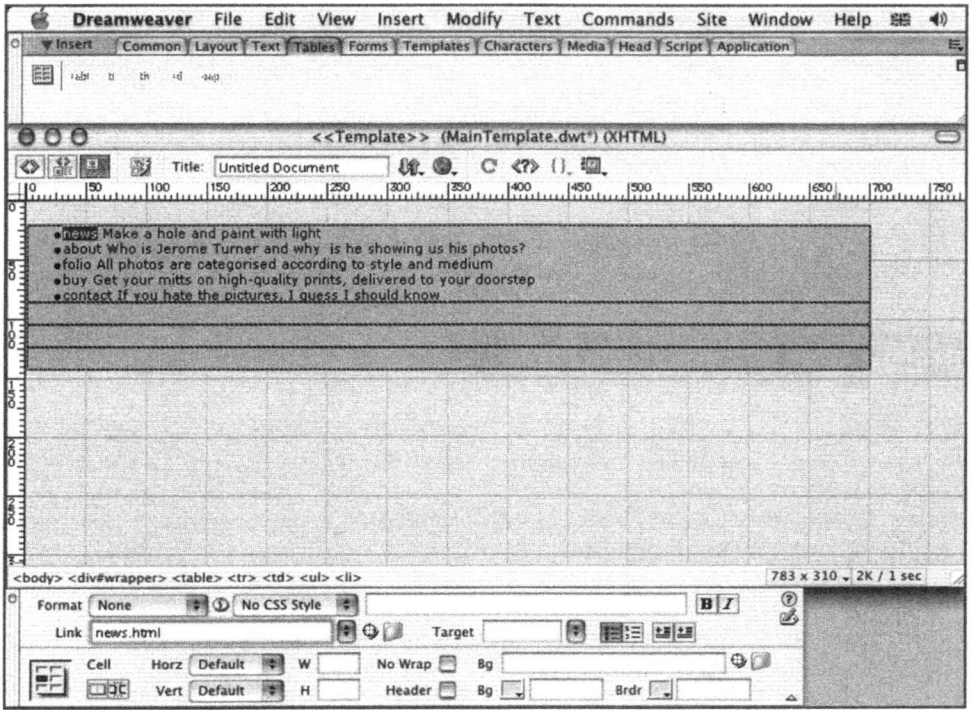

4. We need a set of squares to use as a bullet point. Time for our first graphic – a transparent GIF. Drop the `nav_bullets.gif` file – available from the friends of ED site in the usual way – into the `shared` folder that's within the `assets` folder created in **Chapter 3**.

> *We use a transparent GIF because exported graphics often display incorrectly when people set their monitors to thousands of colours. Therefore we make the blue color transparent, just leaving the white squares, ensuring everything looks good in all browsers.*

5. Changing the bullet points to a graphic simply requires adding a class to the Style Sheet and amending the unordered list tag.

   First, add the following to the Style Sheet:

   ```
   .navList    {
               list-style:   url(assets/shared/nav_bullets.gif) outside;
               }
   ```

   This will ensure the image that you placed in `assets/shared/` in step four will be used as the graphic for each bullet. The value `outside` ensures the bullet is not indented.

Next, we need to add the margin between the bullet points. This is done by adding `margin-top: 25px;` to the `.navList` class. This immediately shows one of the advantages of working with lists in CSS; if you want to change the margin later, you just have to edit this value – much easier than messing about with a load of table cells!

6. Finally, add the class to the unordered list tag. Although you can do this in the Design view, it's probably best to add it in the Code view to ensure it goes in the correct place, which is as follows:

```
<ul class="navList">
```

Formatting the navigation text

Great! We've sorted out our bulleted list. Next, we need to sort out the text itself. We want to give our navigation area a set width, a margin, and create a border at the bottom of the text. To do this, we'll create two **classes** – as we've said, classes can be applied to *multiple elements*, while IDs are specifically applied to *one element*. The first class will sort out the text size, width and margin, whilst the second will sort out the border at the bottom of the text.

> *You might be wondering what the point of IDs is, and why we don't just use classes. Well, for page sections that are only defined once, it's good practice to use IDs, as you can then refer to them later for things like scripting. For example, you could create collapsible navigation by toggling the visibility of `divs` with named IDs.*

1. For our first tag, go to the Code view, and find the text for our bulleted list. You'll notice each line starts with an `<li>` tag. Inside this tag – after the `<li` and before the `>` - add `class="navListBullet"`.

2. For our second tag, after each of these `<li class="navListBullet">` tags, add `<span class="navUnderline">`.

3. Add `</span>` tags just before the `</li>` tags at the end of each bullet to close the area covered by the second class.

Cascading Style Sheets

[screenshot of Dreamweaver template code showing MainTemplate.dwt (XHTML) with HTML markup for navigation list items with classes "navListBullet" and "navUnderline"]

What we've done is to add two classes to the text. We can now go and define these in our style sheet.

4. First of all, we want to sort out the `.navListBullet` class. Here we want to give our bullet points 11px size text, a width of 410px, and a bottom margin of 15px. Add the following to the bottom of your style sheet.

```
.navListBullet
{
font-size: 11px;
width: 410px;
margin-bottom: 15px;
}
```

5. Next up is the `.navUnderline` class. Here, we want to add a border at the bottom of the text, effectively creating an underline. Add the following:

```
.navUnderline
{
border-bottom: solid 1px #666;
display: block;
}
```

The `display: block;` attribute ensures that the line continues for the length defined in `.navListBullet`.

139

> *While this may seem complex, creating a similar effect using tables would have taken far longer, and would have been a pain to implement as you'd have needed a colored background cell for the underline. This would have meant adding an embedded table, and also making updating margins and the color of the underline trickier later on. After all, if you reckon there's too much of a gap between the bullets, you can change that by editing the margin-bottom attribute within* `.navListBullet` *– a far more flexible solution than other methods.*

news Make a hole and paint with light

about Who is Jerome Turner and why is he showing us his photos?

6. If you create a page from the template at this point and preview it in a browser, you get something like the above screen.

7. This is getting closer to our visual mock-up, and all we need to do for this section is change the links to white. Open your Style Sheet, and create an `a:link` element to define attributes for all links in our file:

   ```
   a:link
   {
   }
   ```

8. Inside this element, we can set the font to bold, and set the color, so add:

   ```
   font-weight: bold;
   color: #fff;
   ```

9. We can also ask for a transparent background, and no underlines (by setting `text-decoration` to none), so add:

   ```
   background-color: transparent;
   text-decoration: none;
   ```

10. We also need to define settings for visited links, so create an `a:visited` element:

    ```
    a:visited
    {
    }
    ```

11. Inside this, we're going to add the same settings as last time:

    ```
    font-weight: bold;
    color: #fff;
    ```

```
background-color: transparent;
text-decoration: none;
```

12. Duplicate the above settings for active links (in other works, how the link appears as it's being clicked).

    ```
    a:active
    {
    font-weight: bold;
    color: #fff;
    background-color: transparent;
    text-decoration: none;
    }
    ```

13. Finally, we can change how the links look when the mouse hovers over them with an `a:hover` element:

    ```
    a:hover
    {
    }
    ```

14. Inside this, we can set the background color, and the link color itself (as you can see in the screenshot):

    ```
    font-weight: bold;
    color: yellow;
    background-color: #000;
    text-decoration: none;
    ```

    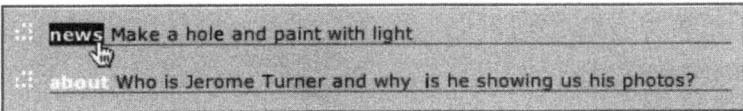

15. All the changes to your CSS file should now read like this:

    ```
    a:link
    {
    font-weight: bold;
    color: #fff;
    background-color: transparent;
    text-decoration: none;
    }

    a:visited
    {
    font-weight: bold;
    color: #fff;
    background-color: transparent;
    ```

continues overleaf

```
text-decoration: none;
}

a:active
{
font-weight: bold;
color: #fff;
background-color: transparent;
text-decoration: none;
}

a:hover
{
font-weight: bold;
color: yellow;
background-color: #000;
text-decoration: none;
}
```

> *Make sure your link styles are in the correct order, as above: Link, Visited, Active, Hover. This is to ensure they all work properly in browsers, as latter styles override former ones. If you struggle to remember the order, you can remember the first letter of each link style via **LoVe And Hate**.*

And that's the navigation taken care of.

Adding the logo

The final thing for the first row is the addition of the logo, which was again exported as a transparent GIF, knocking out the blue background to transparent.

1. Add `jtplogo.gif` to the first row of the page with the Image button under the Common tab of the Insert panel.

2. This will then appear in the Design view, although probably in a fairly random place. This highlights one of the problems on relying solely on visual editing: sometimes the editors make mistakes. The most likely place that Dreamweaver MX has dropped the image is somewhere within your list.

3. Go to the Code view, highlight the entire image tag and move it to just before the `<ul>` tag. Why before? After all, the image is going on the *right* of our list, so it should come afterwards, right? Nope. You remember how we said that instead of straight tables, we were going to use a

better method to position things such as the logo? Well, here's how we do it: we *float* the image to the right of the list using CSS.

4. Add this class to your Style Sheet:

```
.floatRight        {
                   float: right;
                   }
```

5. Back in your template, find the line of code that refers to the image (clicking on the image in Design view is the best way of doing this). Then add `<spanclass="float: right">` to the left of your `img src` tag, and `</span>` to the right of it, so that it looks a bit like this:

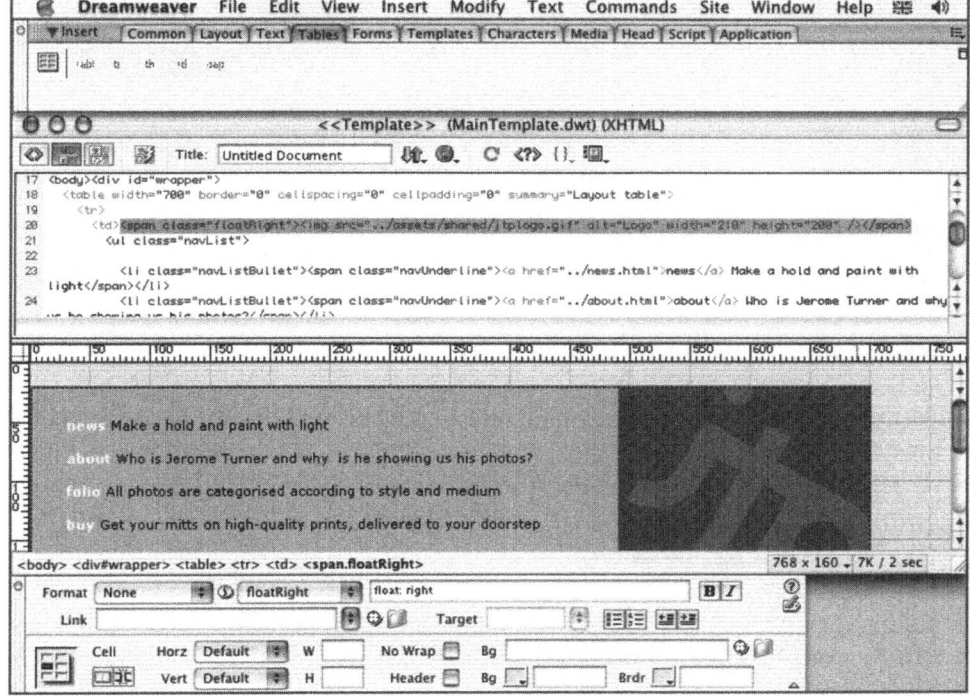

6. Save both files again, and you should see the floated logo displayed. This wouldn't have displayed in Dreamweaver 4, and it's a nice addition to Dreamweaver MX.

Note that 'floating' elements is something that comes in very handy with CSS. For instance, you can float images, thus wrapping text around them, or even entire boxouts, such as the sub-navigation area at www.wireviews.com.

The gray bars

Next we'll define the gray bars and add their content. Note that the two bars are identical in size and color, but the content within them varies. In the top one, we need the title of the site on the right, and the title of the page on the left, which can be done in a similar way to the navigation and logo (with a float). The navigation at the foot of the page is simpler, being centered text.

Adding the gray bars

1. Add a class of rowGray to the second and fourth rows of your table by clicking on the row on the Design view and using the Properties panel (via the `<tr>` tag, so they become `<tr class="rowGray">`).

2. Add this class to your Style Sheet, save both documents, and the two rows will have a dark gray background, onto which we'll put white text at a size of 12px:

```
.rowGray    {
background: #333;
font-size: 12px;
color: #fff;
}
```

3. The text is added by clicking on the cell and typing it in as normal. Note that as the JEROME>TURNER>PHOTOGRAPHY text will be floated like the logo, it needs to come *before* the TITLE text.

4. Dreamweaver MX sometimes has an annoying habit of displaying white text on a white background, so you might need to change the color attribute in the `.rowGray` class while working on it. Don't forget that – as usual – you have to save the file to make this work.

5. Now wrap span tags around both of them, adding a class of `floatRight` to the JEROME>TURNER>PHOTOGRAPHY text and `copyPadding` to the TITLE text. Then define the following in the Style Sheet:

   ```
   .copyPadding    {
   padding-left: 40px;
   }
   ```

   This produces a 40-pixel margin to the left of the TITLE text, to align it somewhat with the navigation list.

6. A final inline style is applied to the JEROME>TURNER>PHOTOGRAPHY text in order for it not to totally hug the right-hand border: `style="padding-right: 5px;"`. You should now have something that looks like this:

```
<tr class="rowGrey">
  <td><span class="floatRight" style="padding-right: 5px;"><strong>JEROME&gt;TURNER&gt;PHOTOGRAPHY</strong></span>
<strong><span class="copyPadding"><!-- TemplateBeginEditable name="documentTitle" -->TITLE<!-- TemplateEndEditable --></span>
</strong></td>
  </tr>
```

7. The second gray bar is much less hassle – it just contains a second set of navigation links for anyone who's scrolled to the bottom of the screen. Click on that cell, and add these, wrapping links around them as normal.

8. Don't apply any formatting to this text via the Properties panel, but add `class="center"` to the table cell containing that text via the Code view.

9. Then add the following to the Style Sheet:

   ```
   .center    {
   text-align: center;
   }
   ```

This aligns the links center, as per our visual mock-up.

A few additions

The gray background looks kind of dull, so we made a GIF of some alternate gray/white stripes in Photoshop. Another thing that might be useful is the addition of a drop-down menu under the main navigation, to provide immediate access to any sub-pages we might include.

1. Add the stripes to the background by setting url(assets/shared/background_stripes.gif) to the background attribute of the body tag within the Style Sheet.

   This will tile automatically, so it doesn't have to be the potential size of the visitor's web browser window. Some browsers choke if you use tiny tiled backgrounds, so this one is around 600 x 300 pixels. Because it's a two-colour GIF, it only weighs in at 4k.

2. Now for the drop-down menu. Click on the last bullet point on the first table cell, hit ENTER and then click the bullet-point on the Properties panel to turn the list off.

3. Add the Form by selecting the List/Menu button under the Forms tab.

4. Select it, then click on List Values in the Properties panel to add values to the drop-down menu. The first one is what's displayed by default and doesn't require a value. Similarly, you can use this tactic to add 'dividers' – Item Labels containing a series of dashes, but with no value.

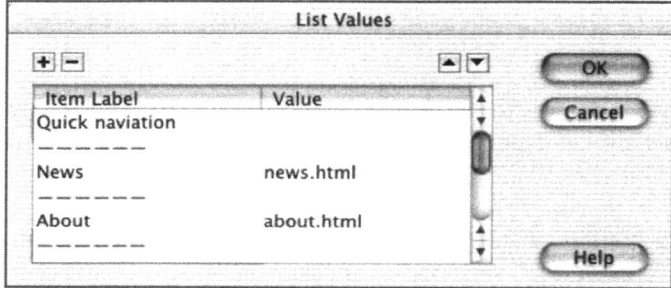

5. Next to the drop-down menu, add a button by selecting the button on the Forms tab.

6. By default Dreamweaver MX will make this a Submit button, which is what we're looking for. Rename it by changing its label to something more snappy, such as Go.

7. The form still won't work, and is a bit of a visual mess, so we need to style it and add functionality via the Code view. Replace the entire <form> tag and its contents with this:

   ```
   <form style="padding-left: 40px; margin: 0px;" name="navForm">
   ```

   This removes the default margins from the form, meaning it doesn't interrupt our layout, and also pads it to line it up with the TITLE text entered earlier.

8. Replace the <select> tag with this:

   ```
   <select name="navLinks">
   ```

   The select tag now has the right name for the JavaScript that we'll add to the submit button to get the form working.

9. Add the following to the <input> tag:

```
style="border: 1px solid #666; background-color: #fff;"
onClick="window.location=document.navForm.navLinks.options[document.navForm.
navLinks.selectedIndex].value"
```

Now the drop-down menu will work as intended (or at least it will when we author the pages it's linking to!)

Creating editable regions

Now our template's design is complete, we need to start adding editable regions, so we can create pages based on it. There are two areas that will be editable on our page: its title, and the content area, and we have to create an editable region for each of these.

Further to that, some of our pages may vary design-wise, requiring a different number of columns. These pages will still need the same basic layout, and it would be useful if changing one template updated the relevant parts of all of them. In other words, we're talking about embedded templates.

1. Select the title area with your mouse. Go to Insert > Template Objects > Editable Region. It's best to not use spaces in the region names, although capitalization such as wordWord is fine.

2. Now, do the same for the content area.

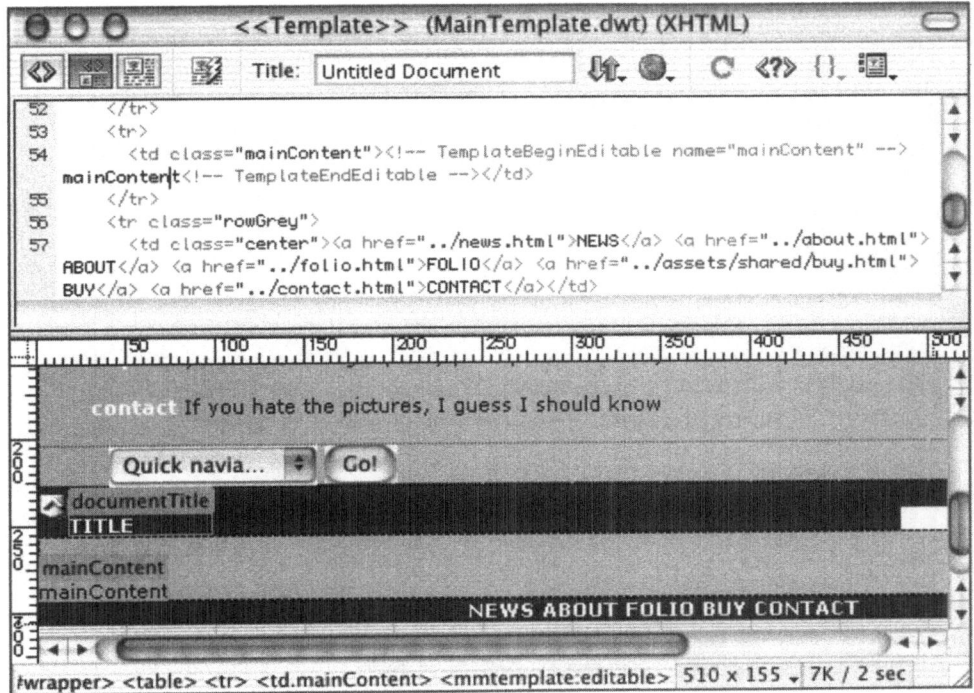

Foundation Dreamweaver MX

> *Editable regions show up on the Design view as titled tabs, and in the Code view as special comment tags that don't affect web browsers, but enable Dreamweaver to keep track of things and update pages. If you don't see the tabs in the Design view, toggle* View > Visual Aids > Invisible Elements.

3. Next, we're going to create a version of our template, but with a two-column content area. First, go to File > New and select our template from the Templates tab.

4. Inside the mainContent editable region, add a two-column table.

5. Both cells require some padding, so use class="copyPadding" for the first (to keep it in line with the TITLE text and class="cellSpacer" for the second).

6. Add the following to the Style Sheet:

   ```
   .cellSpacer       {
        padding-left: 10px;
        }
   ```

7. Finally, create editable regions inside each of the cells, so you should end up with something like this:

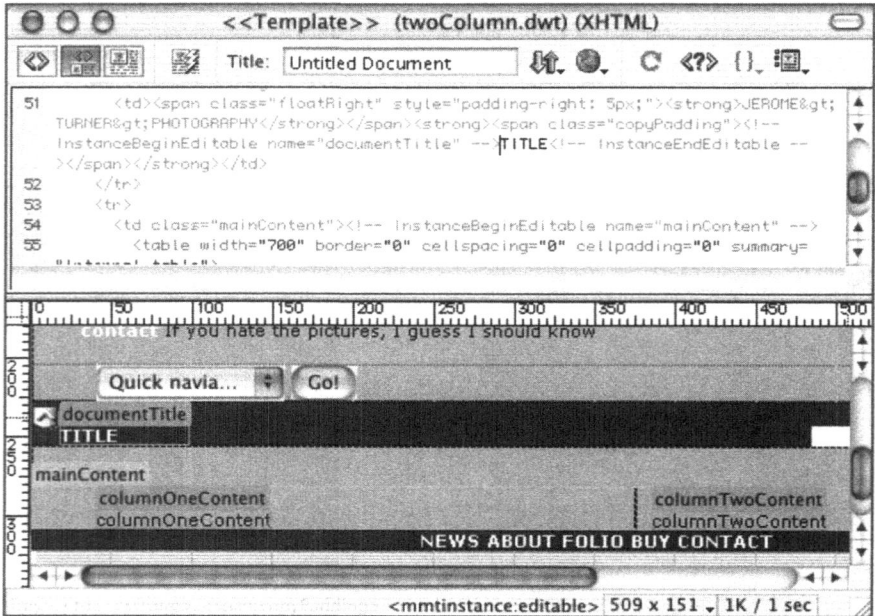

Cascading Style Sheets

When you create a new document based on *this* template, you won't have free rein within the entire content area, but only within the predefined table cells. Using the same methodology, we've also created two more templates for the next chapter: one with a three-column layout, and one with a one-column layout that contains the 40-pixel border to the left.

How they work is like this: make a change to, say, the two-column template, and all associated pages will be updated. Make a change to the main template, and not only will all the site's pages be updated, but so too will the templates that are based on the main one.

Creating pages

To create a new page from the template, simply go to File > New as normal, then select one from the Templates tab.

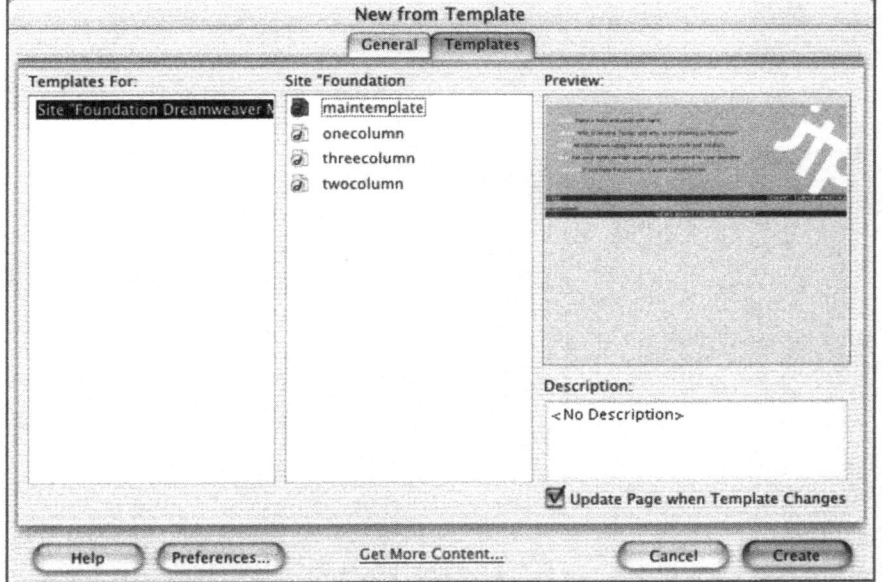

Alternatively, override a page's content with a template via Modify > Templates > Attach Template to Page and select the required template.

If any incorrect gaps have appeared in your pages, check for stray, empty paragraph tags via the Code view and delete them!!

Hopefully you're now at least fairly clear on how to get site templates up and running. As far as the site goes, the main structure, along with most of the donkey work, is now complete. The next chapter looks at adding a number of other assets to the site, including photographs, styled text and more.

Creating Content for our Site

What we'll cover in this chapter

- Using our template and CSS files to create pages for our site
- Adding images and text
- Including Flash and QuickTime content in our site

In the last chapter, we created a CSS file to make sure everything on our site is formatted in the same way. We also created some templates to work with. We're now going to see our hard work pay off as we insert and lay out the content for our site.

In this chapter, we're going to be creating a gallery of photos, and setting up a contact page ready for some extra functionality in the next chapter. We're also going to create two other pages: one with a Flash animation showing how the concept of Pinhole photography works, and the other showing a quick video that will become part of a camera tutorial.

This chapter draws on skills covered earlier in the book so don't be afraid to check back if you're not quite sure about something. We'll also be taking a look at a few extra features, and adding some new file types into the mix, allowing for whole new areas of content.

Organizing our files

We'll need some files before we can start. You can either download the files from the friends of ED site in the usual way, or use the ones that we prepared in the last chapter. You'll need:

- the CSS file:
    - `jtphotography.css`

- the templates:
    - `MainTemplate.dwt`
    - `oneColumn.dwt`
    - `twoColumn.dwt`
    - `threeColumn.dwt`

- the images:
    - `background_stripes.gif`
    - `jtplogo.gif`
    - `nav_bullets.gif`

These should be well organized in your root folder to save hunting around for files later on, so create a new folder within `assets` called `shared`, and use it to store the three images for our template (as mentioned above). Create another folder called `Templates`, and move the templates to there.

> *Dreamweaver only recognizes templates and allows you to select them from the* File > New > Template *list if they're in a folder called* Templates, *so this step is possibly more important than you think!*

You can start to see how things could get complicated without a well-organized file list. Even in the early stages of a site's creation, we have files that relate to earlier work such as the splash page. The Root Folder side of your Site window should now look something like this:

Creating content for our site 6

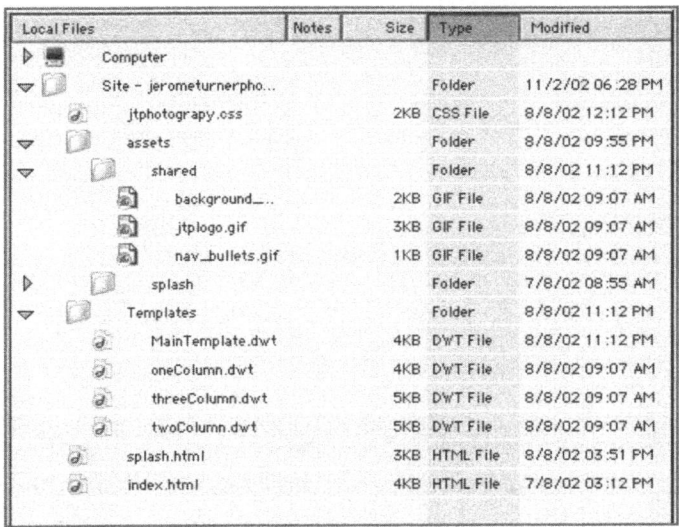

The 'about' page

Let's start working on the first page of the main site. This will be the 'about' page, describing the content, how it affects the user, and what the user can expect.

1. You should already have Dreamweaver opened and be looking at the Site window for the particular project you're working on. Go to File > New and click on the Template tab in the window, as shown. (NB: this is the template tab at the top of the window, next to General, which is *not* the same as selecting the Template Page option from the left-hand column of the General tab.)

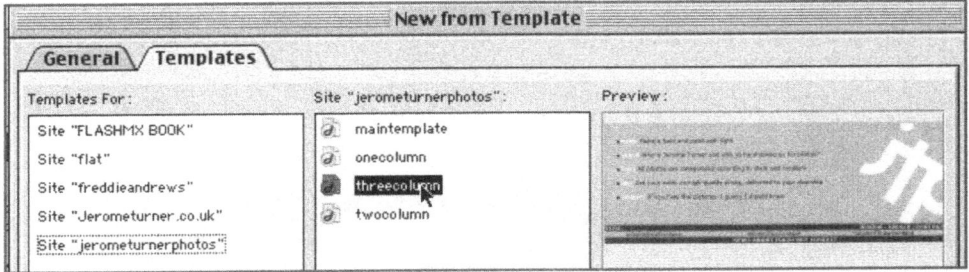

2. Select your site from the left-hand column, and the list of templates that we placed in the Templates folder earlier will appear. Choose the `threeColumn.dwt` template, click Create, and a page like the one pictured over the page will open up.

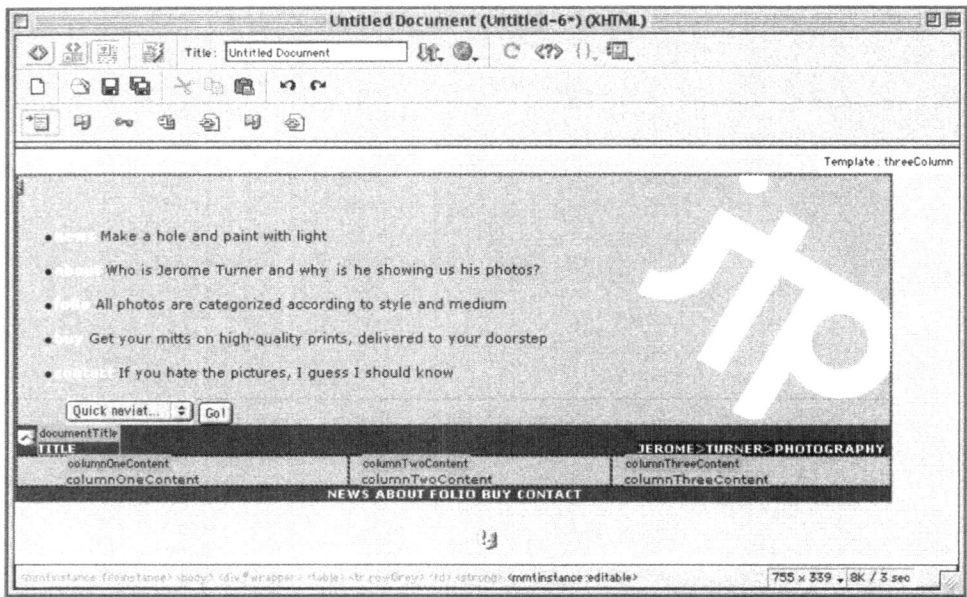

As you'll see from the title of this page, you've now created an untitled HTML document. Just as with Word or other word-processors, you don't create a page from a template by opening the template itself with File > Open, *but by creating a new document (*File > New*) and specifying the template.*

I've prepared some text telling the user about the site and what they can do there (see screenshot below). I did this on paper so that my writing isn't influenced by the space I have to work in – I can always cut bits out in a moment if it doesn't fit. Either use my text, or be creative and come up with some of your own.

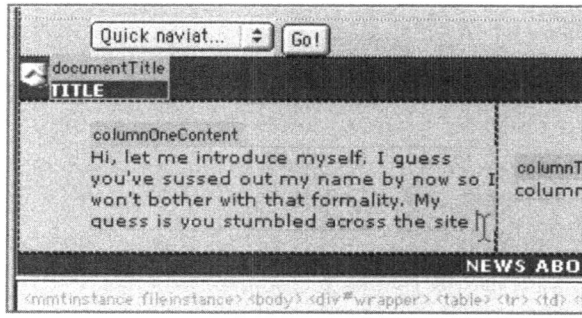

3. Place the cursor inside the first editable region labeled columnOneContent. Before we start typing, we need to check that the CSS will format our text. We set this up in the last chapter, but to check, take a look in the Design panel. Expand `jtphotography.css`, and you should see 10px Verdana listed opposite p, td, li.

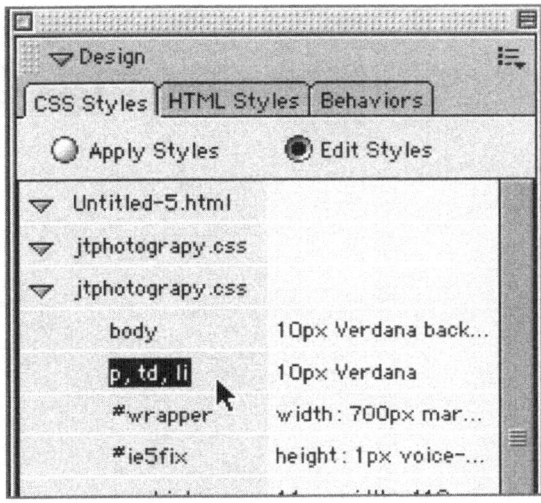

4. Given this, any text that we want formatting by our CSS has to be in the paragraph style, so set this in the Properties window for our text here. As we add further text in this chapter, check that it is set to Paragraph text each time.

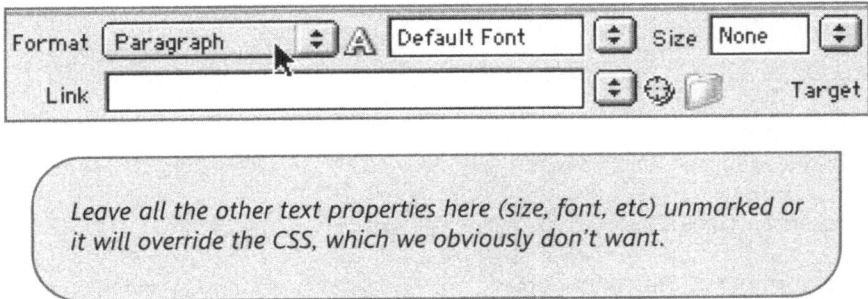

Leave all the other text properties here (size, font, etc) unmarked or it will override the CSS, which we obviously don't want.

5. Delete the text that says columnOneContent, and enter your text. You'll see that the text appears in the font and size specified by the CSS file. When you've typed around a third of the content, move to the next column, and then move to the third when you're ready so that your text is roughly split over the three columns.

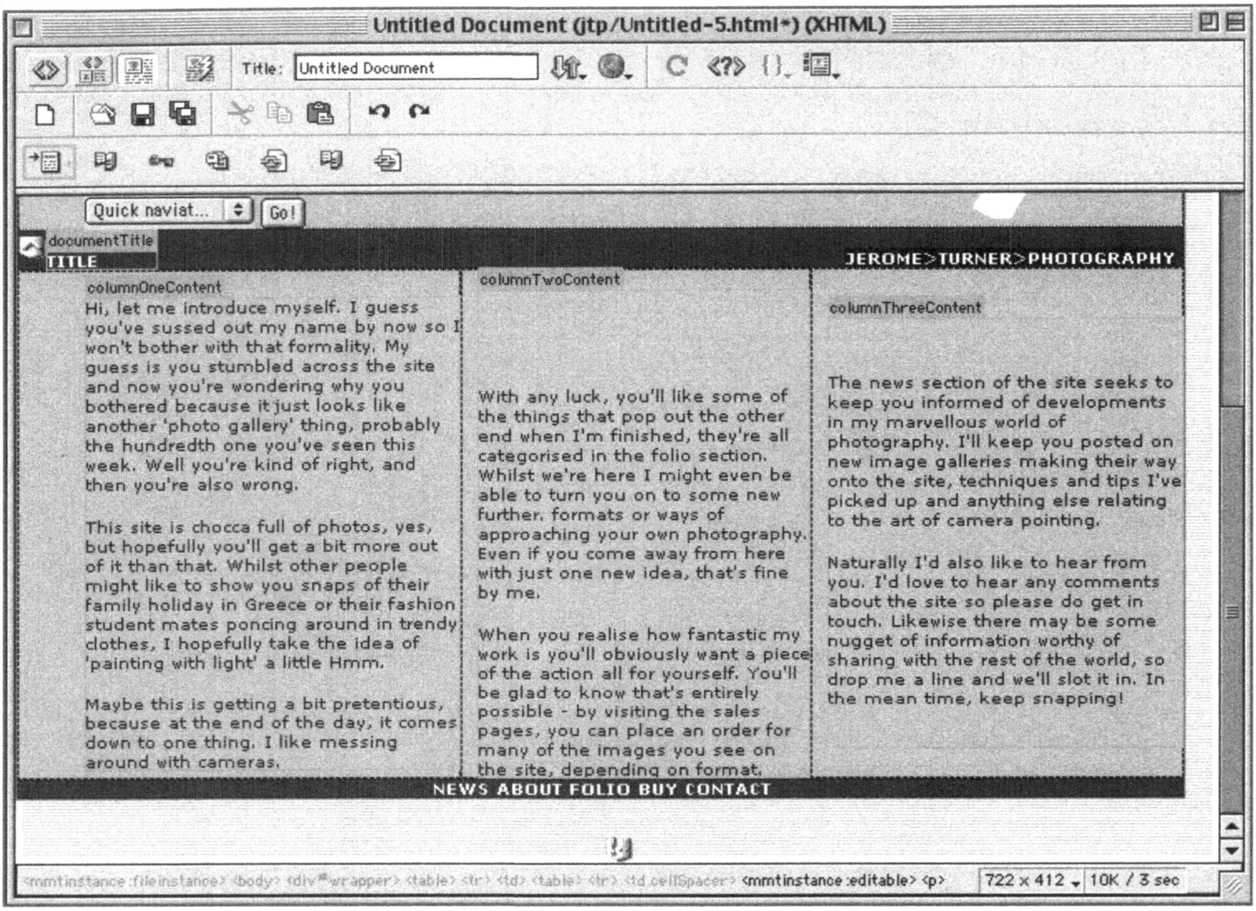

6. Preview the page in your browser. You'll see that there's something not quite right - whilst you have three columns of text, they're not all aligned to the top of the 'content' area.

7. Save the file as about.html.

8. Whilst a lot of the formatting is done by CSS, the position of the text within each of these three columns isn't, so it needs to be altered in the threeColumn.dwt template. Open the template itself by clicking on the file in the root folder list.

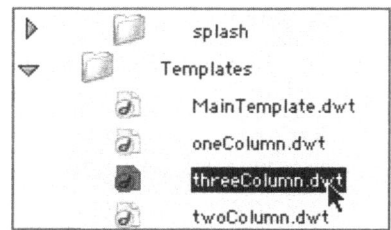

Creating content for our site

9. Place the cursor inside the first column in the layout, just as we did when entering text earlier. The text in the editable region is the occupant of the cell, so highlight the text (as shown) in order to make changes.

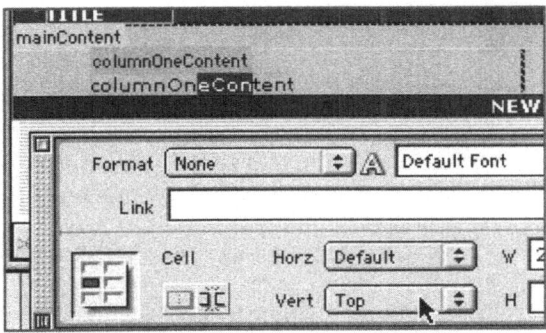

10. Switch to Standard View and change the orientation of the editable region's content to Top in the Properties panel. This won't work if you're in Layout View, so make sure you're in Standard View in the Design window (check by selecting the Layout tab at the top of your screen and seeing whether Standard View is highlighted if you're not sure).

11. We need to save our changes, so go to File > Save. You'll see a box asking whether to update the files currently using the template – Dreamweaver is clever enough to detect which files use this template and ask if you want to apply your changes. Click Update to OK the update on our HTML about file, and close the template file.

12. Go back to the about file we made from the template, and you'll see that the editable regions full of text are all aligned to the top of the cells. Wahey!

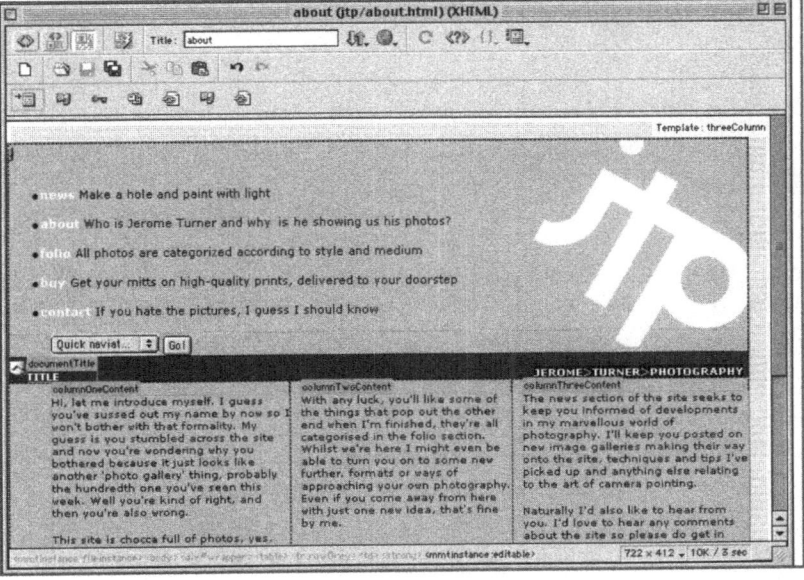

13. Before you forget, change the TITLE in the editable region on the left above column one to something appropriate like 'About'. It's one of those little things you can so easily forget until someone points it out when it's online!

Inserting images

All this descriptive text is very informative, but it might seem a bit too much to start with. Time to drop in a graphic element to break it up a bit. The image I came up with is very simple, a graphic of a camera that seems to fit in nicely to the rest of the site. I saved it as a transparent GIF (you'll remember these from **Chapter 3**), so that the background blends into the Dreamweaver page.

1. Download the camera.gif file in the usual way, or come up with a graphic of your own.

2. Continuing with our ultra-organized theme, create a new folder in assets called graphics and place camera.gif there. We've now got a place to keep non-photographic images, which will be useful when we start using more photos....

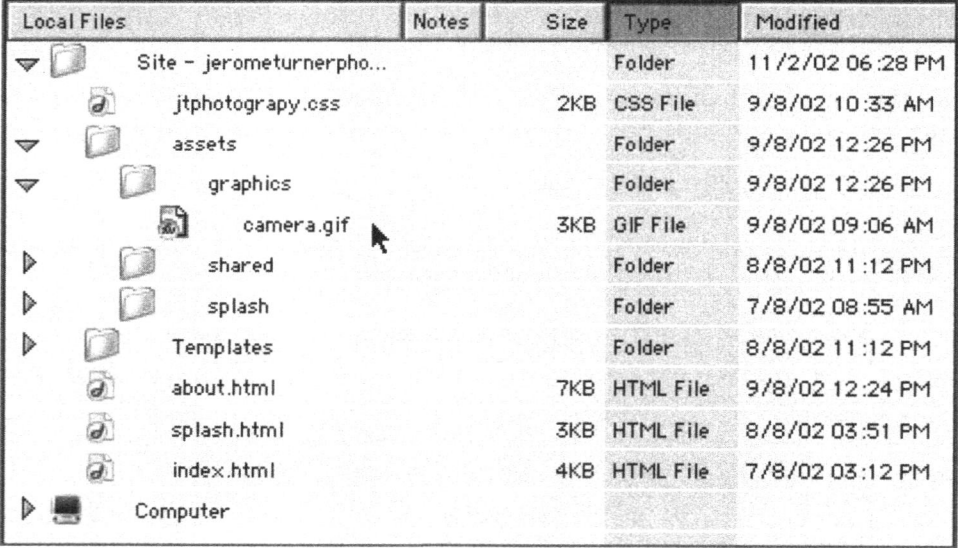

3. I've decided that I'd like the image to go somewhere in the second editable region column. This would make the first two columns much longer than the third, so transfer some of the text from the second column to the third column using cut and paste.

Creating content for our site 6

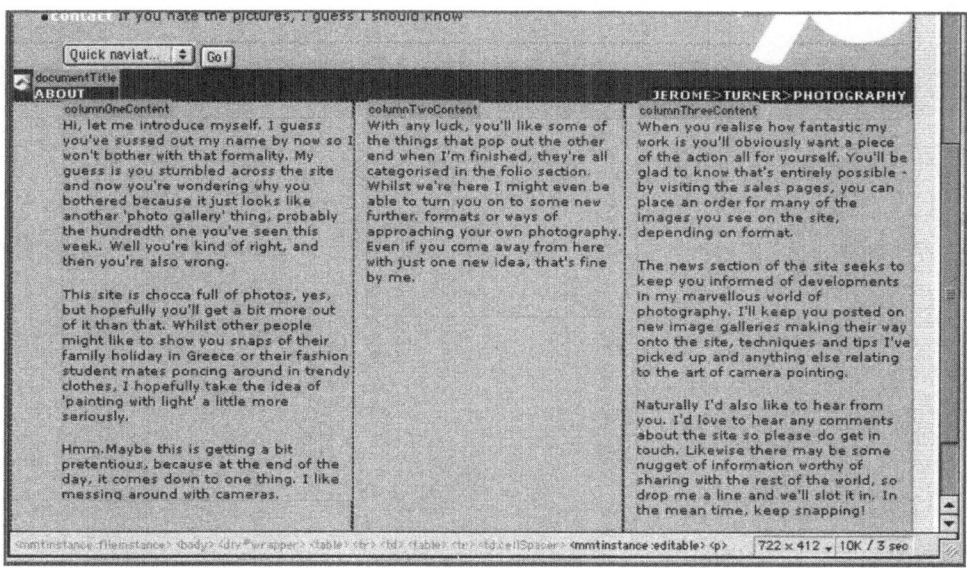

4. We want the image right in the middle of the text, so hit ENTER a few times where you want to leave a space for our picture.

5. Drag the image from the Files (Assets) panel and drop it into the space.

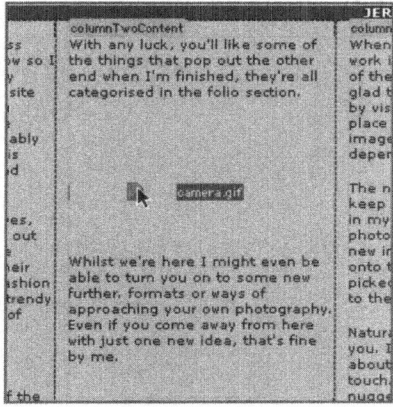

Foundation Dreamweaver MX

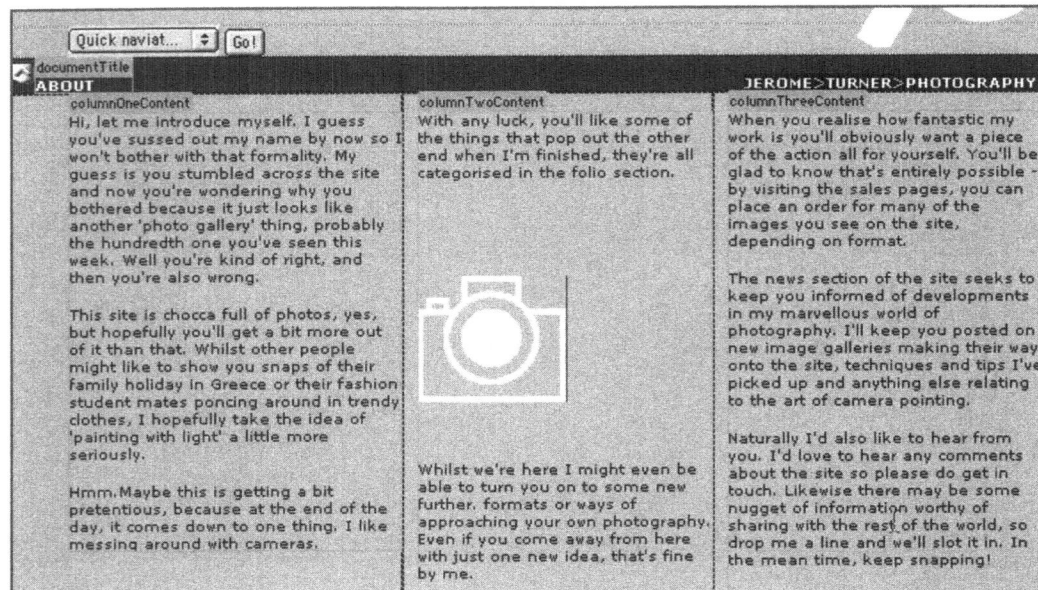

6. We want the image in the center of the column and it isn't, so select the image and click on the Align Center button in the Properties panel.

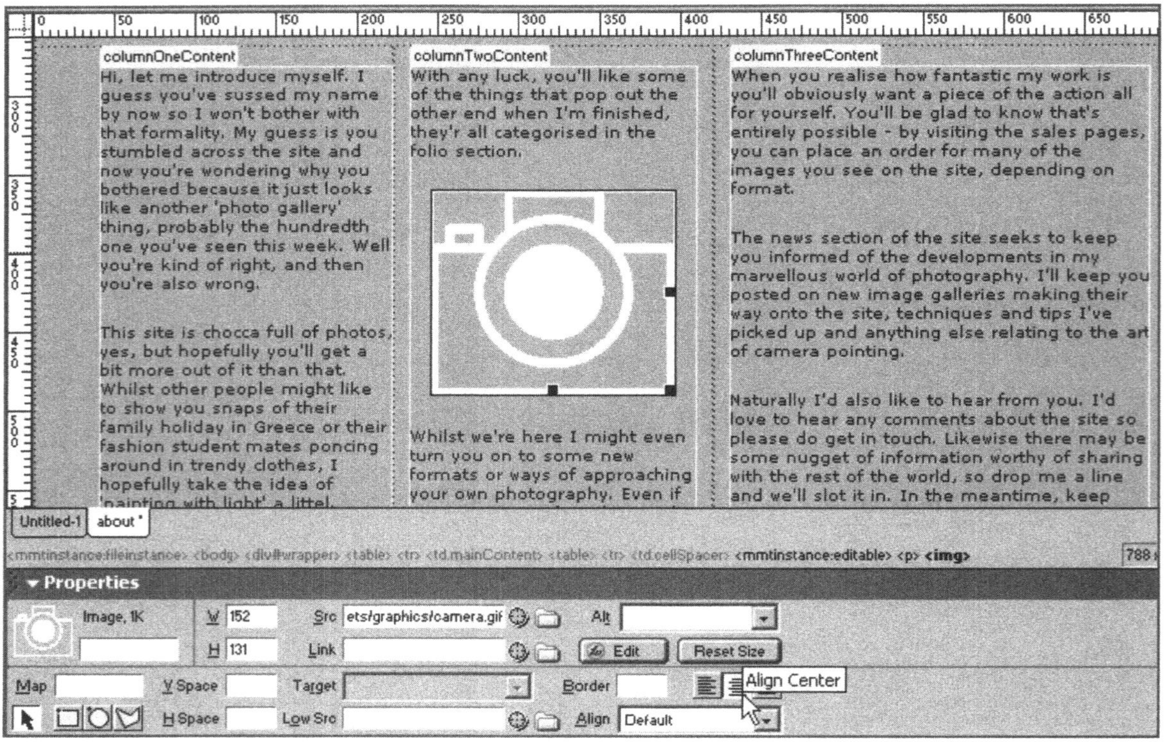

The photo gallery

We've covered one of the core pages of the site, so it's time to tackle one of the most important content areas – the photos. This page is going to be one of the portfolio pages and probably won't be accessible from the main navigation.

Clicking folio would take you to a page giving a choice of different photo galleries. We can come back to this 'gallery selection' page later, which is part of the beauty of working with Dreamweaver. There's no-one telling you how to approach the site: you can do it in an order that suits you.

Creating a thumbnail gallery

My approach to the galleries is going to match the rest of the site – nice and simple, and the CSS will help us along with the formatting.

1. This time, we're going to use the twoColumn.dwt template, so select File > New > Templates to create a new file using this template.

2. It makes sense to put text introducing / describing / labeling the photos on one side of the layout and images on the other, repeating the magazine design inspiration that we saw in the first chapter. Place a table in the first column; make it 1 column wide and 2 rows tall (leave the other values set to 0).

3. Start typing in the top of the two boxes. Again, you can use my text, or come up with something yourself.

Foundation Dreamweaver MX

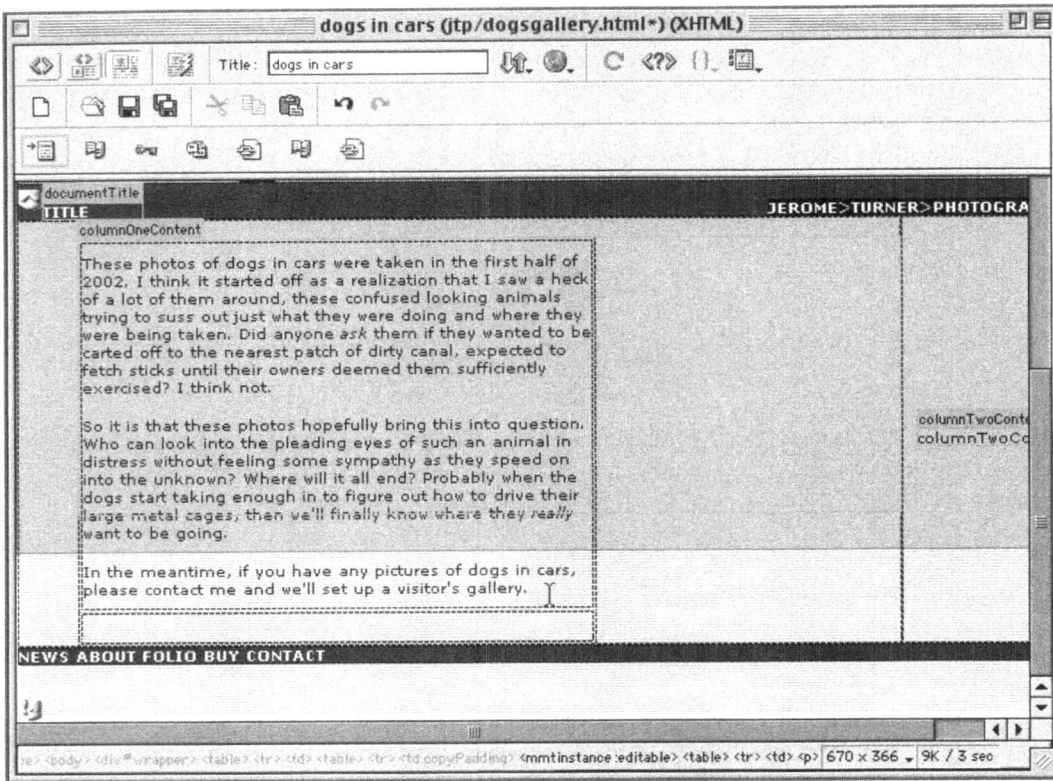

4. You might find as you're typing that the CSS and Template don't always keep up with what you're doing. In the image above, it's a little concerning that I seem to be typing through the background 'gray lines' image. Hit F12 to see how your page looks in the browser to check that everything is in order before continuing.

5. Before we continue, save your page – I've called mine dogsgallery.html.

   In the bottom part of this table, we'll insert descriptions to accompany the gallery of thumbnail pictures that will sit in the right hand column. We'll create the thumbnail gallery first.

6. Create a new directory in the assets directory, and call it photos. Inside this, set up another directory called dogsincars, which is the name of the set of photos we're going to show on this page (if you want to use your own set of photos, go ahead). Copy the dog1.jpg through to dog15.jpg files into this directory.

7. Set up another directory within photos called thumbs, and add the pictures named dog1t.jpg through to dog15t.jpg to this directory.

8. If you're using your own images, you need to open up your image editing program, crop a 60 pixel by 60 pixel detail out of each main picture, and save the result as a JPEG. Each of my thumbnail images are no larger than 8k in size, and you should aim for the same size, before copying them into your thumbs directory.

Creating content for our site

9. In the right hand column, we'll create a table with all of our thumbnails, and one full-size image to whet the appetite of the viewer. Leave the ColumnTwoContent text in place for the moment.

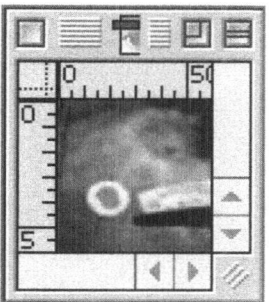

It often makes things easier to leave the placeholder text in place until you've added a few assets to a cell, as you'll discover if you delete the text and add a table, the whole column shrinks to a tiny, tiny size!

10. Now drag the full size `dog1.jpg` in underneath the columnTwoContent text.

Foundation Dreamweaver MX

11. Above the columnTwoContent text, insert a table with 3 rows and 5 columns to hold our thumbnail images. Now you can finally delete the columnTwoContent text.

12. Now drop the thumbnail images into the spaces one by one.

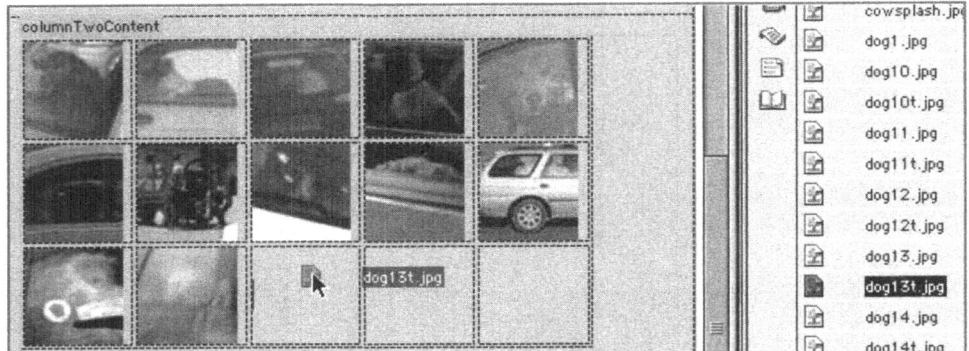

Now you'll need to set the table properties so that the spacing of the thumbnails is the same as mine. Right-click or CTRL-click on any of the blue spaces within the table and select Table > Select Table from the menu that appears. In the Properties panel set the width to 87% and the height to 194 pixels.

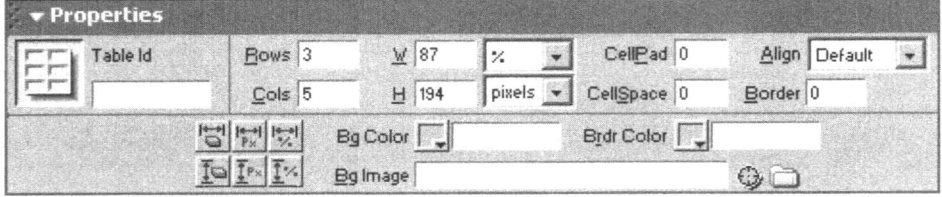

13. We want some labels for our thumbnails in the bottom left cell of the page.

Again, we're going to use those lovely glossy Sunday supplements as inspiration. First, type in the definitions:

Creating content for our site 6

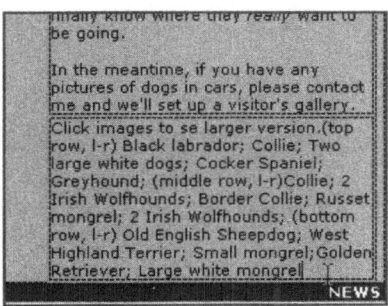

At the moment this text looks as if it follows straight on from the text above it, so we're going to make this a little smaller. We could simply change the properties of this text but I'd rather make an addition to the CSS. At the moment, all paragraph text is formatted in one particular way by the CSS file.

```
p, td, li   {
            font-family: Verdana, Arial, Helvetica, sans-serif;
            font-size: 11px;
            }
```

There are, however, plenty of other formats that can be set up:

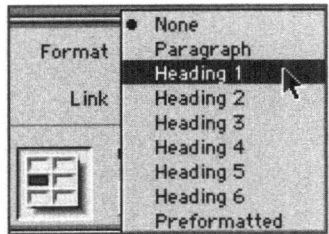

14. We need to alter a definition in the `photography.css` file. Open up the CSS file, and edit the Heading 1 text keeping it the same verdana/arial/helvetica/sans-serif font but with a size of 9 point instead of 11 point. We also set the `font-weight` to `normal` because the default for heading text is usually bold.

```
p, td, li   {
            font-family: Verdana, Arial, Helvetica, sans-serif;
            font-size: 11px;
            }

h1          {
            font-family: Verdana, Arial, Helvetica, sans-serif;
            font-size: 9px;
            font-weight: normal;
            }
```

15. Save the CSS file, and we now have a style controlled by the CSS that can be used for the captions for *all* my galleries and titling images. Highlight our text, and change the format to Heading 1.

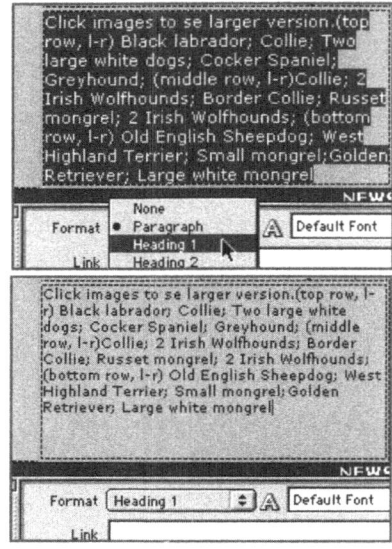

16. Finally, drag the top cell to be a bit taller so that it stands a little apart from the description text, and align the captions to the right.

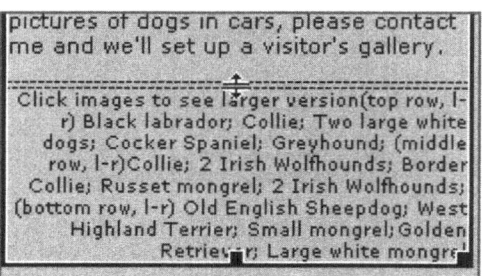

17. Finally, this time we'll override the CSS for the 'Click images to see larger version' instruction by making it into bold using the Bold button in the Properties panel.

18. Test your page in a browser, and it should look like this:

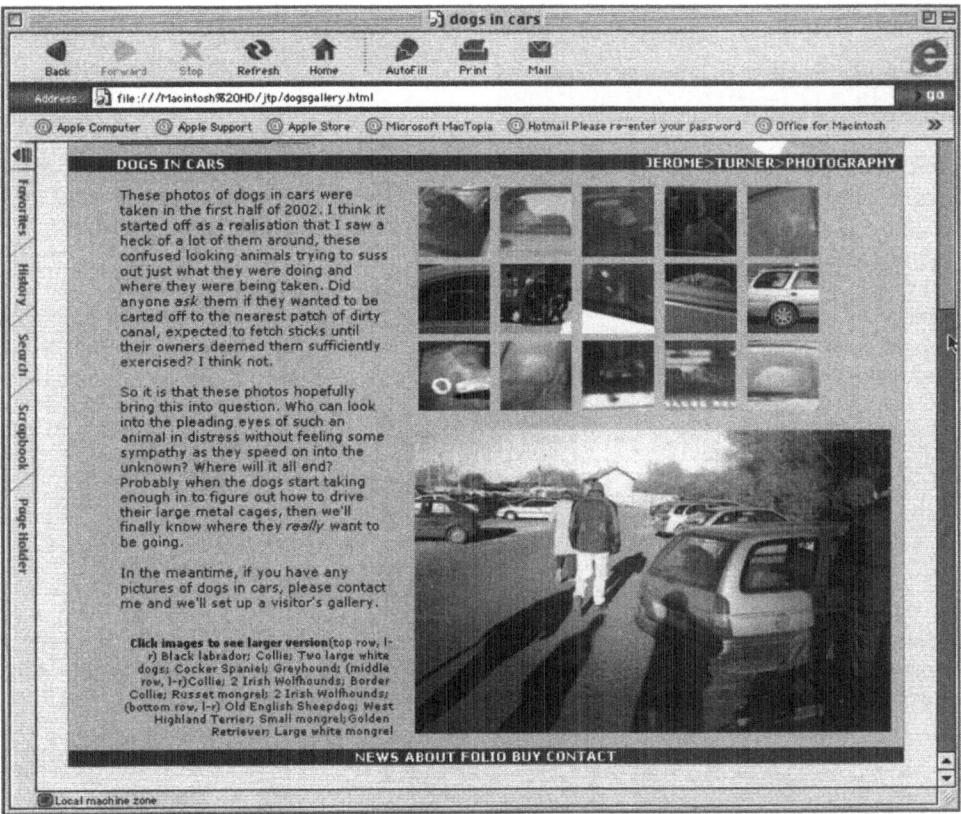

Finishing off the gallery pages

So that's how our gallery pages will look. Now, we just need to make a few minor additions to get the whole thing working. This first page we've come up with shows `dog1.jpg` in full size so it stands to reason we should create fourteen other similar pages, each showing the others in full size too. We also need to make sure we have the navigation in place.

We called the page we've just created `dogsincars.html`, and this will serve as the basis for our series. We're simply going to alter this page, and save it with a new name each time for the other fourteen images. Be careful though: it's probably not worth making a template for our fourteen images, but on larger projects you most certainly should.

If we make a mistake in the spelling for one of our links, we'll have to go through and change it fifteen times, which is irritating but manageable. Make a mistake in a bigger project, and you'll realize the benefits of changing it into a template, where you would only have to change it once.

You could also ask why we haven't done this on some kind of timeline within a larger `dogsincars.html` page. Consider a scenario where John sees the site, decides that he likes the picture in `dog9.html`, and e-mails the link for the page to his friend Frank. When Frank visits the page, he gets a full description, hopefully drawing him into the other pictures and ultimately the rest of the site. There is a specific URL for that picture so that there's no messy navigating to find it.

The gallery page navigation

1. Make sure you add the navigation first, before re-saving the original file 14 times, or you'll have to type in the links each time. Select the first (top left) thumbnail image and make this link to page `dog1.html`. Then the second one links to `dog2.html`, etc until you've got 15 clickable thumbnail images.

2. Then still in the same page change the Title to dog1 and re-save the file as `dog1.html`. The title is what will appear in the top bar of someone's browser when they're viewing the page, so it's important to remember to fill this in!

3. Delete the full size image `dog1.jpg` and replace it with `dog2.jpg`. When exporting these images from Photoshop I made sure they all had the same width of 400 pixels – this way the text on the left isn't thrown out.

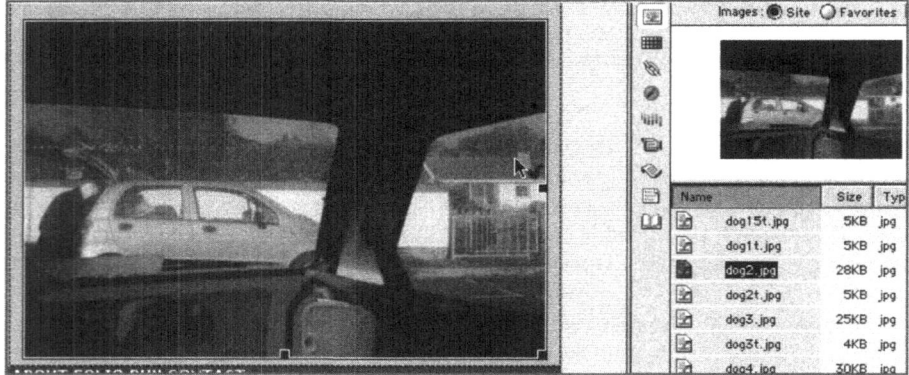

4. Now re-title and re-save again, naming this page `dog2.html`.

5. Repeat this action until you have 15 different pages, each showing a full-size image from the thumbnail gallery.

6. Having created all these pages it's probably a good idea to check that all your links work. The easiest way to do this is to try it in your browser and navigate round as a user would.

Creating content for our site

7. Having created all these new pages, take a quick look at your File list in the Site window. It's probably looking a bit messy, as most of your files will be in the root level of the site. Create a new folder called dogs, and place `dog1.html – dog15.html` in there.

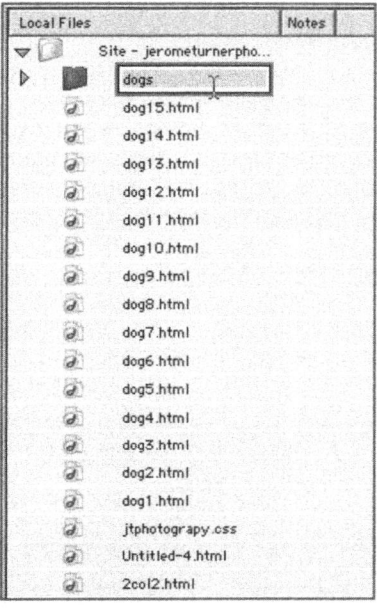

You can quickly select a whole list of files by selecting a file at one end, holding down SHIFT and then clicking on the file at the other end. Drag the whole lot into the new folder just as you would with a single file.

8. As soon as you make any change like this, the instructions for linking and the location of files will change for certain pages so Dreamweaver will ask you if you want to update the files concerned. Click Update and you'll get a running commentary of what's going on. When this is finished, you should find that there's a bit more room in your site files list.

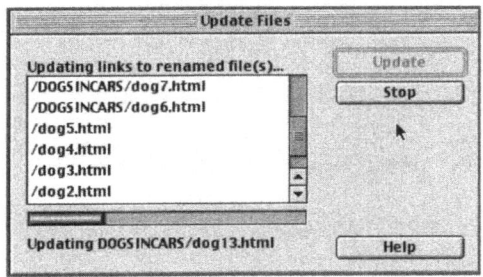

So that's the basis for my gallery page. I'll probably use a similar layout for other photos grouped under the various themes – beaches, landscapes, pinhole photography, and so on - I can come back to them later. Towards the end of this book, we'll be taking a look at how you can construct a system that uses some dynamic content power to create a dynamic gallery that allows you to easily add images into a gallery-type page, so maybe you can come back and add that to the JTP site.

You may have noticed that we haven't built the folio page yet. Well, being as the dogs in cars gallery is the only collection of pictures we have on the site right now, it would seem a bit strange having a folio page with nothing but a link to the dogs gallery on it. Obviously, when there are more galleries up on the site ('Cats in Trees', 'Pigs in Sties' maybe) then we could build a folio page that links to them all. For now though, so that the folio link works on all pages just save your dogs gallery as `folio.html`. This means that whenever anyone clicks folio they'll be taken straight to Dogs in Cars.

In the meantime, what else is there? Well, I'd like to put together some kind of contact page so people can get in touch with me.

Using Form Objects

There is a really simple way of getting people to e-mail you in Dreamweaver. You simply turn a piece of text or an image into a **mailto** link. Rather than entering a URL or page of your site in the Link field of the Properties panel, you type something like this:

This type of link is pretty clever because it automatically opens a user's main e-mail application (e.g. Outlook) and starts a new e-mail message for them to send you. Given that they have to be online to see your site anyway, there's no reason why they can't type it up and send immediately.

However, I want to give my users the option of sending me messages through my own site so they don't get distracted away from the content. This also means those accessing from machines where they haven't got an e-mail application like Outlook set up can get in touch.

Creating the contact page

We're going to do this by dropping in editable elements that have been pre-made for Dreamweaver, the Form Objects. We added one of these to the template in the last chapter in the form of the Jump Menu. The Go! Button to the right is another Form Object.

1. Start off by opening a new file, using the `onecolumn.dwt` template.

2. Delete the placeholding text (as this is only a one column layout, we don't need to leave it there to help us as we did before), and insert a table with 1 column, 3 rows, a width of 100% and the

cell spacing, cell padding and border set to 0. If it doesn't already look like the screenshot, resize the table so it's a little more of a box shape.

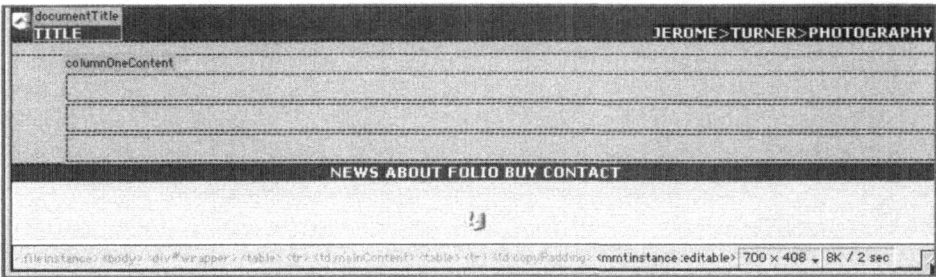

3. In the top cell, enter some text inviting the user to send a message.

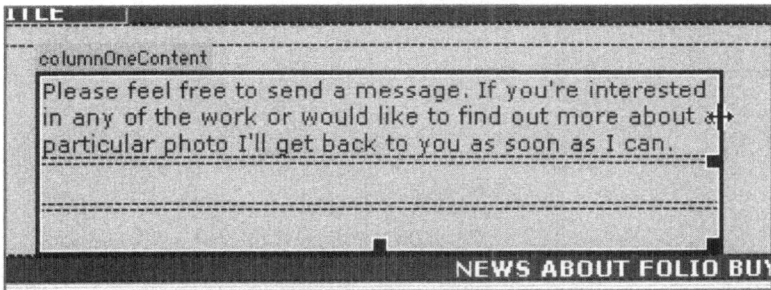

With the text in place, resize the table (by selecting it and dragging the right hand edge of it towards the left) so that it fills about half the width of the screen.

In the second cell, add a text field for people to enter their message - select Insert > Form Objects > Text Field.

4. In the next two pop-up windows (Accessibility Options and Add Form Tag) click OK and Yes.

5. A Text Field graphic will appear on your page. Highlight it and check out the Properties panel.

6. There are a couple of things to do with the text field as it stands. First of all, we want to make sure people can enter a fair amount of text, so change the Type to Multi-line.

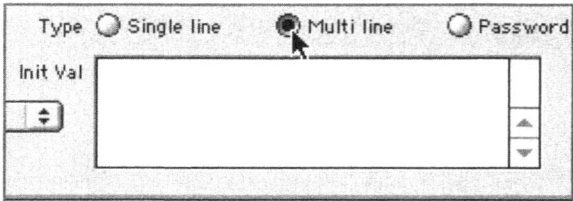

7. The user will probably want to easily see the whole content of their message before they send it, so we need to make the field a little taller. Change the number of lines to 8 with the Num Lines option that appears just under the Char Width box to make the field taller.

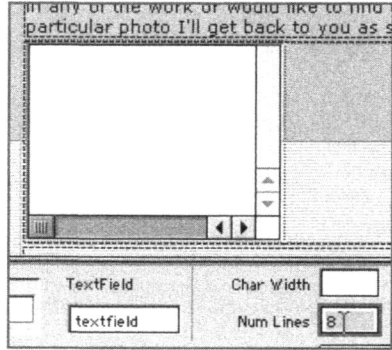

8. Now test the page in your browser by pressing F12 to see how these changes affect the text field. You should be able to type as much text as you want and after typing eight lines, the scrollbar on the right should become active. The text should also automatically go to a new line when it reaches the edge of the field.

9. We can also make the text field a little wider by changing the width, which is measured in text characters (Char Width), to 50.

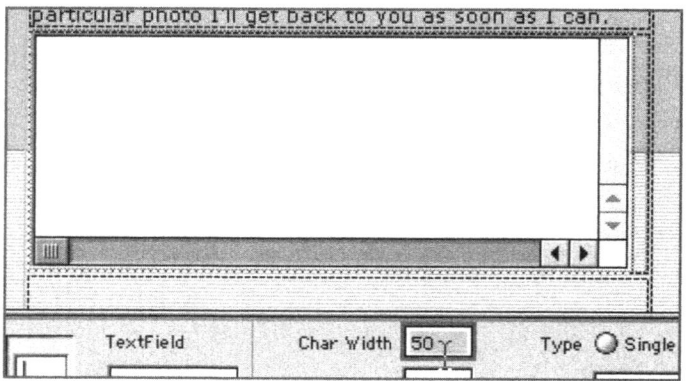

Creating content for our site 6

10. To make sure the user knows what they're doing add some initial text to sit in the Field until they start typing over it. You'll have to do this in the Init Val box in the Properties panel, and not straight into the box in the design view layout you can see.

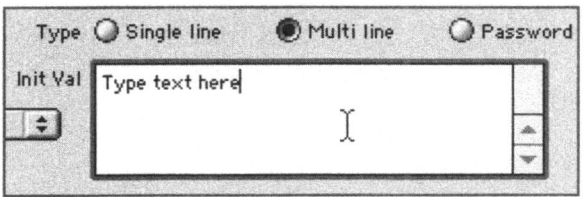

Adding a Submit button to the Text Field

Having laid out a text field, you'll need some way for the user to send the information to you.

If you look very closely you'll notice a thin red border running round the outside of the Text Field object. You can just see it inside the dotted lines in this detail.

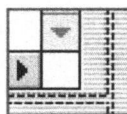

This is the **Form** that was automatically created when you inserted the Text Field. A Form is made up of a group of elements that works together to a particular end. Within the Form we're working with, we have a text Field object and the submit button we're about to add will be a Button object. When the user inputs text to the text field and hits the button the form will send the comments to us(more on how this actually works later).

```
65          </tr>
66          <tr>
67            <td height="129"> <form name="form1" id="form1" method="post" action="">
68              <label>
69                <textarea name="textfield" cols="50" rows="8">Type text here</textarea>
70              </label>
71            </form></td>
72          </tr>
73          <tr>
74            <td valign="top">
```

Highlight the Text Field and switch to Design and Code View for a moment. You can see where the information relating to my Text Field appears. The `<tr>` tags bracket *all* the Form info. The values for `form name`, `id`, `method` and `action` were all automatically defined as defaults when I inserted the text Field.

Adding the button

1. This means that we have to be careful where our button goes. Place the cursor inside the red outline, just after the Text Field.

6 Foundation Dreamweaver MX

2. Insert a Button using the Insert Panel, as shown. Click OK for the Accessibility settings.

3. Highlight the button on the page to see the Properties. We can see that this button may have uses other than submitting the info in this form, but that's what we'd like it to do, so there's no change there.

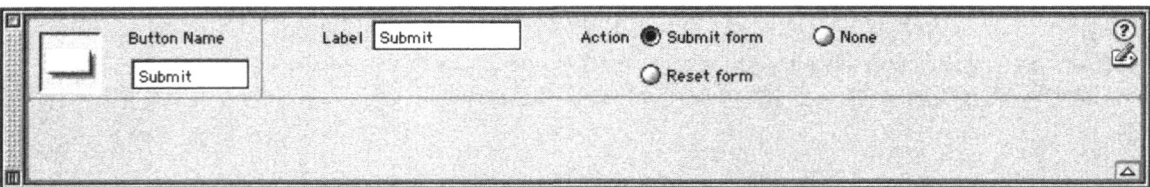

4. Change the label so that it reads Send instead of Submit.

5. Back in the code window, we can see the Submit button (line 71 in my screenshot) within the `form` tags and alongside the Text Field.

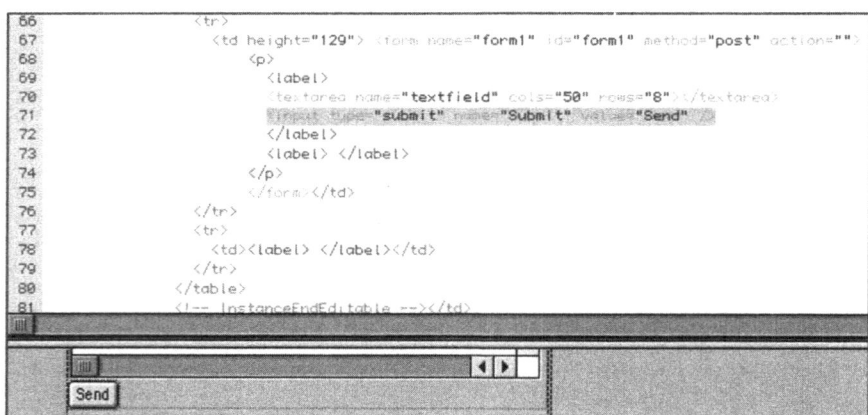

6. In the bottom cell, add some text to round off the whole page.

```
66          <tr>
67              <td height="129"> <form name="form1" id="form1" method="post" action="">
68                  <p>
69                      <label>
70                          <textarea name="textfield" cols="50" rows="8"></textarea>
71                          <input type="submit" name="Submit" value="Send">
72                      </label>
73                      <label> </label>
74                  </p>
75              </form></td>
76          </tr>
77          <tr>
78              <td><label> </label></td>
79          </tr>
80      </table>
81      <!-- InstanceEndEditable --></td>
```

[Send]

It's only a small page really, but it will be invaluable in helping me find out what people think of the site. You may be wondering how we recieve the comments that the user enters into our contact form. Well, one of the best ways of retrieving this data is by setting up a database to hold all the comments. The database will be stored on our web server and we can access it to read all the comments that have been sent.

The process involved in setting this up is a little beyond the scope of this chapter. It requires the use of dynamic content techniques that we'll be looking at later in the book. We show you exactly how to set up a contact form using a MySQL database in Chapter 10. Once you've read that chapter, you'll be able to come back to this contact page and set it all up so that you can view the comments users send.

When to start using other file formats

Back in **Chapter 3** we started to address the problem of using files outside of the Dreamweaver/HTML remit. We can all view HTML text and images without the aid of anything more than a standard web browser, but when we start talking about Flash animation or QuickTime videos it's a different story. The user will need to have a 'player' downloaded to their machine in order to view the Flash or QuickTime content.

As we discussed in **Chapter 3**, there will be a small proportion of users unable to view such content, and you should take a good look at the projected audience for your site before taking the decision on whether to include such content. With our photography site, it's a bit of a no-brainer. We're creating a site where the emphasis is on visual appeal, and – as we'll see – these elements will certainly add to that.

Either way, it's always important to inform your users what they need to download to be able to view what's in the site, as we did in **Chapter 3**. Should you want to cater to both a plug-in capable and a non plug-in capable audience, then you could also look at creating two alternative sites: one with content that needs a plug-in, and one without that content. You would then offer users a choice as to which site they entered via the splash page. We're not going to do that here, but it's an option worth bearing in mind for the future.

Flash Files

We'll look at QuickTime in a moment, but given all this fuss about plug-ins, what does Flash offer that you can't already find in Dreamweaver? The main answer to this is probably **animation** – if you want your site to look a bit more exciting and interactive then it's probably something worth considering using some motion graphics created in Flash.

> There are actually a multitude of things that can be achieved in a Flash file – far too many to go through here. For a peek at some examples check out www.flashkit.com and www.macromedia.com/software/flash, the latter of which will allow you to download a fully functioning thirty-day trial version for free.

We're not going to take you through how to create content in Flash here – Flash is a sophisticated and powerful piece of software, and there are entire books (including, of course, the highly acclaimed *Foundation Flash MX* from friends of ED) that deal with this. What we want to do is show you how to successfully include Flash content in your Dreamweaver files. We'll do this by taking you quickly through the options you need to be aware of when exporting Flash files, and then looking at placing a Flash file into Dreamweaver.

Those of you who don't have a copy of Flash at the moment can download the free trial version from the URL mentioned earlier and discover a fascinating new world of motion graphics. If you can't take that level of excitement, then simply skip the next section and join us again at the **Using Flash Files in Dreamweaver** heading.

Preparing SWFs for Dreamweaver

Flash animation can be as simple or complicated as you want. Using Flash, you work with files that have an FLA extension. When you export these for use on the web (a process which compresses the file size, amongst other things), Flash generates a file with a SWF extension. It is these SWFs (pronounced *Swiffs*) that can be imported into a Dreamweaver file. When creating these SWFs for Dreamweaver, there are a few things to look out for, and that's what we're going to quickly cover here.

1. In Flash, open up your Flash file (or take a look at animation.fla), and select Modify > Document. You should see a panel like the one pictured, giving some key information that will influence how the file is used and seen in our Dreamweaver page.

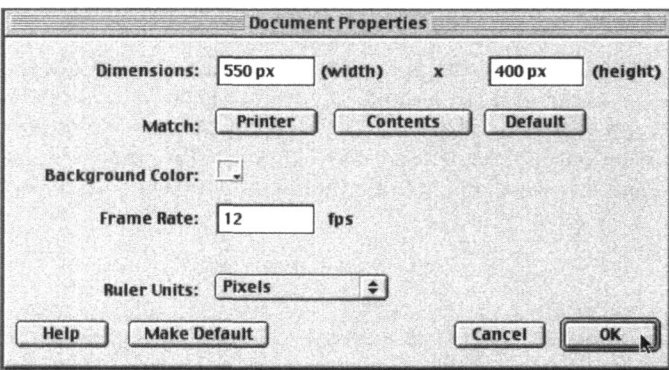

Creating content for our site

2. First, the dimensions. The default size of 550 by 400 pixels can be altered to fit the space in your Dreamweaver page. For example, if you were just creating a button for your navigation you'd make it something more like 40 by 20.

> Note that you need to change the size **before** starting your Flash project. Changing the document size after authoring your Flash content will change the size of the stage on which your content displays, but not the size of the content itself.

3. As we discussed earlier when looking at JPEGs, the background color is also important. If your SWF is supposed to look like it is in a box then you don't have to worry too much about the color, as long as it fits the scheme running throughout your site. If you're doing anything else, then you'll want to select the palette that is brought up by clicking on the Background Color, and enter a HTML color that matches that in the Properties panel in Dreamweaver.

4. There is another option: you can export your SWF as a transparent GIF at the cost of some fairly severe quality loss. Matching background colors really is the best option, but if you decide to give this a try, you can do it by selecting File > Export Movie, choosing Animated GIF, and checking the Transparent box – as shown below.

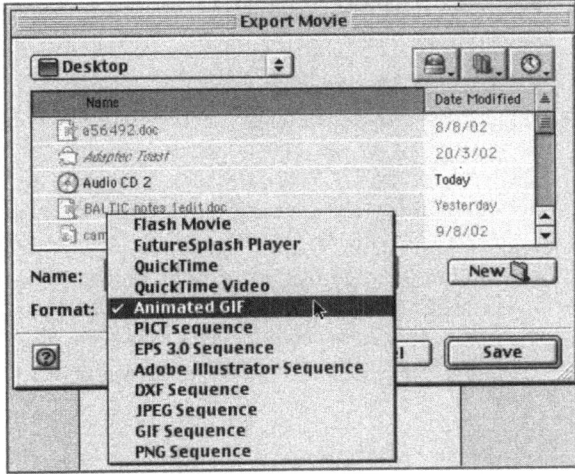

5. Finally, we can also set the speed that the animation runs at from the Document properties box. This is measured in frames per second, or FPS; 12 fps is the default and should only be adjusted if you feel it's really necessary.

6. Once you've sorted everything out, choose File > Export Movie, and pick Flash Movie from the list.

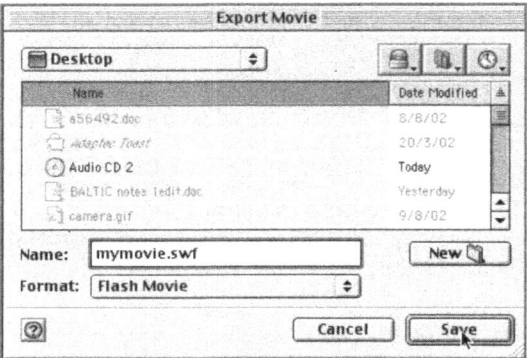

7. Press Save, and you'll be presented with a final window, giving you a few more options.

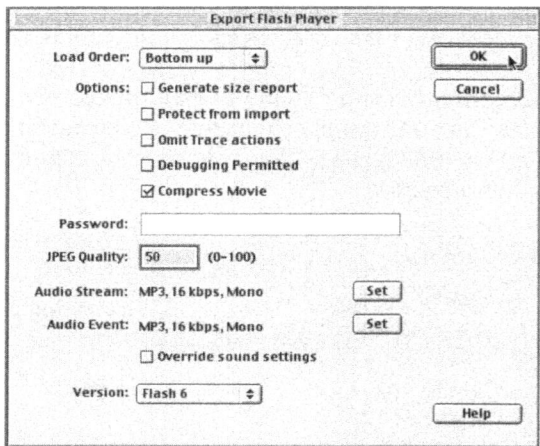

8. There are only two settings that concern us here. The first is the JPEG Quality setting, which sets the overall quality of the image/s in your movie. You can see in the screenshot that I've set this to 50, but you'll probably need to play around a little to determine the optimum setting for your movie. You can usually get away with reducing this to around 80 without too noticeable an effect.

9. The other setting is the Version, and how you want to set this is a little dependent on the Flash file you're dealing with. Why would you want to set it to an old version of Flash? Because it's been around longer, more people have the Flash 5 player than the Flash 6 player. If your Flash file uses some of the new MX features, you may well have no choice but to use the Flash 6 setting, but if your file is fairly generic, you may want to experiment by creating a Flash 5 and a Flash 6 version. If both work, go for the Flash 5 option.

Creating content for our site 6

In case your wondering, the current version of Flash is called **Flash MX**, *but the Flash Player – the plug-in that you need to view Flash MX content in your browser – is called* **Flash 6**. *Whereas you used to need a Flash 5 player to view Flash 5 content, you now need a Flash 6 player to view Flash MX content.*

Using Flash files in Dreamweaver

For my site I've created an animation that illustrates how to put together a pinhole camera for home use. It's a pretty simple piece, so I've saved it as a Flash 5 file. I've also noted that the file dimensions are the default 550 by 400.

1. Import the `animation.swf` file into the site, and store it in the root site directory.

2. Open a new file using the `onecolumn.dwt` template. As usual, delete the holding text and leave the cursor in the editable region.

3. Place a table of 2 columns by 2 rows in the region, as we'll want to add some text as well as the animation. As we'll see, SWFs and QuickTime movies are treated exactly like images as far as layout in Dreamweaver is concerned.

4. In the first cell, add some text, in the paragraph text style. Again, either copy mine or create your own.

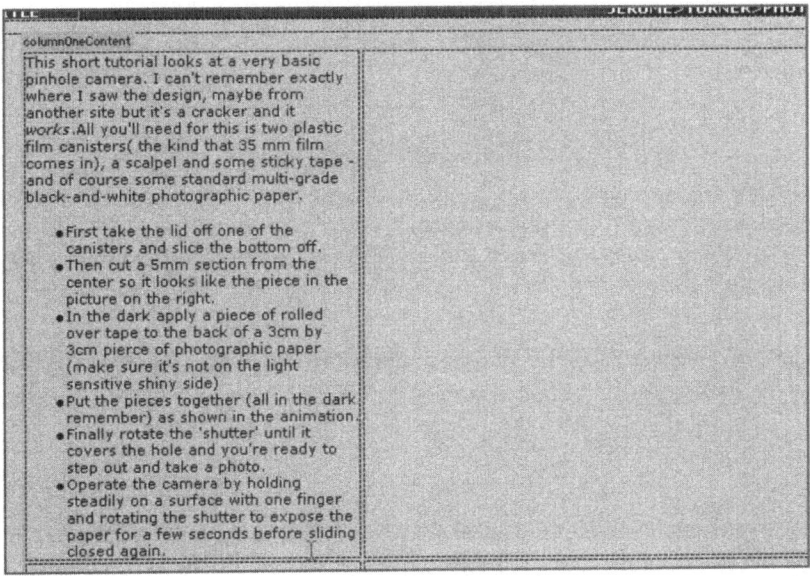

179

5. In the Assets panel, find our SWF by clicking on the Flash icon on the side – it's the red one just under the links. If it doesn't appear, you may need to click on the circular arrow button in the bottom-right hand corner to refresh the list.

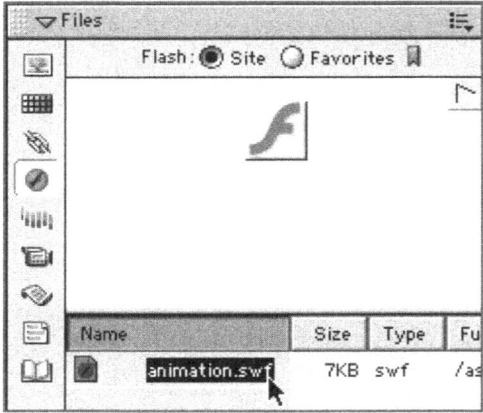

6. Drag the file directly into the second cell of the table, just as if it was an image.

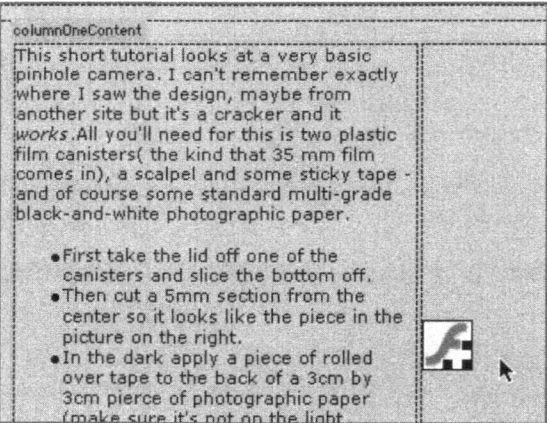

7. Dreamweaver might recognize the size of your Flash file, in which case the 550 by 400 dimensions will come up in the Properties panel. Otherwise, you might notice that your SWF appears as a tiny icon as in the screenshot above. If it is, you need to tell Dreamweaver the dimensions by selecting the Flash icon, and entering the width and height in the Properties panel.

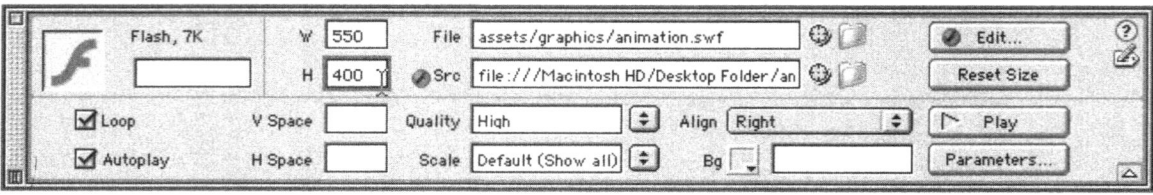

Creating content for our site

8. The SWF still appears as a gray rectangle. It'd be good to see it working in the page, so hit the Play button at the bottom right of the Properties panel (and Stop when you're happy).

9. There are a few other options in the Properties panel: Loop makes sure that the animation loops rather than just playing once. Autoplay means that Dreamweaver will start playing the SWF at the first frame.

10. If you now test your file in your browser, you should see the Flash animation embedded within the page. It's a fairly big file in terms of page size, so it throws things out a bit in my version. Move some of the text around, and then merge the cells (by selecting both cells and using the icon at the bottom left of your Properties panel) so that there's enough space for the SWF.

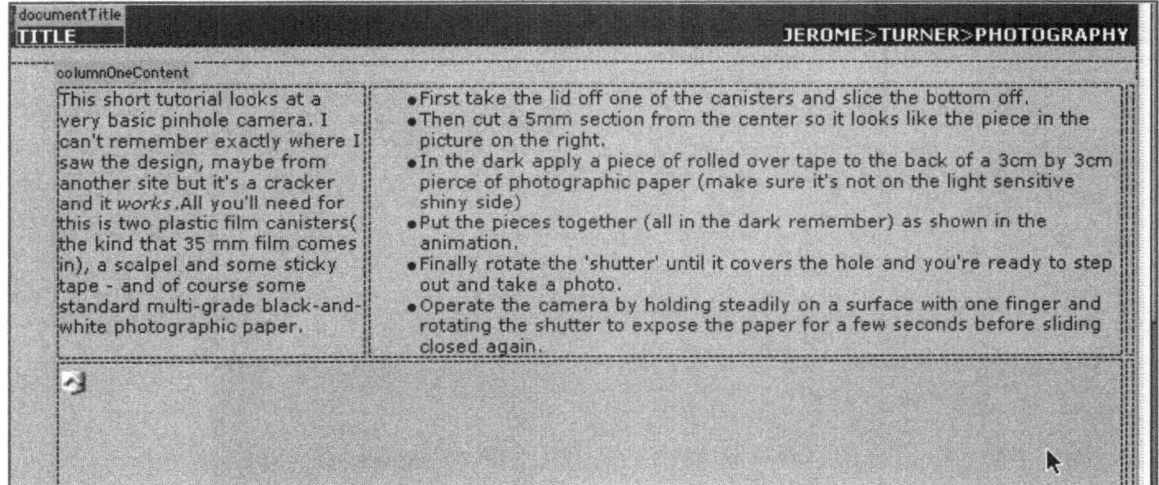

11. Save your file, and there you have it: you're using Flash in Dreamweaver.

Using Flash buttons and text

As Dreamweaver and Flash files work so well together, Macromedia have included the ability to use some Flash elements such as buttons and text without diving into Flash itself at all. Flash work can get pretty involved so it's nice to feel you can rustle up these little snippets without opening another application. If you go to the Insert > Media panel, you'll see a few options depicting the Flash logo. We're going to use a Flash button here.

1. Place the cursor in one of the remaining cells at the bottom of the table.

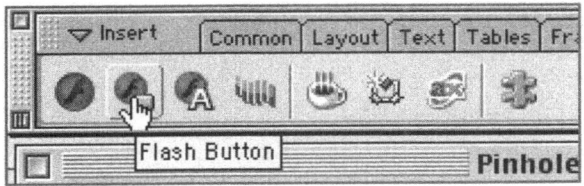

Foundation Dreamweaver MX

2. Select Flash Button from the Insert > Media panel at the top of your screen, as shown. The following pop-up gives pretty much any option and design style you'd expect from a Flash button.

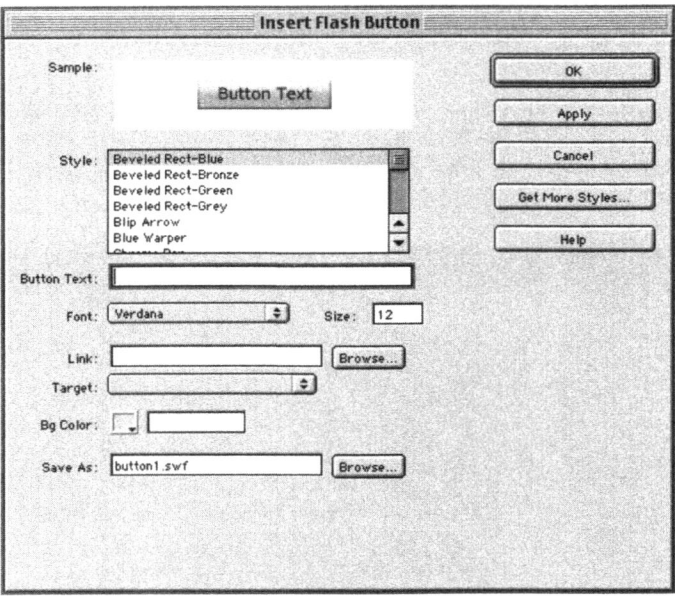

3. Choose a Style – I've used Beveled Rect-Blue here.

4. Enter More About Pinhole as the Button Text. Select Verdana, 12 pt size.

5. Direct the button towards a link either by finding the page you'd like it to link to by browsing or type by hand in the link box. Why not use this example button to link back to the dogsgallery.html page we made up earlier? In real practice these buttons can be used in the same way as any other but this at least gives us an idea of how they work.

6. Set the Bg Color of the button so it matches your site.

7. In the bottom panel of the window, use Save As to save the button in the root folder. I've imaginatively followed Dreamweaver's lead and called my button button1. This has to go in the same folder as your html page. This is a bit of a pain in terms of organization, as it means you have odd SWFs floating around, but try storing it elsewhere and you'll get a warning like this:

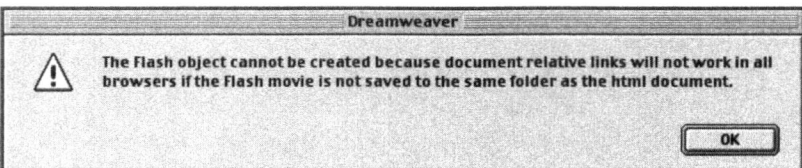

Creating content for our site

8. Click Apply and you'll see the button previewed in location on the page (not in the window at the top of the Panel you can see, actually on the page – so you may need to move the window to see this).

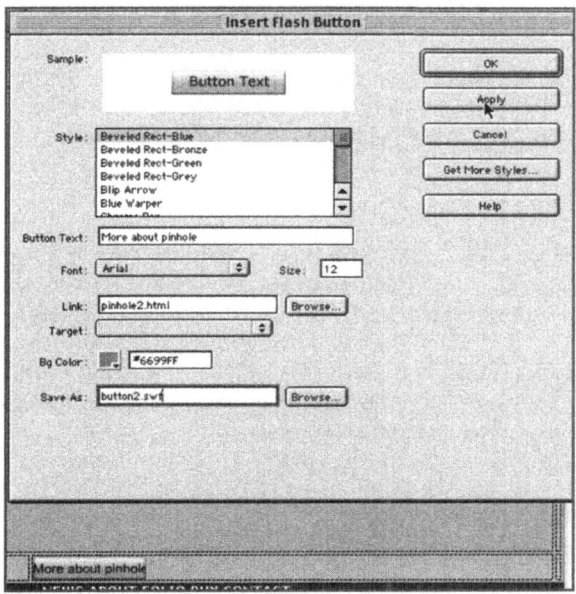

9. You'll see that we need to make the text smaller, so try a lower point size, and hit Apply until you get something that fits. Click OK when you're done. If you click OK before everything is perfect, double-click the button to open it up again.

10. The SWF now sits in the page and has been saved to your Root folder. To see it in action test in your browser with F12 as normal.

11. Sometimes, you might want to try using Flash text to get a different effect. In that case, the options are pretty similar, and once again, you can edit it by double-clicking on it in Design view.

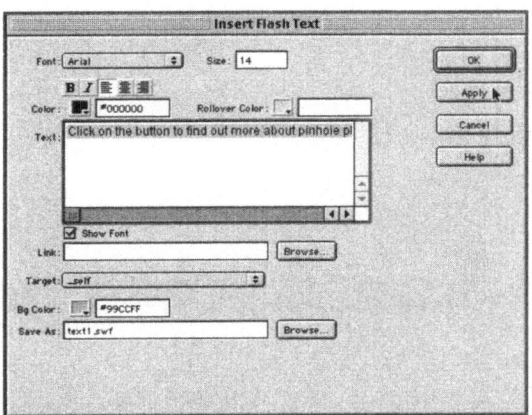

Foundation Dreamweaver MX

> *If your SWF was created in Flash MX, then you can edit it by selecting it and clicking the* Edit *button in the Properties panel.*

This is only an introduction to using Flash content in Dreamweaver, but you should have begun to see the possibilities it opens up. With the increasing integration between the members of Macromedia's MX Studio, this is something we're surely going to see more and more.

QuickTime files

The other file type we'll deal with is the most commonly used way of showing video on the web – a QuickTime file. I've made a short video that illustrates the opening mechanism of my SLR camera, which will hopefully be one in a line of tutorials on the site, and turned the video into a QuickTime file.

The process of exporting the QuickTime file from your editing application can be fairly easy. In most cases, you can hit Export Movie or something similar, and you'll be faced with a number of pre-sets. I've chosen Web Movie, Small from the iMovie presets in the screenshot. Take a note of the dimensions of your movie - as with the SWF we used, this will become very useful later on.

Inserting a QuickTime file

As with the other exercises, you can either use my video (available in the usual way from the friends of ED site), or one of your own. QuickTime files can become huge far quicker than any other assets you'll use in Dreamweaver, so watch those file sizes.

1. Create a new folder in the `assets` folder, call it `video`, and drop the `cameraopener.mov` file in there.

2. Open a new file using the single column template, and drop a table with 2 columns and 1 row into the editable region.

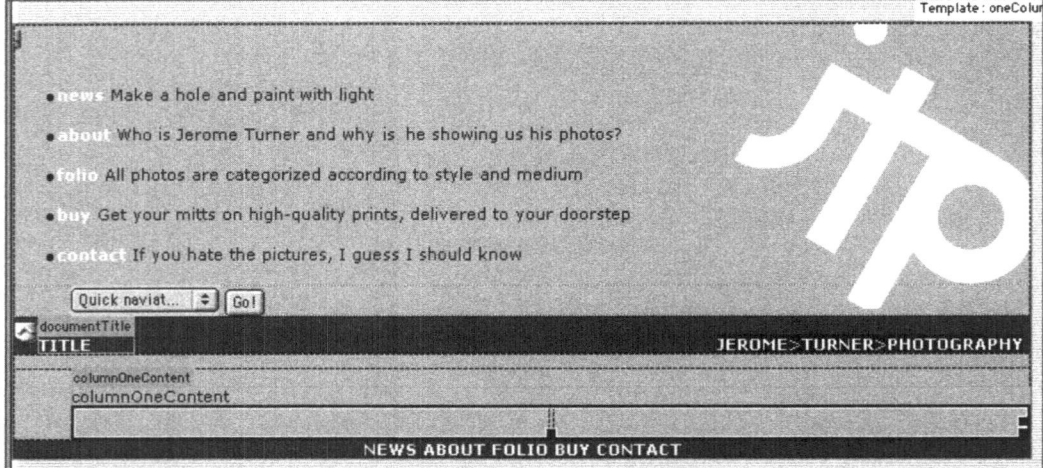

Creating content for our site

3. Go to the Movies category in the Files panel and drag it into the first cell. Again, you may well have to refresh the list of video files in the panel to get the video file to appear.

> *Once you start using a lot of video files in a site, you'll find the Play/Stop button in the top right-hand corner of this panel is very useful.*

4. My page looks like the one shown – as may have happened to your SWF earlier, our QuickTime file is 32 by 32 pixels.

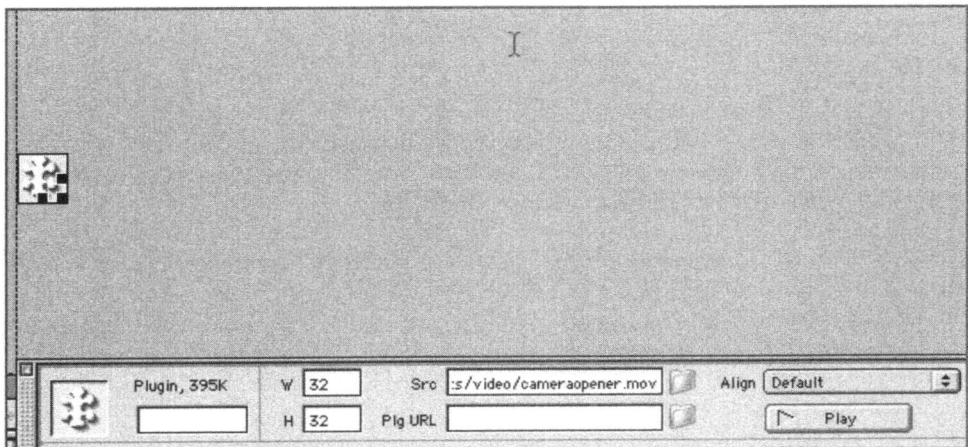

If you've forgotten the dimensions we saw earlier, hit the Play button on the Properties panel to see the video. Now, enter new W and H values until you match the size of the window to the file. If your video file suddenly disappears during this process, simply press Stop on the Properties panel, and then Play again.

5. You'll now have a video file, complete with the video controls that are displayed by default by a QuickTime file along the bottom. That really is all there is to it.

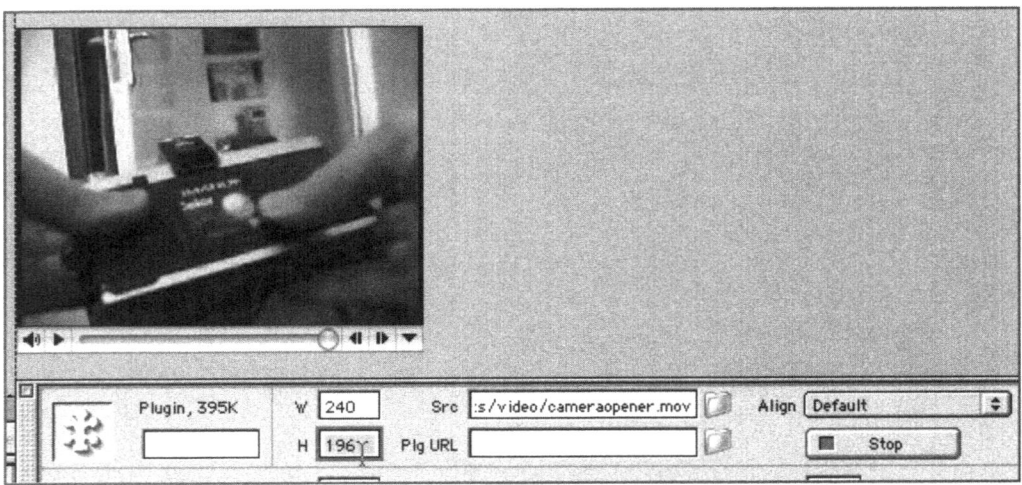

If you are using a set of dimensions from the export process, remember that you need to add 16 pixels to the height value to allow for the VCR type controls that appear by default at the bottom of a QuickTime file.

Summary

After the heavy work creating templates and style sheets in the last few chapters, we've been able to cash in on all our hard work and get started on the visual side of the site. Adding new pages to our site in this chapter has been an absolute cinch with our templates and style sheet – without them, this would probably have been about four different chapters!

We've seen how to add images and text, but we've also explored how the creative and appropriate use of Flash and QuickTime content can really take a Dreamweaver page to a new level. In the next chapter, we'll be taking a look at that code window and the stuff that's been hidden in the background so far in order to add the finishing touches to our site.

Creating content for our site 6

The Code Window

What we'll cover in this chapter

- *Setting Code view preferences*
- *Use the tag editor*
- *Inserting JavaScript*
- *Creating and use Snippets*

One thing that almost universally scares people when they start to work with the web is **code**. Whether it's the barrage of acronyms you have to contend with – ASP, PHP, XML, HTML, JSP, CSS, and so on – or the fact that using code seems so alien to *graphic* design. However, without learning how to manipulate code directly, your web designs will often fail to be cutting edge, and will rarely be as optimized and streamlined as they could be. Code also enables you to do a whole bunch of cool things that are difficult – or even impossible – when using visual editing tools. In the long run, many of these can also save you time and effort, thus making a bit of initial pain very much worth your while.

Directly writing or editing web page code can also offer you a great deal of precision, something visual tools can often lack, as we saw in the chapter on Style Sheets.

This doesn't mean you have to uninstall all your favorite applications just yet though. The Dreamweaver MX update brought with it a number of extremely useful enhancements with regards to working with code and, of course, you can rapidly toggle your view via the toolbar at the top of each document window:

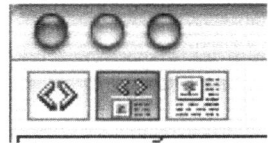

The left-hand icon in your Dreamweaver toolbar enables the Code view; the right-hand icon, Design view; and the middle icon, Code and Design view, which is often referred to as 'split pane' view. While it's usually best to get in the habit of working in the latter view, it's useful to flick to Design view when working purely on strictly visual elements. Likewise, when working solely in Code, it's often useful to work in Code view, as this presents you with a larger window, thus enabling you to see more code at any one time. This is what we'll mostly be doing in this chapter.

Code preferences

As you might expect, Dreamweaver has a number of preferences relating to the Code view. It's worth taking the time to familiarize yourself with these options, as although they may often seem decorative or even intrusive, most make your job a whole lot easier.

Code coloring

You can access this window via Edit > Preferences..., under Code Coloring. By default, Dreamweaver MX assigns certain colors to specific tag types, CSS values and so on. This enables you to quickly pick things out from a soup of code, such as links and image tags.

To modify the colors used for a particular language (e.g. HTML), just click on HTML in the Document Type pane and then click Edit Coloring Scheme.

The Code Window

You can edit the settings via the Text Color drop-down menu on the right-hand side of the dialog box, along with making specific tags bold, italic and underlined if that takes your fancy although, you tend to avoid making things bold, italic and so on, as this usually ends up being confusing.

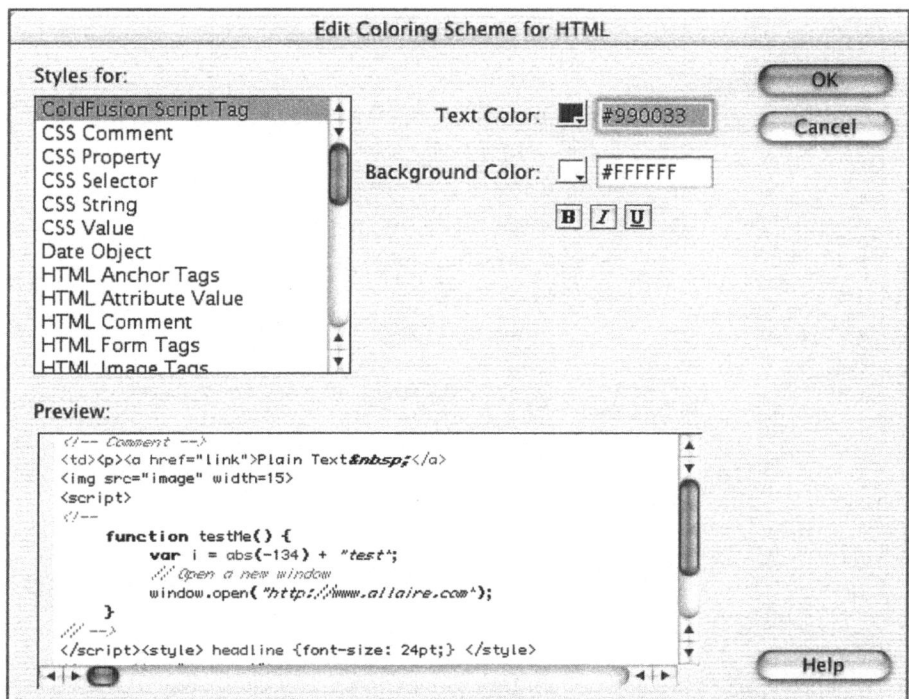

While you'll probably never need to edit these colors, anyone used to working with code in another application might want to change the colors to suit whatever they're used to.

Formatting

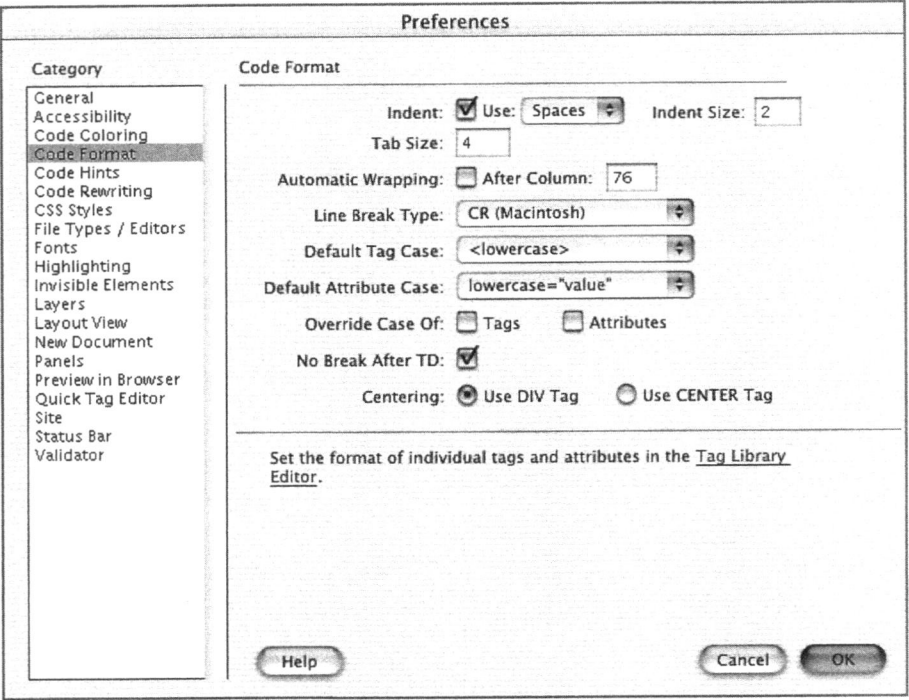

The Code Format preferences are perhaps a little more important. While several of these can be ignored, or changed to your own personal preference, *always* turn off Automatic Wrapping. There is simply no need for this, because although it may in some cases make your code look a little nicer when viewing the source in a Web browser that doesn't support line wrapping, it can cause errors in your site. This is because some browsers parse the white space created by Automatic Wrapping, causing odd gaps to appear in your pages. Admittedly this is rare, but when it does happen it's infuriating and getting the Automatic Wrapping spaces out of your pages (by deleting it) is a long-winded and tedious task.

> *Line wrapping means that lines of code fit within the current window. Some browsers, such as Internet Explorer for Windows, use source code editors (in this case, Notepad) that don't initially display line wrapping. The upshot is that you have to scroll horizontally while perusing code. However, seeing as this won't affect you as a designer then you shouldn't worry about it. After all, you'll always be using Dreamweaver MX for viewing your source code, not a browser.*

Dreamweaver's default settings for tags and attributes are both lower case and you should leave this alone, even if it's often easier to make out tags in UPPER CASE. The reason is that XHTML calls for lower case for all tags and attributes – apparently, upper case is now old hat. Don't worry too much if you miss a few of these. Once we've finished working through this chapter, we'll use Dreamweaver's Update function to ensure all pages comply with the selected DTD (Document Type Definition) in our templates.

Other settings include the ability to indent code – a good idea if you want to be able to edit anything with ease – change the Line Break type, and enforce No Break After TD. Messing about with line breaks probably won't make a lot of difference to your sites unless you're sending them to someone who's working on a different platform to you. It's usually best to ensure this fits your system, be it Macintosh, Windows, or Unix. No Break After TD should generally be left on. It ensures that whatever content goes inside table cells won't be indented, and therefore no odd little spaces will appear in your layout. Again, some browsers will present a gap if you have code like this:

```
<td> <img src="an_image.jpg" height="100" width="100" alt="Image" /></td>
```

...and some won't. It's never a good idea to leave these things to chance.

The final option concerns centering, and seeing as the `<center>` tag is now deprecated, you should set Dreamweaver to use the DIV tag (although, as we've shown, centering is better controlled via your CSS for specific element placing).

Code hints

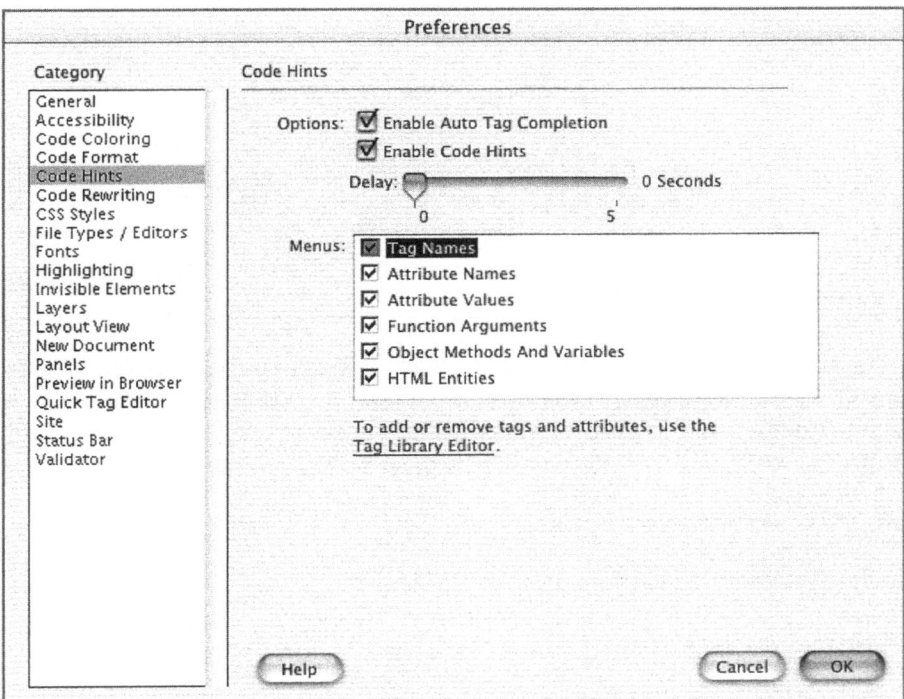

Code Hints lets you quickly insert tag names, attributes, and values as you enter code.

Foundation Dreamweaver MX

These are new in Dreamweaver MX, and we'll be covering them later on in the chapter. In the meantime, unless you have a photographic memory or a fetish for typing HTML attributes, it's best to leave them on. The same goes for Auto Tag Completion. Setting the Delay to 0 is also a good idea, as you'll be able to write code rapidly by mostly using the arrow keys and ENTER on your keyboard. Again, we'll show you how to do this later in the chapter.

Code rewriting

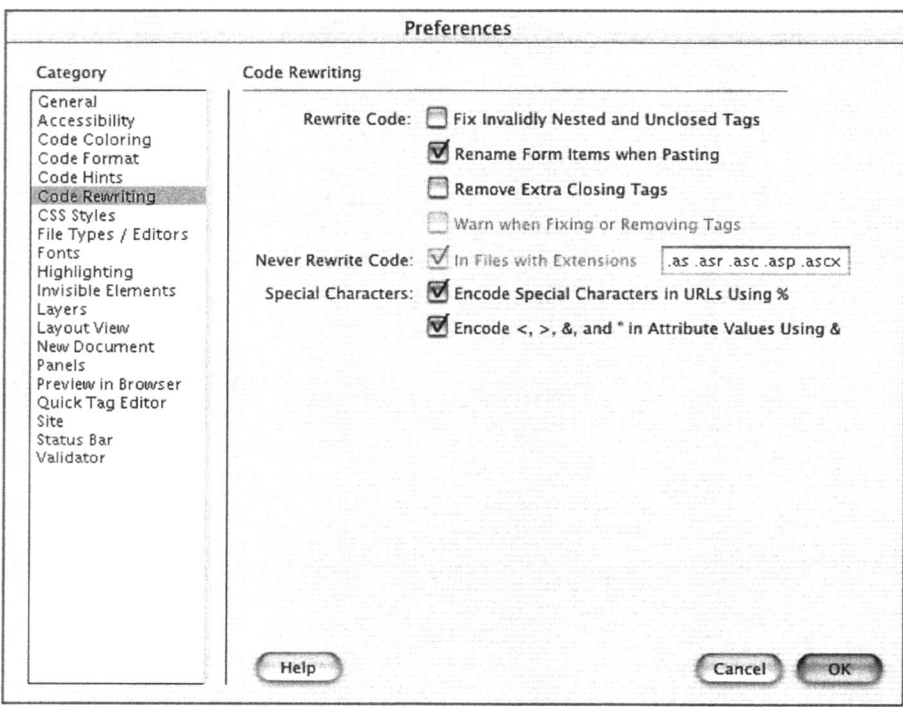

This determines what Dreamweaver does when opening documents. After you've worked with code for a while, you'll be the best judge of which of these options to enable and disable. Dreamweaver MX sometimes gets confused with regards to nested tags, so the first option is usually best left disabled. However, if you're using Code Hints and continually getting extra closing tags, such as:

```
<p>I am a paragraph.</p></p>
```

... then you should check the Remove Extra Closing Tags box.

Internal preferences

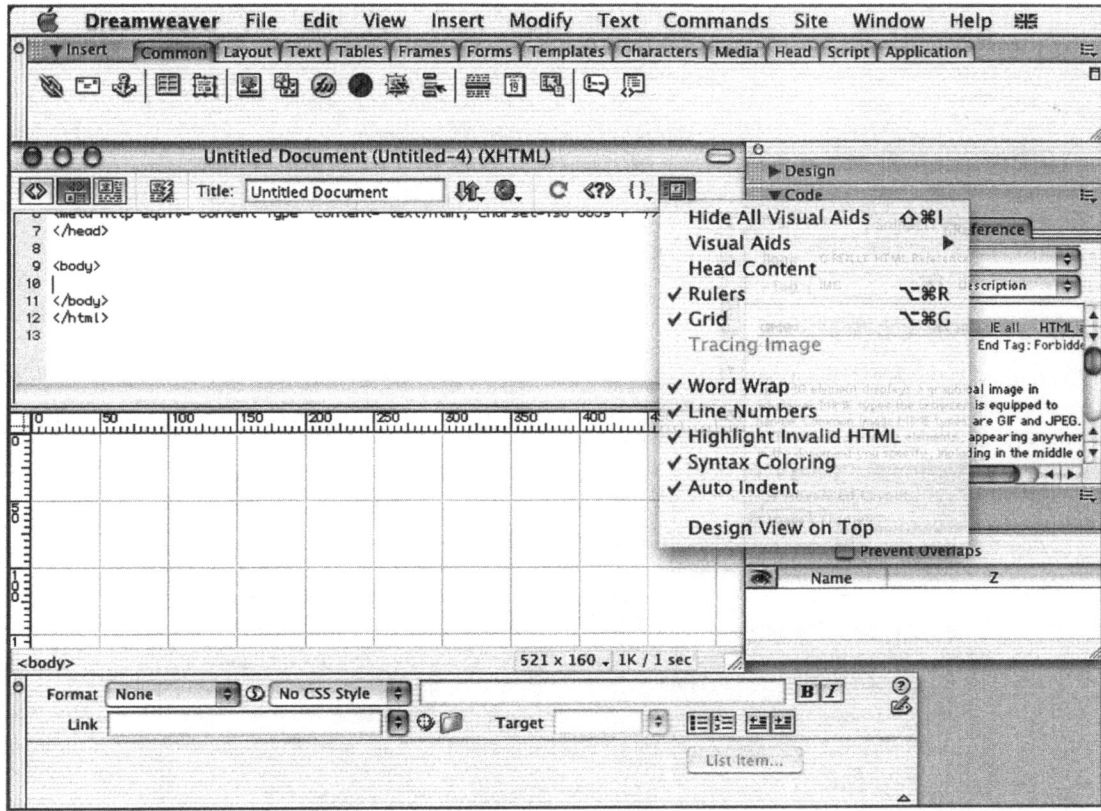

Each window also has a View Options drop-down menu that provides you with access to the options seen in the above screen grab. To make your life easier, just turn everything on. Word Wrap means you won't have to scroll the Code view horizontally, as it will 'soft wrap' to your window width. Line Numbers are helpful with debugging, as is highlighting invalid HTML. Syntax Coloring should only be disabled if you enjoy looking at a sea of black characters and auto indent means you get something like:

```
<table width="700" border="0" cellspacing="0" cellpadding="0"
summary="Layout table">
   <tr>
     <td><span class="floatRight"><img src="assets/shared/jtplogo.gif"
alt="Logo" width="210" height="200" /></span>
       <ul style="list-style:  url(assets/assets/shared/nav_bullets.gif)
outside; margin-top: 25px;">
```

Foundation Dreamweaver MX

... rather than:

```
<table width="700" border="0" cellspacing="0" cellpadding="0"
summary="Layout table">
<tr>
<td><span class="floatRight"><img src="assets/shared/jtplogo.gif"
alt="Logo" width="210" height="200" /></span>
<ul style="list-style:  url(assets/assets/shared/nav_bullets.gif)
outside; margin-top: 25px;">
```

... which makes it much easier to spot nested items and generally find stuff within your code.

Working with code

The first thing to point out when working with code is this: don't panic. Always take regular back-ups of your pages and store them in a safe place, which is *outside* of your web site folder. At the very least, this should be done daily. If you're working on a particularly complex piece of code and slightly unsure what you're doing, save 'milestones' when you get specific things working. Then if you do make an error that causes problems, just revert to the previous version.

> *The reason you should store back-ups elsewhere is otherwise Template changes will affect the backed up pages along with the ones you're working on. But remember, if you're trying to test code that you've saved elsewhere and it has direct links to other things in the site, those links may not work because you've changed the location of the file. All relative links will need to be tested from your web site folder.*

One major element of the Dreamweaver package – and something that is often overlooked – is that Macromedia thoughtfully provided a slew of reference materials within the application for the budding designer.

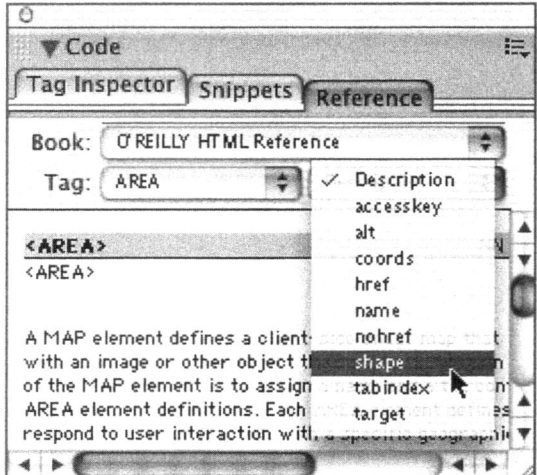

SHIFT + F1 will focus the Reference panel, and then all of the above guides will be available via the drop-down menu. Along with being a great way to check up on specifics within HTML, CSS, JavaScript and more, this panel is also a good way to learn. For instance, the HTML reference includes a brief description of each tag, lists all the attributes, and points out anything that is now deprecated (removed from the official HTML specification, as drawn up by W3C).

Adding tags

Although raw coding usually gives you a greater degree of control – at least if you know what you're doing – it can be rather dull and time-consuming. Dreamweaver MX does away with the bulk of the tedium by its Code Hints innovation. This simple concept is basically a context-sensitive drop-down menu that appears under any given tag that you're adding. By using the arrow keys, you can usually key in tags and attributes remarkably quickly, and it can even point out things you may have forgotten, as we'll see below.

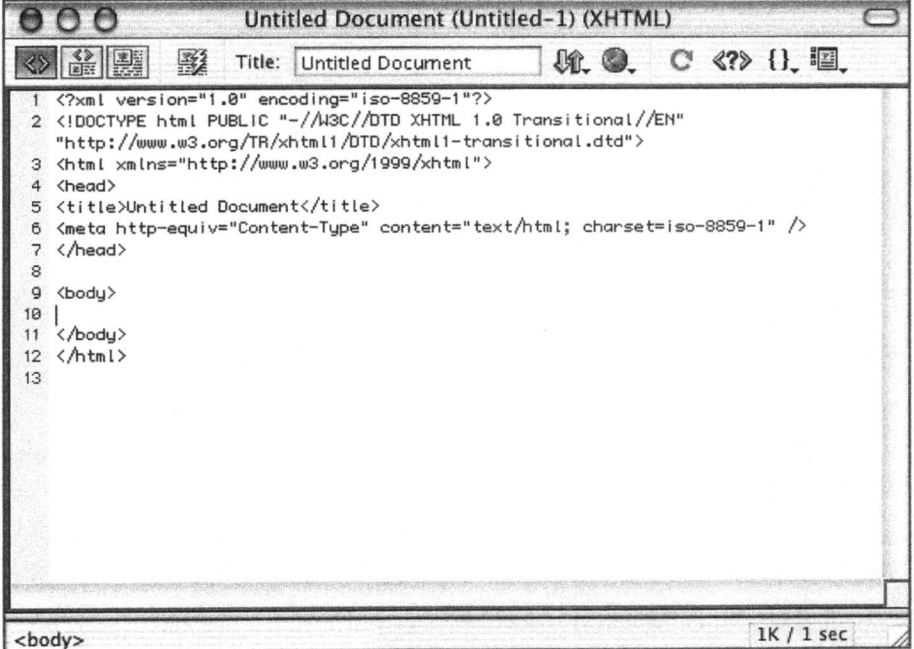

Here's a new XHTML document. This isn't attached to any site, and doesn't use any templates as yet. It's just the most basic XHTML document you can get, as set up by default in Dreamweaver MX.

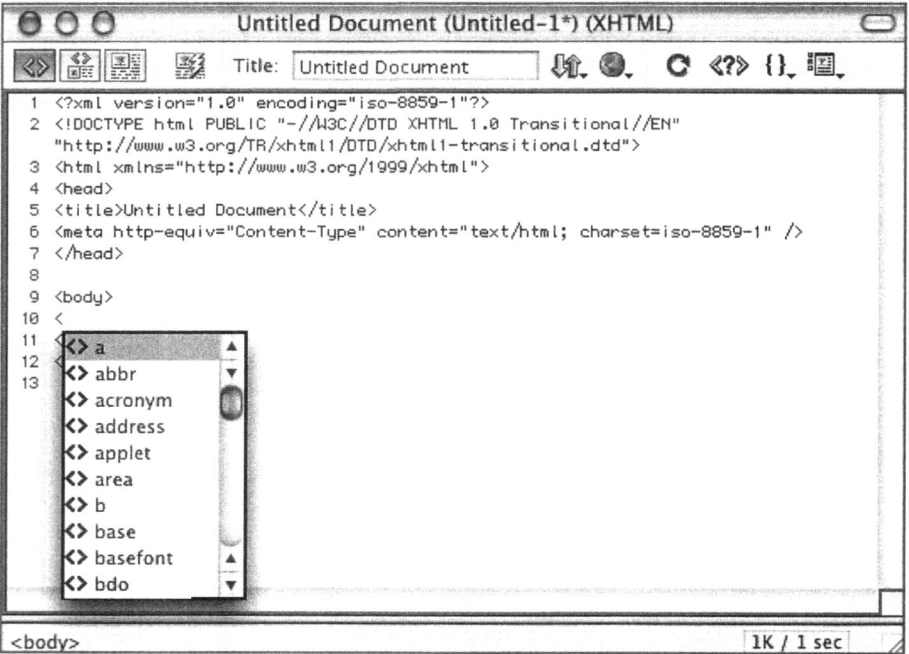

As you have already seen, HTML tags are enclosed within 'less than' and 'greater than' symbols. An opening tag looks like this: `<tag>` and a closing tag has a forward slash added, like this: `</tag>`. Even when just typing the former in, so as to open a tag, the Code Hints drop-down menu appears, providing you with a list of all available tags. At this point, it's not worth your while scrolling through the entire list to select your tag, so type another letter.

> *Elements without any de-facto content still need to be closed within XHTML. Whereas in HTML, you could do this:* `<p><img src="myImage.jpg"></p>`, *in XHTML you need to do this:* `<p><img src="myImage.jpg" /></p>`. *Note the trailing slash on the image tag. The same is true for meta tags, line breaks (*`<br />`*) and several other tags. If in doubt, check out the guides within the Reference panel. Also note that when closing tags without content, it's best to leave a space before the slash, otherwise older browsers, such as Netscape Navigator 4, choke and don't display the tag accurately or at all.*

Here, we've typed 'p', which scrolls the list down to <>p indicating a paragraph tag. At this point, you could move up or down the list, select a different option, and hit enter to activate it. Once you've gotten the hang of where tags appear in the list, it can actually be quicker to start with the wrong letter. For instance, to get to the <option> tag, you'd have to type 'o', which would highlight the first tag starting with that character (<object>). After that, you'd need to hit the down arrow three times, whereas if you started with 'p', you'd only have to use the 'up' arrow once, in order to get to <option>. Whether it's borne out of laziness or efficiency, it's a handy tip.

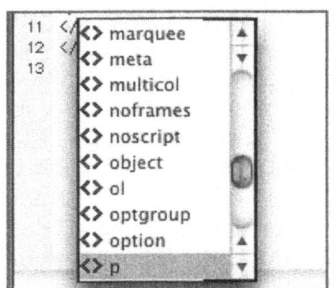

> *Of course, as this is a context-sensitive menu, it gradually works out what tag you're typing, so for <option> you could easily type 'op' to get to the tag. Sometimes it's quicker to do this, whereas other times, using the arrow keys will be more efficient. Try the various different ways of working and see which works best for you.*

Next, just type a space after your tag, and the drop-down menu changes to highlight a whole bunch of attributes that are associated with the tag. Again, using the arrow keys, you can select one of these, or begin typing to 'snap' the selection to a particular word.

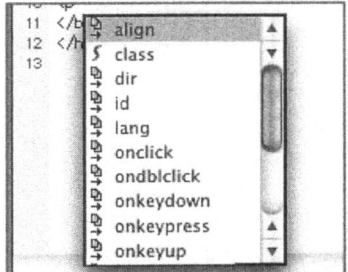

Here, we've chosen 'class' in order to utilize styling from our CSS file. However, this is a totally new page, and we've not yet attached the Style Sheet. As you can see, Dreamweaver MX not only helpfully reminds us of this, but also provides options to Refresh, Edit, or Attach Style Sheet from the drop-down menu. (Note that attaching the CSS file at this point will create a full link to the file on your hard drive, so you should save the XHTML document prior to attaching it. However, Dreamweaver MX will automatically update the link should you save it at a later point.)

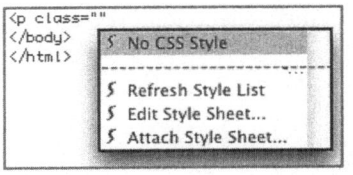

The CSS has now been attached, but going back to the tag won't always bring up the drop-down menu again. Sometimes you'll have to delete and re-enter the attribute. Upon doing this, the various classes we defined in previous chapters are highlighted.

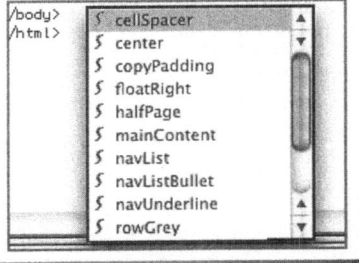

199

Hitting ENTER adds the class and closes the attribute with a second quote mark. If you add another space, you are given the opportunity to add more attributes to the tag. If you add a > symbol in order to close the first part of the tag, Dreamweaver MX automatically closes the tag by adding `</p>`. You then add your content in-between. Note that this can sometimes be a bit awkward when trying to add code around information already in your HTML document, such as table cells. For instance, when you have the following:

```
 9
10  <body>
11  <p class="copyPadding">|</p>
12  </body>
13  </html>
14
```

```
10  <body>
11  <p class="copyPadding">Some Web site copy.</p>
12
13  I want to be in a table cell.
14
15  So do I.
16
17  </body>
18  </html>
19
```

... when you add the table itself, and the associated attributes, the tag is closed prior to the content:

```
10  <body>
11  <p class="copyPadding">Some Web site copy.</p>
12
13  <table border="0" cellpadding="0" cellspacing="0" summary="A table for content">
    </table>I want to be in a table cell.
14
15  So do I.
16
```

Rather than constantly deleting and entering tags, it's usually simpler to set up the entire table, and then select and drag content into it once you're done:

Set up the table

```
10  <body>
11  <p class="copyPadding">Some Web site copy.</p>
12
13  <table border="0" cellpadding="0" cellspacing="0" summary="A table for content">
    <tr><td></td><td></td></tr></table>I want to be in a table cell.
14
15  So do I.
16
17  </body>
18  </html>
```

Select your content and drag it to its final location

```
12
13  <table border="0" cellpadding="0" cellspacing="0" summary="A table for content">
    <tr><td>k/td><td></td></tr></table>I want to be in a table cell.
14
15  So do I.
16
17  </body>
18  </html>
```

Admire your handiwork!

```
11  <p class="copyPadding">Some Web site copy.</p>
12
13  <table border="0" cellpadding="0" cellspacing="0" summary="A table for content">
    <tr><td>I want to be in a table cell.</td><td>So do I.</td></tr></table>
14
15
16
17  </body>
18  </html>
```

Also, remember that if all this viewing code is becoming a bit eye-boggling, you can always switch to Design view to check out an approximation of how things are looking (although it's always more accurate to test your pages in a range of Web browsers rather than relying on the built-in preview).

> *While in these early stages of your coding career you might want to use Code and Design View as your default view, that way you have the best of both worlds.*

Because Dreamweaver automatically closes tags and then assumes you're going to add content, be careful not to end up with something like this, which has incorrectly nested two table cells within each other rather than placing them next to each other:

```
<table><tr><td><td></td></td></tr></table>
```

Although this may not look like a huge mistake, something along these lines can throw an entire web page layout.

The tag editor

Of course, if you're relatively new to HTML, there's going to be a lot of trial and error when playing around with various tag attributes. Therefore, it's perhaps a good idea initially to check out Dreamweaver's Tag Editor. Simply select one of your tags in Code view and go to Modify > Edit Tag.

In this dialog box, almost every aspect of every tag can be edited, and attributes are logically grouped, in order to make it clear to the user whether, for instance, they are specific to browsers, tie into the CSS, and so on. Generally, browser-specific stuff should be ignored unless authoring for an audience that is known from day one (such as a corporate Intranet, where all the users have the same browser).

Two further areas of information are available via the arrow switches: Tag Info displays information about the tag you're editing, as found in the Reference panel; Events enables you to add JavaScript events (although you have to type in the contents yourself).

Once you click OK you're returned to the Code view, with all your changes in place.

JavaScript

Working in the Code view means that you have more control over client-side scripting, such as the addition of JavaScript. While as with any computer language, JavaScript can potentially be very complicated, there are also simple uses for it that can greatly benefit your site. Once again, Dreamweaver MX enables you to rapidly add scripts, without the need for scripting experience, via a combination of panels and menu items.

There are various methods of achieving this. Designers more used to working visually might want to start with the Behaviors Panel via Window > Behaviors (SHIFT + F3).

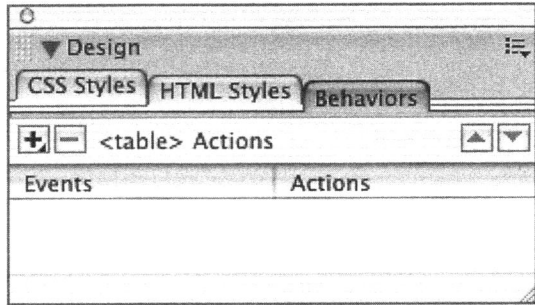

Adding a behavior is a simple process: click inside a tag in the Code view and then use the drop-down menu under the [+] sign in order to add JavaScript events, such as the ever-popular 'text in the status bar', pop-up windows and so on.

> You must always remember that JavaScript is case sensitive.

If you venture into writing your own JavaScript, you should pay particular attention to syntax, as forgetting a ";" can allow the code to work in IE, but not in Netscape. At this point in your Dreamweaver career, unless you're already familiar with JavaScript, you'd be best off using the Behaviors, then work up to writing your own code once you begin to understand it more.

Using a simple Javascript behavior

For instance, to add text that appears in the browser's status area when you mouseover a link, follow these steps:

1. Click inside the tag you want to add the behavior to, then use the drop-down menu to go to Set Text > Set Text of Status Bar.

The Code Window

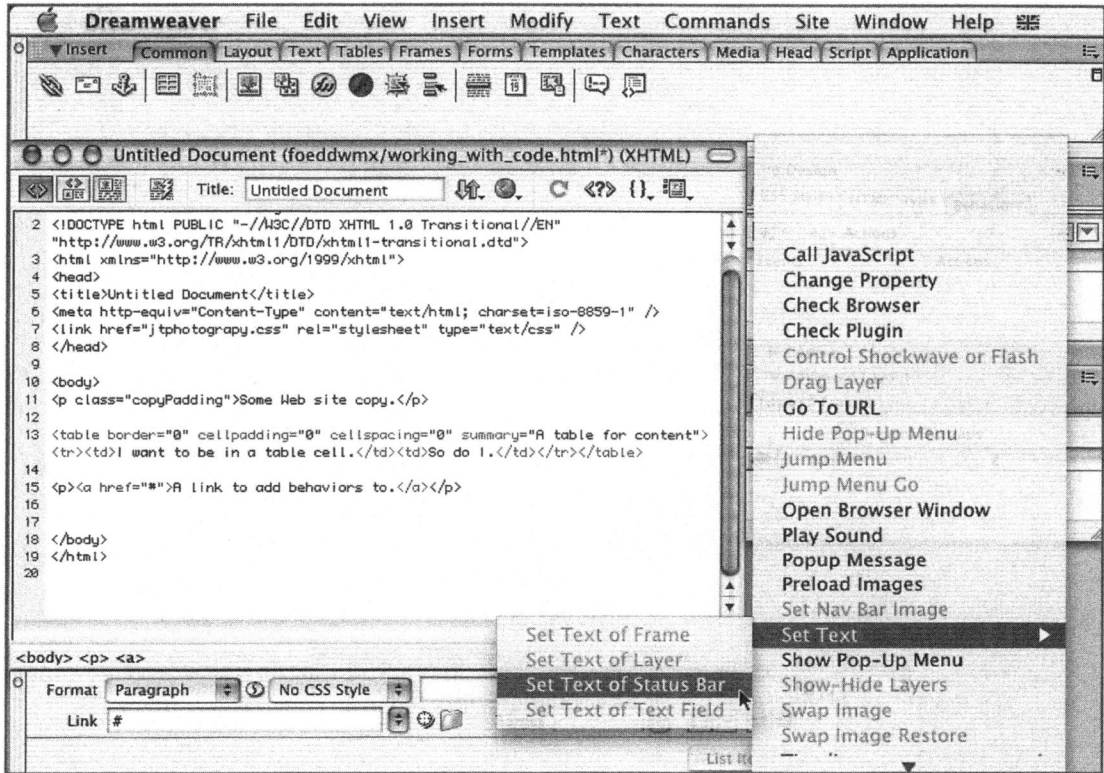

2. In the dialog box that appears, add the text. Don't write too much, otherwise people using small screen resolutions won't be able to read everything.

3. The <head> area of your document will now have some JavaScript that Dreamweaver has automatically created.

```
 8  <script language="JavaScript" type="text/JavaScript">
 9  <!--
10  function MM_displayStatusMsg(msgStr) {
11    status=msgStr;
12    document.MM_returnValue = true;
13  }
14  //-->
15  </script>
16  </head>
```

7 Foundation Dreamweaver MX

```
18  <body>
19  <p class="copyPadding">Some Web site copy.</p>
20
21  <table border="0" cellpadding="0" cellspacing="0" summary="A table for content">
    <tr><td>I want to be in a table cell.</td><td>So do I.</td></tr></table>
22
23  <p><a href="#" onmouseover="MM_displayStatusMsg('Text for status bar!');return
    document.MM_returnValue">A link to add behaviors to.</a></p>
24
25
26  </body>
```

Your tag will now contain an 'onmouseover' script that references the JavaScript in the <head> of the document, along with containing your code. To edit the status bar text, it's usually quickest to just do this within the Code view rather than messing about with the Behavior panel again, although if you double-click on the behavior in the Behavior panel, you can access your text that way, too.

> *JavaScript functions are best kept in the <head> section of the page, however, JavaScript can be used throughout the page by enclosing it within <% %> tags.*

However, beware that some characters are illegal in JavaScript and if you use them, your text may not show up. Amongst the most common illegal characters are the following:

#
%
&
=
'
?
:
;
'
"
[ ]
{ }

These characters need to be 'escaped' by use of a backslash. For instance, here's what happens when we try and add a phrase with quotes and apostrophes:

4. Adding some text.

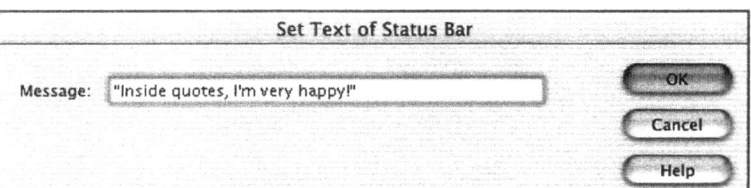

5. Viewing the code

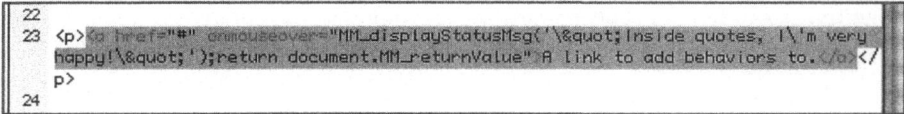

Dreamweaver has automatically added backslashes (\) prior to the characters. This 'escapes' the meaning of those characters, which in layman's terms simply means a Web browser will display the character de-facto rather than trying to work out what it means in JavaScript (and thus terminating the tag when it comes across the apostrophe).

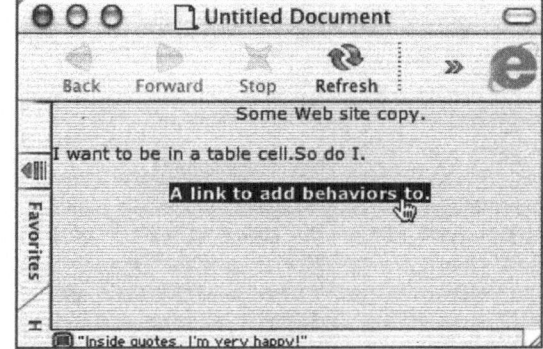

While this can be useful, it's still not perfect. For instance, the status bar text sits there permanently until you mouseover something else that changes it. What we want to do is return the status area to blank space once the mouse moves off the link. To do this, we'll need to add the behaviour again and then modify it. Read on...

6. Add your text in the same way as before, but this time leave the Set Text of Status Bar dialog blank.

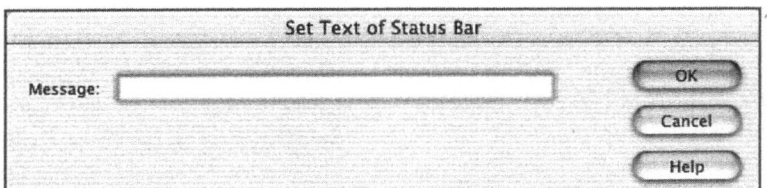

Now we need to change the **event** which triggers the behavior.

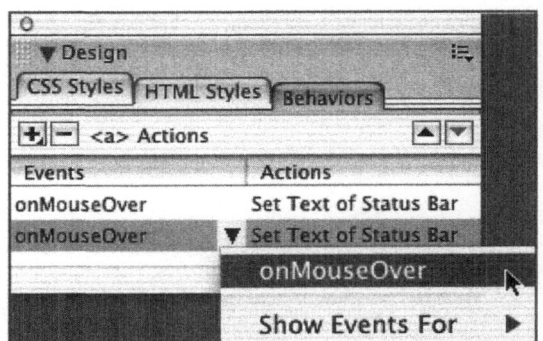

7. We'll use the drop-down menu as shown to change the behavior. Oddly, Dreamweaver MX defaults to events for *very* old browsers, which only gives you access to onMouseOver. To change this, go to Show Events For and select something a little more modern.

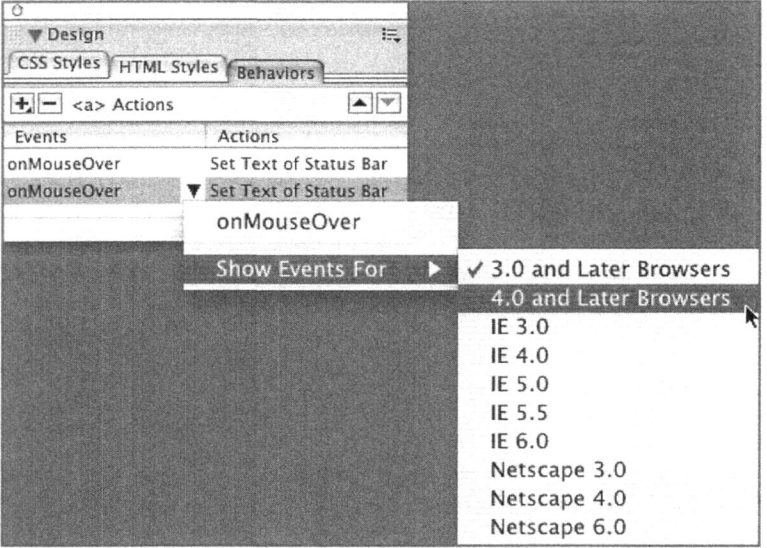

8. You'll then be able to select onMouseOut for the blank status bar text. You can probably guess what onMouseOut means; it just means that in the same way as our first behavior sets the status bar text when we move our mouse over the link, this behavior clears the text (or rather, sets it to nothing) when we move the mouse off the link.

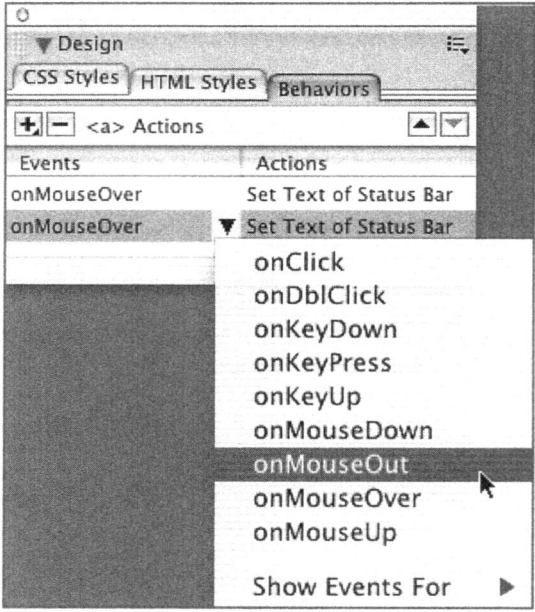

9. Finally, test the page in a browser (F12) to ensure everything's gone to plan!

The Code Window

> *With more advanced features in your page, such as behaviors, it's even more important to test it in as many browsers as you can. This is why Dreamweaver allows you to set a Primary browser and Secondary browser in the Preferences. So Dreamweaver makes it easy for you to test in Internet Explorer and also Netscape in a snap!*

You can add as many behaviors to each link as you like, but try to avoid doing too much, otherwise you might end up confusing your site's visitors. In Dreamweaver MX, deleting a behaviour is even easier than creating one; simply select it in the Behavior panel and click the [-] icon.

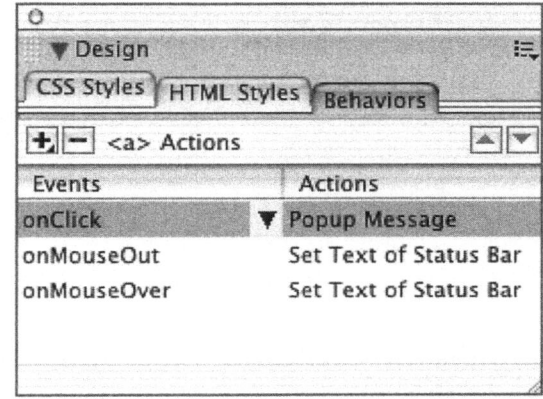

Raw coding

Of course, you can always add your own code instead of using the built-in behaviors. In some cases, this may actually be beneficial. While the bulk of Macromedia's code is extremely streamlined, some, such as the status bar text JavaScript could possibly be better.

This is what Dreamweaver produces from the built-in behavior (along with some additional scripting in the `<head>` of the document).

```
<a href="a_page.html" onmouseover="MM_displayStatusMsg('Explanation of
link');return document.MM_returnValue" onmouseout="MM_displayStatusMsg('');
return document.MM_returnValue">This is a link</a>
```

If you had hand-coded this, you would end up with the following:

```
<a href="ADDRESS TO LINK TO" onmouseover="window.status=('STATUS BAR
TEXT');return true" onmouseout="window.status='';">LINK TEXT</a>
```

This is a third shorter than when using the built-in behaviors, although this won't always be the case. For instance, Macromedia's built-in JavaScript for image rollovers is excellent, and although complex, is extremely streamlined. As always, try various methods and work out which suits you, and balance that with trying to make the smallest pages possible, in order to reduce download times.

Now you're maybe wondering why you would bother with typing all that out when you can use a simple behavior. Well, who says you have to keep typing it out? Say you're using six of these links with status bar text in your page. Once you've added this code you can reuse it, changing the status text in a flash. It might actually end up being quicker than using the behaviour panel.

To save even more time, Dreamweaver has a function called Snippets. Snippets are pieces of code that you use frequently and have saved for future use. All good HTML or code editors use snippets as a time-saver and Dreamweaver MX is no exception. Let's find out more.

Snippets

Bring up the Snippets panel via SHIFT + F9 and you'll see there are already a number built-in. You could spend an hour looking at all the neat functions and features you can paste into your code, but finish the chapter first before you go off to play!

Here's how to make two Snippets that are based on the JavaScript example that we worked on in the 'Raw coding' section:

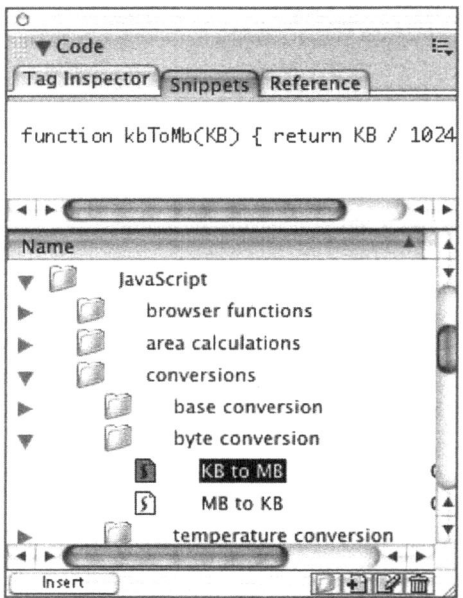

Creating and using Snippets

1. From the drop-down menu on the right of the Snippets panel, select New Snippet.

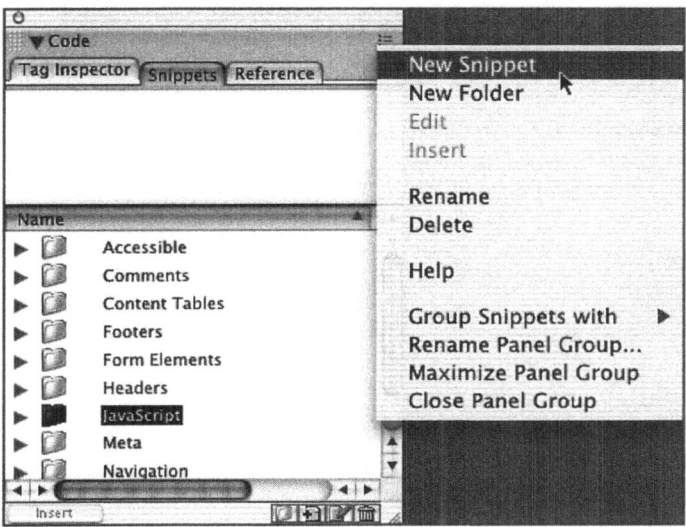

2. Now let's edit the Snippet.

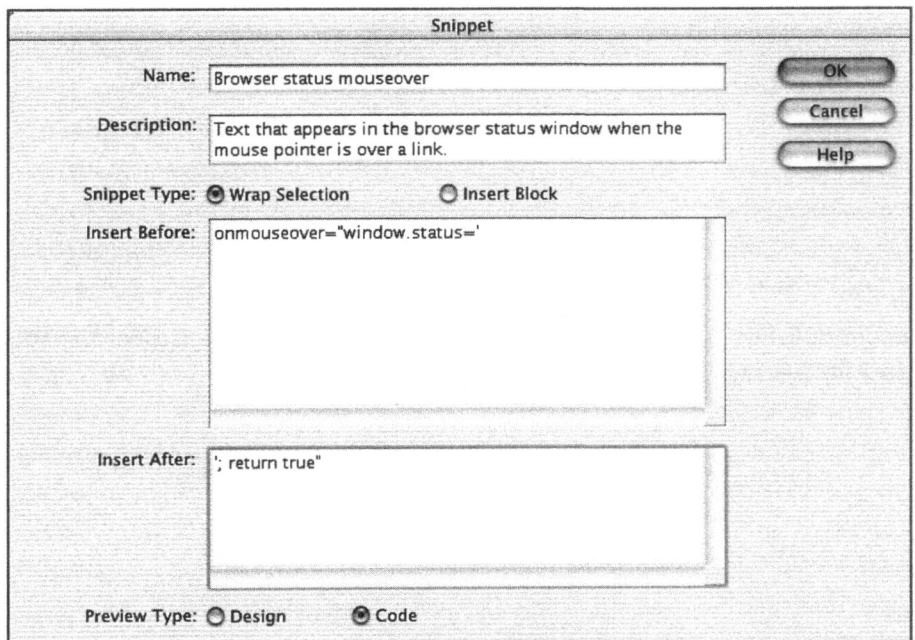

The first two fields are pretty self-explanatory; give your Snippet whatever Name and Description you want. The Snippet Type enables you to Wrap [it around a] Selection, such as an HTML tag, or Insert Block, which adds your Snippet as a block element (such as a paragraph tag).

Insert Before and Insert After simply say which parts of the script should be inserted before and after your selection. We're making something that will wrap around 'browser status area' text, so Insert Before contains everything up to and including the first window.status quote and Insert After contains the second quote and what follows.

3. Now that you've defined the Snippet, let's go back to our page to try it out. Delete the link from the previous example or just add another underneath. In the Code view, type the status text that you want to be displayed into your anchor tag (link) and select it.

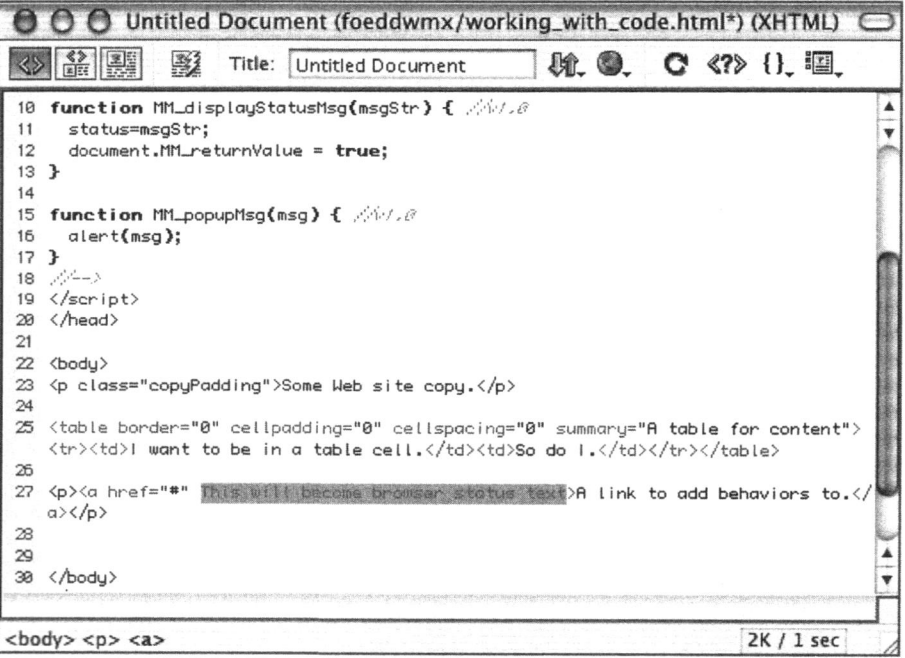

4. Now to add the Snippet. Simply drag the Snippet over your selection and your code will magically wrap around the text you typed earlier!

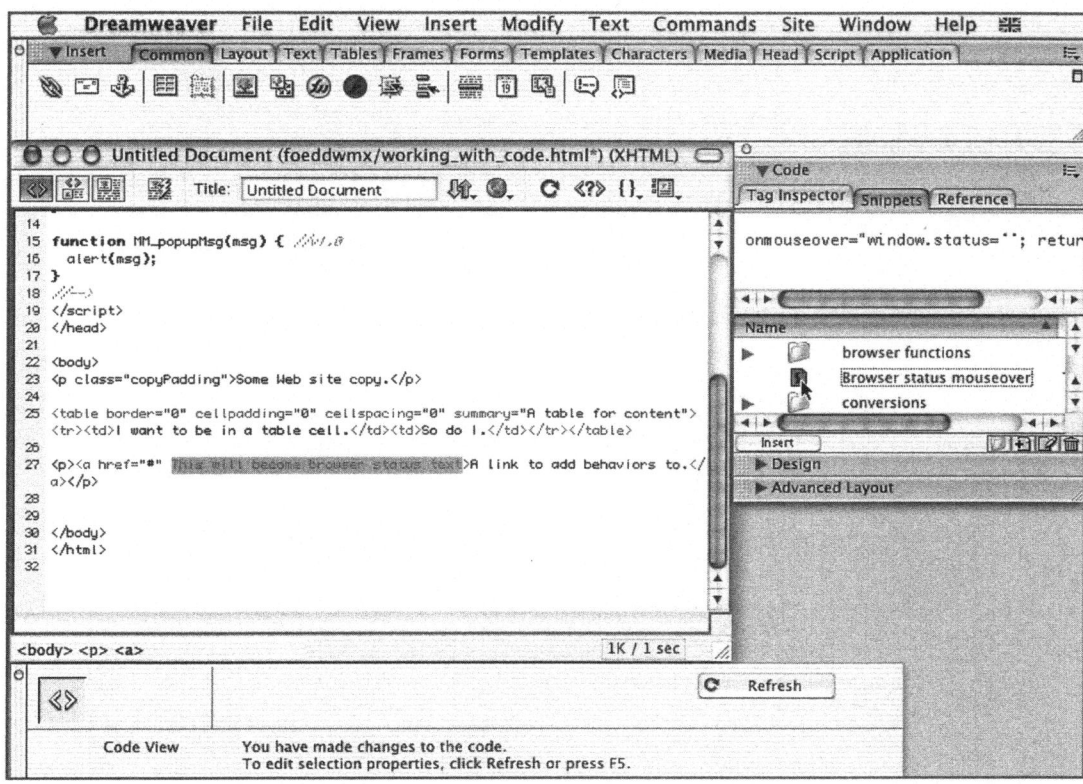

5. But what about the mouseout code? Of course, these first four steps only add the onMouseOver code, so you need to create another Snippet for the onMouseOut JavaScript, as below. This doesn't need to be wrapped around a selection and can be just dragged straight into the anchor tag.

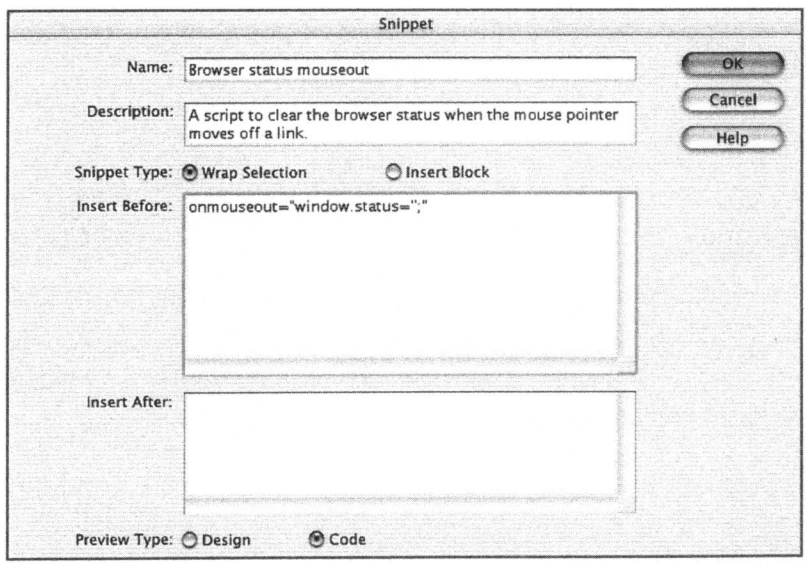

Note that `window.status=` is followed by two single quotes with nothing in-between them and *not* a double quote.

> *Of course, Snippets can contain anything you want, so you can add huge chunks of HTML, JavaScript, and even inline CSS. If you fancy a break after all this coding, take a trip through the Snippets panel's pre-supplied code chunks. You'll find everything there from browser detection, to cookies and ready-made drop-down menus!*

Getting your <head> checked

After you've added a few JavaScript behaviors, you'll soon notice that the `<head>` section of your HTML document contains a whole bunch of code. Here's a version of the page we were looking at earlier in this chapter:

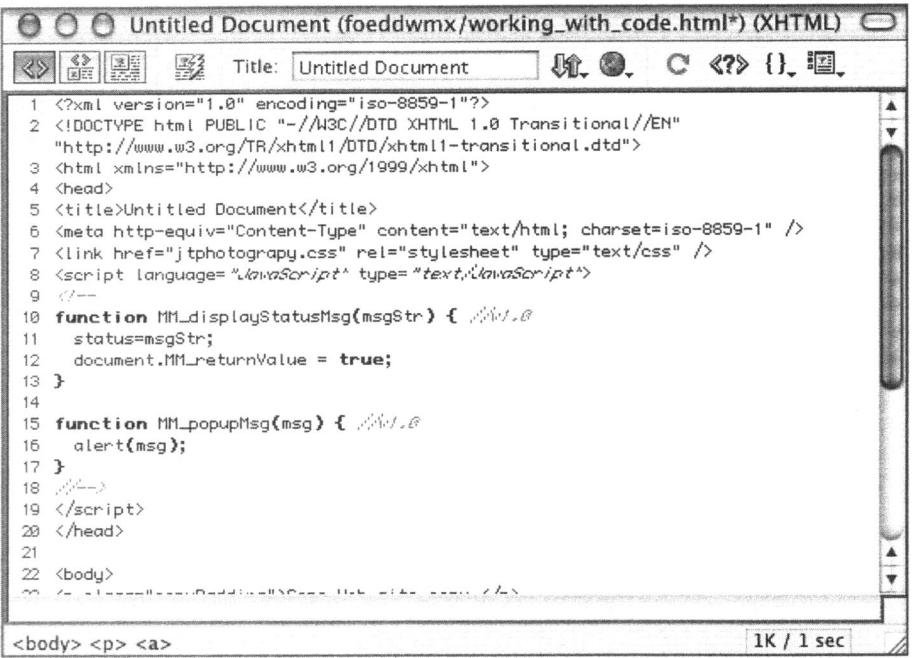

Now, imagine having this code on *every* HTML page where you're using JavaScript events. Not only would this increase download times, but it would fast become a pain to keep everything in check. Updating the scripts at a later date would also be tricky, even with Dreamweaver's Find and Replace functionality. The solution is simple: in the same way that the CSS is separated from the HTML documents by using an external file, you can also do this with JavaScript.

> *Of course, templates mean that you could, in theory, amend JavaScript site-wide in seconds, but it's still better to use external scripts to keep page weights down.*

Here's how to make an external script:

Setting up a JS file

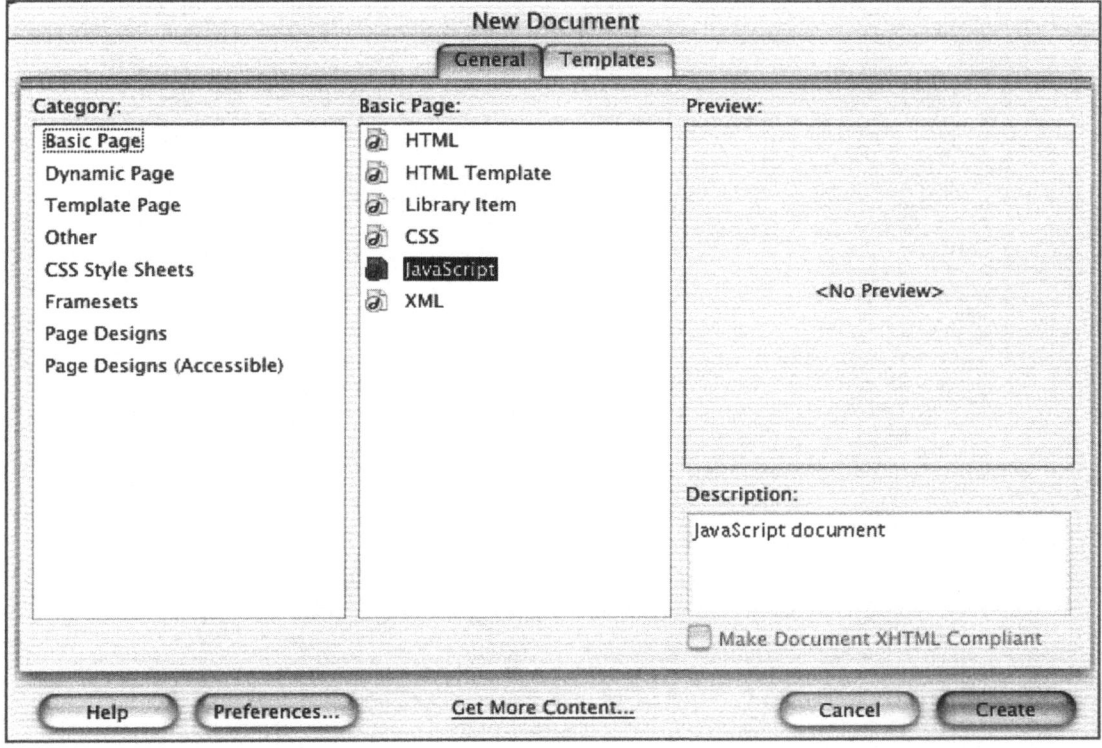

Foundation Dreamweaver MX

1. Create a new JavaScript document, as above (File > New), and save it with whatever name you choose, ensuring it has the extension `.js` (such as `global.js`). (Dreamweaver MX should add this extension for you by default.)

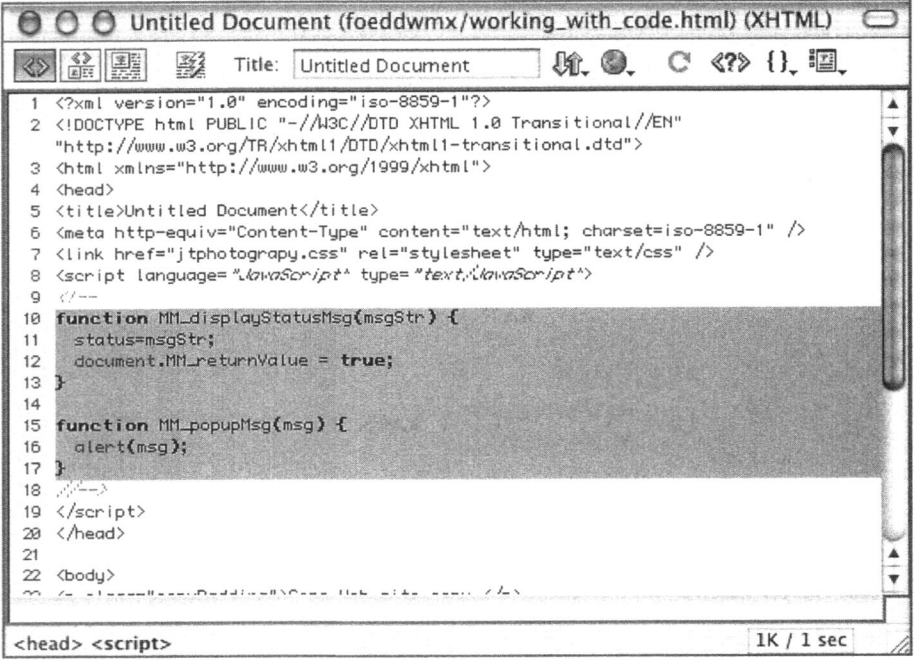

2. Select everything between the `<!-- -->` tags in your HTML document and Cut the section.

> *If you've been wondering what these `<!-- -->` tags do, it's quite simple. These HTML comment tags are generally used for the designer to make notes in. For example, you might include `<!–Browser Status Message -->` above the status code to remind you what it does. This is useful if you're scanning your code looking for a particular section. Dreamweaver sometimes also uses comments to store information, such as Template regions.*
>
> *In this case, we're "commenting out" the JavaScript code so that older browsers which don't support JavaScript will ignore the code. Such browsers will automatically ignore unrecognized tags such as the `<script>` tag. Our comments tag is used to ensure that these browsers do not interpret our JavaScript functions as actual text and print them at the top of our web page! This does happen, although it's increasingly rare as new browser penetration increases.*

3. Paste the scripts into the JavaScript document you saved in Step 1. Save and close the file.

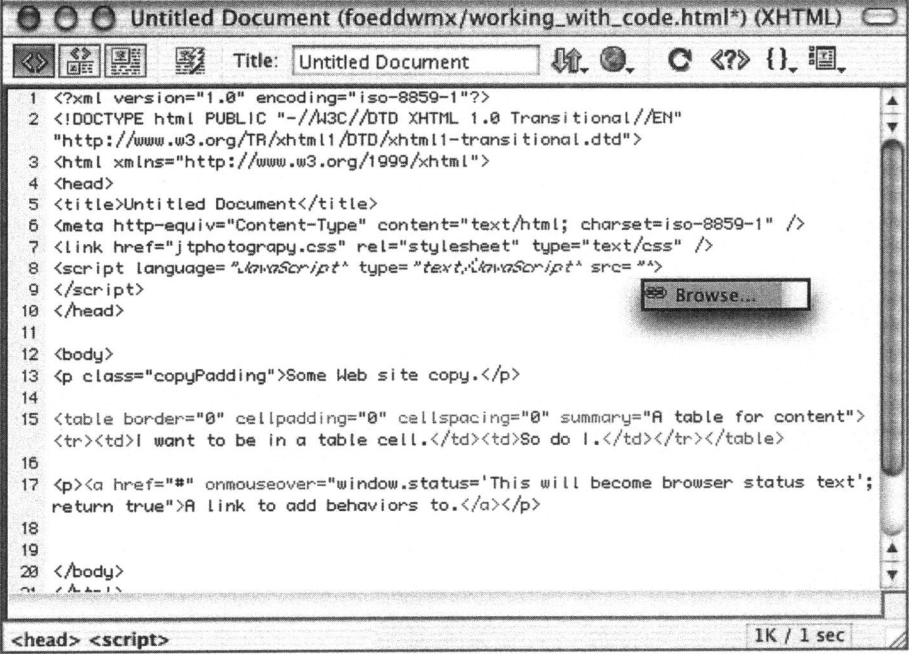

4. In your HTML document, delete everything within the `<script>` tag and add a link to the JavaScript by adding an **src** attribute (see above) and browsing to your JavaScript file.

> Note that when you add new JavaScript behaviors, you can just cut and paste them from the `<head>` of the working HTML document to your external JavaScript file.

Our case study site

You've now got some idea about how best to set up and use the Code view, along with some knowledge of using built-in Dreamweaver functionality to assist you. We're now going to take a look at what we've created so far, in order to see how we can improve the site by using the Code view. We can definitely improve on some of the pages in our case study by making use of Code view. We'll take each page that needs attention in turn.

The contact page

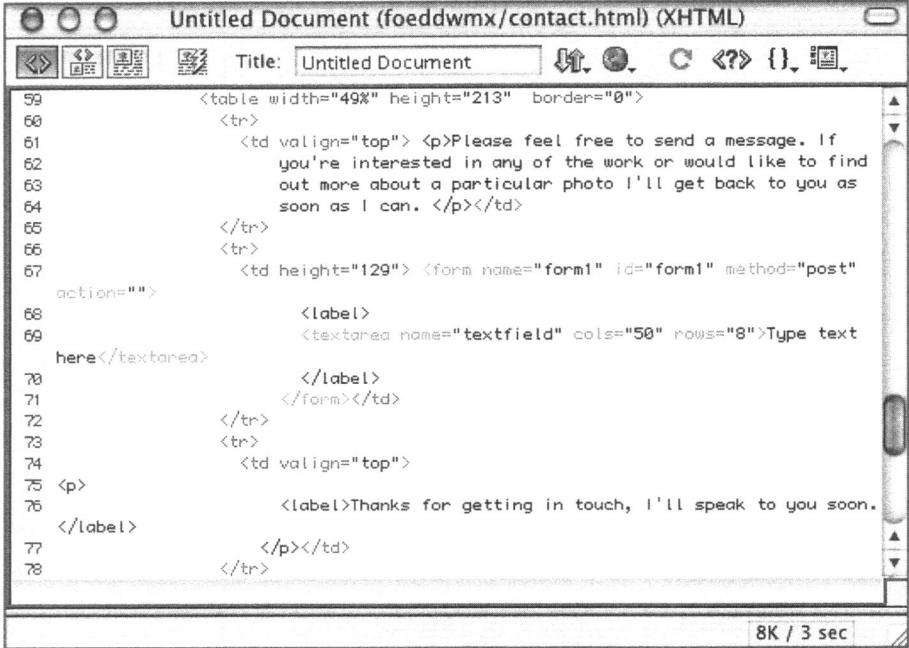

This has a number of things that can be tweaked. Firstly, table heights shouldn't really be defined when you have text and form fields in them, as browsers on various platforms have different line-spacing and spacing around forms.

In retrospect, there's also not a great deal of point in having a table at all, as you can get the same effect of only using half the page with CSS and with far less code.

Upgrading our layout to CSS

1. Define a new style by clicking inside the first paragraph tag and using the Properties panel to add a New CSS Style.

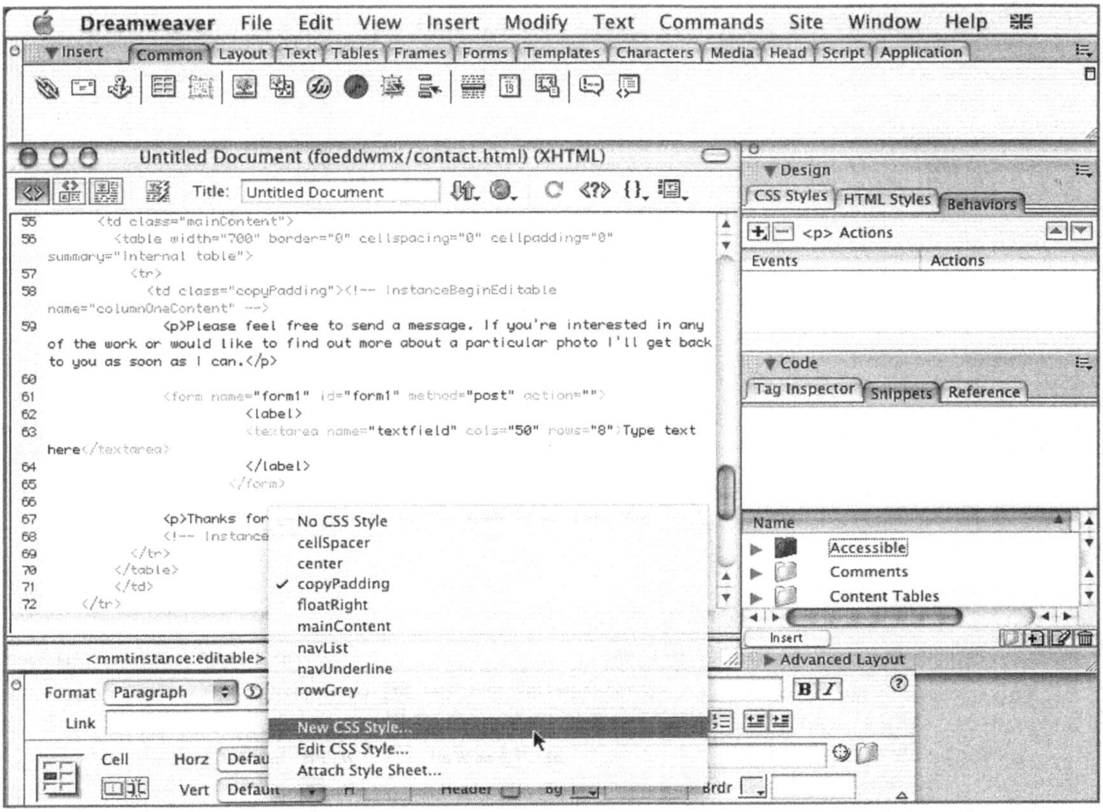

The Code Window

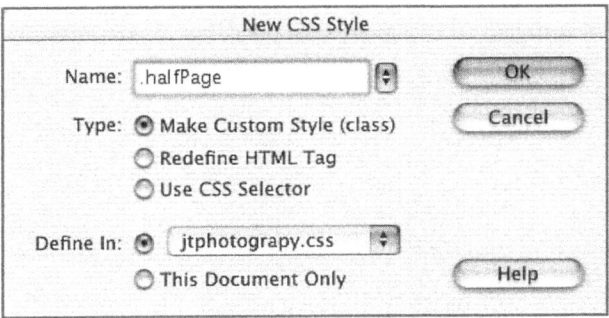

2. Name the style .halfPage and leave the other options alone. We want this to be a reusable style (already set in Type); to finish off, Define in jtphotography.css.

3. Time to set the padding.

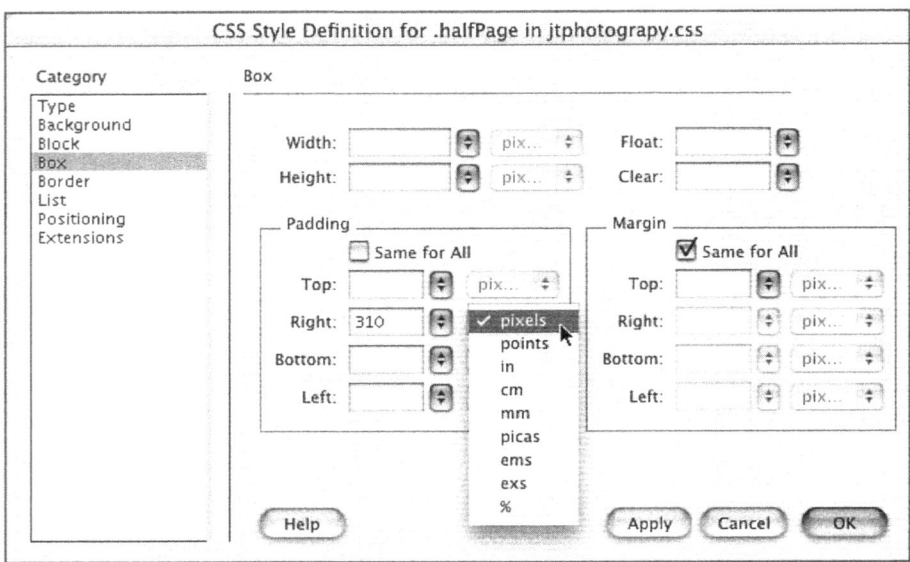

To achieve the 'half page' effect, we only need to set one attribute: the right-hand padding on the paragraph element. This is found under Box in the Category listing. The setting needs to be half the width of the available space. Our main table was set way back at the start of this project at 700 pixels and the columns leave 40 pixels left and right. Therefore our padding needs to be (700 − (2 x 40))/2, which is 310 pixels.

4. Hit OK and check your code. You'll see class="halfPage" added to the first paragraph tag. You need to add it to the second in order to give it consistent padding.

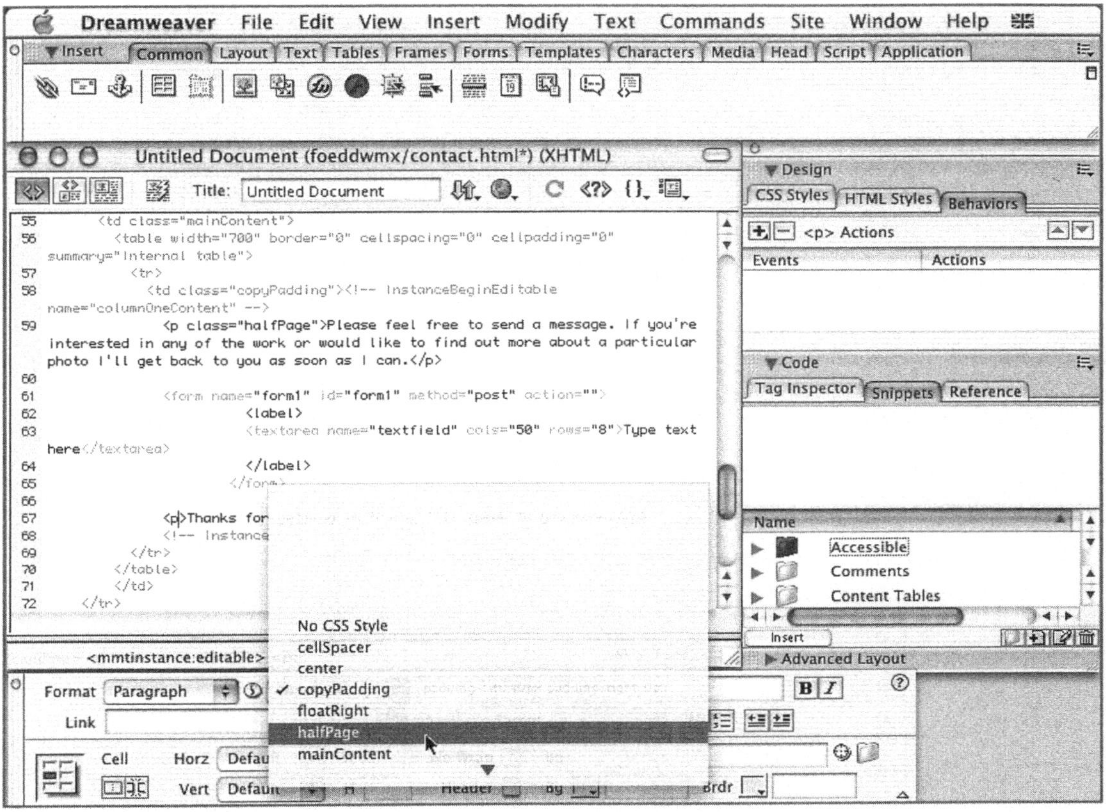

5. Check in a browser or two using F12 or Preview/Debug in Browser.

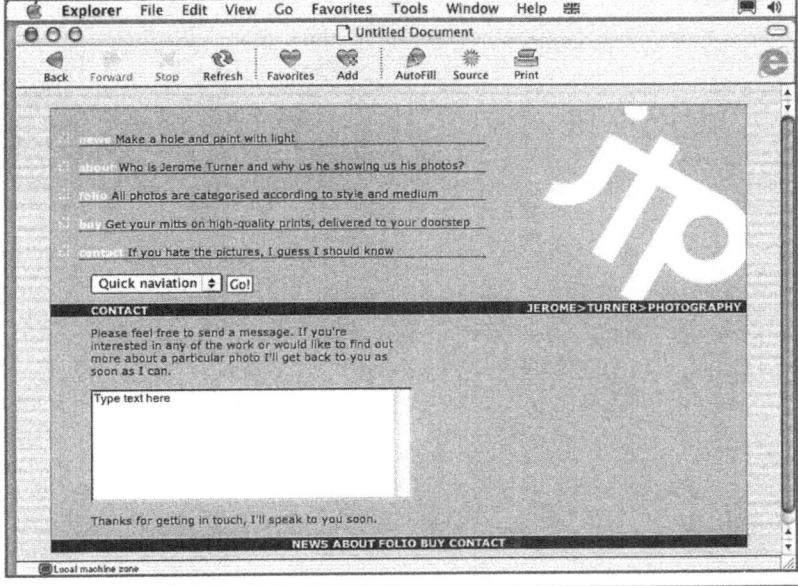

> *Always make sure everything's going to plan by checking in a browser at regular intervals. The above page is the edited one, with table removed and CSS padding in place. It looks more-or-less identical to the previous one, but should you later decide to extend the padding, for example to line up with the gray underlines on the navigation at the top, you only need to edit the padding-right attribute of .halfPage in the CSS file...*

Dogs in cars

The final page – or rather set of pages – we're going to look at is the Dogs in Cars one.

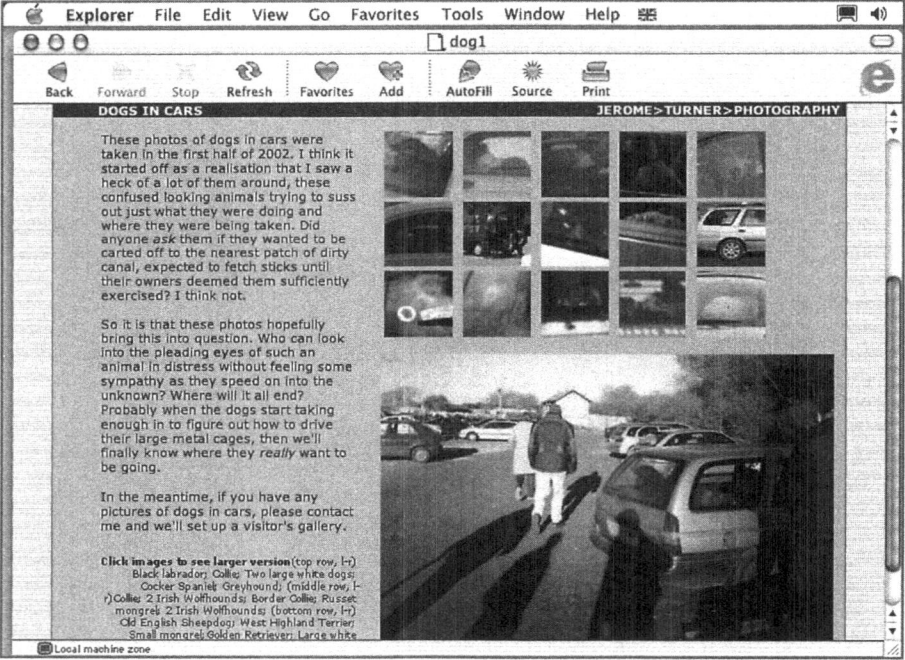

The code for the first column (the text) ends up looking like this:

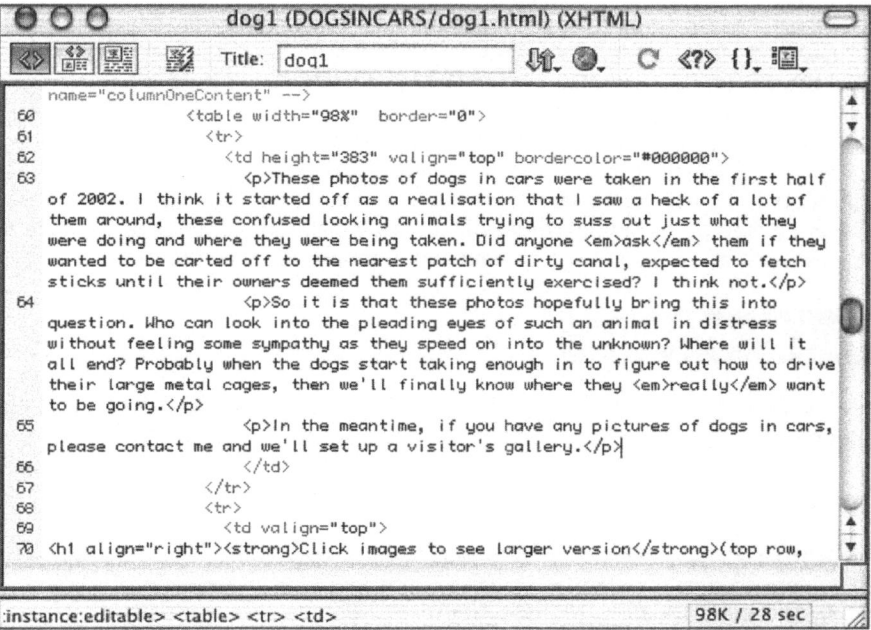

The table is superfluous and can be removed. It doesn't assist the formatting in any way and just adds extra, unneeded code that may even cause some inconsistency across various Web browsers.

Remove it and you end up with this:

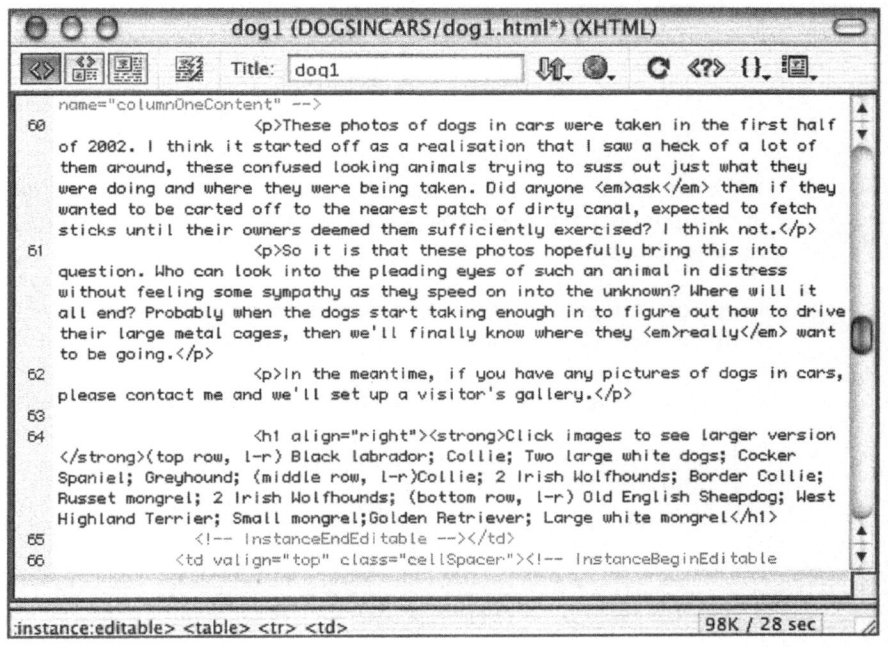

... which is much better.

A rather more interesting area to experiment with is the column on the right, which contains all of the images. You'll remember that a set of almost identical pages was made, the only difference in each being the 'zoomed' image. This had the advantage of you being able to e-mail a specific page to someone, and them perhaps going to the site and being interested enough to explore the other pages. However, this does have the disadvantage of being somewhat inflexible when it comes to updating.

Another method is to use some JavaScript to 'swap out' the main image when you click on the thumbnails. With regards to loading time, this doesn't make any difference, but the site will seem a little more seamless, as you won't see a 'jump' when moving between pages.

JavaScript swap Shop

1. The first thing you need to do is take a copy of one of the pages and then add this to its `<head>` section, within the editable area that Dreamweaver sets up by default:

   ```
   <script type="text/javascript" language="javascript">

   <!-- This HTML comment hides me from non-supporting broswers

   // This is a JavaScript comment
   // Foundation Dreamweaver MX - Swap Image function

   function swapPhoto(photoSRC) {
       document.images.imgPhoto.src = "assets/photos/dogsincars/" + photoSRC;
       }

   // -->
   </script>
   ```

   The script is a very simple function that when called looks for an image called `imgPhoto` within the current document, and changes its `src` (the location of the displayed file) depending on the variable `photoSRC`.

2. Those of you getting ahead of yourself probably already know the next step: adding the attribute `name` to the main image on the page and calling it `imgPhoto`.

   ```
   115            </tr>
   116          </table>
   117          <p><img src="assets/photos/dogsincars/dog1b.jpg" width="400" height="252" name="imgPhoto" /></p>
   118                 <!-- InstanceEndEditable --></td>
   ```

3. Finally, we have to amend the links for each of the thumbnails. Instead of going to a new page, they'll now call the script we've just added to the page.

The code for the first thumbnail currently looks like this:

```
<a href="dogsincars/dog1.html"><img
src="assets/photos/dogsincars/thumbs/dog1t.jpg" width="60" height="60"
border="0" /></a>
```

We'll change it to this:

```
<a href="javascript:swapPhoto('dog1.jpg')"><img src="assets/photos/dogsin-
cars/thumbs/dog1t.jpg" alt=" thumbnail" width="60" height="60" border="0"
/></a>
```

4. Instead of a link to a file, we call our JavaScript function swapPhoto. In brackets and single quotes we add the filename of the image we want the thumbnail to access. Of course, with what you learned earlier in the chapter, you can always add a few more things to the link, such as browser status text, and more:

```
<a onmouseover="window.status='Our first dogs in car photo.'; return true"
onmouseout="window.status='';" href="javascript:swapPhoto('dog1.jpg')"
title=" Our first dogs in car photo.">
<img src="assets/photos/dogsincars/thumbs/dog1t.jpg" alt="thumbnail"
width="60" height="60" border="0" /></a>
```

Two more additions that we've made are the title attribute within the anchor <a> tag and the alt attribute within the image tag. You're maybe familiar with the latter – it provides non-graphical browsers with a text description of the image, and graphical browsers something to display while they load the image, and also when people 'mouseover' the picture. The title attribute might be less familiar and displays its value when you mouseover an ordinary text link – pretty useful. It's often good to include the same content here that goes in your browser status text.

5. We end up with something like below:

7   Foundation Dreamweaver MX

Moving the mouse over the thumbnail shows the pop-up, due to the `title` attribute and clicking it replaced the main image with the full version – all on one page. A fairly elegant addition to our site, wouldn't you say?

The only thing that remains to be done on this page is sorting the alignment problem with regards to the thumnbnails and images (the main image is a little too far to the left). This happens because cellspacing wasn't defined in the table tag encompassing the thumbnails. Again, different browsers then make their own interpretation as to how to layout the table.

6. Finally in this exercise, add `cellspacing="0"` to the table tag as shown:

```
75
76                <!-- InstanceEndEditable --></td>
77          <td valign="top" class="cellSpacer"><!-- InstanceBeginEditable
   name="columnTwoContent" -->
78                <table cellspacing="0" cellpadding="0" border="0"
79                <tr>
80                    <td height="62"><a onmouseover="window.status='Our first dogs
   in car photo.'; return true" onmouseout="window.status='';" href=
   "javascript:swapPhoto('dog1b.jpg')" title="Our first dogs in car photo.">
81  <img src="assets/photos/dogsincars/thumbs/dog1t.jpg" alt="thumbnail" width="60"
```

Now there's no misunderstanding, and the page ends up with all images lined up as they should be:

Updating site pages

Over the course of this chapter we've tweaked a number of pages, and you may have also made a few amendments to the templates along the way. Now we're tidying up loose ends, this is an ideal time to update the site pages. What this does is ensure the pages that are based on templates all comply with said templates. It also ensures that any tags you've added comply to each document's DTD, so if you've missed a closing slash from the odd `<img>` tag, Dreamweaver MX will automatically sort that for you.

1. First off, you should close any open pages. You'll see why shortly.

2. The next thing to do is go to Site > Site Files, which shows the files for your web site.

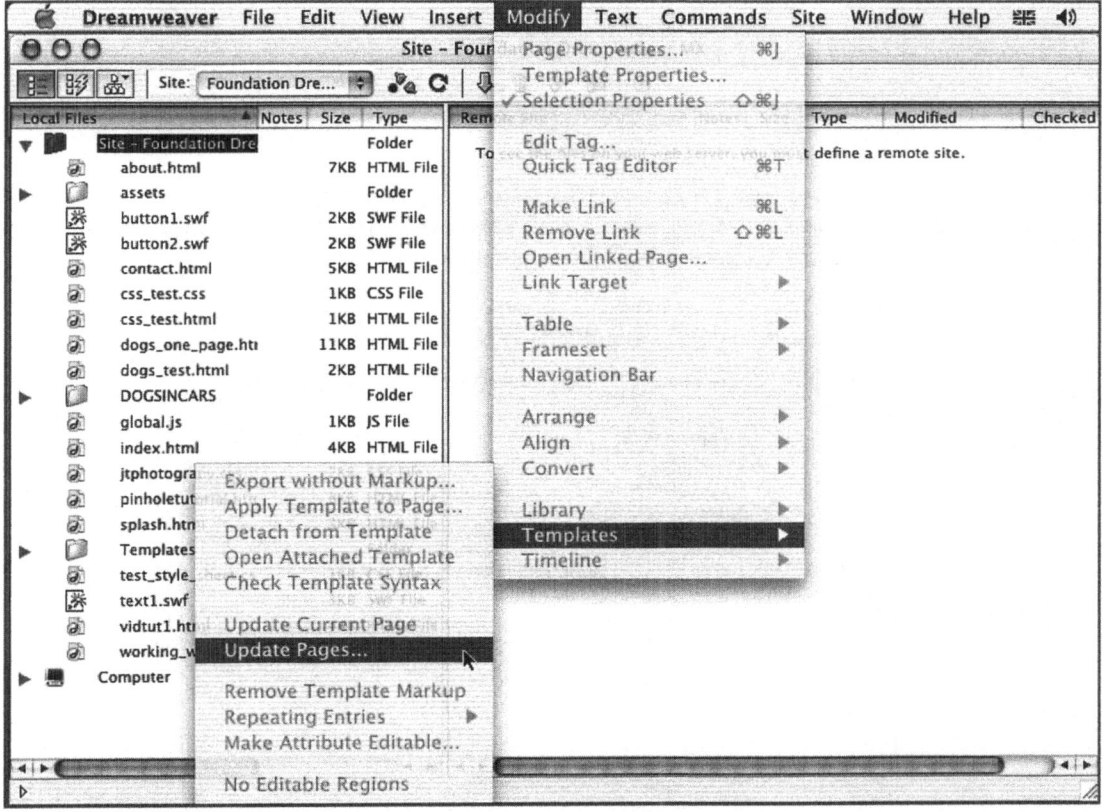

3. Go to Modify > Templates > Update Pages and you'll get the following dialog box:

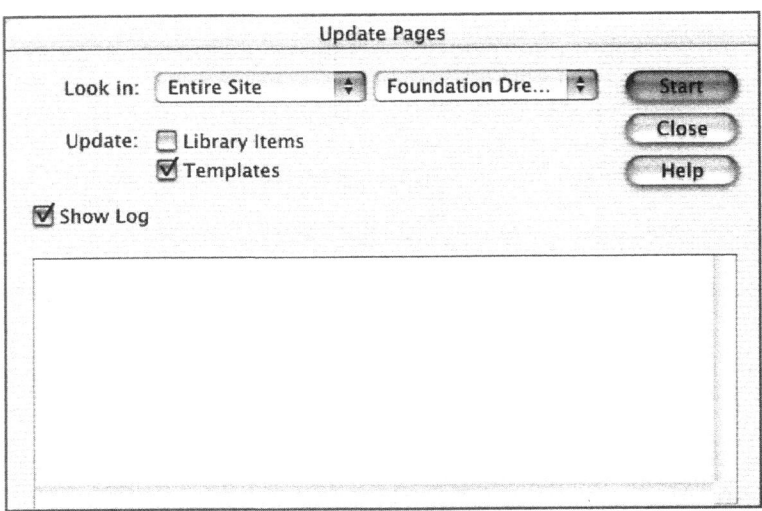

4. You can use the first drop-down box to update a selection of files that only use a specific template, but the default setting checks all the files on the site. Hit Start and the application will begin working through all your files, checking that everything's okay.

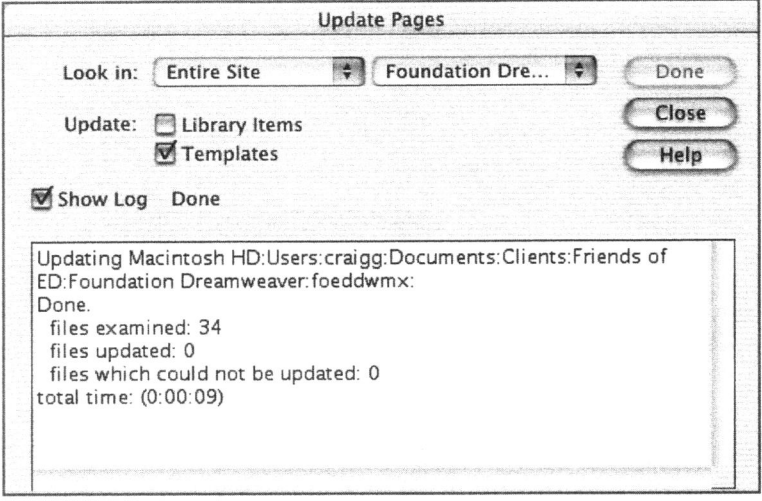

The results will be displayed to you as above. In this case, nothing needed to be updated, but that may not always be the case. If you regularly modify your templates, it's a good idea to run an Update every now and again just to ensure all your pages are up-to-date.

> *If any of your site's pages were open when you run* Update Pages, *the changes will have been made but you'll have to manually save them. It's usually best to close all pages when updating the site.*

Further validation

Those of you who really want to make sure your site is compliant and up-to-scratch with regards to web standards can go one step further by visiting the W3C. The World Wide Web Consortium is the organization that makes the rules with regards to mark-up and how it works, the standards browser makers should follow, and so on. Its site at www.w3.org provides a number of useful tools to check your pages further, including validators for (X)HTML pages and CSS files.

Of these, the CSS Validator is perhaps of the most use. You can validate your cascading style sheet by URL, with a text area, or by uploading it, and the site will return a report by whatever criteria you give it. Rather than just reporting on errors, it will also make suggestions to improve your CSS file. While not implementing these won't make your CSS invalid, taking advantage of the recommendations will most likely ensure your CSS is more compliant within the range of Web browsers available today.

The W3C Validator is completely free-to-use and very useful.

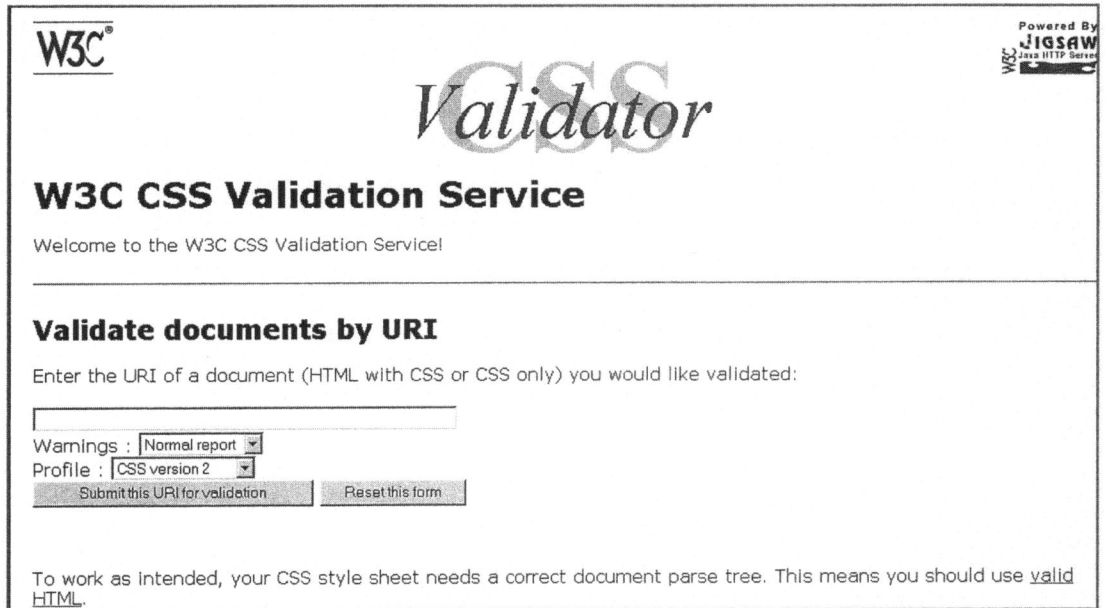

W3C also offers a validation service for (X)HTML documents. While Dreamweaver itself has a built-in function for checking pages, it's somewhat flaky, and W3's validator is far superior. However, even better is the application called Tidy.

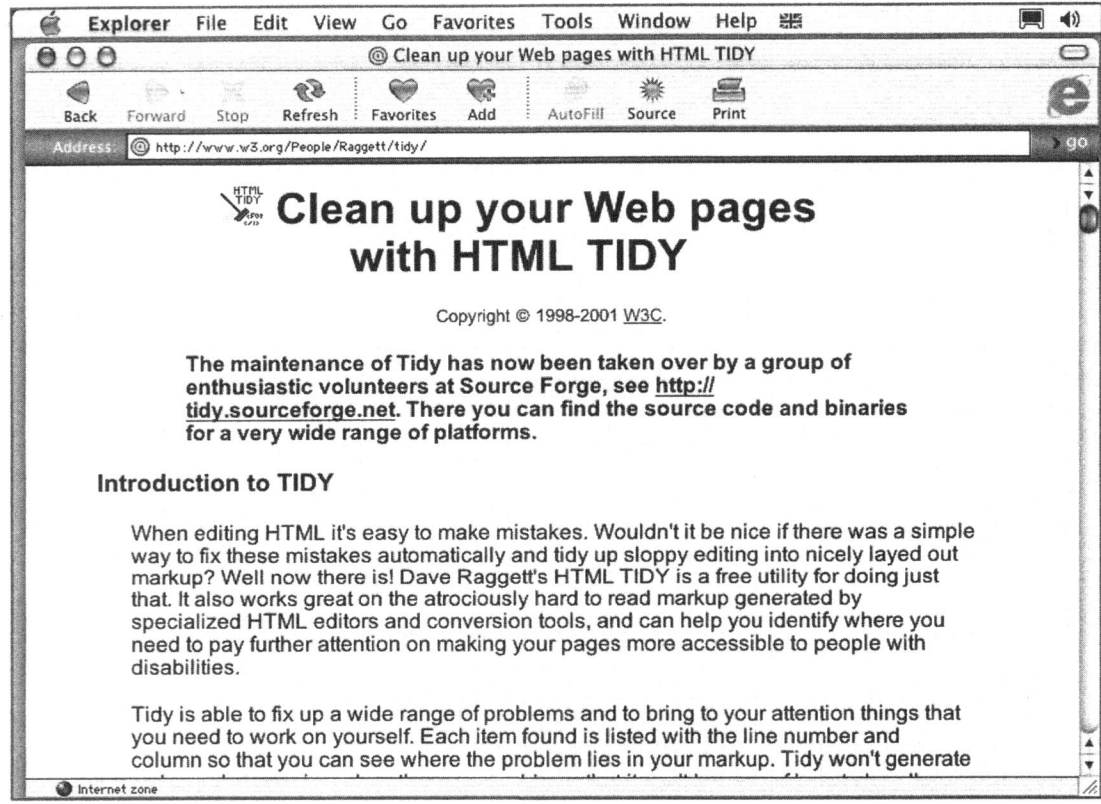

This offline tool is available for a number of platforms and goes through your pages looking for errors, amending your code (if you configure it to) and generally offering useful advice. We'd suggest though reading the documentation very carefully prior to using it, as it's a very powerful tool, and you wouldn't want it making any unwanted changes to your precious site. However, in careful hands, it's extremely useful. As well as coming as a standalone application, it's also available in plug-in format for the likes of BBEdit Lite for Macintosh.

Loose ends

While nothing to do with the Code view as such, now's a good time to make a few other small amendments to the site. Working in Code view usually gives you a keen eye for small details and a few things became apparent when updating the site when looking at the site's files.

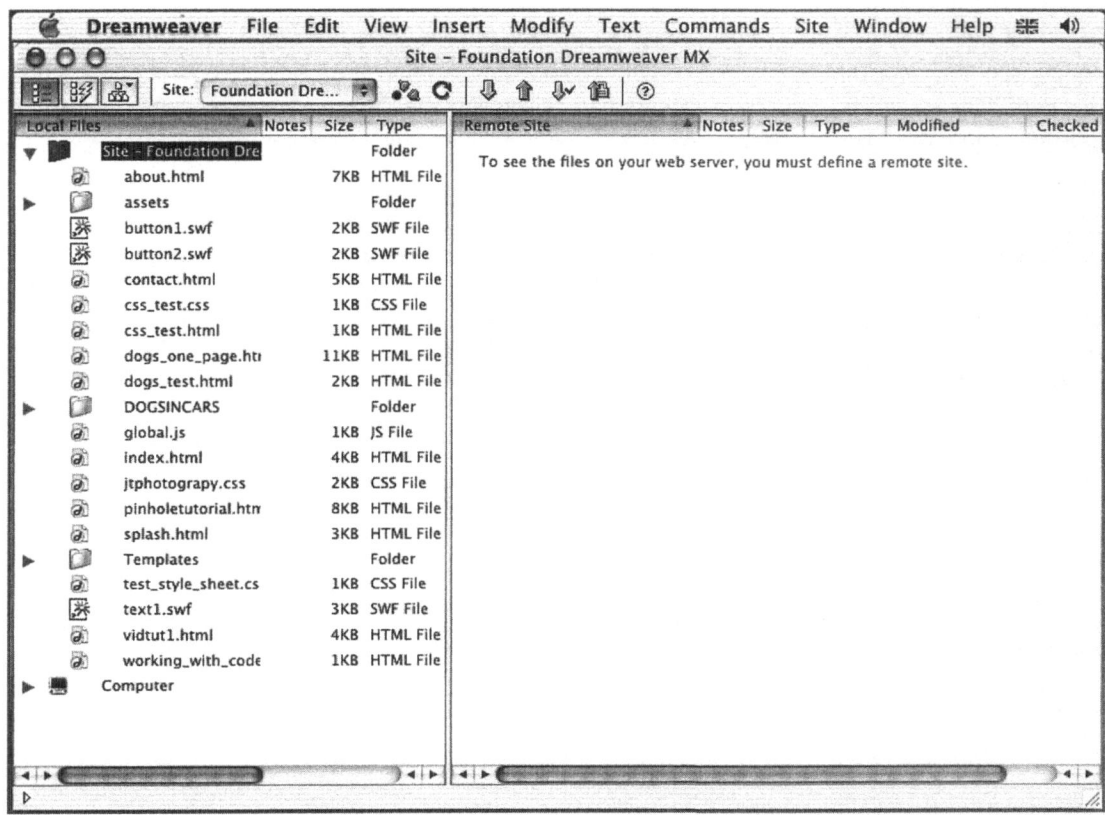

Earlier, we stressed the importance of being tidy and organizing your files, but we've made a bit of a mess here. The Flash files should really be tucked away in the assets folder and the DOGSINCARS folder written in lower case.

> *While it's really up to you whether you want to use* UPPER CASE, *lower case or a combination of the two for files names, some servers — particularly Unix-based ones — are case sensitive. Therefore they will treat Document.html, document.html and DoCuMeNt.html differently. With that in mind, it's usually best to stick to lower case only for Web files, and use underscores (_) for any required spaces for filenames such as my_best_picture.jpg.*

Amending these is easy. We can make a new folder inside the assets folder for the Flash files and drag them in there. Furthermore, we can rename the DOGSINCARS folder. Dreamweaver will then rummage through the site and update all relevant links accordingly.

Summary

So that's the Code view thoroughly checked out and the site polished accordingly. Hopefully you're now more confident in delving into code rather than relying on the Design view, and you've seen how important, and easy, it is to tweak and amend the time-saving behaviors Dreamweaver offers.

Dreamweaver's visual tools make our jobs so much easier, but a familiarity with the code it generates is also essential. You don't have to be able to write this code, but an ability to troubleshoot and make simple edits in the Code view will help optimize your pages and keep them in pristine shape!

The rest of the book will build on what you've learnt so far about visual design in Dreamweaver by giving you a thorough introduction to dynamic content concepts. You'll be learning all about PHP and MySQL and how they can be integrated into your Dreamweaver work.

The Code Window 7

Introducing Dynamic Content

What we'll cover in this chapter

- Learning about dynamic content
- Installing Apache and PHP
- Testing our installation

In previous chapters, we've learned how to design and create pages using Dreamweaver MX. What we haven't covered is what to do if you want to create a site that gathers and processes information from the user. Dreamweaver has the ability to deal with a whole range of dynamic elements to allow this to happen, and this is what we're going to learn about in the rest of this book.

We know that you've probably never done this before, and it's a bit scary, but please stick around and take a look – it's much, much easier than you think and you're missing so much of Dreamweaver if you restrict yourselves to the layout and design tools.

In this chapter, we'll take a look at the range of technologies available to us, install our choice onto our machine, test that this works, and look at what to do if it doesn't work.

How do dynamic sites work?

Now that we have an overview of the next few sections, we must begin with an overview of the conceptual leap involved when we start looking at dynamic sites. Take a look at one of the most interactive sites on the web, amazon.com. Load the home page, and you'll see tons of features that allow the site to tell you what you will like and how to get it.

How does the site know all of this? It tracks where you go on their site, and then **stores** this information. Amazon is able to generate 'recommendations' based on this information. It's also able to look at what other people have done, compare that to you, and create recommendations from this. Every time you visit, Amazon will add some more information.

How does Amazon do this? It stores the information in a database, and uses some sort of dynamic technology to communicate between the database and the site, to move the information around so that that it can store and use it. This "dynamic technology" can be one of a number of different languages. Popular choices include PHP, ASP, ColdFusion, and Perl.

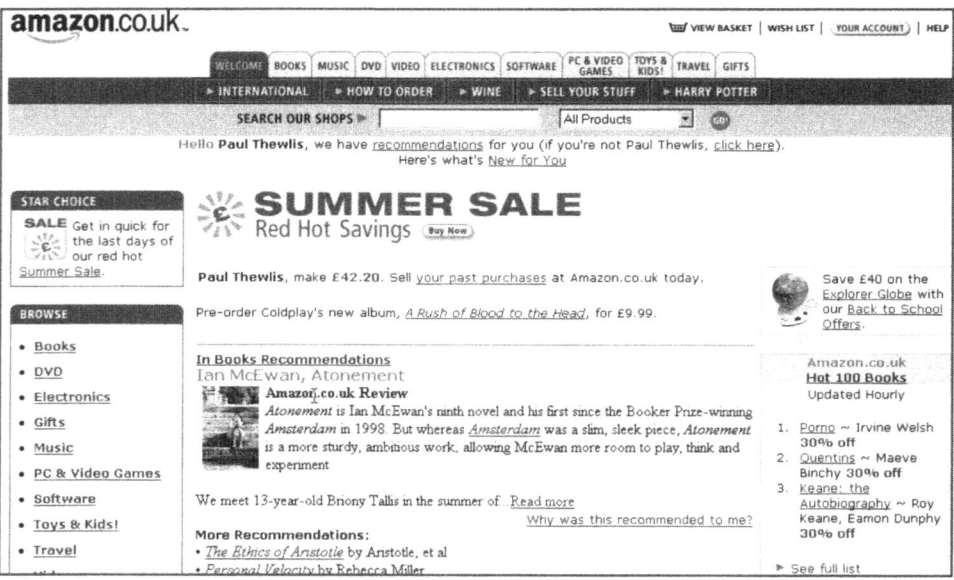

Which language is best?

So which one of these languages is best? That's a debatable issue – ask that question anywhere where there are people who are involved with web design or development, and you'll get several different answers, and a very heated argument. There are different strengths for each option.

ASP, and now the greatly enhanced new **ASP.NET** are a very popular choice. You'll have to cough up for some third-party software, though, and as it's a Microsoft product, you're generally excluding Mac owners from the equation.

Macromedia's **ColdFusion** has previously not been as popular as some options in the past, but with the new MX version integrating with Flash and Dreamweaver, and a reputation for ease of use, it looks set to take an increased share of the market. Running against it for the moment are the cost, and the greater difficulty in finding hosts for ColdFusion sites.

As you've probably guessed, we're going to be using **PHP** for the purposes of this book – it's free, it's cross-platform, and it's widely used. Past versions of Dreamweaver haven't offered support for PHP, but Macromedia have thankfully included support for it in Dreamweaver MX. In a benchmark test, ZDNet (www.zdnet.com) pitted the major programming languages against each other in an output battle. The results were that:

- PHP pumped out about 47 pages per second
- Microsoft ASP pumped out about 43 pages per second
- Allaire ColdFusion (now Macromedia ColdFusion) pumped out about 29 pages per second
- Sun Java JSP pumped out about 13 pages per second

The higher the output, the more efficient the language, so – whilst this is only one test (and it was using an old version of ColdFusion) – we can see that PHP holds its own in the company of others.

As we'll be seeing, PHP pages are treated just like regular HTML pages and you can create and edit them in the same way as you normally create regular HTML pages. Your server will, however, need support for PHP activated so that all files ending in .php are handled by PHP.

We'll be using the MySQL database in combination with PHP, and this is also available for free. You can use other types of databases, like Microsoft Access, but PHP was written to work with MySQL so it's much easier this way. You'll get a better idea of how things work as we go through some exercises after installing PHP and MySQL, but the diagram over the page should give you a good idea.

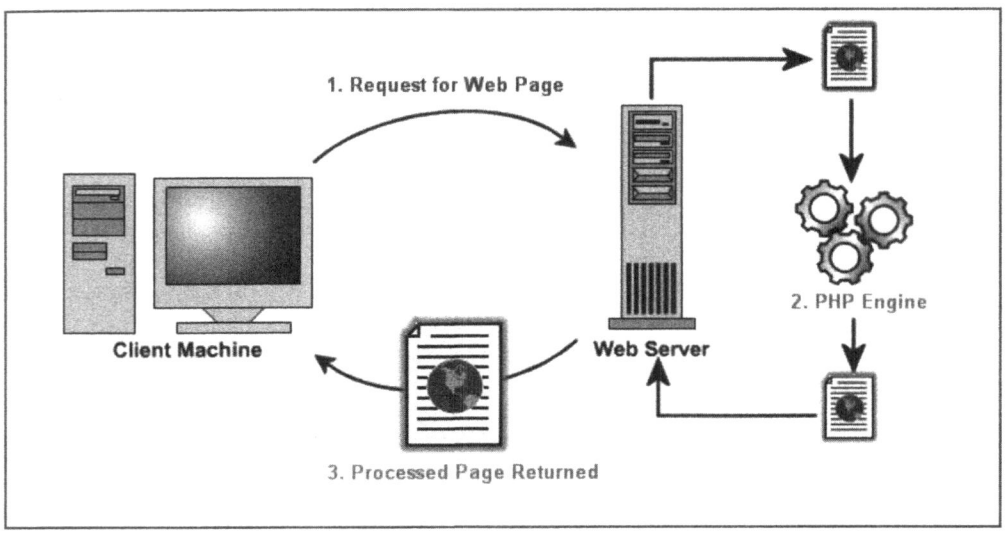

ASP coders

Although we're not going to use ASP code in the following examples, we do recognize that some of you out there are going to want to use ASP with Dreamweaver. Our main aim in the following chapters is to give you grounding in how easy creating dynamic content in Dreamweaver can be, rather than to train you up in any particular language, so you will be able to apply the concepts you learn to any language.

If you still want to use ASP instead, and are confident enough to go ahead with that, that's great, though you'll want to skip the remainder of this chapter. Dreamweaver offers greater online support for ASP than for PHP, including the Wrox ASP 3.0 reference – accessed by opening up the tab on the right handside labeled Code and clicking the Reference tab. Beginners might also be interested to know that PHP does have an ASP tag emulation mode created by www.zend.com.

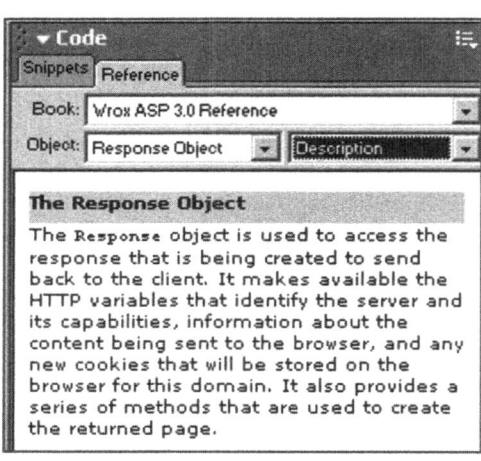

Installation

This is the first phase in installing the software you'll need to tackle the tutorials in the rest of this book. In this chapter we'll be installing PHP, and Apache, the web server for PHP to run on. Later, we'll also install MySQL and phpMyAdmin.

To some, the thought of installing PHP may seem a daunting task. Now, add to that the perceived complexities of an Apache web server and you can almost smell the fear. You know what I'm going to say now? Exactly what you want me to. It's really not so hard.

This installation section should mop up the vast majority of installation spills but, if you do hit an insoluble problem, check out the technical support addresses in the introduction and get in touch – we'd be delighted to help. The online documentation that comes with the downloads, and web sites and forums like friends of ED's www.phpforflash.com can also offer valuable help.

As we mentioned earlier, both Apache and PHP are free for both commercial and non-commercial use. This fact alone has contributed to the success of both Apache and PHP. Add in the functionality offered by both products, and you've got a winning combination.

Be aware that this process is a little different for Macs and PCs, so you're only going to need to read one of the two following sections. PC readers can read straight on, Mac users need to skip to the big heading reading **Switching on PHP in Mac OS X** a few pages away.

Installing PHP and Apache on a PC

Before you can begin the installation you need to make sure you have the latest versions of the software. You can download Apache from the developer's web site at:

http://httpd.apache.org/dist/httpd/binaries/win32/

The current version at the time of writing is 2.0.40. There have been some reports of problems with 2.0.40, so to be on the safe side we'll stick with version 1.3.26, which has a solid reputation. Download the 1.3.26 Win32 binary version of the software; this is a Windows specific version, providing a nice friendly Installation Wizard. This will probably be the larger version of the 1.3.26 options as a result, and will be called something like `apache_1.3.26-win32-x86-no_src.exe`.

Once you've got Apache, you need to go to:

www.php.net/downloads.php

to download PHP. Unlike Apache, there are differences between the ways in which different versions of PHP handle things, so this time, we do want the most recent version. At the time of writing, this is 4.2.2, and you will need this version or newer for some of the code in later chapters to work as intended.

Each new release of PHP brings improvements (and the inevitable bug fixes!), so keep your PHP installations up to date where possible. It's free, after all, so there's no reason not to get the latest one.

At the time of writing, there were two types of installation files listed under Windows Binaries on the PHP web site:

PHP 4.2.2 zip package [5,275Kb] - 22 July 2002
(CGI binary plus server API versions for Apache, Apache2 (experimental), ISAPI, NSAPI, Servlet and Pi3Web. MySQL support built-in, many extensions included, packaged as zip)

PHP 4.2.2 installer [913Kb] - 22 July 2002
(CGI only, MySQL support built-in, packaged as Windows installer to install and configure PHP, and automatically configure IIS, PWS and Xitami, with manual configuration for other servers. N.B. no external extensions included)

For the purposes of this chapter we'll be using the zip package (the first option), and installing a few parts of PHP manually. This isn't nearly as scary as it sounds, and it means we become more familiar with how PHP is organized than we would with a point-and-click installer – which can only be a good thing.

Installing Apache web server for Windows

Assuming that you've successfully downloaded both Apache and PHP installation files from their respective sites, we're ready to begin our installation.

1. To begin, double-click the Apache installation file to start the Installation Wizard. The screenshot shows the Apache Installation Wizard, displaying the version of Apache we're about to get friendly with. Click Next to continue with the installation.

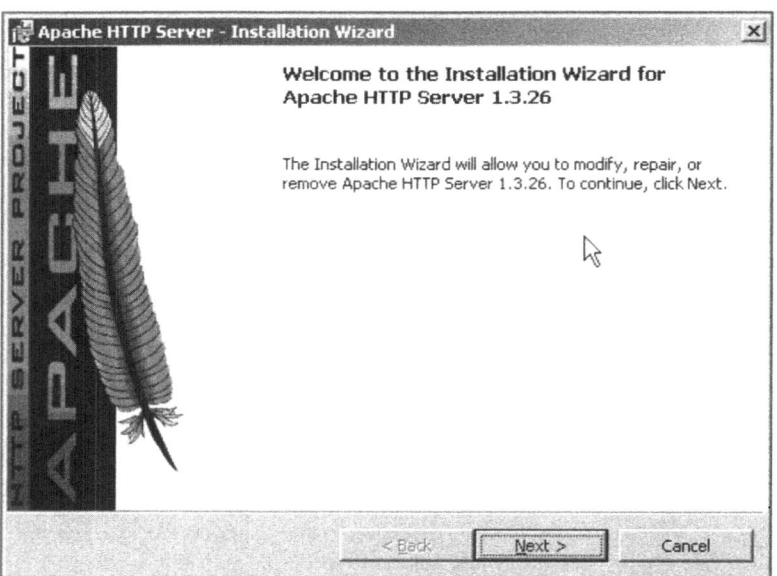

2. Next, you'll see the Apache License Agreement screen. Because Apache is freely available the restrictions of the agreement apply mainly to those wanting to redistribute the Apache software but, as with all software, it's important to read the terms and conditions of use.

Introducing Dynamic Content 8

3. If you intend to use your Apache server as a production web server, read this screen:

    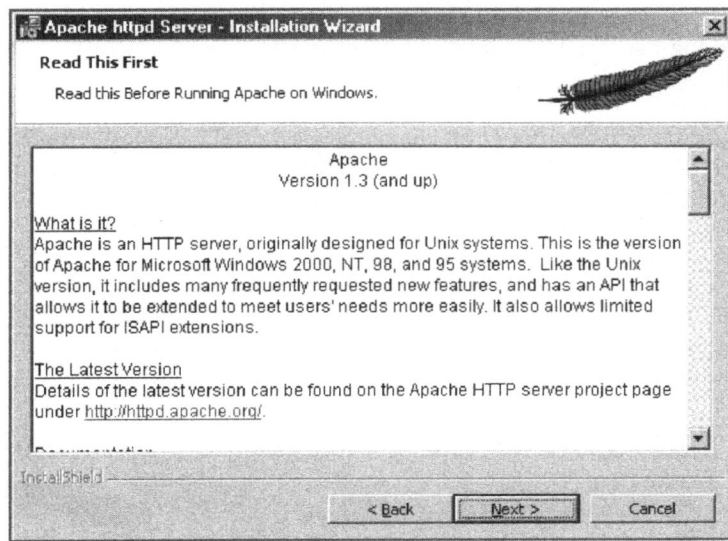

    The Windows version of Apache is not considered by its developers to be a production-ready product. For one, the code has not been optimized for performance, and there are a few remaining security issues. For our development purposes, it's fine.

4. OK, that's the initial froth out of the way – here's the interesting bit of the installation. The image below shows the Server Information screen. This is where you'll configure your web server. Replace the contents of the text boxes with your settings, your server name, your domain and so on. Unless you know other details, type 'localhost' in the top two boxes and your e-mail address in the bottom box.

    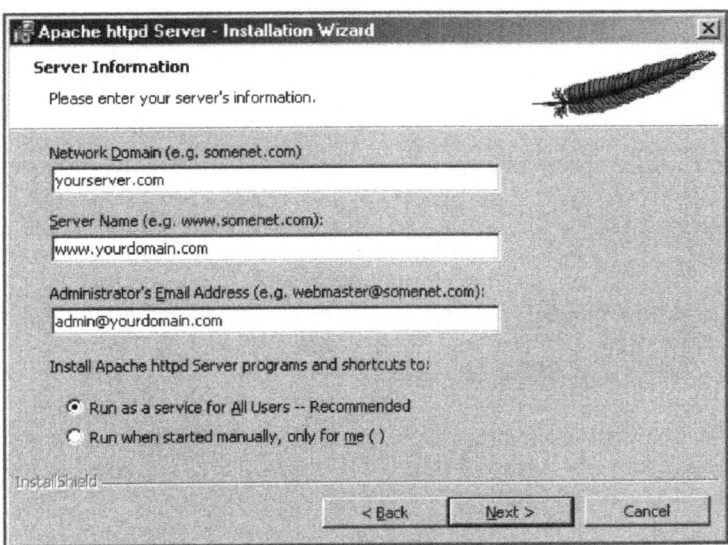

Foundation Dreamweaver MX

5. The final part of the Server Information screen allows you to install the server icons and start-up options for all users, either on a shared system or simply for the current user. If you select the Run as a service for All Users on an NT or Windows 2000 system the Apache server runs as a service in the background and you don't need to worry about starting the server before you can use it.

   If you are using Windows 95/98/ME you can select either of the options, but Apache will not run as a service and will need to be started manually. You can replicate the functionality offered by running the web server as a service by adding the `apache.exe` to the Start-up menu, so that it starts every time you start your computer.

6. Click Next and you'll be presented with the screen shown. On the previous screen, you provided all the information the Apache installer requires to complete a successful installation. This screen displays the Setup Type options. Unless you want to remove the Apache documentation, select the Complete option.

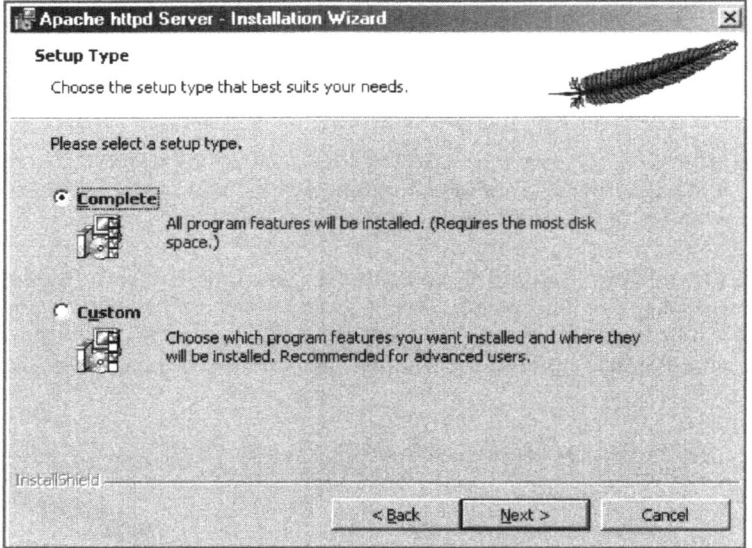

7. Click Next to select where you want your web server to be installed. By default, it will be installed to `C:\Program Files\Apache Group\`. It's as good a place as any and I recommend that you use this if possible, as it will make troubleshooting easier if something does go wrong at a later date.

8. Click Install and the installer will go off and do its worryingly will-it-won't-it thing for a moment, including a few strange DOS window things. When it's stopped, click Finished. Well done! Your first Apache Web Server install is complete.

9. Now for the acid test: does our web server actually work? Open a browser window and type `http://localhost` into the address field. `localhost` is a way of referring to the local machine – in this case our Apache web server.

Introducing Dynamic Content 8

If all went well you'll see the Apache test page in your browser:

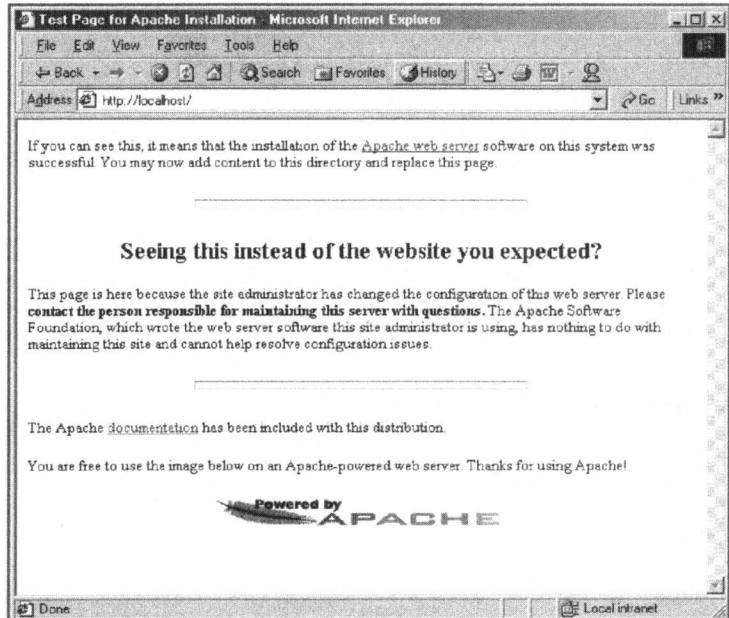

If your browser looks like the one above, perform one final, crucial step: sit back, put your hands behind your head and smile smugly. Your Apache install was completely successful.

Troubleshooting tips

If you don't see the Apache test page then you need to check that your web server is running. When running Apache *not as a service*, you'll see it running on your Windows task bar (see image below). If you don't see Apache running in your task bar, you can start it by selecting Start > Programs Menu > Apache httpd Server.

> It's worth noting that if you start the server manually the DOS command line window will remain on screen while the web server is running. Please don't sit waiting for the DOS window to vanish: it won't.

If you installed Apache on WindowsNT\2000 as a *service*, then check that the Apache service is running in Control Panel > Services (NT) Control Panel > Administration > Services(Windows2000). If the service is not running, then start the service and then try connecting to `localhost` in your browser again.

8   Foundation Dreamweaver MX

If you're still having problems with your web server, you'll find lots of support information on the Apache website at www.apache.org.

Installing PHP on Apache for Windows

As we've already successfully completed the Apache web server installation your confidence levels should be sky-high right now. While we're on a roll, let's dive straight into installing PHP.

1. Double-click the PHP4 installation file we downloaded earlier. You'll need Winzip (www.winzip.com) or something similar to extract the files. If you extract them straight into the root directory of your main drive, you'll find all your files in a folder called something like `php-4.2.2`. For ease of use, rename this directory `c:\php`. If all goes well, then the contents of your folder should look something like the image below.

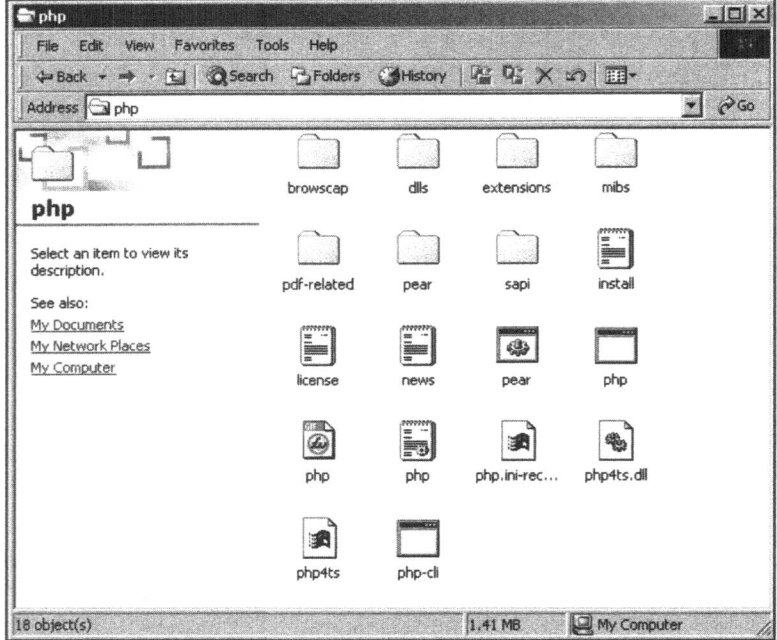

2. Rename the file `php.ini.dist` to `php.ini` and drag it over to our main windows directory (it'll be called `C:\WINDOWS` or `C:\WINNT` for NT based systems)

3. Copy the file `php4ts.dll` to your Windows system directory – for example `C:\WINDOWS\SYSTEM`, or `C:\WINNT\SYSTEM32`.

4. We've installed the Apache web server and PHP4. What we need to do now is tell Apache that we've installed PHP on our system and where it can be found. Go to the directory where you installed the Apache web server - `C:\Program Files\Apache Group\apache\conf` - and open the `httpd.conf` file in Notepad (or any other simple text editor).

Introducing Dynamic Content

5. We need to modify this file. I know, I know – it's another scary bit – but it's only one *little* change, and it is *absolutely necessary*. Once you've got it open, find the section shown below (hint: using the Find option to search for "ScriptAlias" will save you much scrolling):

    ```
    # ScriptAlias: This controls which directories contain server scripts.
    # ScriptAliases are essentially the same as Aliases, except that
    # documents in the realname directory are treated as applications and
    # run by the server when requested rather than as documents sent to the
    client.
    # The same rules about trailing "/" apply to ScriptAlias directives as to
    # Alias.
      ScriptAlias /cgi-bin/ "C:/Program Files/Apache Group/apache/cgi-bin/"
    ```

6. At the end of the section shown above, add the following line (if the last line of the section above is not there, add that as well):

    ```
    ScriptAlias /php/ "C:/php/"
    ```

    The paths in quotes should represent the paths where you installed Apache and PHP. This may be different, depending on where you installed the applications, so check that this is correct before proceeding.

    > *Note the use of forward slashes "/" where Windows would normally use back slashes "\". This dates back to Apache's UNIX roots, and needless to say, mixing them up here will result in some not terribly happy results.*

7. Now find this section (again, using Find might save your mouse):

    ```
    # AddType allows you to tweak mime.types without actually editing it, or to
    # make certain files to be certain types.
    #
    ```

8. At the end of the section shown above, add the following lines:

    ```
    AddType application/x-httpd-php .php
    AddType application/x-httpd-php .php4
    ```

    This tells Apache what file extensions it should treat as PHP files - in this case anything that ends in .php or .php4 is a PHP file as far as Apache is concerned.

8 Foundation Dreamweaver MX

9. Now find the section shown below. (This is the last one, I promise.)

   ```
   # Action lets you define media types that will execute a script
   ➥ whenever
   # a matching file is called. This eliminates the need for repeated URL
   # pathnames for oft-used CGI file processors.
   # Format: Action media/type /cgi-script/location
   # Format: Action handler-name /cgi-script/location
   ```

10. At the end of this lot, add the following line:

    ```
    Action application/x-httpd-php /php/php.exe
    ```

11. Save the file and close your text editor.

12. All modifications to the `conf` file require a restart of the web server, so go and do that now by selecting Programs > Apache HTTP Server > Control Apache Server > Restart.

OK, let's recap on what we've achieved so far. By modifying the `httpd.conf` file we've told Apache about our PHP installation, and we've also told Apache what file extensions to treat as PHP files. That's it! Your PHP installation is complete. Now all we need to do is test it, so unless you want to install PHP on a Mac as well, proceed to the **Setting Up Dreamweaver and Testing PHP** heading.

Switching on PHP in Mac OS X

"Switching on PHP?" – didn't the PC folk have to install it? Believe it or not, PHP has already been installed for you as part of the standard Mac OS X installation. All you have to do is switch it on.

If, like me, you're not a Unix person, then until now you might have avoided the dreaded Terminal application altogether. Switching on PHP in OS X means that we're going to have to dip our toes in the water and open up Terminal. As most Mac users are used to working with nice graphical things, and not horrible command-lines, we're going to take things very slowly here.

We'll start with Apache, before learning just a little bit about the Terminal and vi applications. We'll then be able to log in and set up everything that we need, creating a backup file along the way in case we get things wrong.

Starting the Apache web server

The first thing to do is switch on the Apache web server. As you might have guessed, this is also pre-installed and is a little easier to switch on than PHP.

1. Select the Sharing control panel of the System Preferences (Apple Menu > System Preferences).

2. In the Sharing control panel, click Start to begin the Web Sharing. This activates the Apache web server.

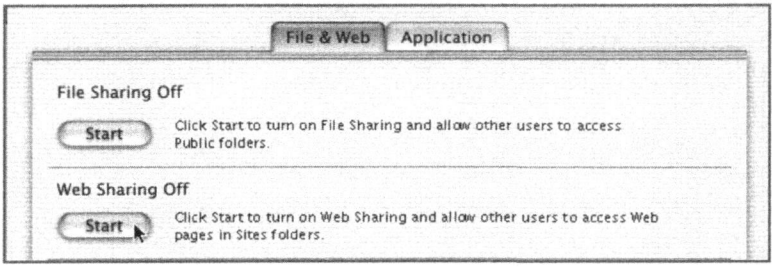

That's it for Apache – pretty easy so far. The next thing to do is to get in a little practice with the Terminal application.

The Terminal application

The command-line provided in the Terminal application allows you to access the Unix shell. A slightly more enlightening way of putting this is that the Terminal provides an alternative way for the User Interface (called Aqua) to work with your system. Instead of using a mouse and windows, the Terminal application allows you to interface with your Mac using the command-line.

Remember *War Games*? Well, it's a bit like that... kind of. You don't get to accidentally start World War Three, but working through the Terminal can still be pretty deadly if you do the wrong things. For this reason, only people logged in as the SuperUser of a system (called root) can make amendments to system files, like the one that we need to change to get PHP running.

Before logging in as root, we'll have a little play to get you familiar with the world of keyboard interfacing.

> *Before we use the Terminal application, make sure that you have administrator rights for your machine. You'll eventually need root rights too, but we'll get to that in a moment.*

Open the Terminal application. This is located in your Macintosh HD > Applications > Utilities, and looks a little like this:

Once you have it open, you'll be faced with a window like this (with an obvious user name difference!):

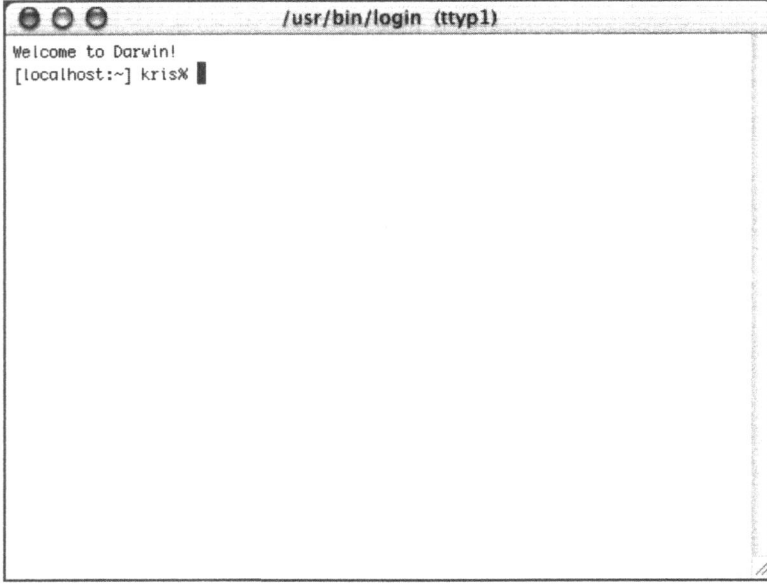

This is the much-dreaded command-line interface. Remember that you can't do any damage when you aren't logged in as root, so don't worry.

The first thing to point out is that the command-line is not like using a cushy word processor. You can't click somewhere and expect the cursor to go there. The best thing is to look at each line, such as....

[localhost:~] kris%

.... as being an individual line for waiting for a command – hence the name command-line!

Using the Terminal

If you're a hardened Unix or vi user, then you might want to skip the next few exercises, otherwise let's have a look at what the Terminal offers us.

1. With the Terminal open, type `ls` into the command-line, so it looks something like this:

   [localhost:~] kris% ls

2. Press return. The `ls` command simply displays a listing of the files in the current directory. Here's the directory listing of my user folder (not that exciting, eh?):

Introducing Dynamic Content

```
[localhost:~] kris% ls
Desktop              Music                  Sites
Documents            Network Trash Folder   TheVolumeSettingsFolder
Library              Pictures
Movies               Public
```

3. After this listing another command-line is shown, ready for the next command. Type

    `cd`

    followed by the name of a folder from the previous list. (I used `cd sites`).

    This command will change the current directory to the newly specified folder. Our current folder location is shown in the square brackets in the command line.

4. Now type `ls` again, and the content of the folder will be revealed:

```
[localhost:~] kris% cd sites
[localhost:~/sites] kris% ls
images       index.html
```

Okay, I've not exactly set your world on fire with the Terminal application, but at least you can see that it has potential. To switch on PHP, we need to use the **vi** text editor, which we call from the Terminal. The vi editor is a little strange at first, but it will soon become familiar...

Using vi

vi is a text editor commonly used by Unix folk. It might come as a bit of a culture shock, but it's not as complicated as it looks.

1. To help us get familiar with vi, we'll need a plain text file. Either find one on your system, or create a quick bit of text in TextEdit, and make sure you save it in plain text format.

2. Save the text file in your active Users folder (Macintosh HD > Users > <username>), as this'll make it easy to locate and open. If you save it elsewhere, you'll need to navigate to it with the `cd` command.

3. Once you have the plain text file in the current command-line directory, type the following into the terminal window:

    `vi <filename.txt>`

    The file I'm using here is called `dreamweaverMX.txt`, so here's what my command looks like:

    `vi dreamweaverMX.txt`

Foundation Dreamweaver MX

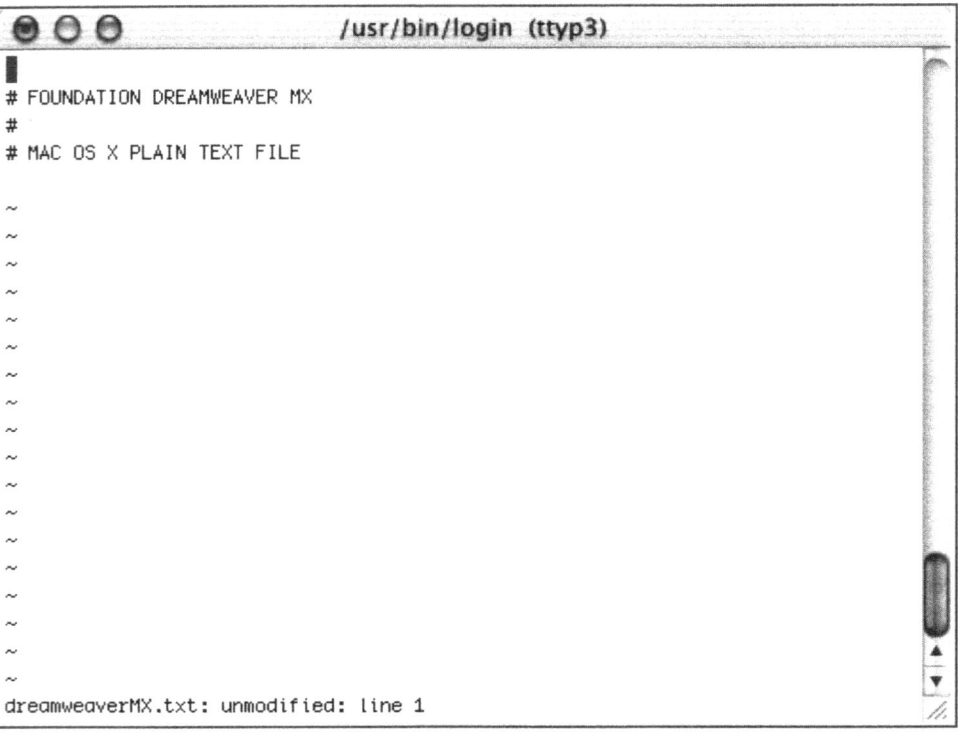

4. You should be faced with something like the screenshot in the Terminal window. vi has opened our text file ready for editing. Use the following keys to maneuver around (you'll find this easy if you've ever played Quake without a mouse):

   H - Left
   L - Right
   K - Up
   J - Down

5. If you find this a little slow and want to skip large amounts of text, use CTRL-F to scroll down a page and CTRL-B to go back a page. When we get there, you'll find that the configuration file is rather large, so this might be useful information.

6. To delete characters, use the x key. We'll be using this later to delete the comment characters (#) from the configuration file.

7. The next essential element of any text editor is the ability to insert text. Although we won't need to write to the configuration file, this bit seemed quite important (especially if you make a mistake). The keys to switch the text edit modes on and off are:

   SHIFT-R – to enter insert characters mode
   ESC – to exit insert characters mode

Introducing Dynamic Content 8

8. vi is pretty extensive, but we've seen all we need to know apart from the save commands, which we'll cover when we need to use them. Type

    :q!

    To quit and close the current vi session without saving.

We're almost ready to edit the config file, but first we need to login as the root user. As we mentioned earlier, doing anything significant to configuration files requires you to log in as the SuperUser, or root user. In the event that you have never logged in as the root user, you'll have to follow the next section to perform it for the first time. If you've already logged in as root in the past, skip the next exercise.

Logging in as root for the first time

If you've never logged in as root before, then it'll be switched off by default as a security precaution. You'll need to enable it system-wide in Mac OS X (as with the previous exercise, you'll need to have administrator rights for this).

We're going to use another application that you might not have used: the NetInfo Manager. As with the Terminal application, this is located in Macintosh HD > Applications > Utilities:

NetInfo Manager

1. Open the application, and you'll be faced with a rather confusing looking window:

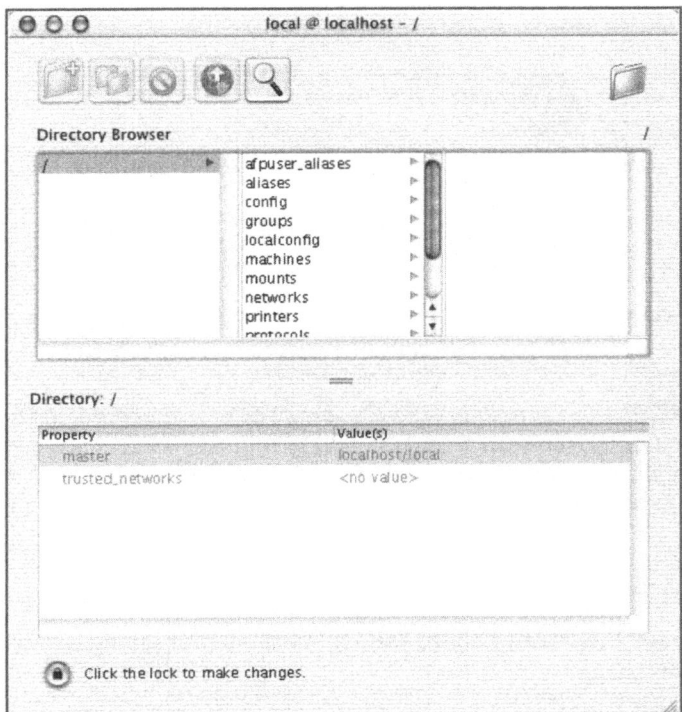

2. Luckily, we don't have to work with this, as we just need to use one of the application menus. Select Domain > Security > Authenticate:

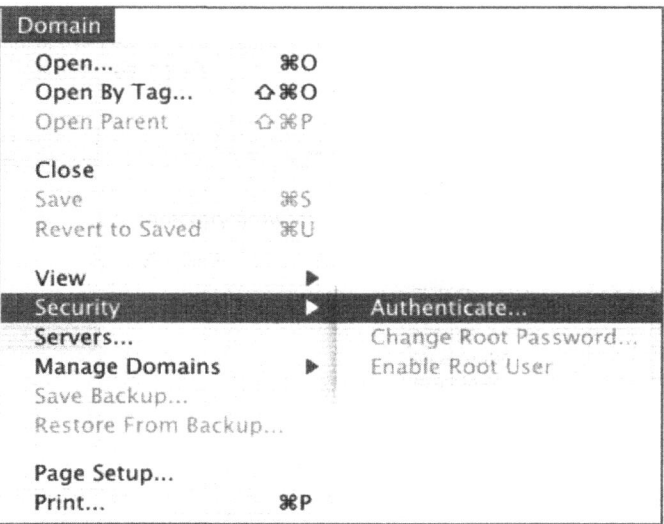

3. This starts the process of enabling the root user login - you'll need to authenticate your administrator short name and password:

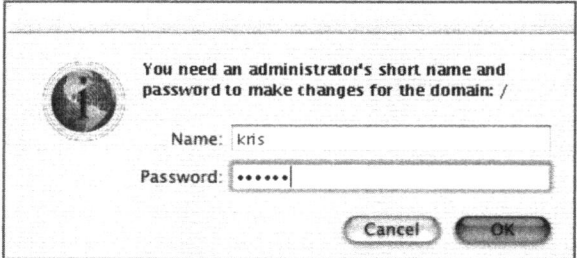

When you've done this, you'll need to give the root user a password.

> WARNING!!! This is the one password that you should never forget and no-one can remember for you. The root user has access to your whole system, and if you forget this, then it might have repercussions for later Mac OS X use. I don't care how – just don't forget it!

4. Once you've read the warning above and let it sink in, proceed by entering a password, typing carefully as you go.

Introducing Dynamic Content   8

5. Once the root user has a password, we can proceed to enable root user access. Select Domain > Security > Enable Root User:

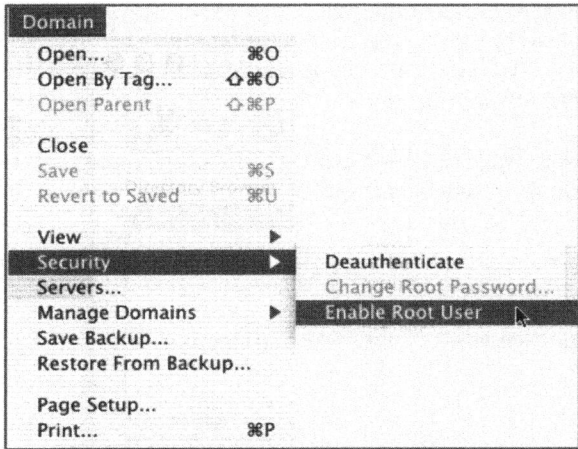

You've now enabled root login. This enables us to log in as root through the Terminal, and will allow it forevermore (well, until you disable it through the Net Info Manager at a later date). When you've done this, you might get the following dialog:

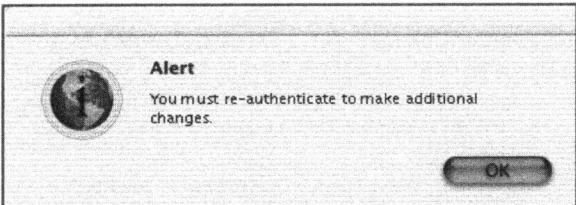

This basically informs you that you need to re-authenticate as an administrator to change the status of the root user at a later date. Now that we've logged in the root user, we can go ahead and log in through the Terminal as root.

> *Unless you're making any significant changes to configuration files, or are installing any software that requires root login, you shouldn't need to log in as root that often – which makes remembering that password for when you do even more important....*

253

Backing up the Apache configuration file

To enable PHP, we're going to use our newly discovered vi skills, while logged in as the root user. This will enable us to make some changes to the configuration file to get everything working. Before we do this, we're going to make a backup of the original config file, something that we can revert back to in the event of any unforeseen circumstances.

1. To back up this file, we need to log in as the much touted root user. Open the Terminal application, and enter su- (short for Super User) at the command-line:

   ```
   [localhost:~] kris% su-
   ```

2. You'll be greeted and asked to confirm the command with a 'yes' or 'no'. Press the Y key for yes:

   ```
   OK? su?
   ```

3. Now, you'll have to enter the root user password:

   ```
   OK? su? yes
   Password:
   ```

   If the authentication was correct, then you'll see the command-line from a root perspective, and we're ready to back up the configuration file.

   ```
   [localhost:/Users/kris] root#
   ```

4. Enter this line to change the current directory to the required one (make sure you place all the slashes in correctly):

   cd /etc/httpd/

5. Now type ls to get a directory listing:

   ```
   [localhost:/users/kris] root# cd /etc/httpd/
   [localhost:/etc/httpd] root# ls
   httpd.conf           httpd.conf.prefix    magic.default        mime.types.default
   httpd.conf.default   magic                mime.types           users
   ```

6. The file httpd.conf is the file that we need to modify, and therefore is the one that we need to back up. For the backup name we'll comply with tradition and add the .bak extension. Type this into the command-line:

   cp httpd.conf http.conf.bak

   The cp command is short for copy. The parameters for this command are:

Introducing Dynamic Content

```
cp <original filename> <duplicate filename>
```

In other words, our code takes the original filename and produces a backup copy with the different specified name. Easy, huh?

7. Once you've done this, type ls to get the file listing again:

```
[localhost:/etc/httpd] root# cp httpd.conf httpd.conf.bak
[localhost:/etc/httpd] root# ls
httpd.conf            httpd.conf.prefix     mime.types
httpd.conf.bak        magic                 mime.types.default
httpd.conf.default    magic.default         users
```

You'll see the newly copied `httpd.conf.bak` file, along with all the other files and folders. We can now safely go ahead and change the original file, with the safety net of a backup file if all goes wrong.

Editing the httpd.conf file with vi

Now that we have a backup file and we're logged in as root, we can use vi to edit our config file. If you can't remember how to delete and move around in vi, check back to our earlier exercise.

1. To open up the `httpd.conf` file in vi, enter the following into the command-line:

```
vi httpd.conf
```

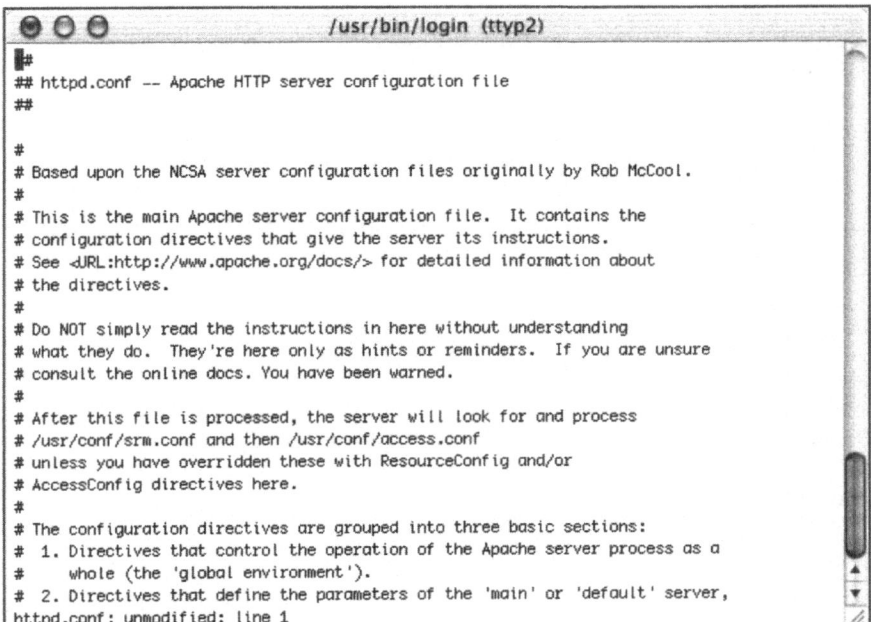

Foundation Dreamweaver MX

You should see something like the screenshot on previous page. As we said earlier, every line with a # is a comment line. This initial text is just the pre-code introductory stuff.

2. There are a few lines in this file that we need to find and uncomment, so that they actually run. First, find the following line:

   ```
   # LoadModule php4_module        libexec/httpd/libphp4.so
   ```

3. When you have it in your sights, remove the # from the start of the line, leaving this:

   ```
   LoadModule php4_module        libexec/httpd/libphp4.so
   ```

4. Now locate this line and remove the comment # from the start of it:

   ```
   # AddModule mod_php4.c
   ```

5. Do the same for these two lines (which will be found together):

   ```
   # AddType application/x-httpd-php .php
       # AddType application/x-httpd-php-source .phps
   ```

6. Once all are uncommented, you need to save the file and quit by typing:

   ```
   :wq
   ```

   ... and pressing enter. Don't expect to see any confirmation that you've saved or exited here – because there isn't any! The best way to check if your changes have taken place is to reopen the file and to check the lines that you uncommented.

7. Type `exit` twice to quit the root user and the current command-line session. Then quit the Terminal application.

8. Finally, restart the Apache web server through the Sharing control panel (click Stop and then Start), so that it restarts and recognizes the changes we've just made.

Okay, you've done it - PHP has been switched on, and you're ready to test the installation has taken place.

Using PHP in Dreamweaver

This is the point at which Mac and PC users can join back up again. We should now have Apache and PHP installed nicely on our systems, so that we can leave that murky world of install instructions and text files behind and return to the cosy confines of Dreamweaver.

It's very easy to set everything up in Dreamweaver.

Introducing Dynamic Content

Testing PHP

1. Open up Dreamweaver. Go to File > New and then select Dynamic Page from the Category menu on the left. (You may need to select the General tab at the top first, instead of the Templates one that we've been using in previous chapters.) From the Dynamic Page menu on the right, select PHP, and then click Create.

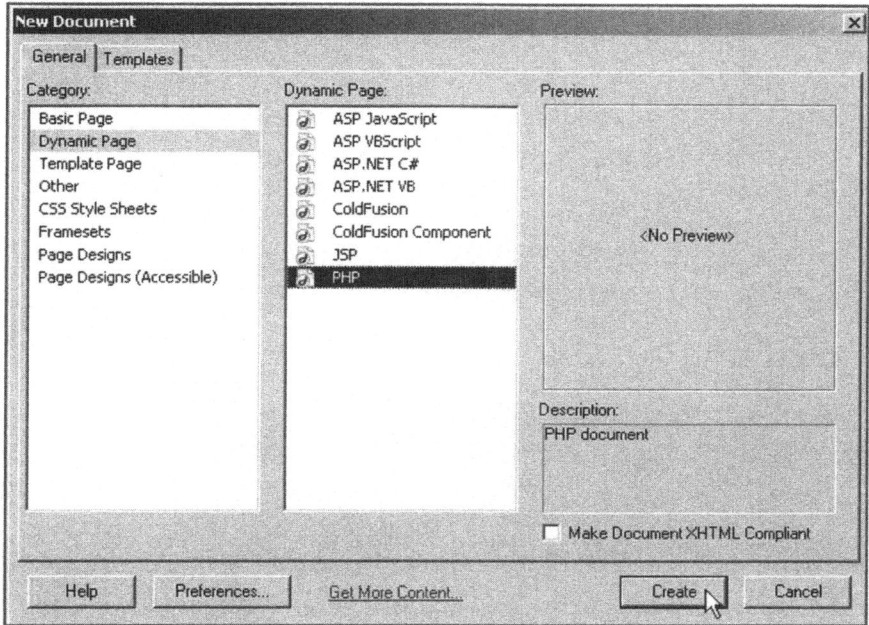

2. If you aren't already in Code and Design view, select this.

3. Between the <body> tags in the Code View enter this line (don't worry about what it all means at this stage; we'll come back to that):

```
<?
    echo "Hello World!";
?>
```

Foundation Dreamweaver MX

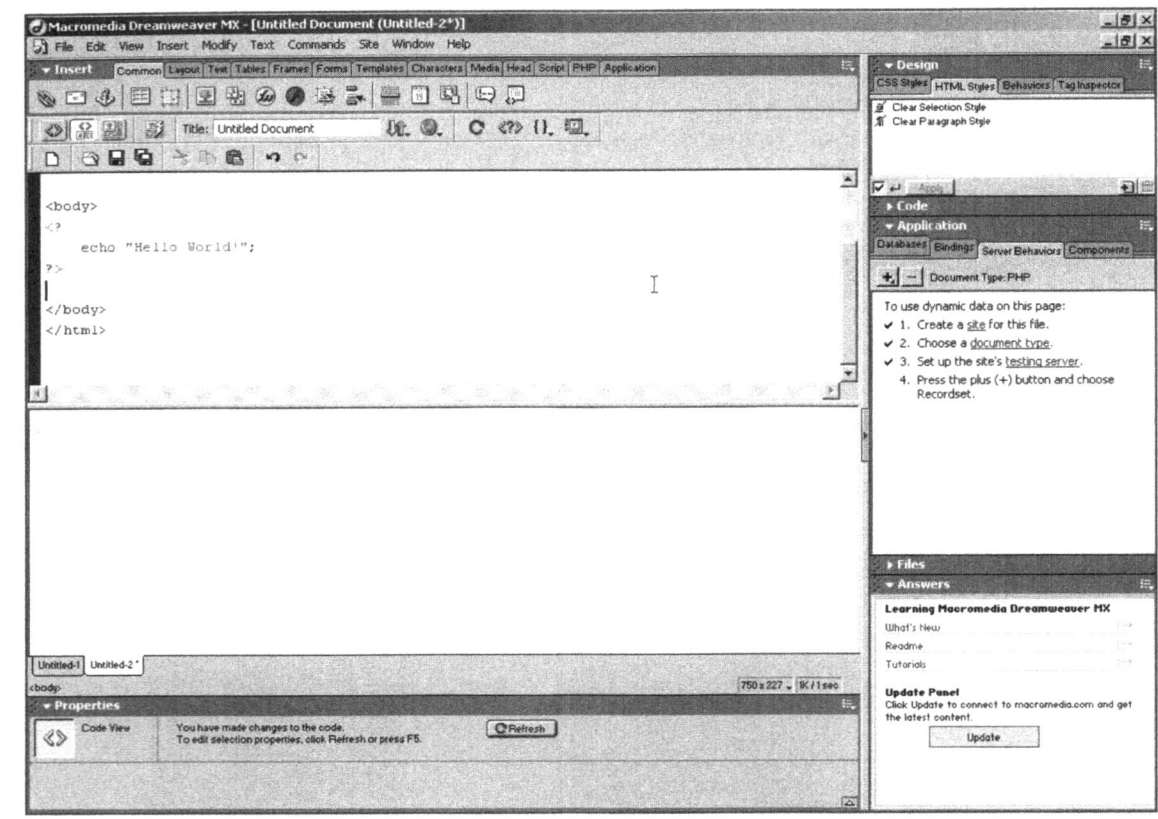

4. Save this file as test.php in the root directory of your web server. For PC users who followed the installation instructions to the letter, this will be C:\Program Files\Apache Group\apache\htdocs. For Mac users, this will be Macintosh HD > Users > <Username> >Sites.

> It's important to note that these directories are your root directories. These are the folders in which you should save all the PHP files we create.

5. PC users, point your browser at http://localhost/test.php. Mac users, point your browsers at http://127.0.0.1/~username/test.php, adding your username in place of the "username" text in the URL. You should get something like this:

Introducing Dynamic Content 8

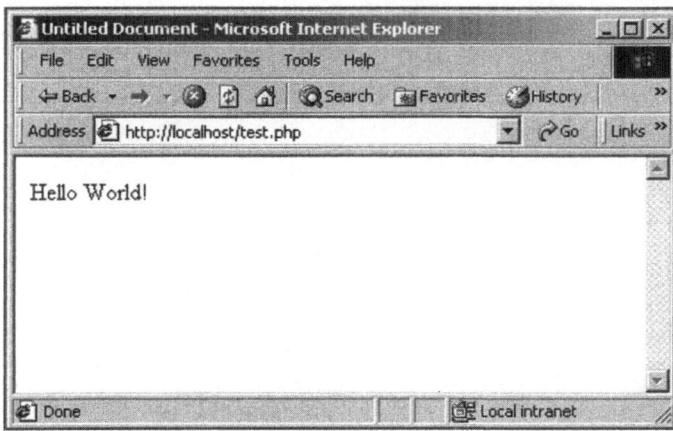

6. Let's do a final test to check our PHP installation. Create a new file in Dreamweaver just like the last one.

7. Instead of typing:

   ```
   <?
        echo "Hello World!";
   ?>
   ```

   Type:

   ```
   <?
        echo phpinfo();
   ?>
   ```

8. Save this file as `phpinfo.php` in the same directory as `test.php`.

9. Load it up in your browser and you should get something that looks like this:

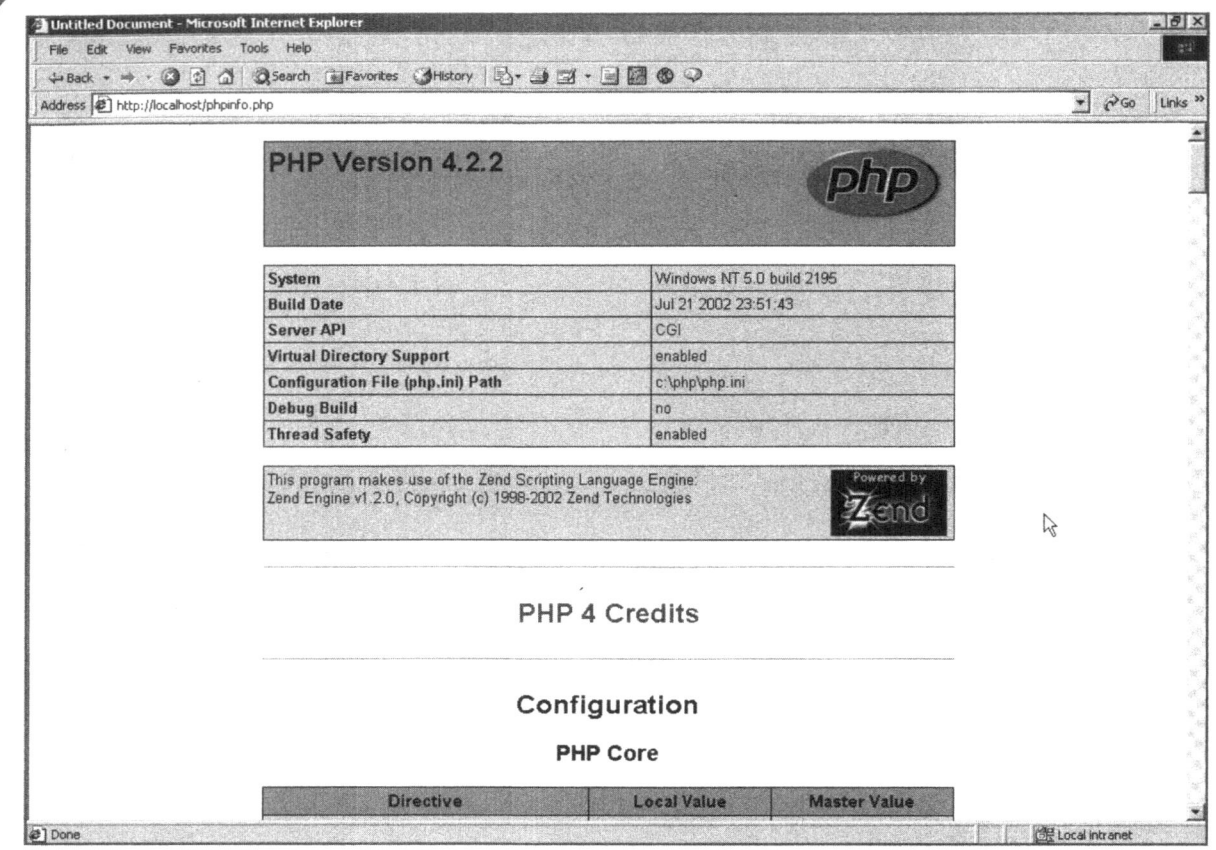

If your browser window looks like the one above then you're onto a winner, and you can assume the position of self-satisfaction. This screen basically tells you what version of PHP you're running at the top, and some other details that you don't need to worry until later on.

Troubleshooting

If your installation failed, here's a couple of things to try:

PC users: check that all modifications made to the `httpd.conf` file used the forward slash syntax instead of the normal backslash:

```
ScriptAlias /cgi-bin/ "C:/Program Files/Apache Group/apache/cgi-bin/"
ScriptAlias /php/ "C:/php/"
```

Mac users: check that the changes to the `httpd.conf` file were successfully saved. You could also return to the backup file, and try again.

Users of both platforms need to make absolutely certain that they restarted the web server after making changes to the configuration file, as changes to the configuration only take effect when you restart the web server. Start it again just to be on the safe side.

If you're still having problems, support is available from the developer's web sites:

Apache – www.apache.org
PHP – www.php.net

Or you could take the easy way out. This involves a simple search for a web hosting company that you can use to test your scripts. Here are a few examples, in no way guaranteed by friends of ED:

Free:
www.free-php-hosting.com/
http://free-php.cjb.net/
www.oinko.net/freephp/link.php

Paid:
www.phpwebhosting.com/
www.dotservant.com/
www.xcalibre.co.uk

Summary

This chapter has been hard work, and you've been introduced to some new concepts, not to mention scary stuff like editing config files. You deserve a rest before the next chapter, but don't leave it too long. Now that you have PHP and Apache up and running, we can start beginning to unwrap the incredible power that Dreamweaver offers your web sites.

Using PHP and Apache

What we'll cover in this chapter

- Setting Dreamweaver up to test our PHP
- Learning the basics of PHP
- Creating forms with PHP and Dreamweaver
- Building a guest book using PHP and Dreamweaver

In this chapter, we'll take a look at how PHP works, and use our PHP/Apache installation to write a guest book that processes a form and e-mails both you and the user.

Defining a Server Model

First, though, we've got to set up Dreamweaver so that we can test our PHP pages from within Dreamweaver, rather than just running our PHP files from outside.

1. Create a new folder in your root directory where Apache stores your web pages. Call the new folder `friends_of_ed`.

2. Open the site wizard that we saw back in the early chapters of the book (select Site from the top menu and then select New Site from the drop down menu if you can't quite remember that far back).

3. Once the wizard is open (if you don't see the wizard as below, make sure the Basic tab is selected) you'll be asked to provide a name for your site. Name it `foe_book`, and click the Next button.

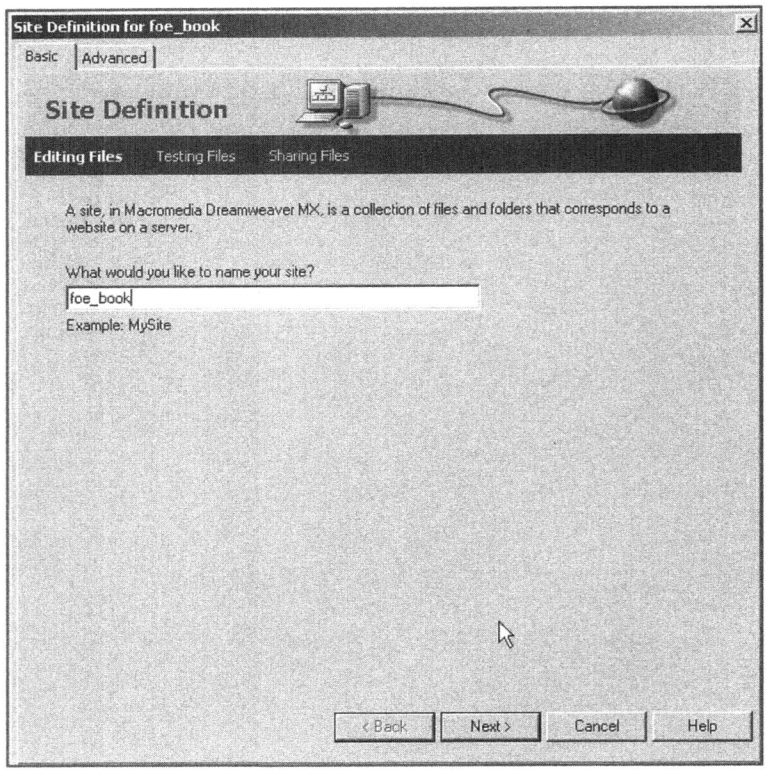

4. In the next page, you are given an option of whether you wish to use a server technology or not. We have to select the second option: Yes I want to use a server technology. Once this option is selected, a menu will appear. Select PHP MySQL, and click Next.

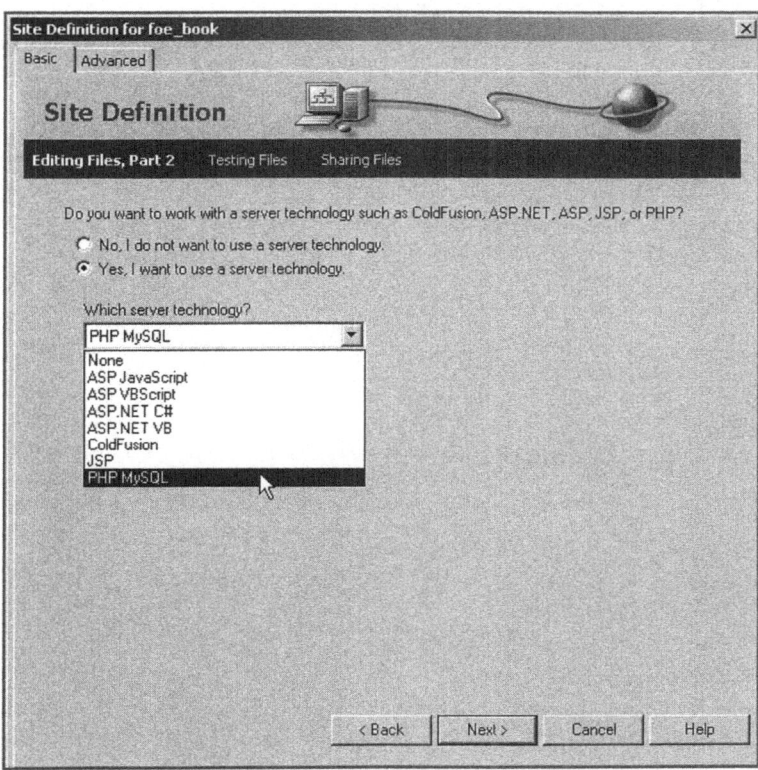

5. The next thing we have to do is to tell Dreamweaver where we will store our files during development. In our case, we have Apache/PHP and MySQL running locally, so select the first option from the list.

6. For our PHP pages to execute, we need to store them in the root directory where Apache stores your web pages. Click on the folder icon and browse to the root directory. Double click on the folder we created earlier (friends_of_ed) and press Select.

> *Dreamweaver will create two folders called* _mmserverscripts *and* Connections *within our defined folder, and these folders will hold the necessary information when we connect to our database in the next chapter.*

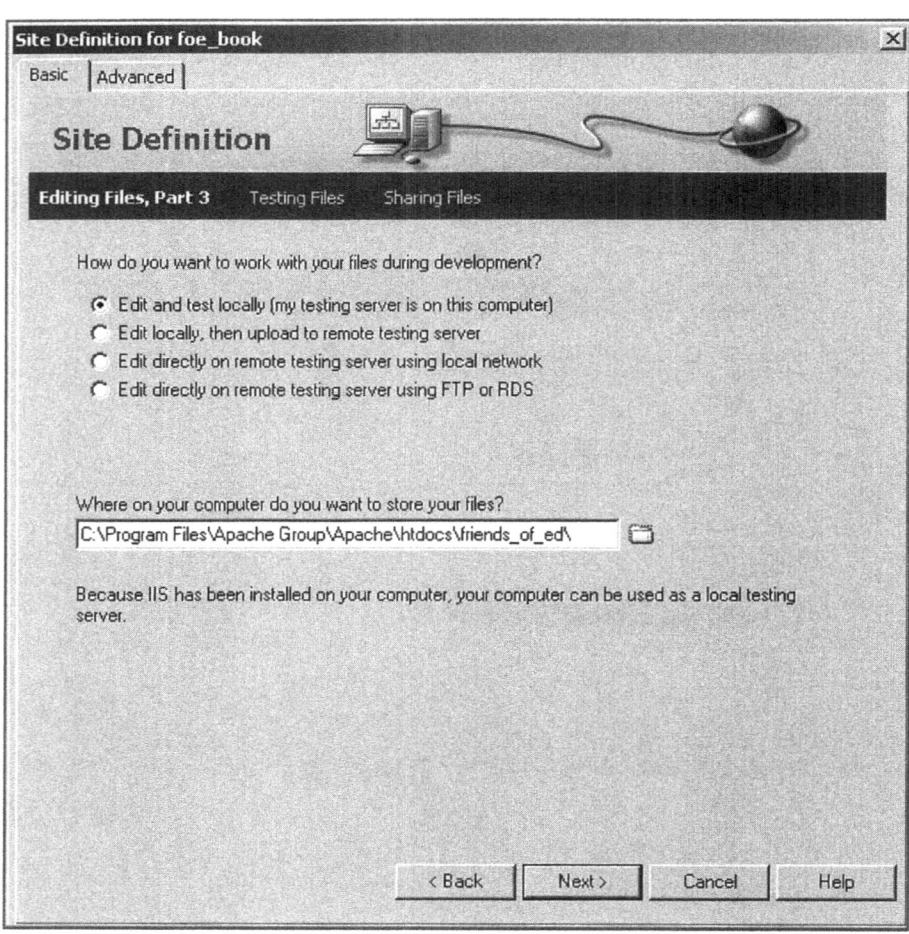

Using PHP and Apache

7. Click Next, and we now have to enter the path to our root folder: http://localhost/friends_of_ed. Don't click Next quite yet, though.

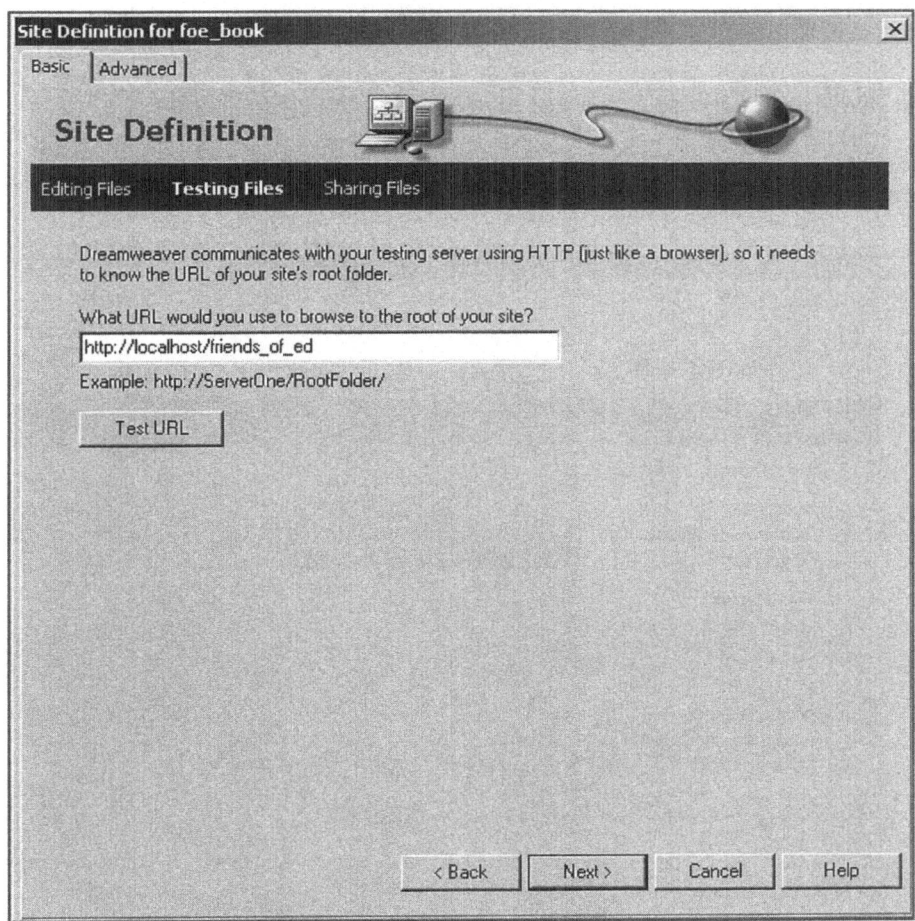

8. Press the *Test URL* button. If we configured everything correctly, then you should get a dialog box telling you that the URL Prefix test was successful. If not, and you get a message similar to the one pictured, make sure you have entered the correct path to the folder we created.

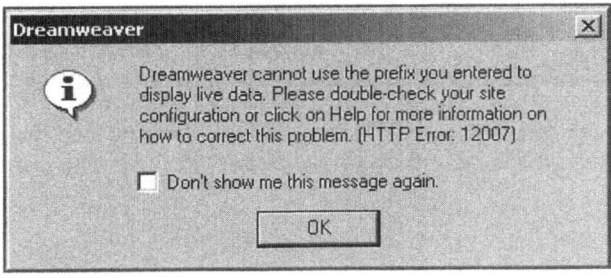

Foundation Dreamweaver MX

If your path is correct and things still go wrong, then repeat steps 1 to 4. If Apache isn't running you'll get a different error message at this stage, and you'll need to start Apache.

9. Once you get a successful Test, click OK to close the message box, and then Next

10. On the next screen of the wizard we want the second option from the two available because our files are stored locally, so select the No radio button and click Next.

11. The last screen is a summary of the information you've provided. Read through it to ensure your information is correct and click Done.

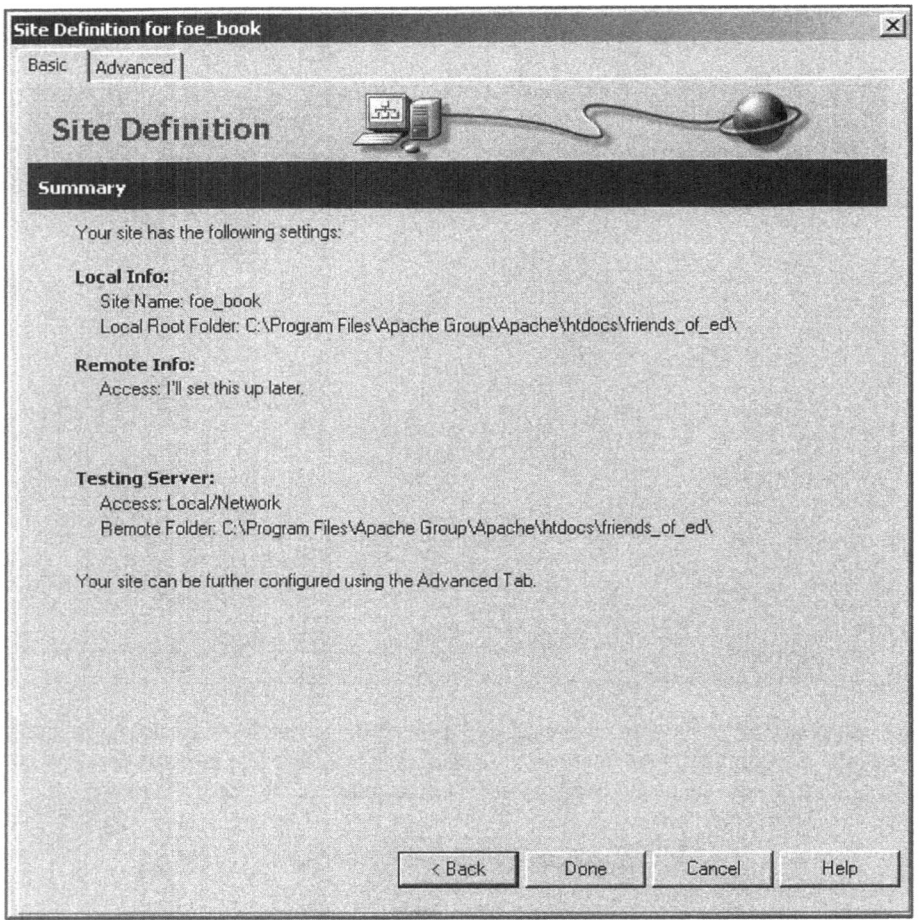

12. As a test, copy our phpinfo.php file from the last chapter into the new foe_book directory. Open it, and preview it in your browser – now we don't have to move out of Dreamweaver at all.

Using PHP and Apache

An introduction to PHP

We're going to start our introduction to PHP by looking at three important factors to bear in mind start tags, semi-colons, and comments. We'll then proceed to take a look at the key parts of PHP that we'll be using in our exercises.

You must always begin your PHP code with a **PHP start tag** so that the server knows that PHP is coming. You can use <?PHP or simply <?. When you're done with the code and want to switch back to HTML, you can just type the PHP end tag, which is ?>.

PHP allows you to embed PHP code in regular HTML pages and execute the embedded PHP code when the page is requested. It's not uncommon to see something like this:

```
<HTML>
Hi There, <?PHP echo $username; ?>
</HTML>
```

If $username=Matt (more on this in a moment) and someone views the source code of the site, PHP will check the value of username, and enter it in. All the user will see is:

```
<HTML>
Hi There, Matt
</HTML>
```

> *Each line of PHP must end with a semicolon. This is important to remember, as it's by far the most common mistake made by new programmers.*

A **comment** is text that you insert in your code to describe what the code is doing. When you run your code, comments are ignored. This might not seem immediately useful, but when you come back to your code to try and fix it, or re-use it – and particularly when other people are going to be looking at your code – it becomes invaluable.

More importantly, it's very easy to do in PHP - just add // before the comment. For example:

```
<?PHP
// this is a comment
?>
```

9   Foundation Dreamweaver MX

If you want to comment on more than one line, you can type /* to start the comment and */ to end it. Dreamweaver has a special PHP bar that automates frequent PHP tasks for us, and this is one of them. Select PHP from the Insert bar at the top of the screen, and you'll find it to the right of the echo button, as shown.

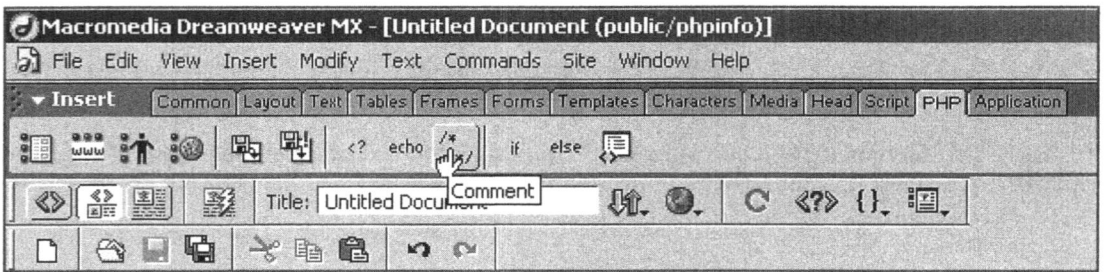

Variables

All that information we were talking about when we looked at Amazon in the last chapter has to be stored somewhere so that we can move it around. The way that we pass information within and between PHP scripts is by storing it in **variables**. A variable is a symbol or a name that represents a value.

Your wallet, for example, holds money. The actual money it holds goes up and down and changes from time to time. Equally, your fridge holds foodstuffs (and maybe the odd liquid). The content of your fridge will change depending on when you last went to the shop, whether you're on a diet, and so on...

Variables hold information in the same way – they're created to hold a type of information (you probably wouldn't go putting cash in your fridge, and yoghurt in your back pocket, would you?), but that information can change. Say Amazon has a variable called "MattS", then it could change from "loggedon" to "loggedoff", or even from "well-off" to "poor" as I spend more money on that elusive complete collection of friends of ED books.

You'll have come across this before – remember your algebra math lessons in school? In the expression $a+b$, a and b are variables, and they can represent any number.

Each variable has a **name** and a **data type**.

Variable names

PHP imposes some constraints on how you name your variables. The simple rule to remember is that you can only use alphanumeric characters and the underscore character in your variable names, and that the first character *must not* be a number! You can see some examples of some good and bad variable names in the screenshot...

Using PHP and Apache

```php
?>
    // This file is in the downloads as badvarnames.php
    $1stNumber = 15;        // Bad! Cannot start with a number!
    $your name = "Steve";   // Bad! Spaces not allowed!
    $sun&moon = true;       // Bad! Alphanumeric and _ only!

    $firstNumber = 15;        // Good!
    $your_name = "Steve";     // Good!
    $sunAndMoon = true;       // Good!
    $_test = "Good";          // Good! Can start with _
?>
```

Variable data types

PHP variables have three data types:

- **Integers** are used to store whole numbers (in other words, numbers with no fractional part) within a range of approx. -2,000,000,000 to +2,000,000,000. An example of an integer might be 5.

- **Doubles** (also known as float or real numbers) are used to represent numbers that have a decimal value or an exponential part, for example 2.765 or even 2.0.

- **Strings** are used to represent non-numerical values and are encased in quote marks, such as "I am a non numerical value" or even "2"!

You don't really need to worry too much about this - what's nice about PHP is that, unlike other programming languages, it auto-detects what data type the variable is. This means that you don't have to define an integer as `int $number=2;`, but just use `$number=2;`.

> *Variables are case sensitive - so* $name, $NAME, *and* $Name *are all different as far as PHP is concerned.*

Creating variables

This is all getting a bit confusing, so it's time to put what we've just learnt into practice.

1. Open a new PHP file in Dreamweaver by selecting the Dynamic Page and PHP options from the New Document dialog box.

2. Enter the following code after the first `<body>` tag in the code window:

```
<?

// Define Variables
$username=deviantART;
$password=dotcom;

?>
```

3. We're going to use `echo` to display the values of the two variables we've set up. Before the end `?>` tag of the code you've just entered, add this comment and line:

```
// Sends text and variables to the browser.
echo "<b>Username:</b> $username<BR><b>Password:</b> $password";
```

Dreamweaver MX has an `echo` button on the PHP toolbar that you might like to use in the future. Here, it's easier just to type it, as the toolbar will also insert a needless pair of `<?php ?>` tags.

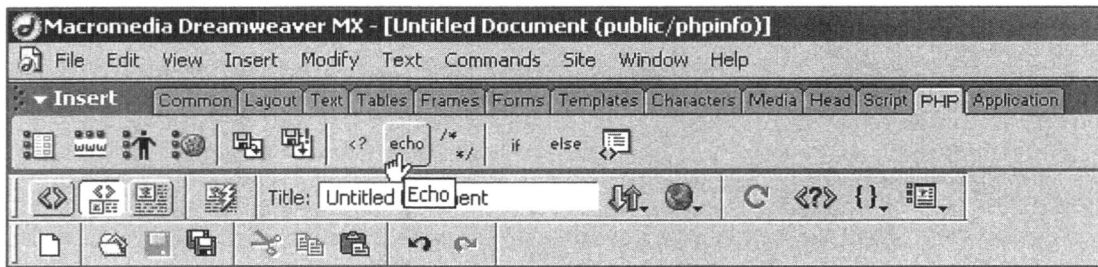

4. Test the script, and you should get something like this:

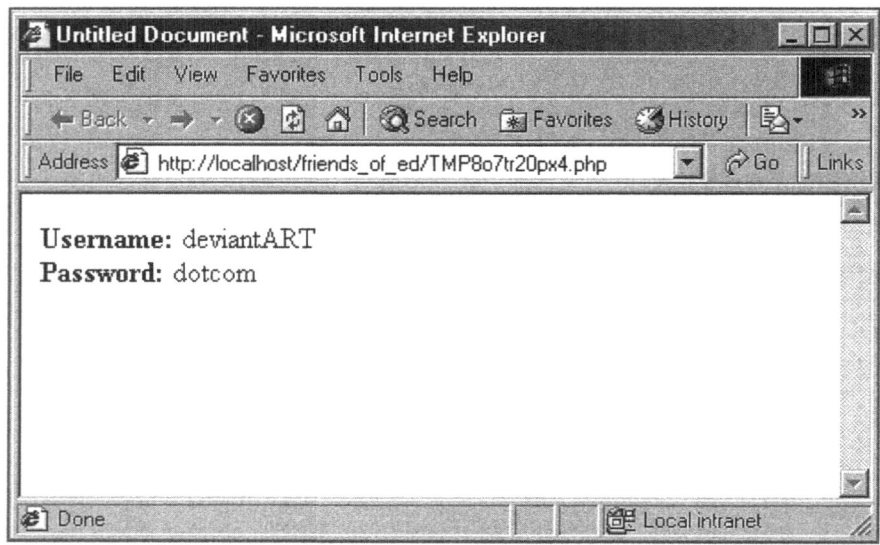

Great! We've created our variables. Now let's see what we can do with them... **Operators** take variables and 'operate' on them.

5. We'll start with the simple mathematical operators that add, subtract, divide, and multiply. Delete the last script, and enter this one into your code window:

```
<?

$add1 = 1;
$add2 = 2;
$sum=$add1 + $add2;
echo $sum;

?>
```

6. Test this in your browser, and you should see just the number 3 displayed. That's because the variable $sum simply takes the other variables, $add1 and $add2, which are 1 and 2 respectively, and adds them using the operator +, giving us 3.

7. Now we can take what we've learned and do pretty much any kind of math that we can think of. Here's a slightly more complex example, so replace your previous script with this:

```
<?

$number = 3;
$number2 = 2;
$multiply = $number * $number2;
$divide = $number / $number2;
$subtract = $number - $number2;


echo "$number times $number2 equals $multiply <BR>";
echo "$number divided by $number2 equals $divide <BR>";
echo "$number minus $number2 equals $subtract <BR>";

?>
```

8. Test this in your browser, and you should get something like this:

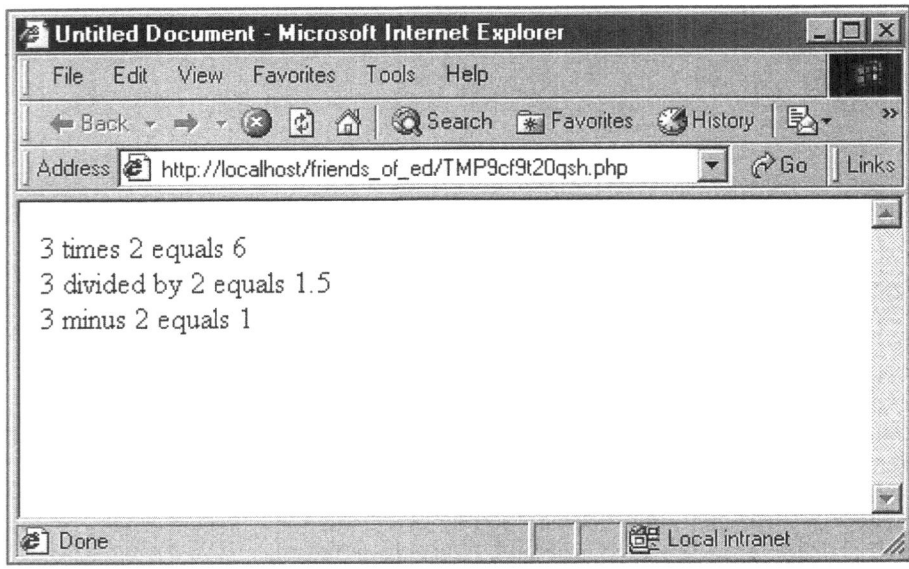

9. This time, let's try some string variables instead of numerical ones. Enter this script, and test it in your browser:

```
<?

$string1="Hello World!";
$string2="How are you?";
$string3="I'm doing well.";

echo "$string1 <BR> $string2 <BR> $string3";

?>
```

Using variables in other scripts

Once you start getting into the swing of things, you'll be using variables all over the place, and it's then that our first problem arises – what if you want to use a variable you created in one script somewhere else? Say, for example, that I had a variable storing a user's login name for the entry screen, but also wanted to use it in the main site to greet the user – what would I do? The answer is to make one file to hold all the variables for a project, and include that file in each script.

Including files

Let's see how we can do this. If we `include` a file in a PHP script, then it parses or pastes the file you're including into that line - so we just need to make a script to hold our variables, and then `include` it in our other scripts.

1. Create another new PHP file in Dreamweaver, and type the following code between the Body tags:

   ```
   <?
   
   $greeting="What's going on?";
   $greeting2="How are you today?";
   $greeting3="Good morning.";
   $greeting4="Good afternoon.";
   $greeting5="Good evening.";
   
   ?>
   ```

2. Save this file as `greetings.php`.

3. Replace the code above with this:

   ```
   <?
   
   include("greetings.php");
   echo "Hello World!<BR>";
   echo $greeting;
   
   ?>
   ```

4. This time, save the file as `hello.php` (make sure that it's in the same folder as `greetings.php`).

5. Test your `hello.php` file in a browser:

   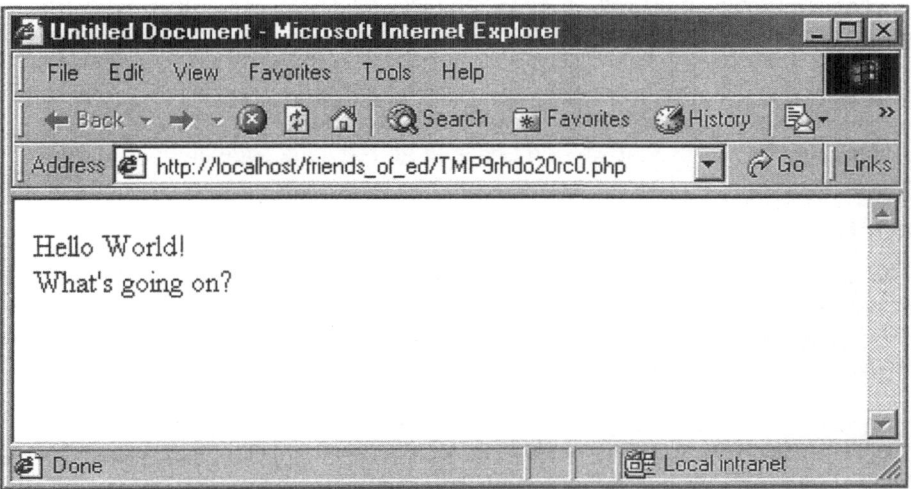

6. Back in Dreamweaver, alter the greeting in the last line to

   ```
   echo $greeting2;
   ```

7. Save this file, and test it, and you'll see that it pulls the relevant greeting out of our original `greetings.php` file.

You can also `include` HTML files in your PHP scripts. You could use what we learned in the early part of the book, and create a graphical header that you wanted to use for all your site files, for example. You could then use:

```
<?

include("header.html");

?>
```

in each file that you wanted to use the header in. Dreamweaver makes this even easier for you by providing an `include();` button on the PHP bar.

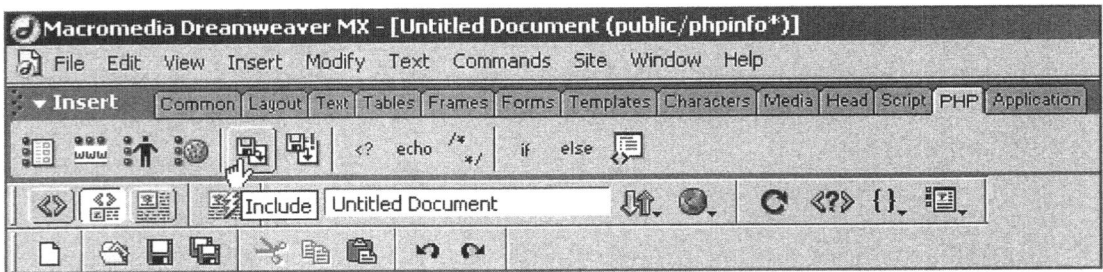

These are very simple ways of using the `include` statement, but you can see how useful it can be in large sites. If you need to change something, instead of having to go through each individual file, you can simply change one file and it will affect all the files that `include` it. Most webmasters use this for navigation bars, usernames, passwords, or anything that has to be used repeatedly throughout the site.

www.deviantART.com, the site I started with a friend of mine, uses a 'config' file that holds URLs, usernames, and any small sections of code that we have to use on a daily basis. We `include` this in all our other files, and this means that we don't have to go re-typing code all the time.

Forms and PHP

Another way that we can pass variables around is through **forms**, and this is a good way to get input from users and then store or process the information. When you set up a form, each type of input has a value. When the form is submitted, it names variables after each field and stores the information that the user entered in those variables.

For example, if we set up a form with a space for me to enter my name, we might call that space "name". When someone entered their name into that space on our site, and clicked a button to submit it, PHP would store that person's name in a variable called (you guessed it) $name.

There are two ways of moving information from the form: **GET** and **POST**. You've probably noticed that, on web sites like Amazon, the URL looks something like this when you bookmark a page: www.amazon.com/redirect.php?url=http://www.whatever.com.

Using PHP and Apache

This is a perfect example of a form using the GET method, as GET places the variables in the URL after a question mark. Most sites use the GET method, so that people can easily access the page again when they bookmark it. You can use POST to hide variables from forms, which is good if you are submitting anything you don't want people to see (don't go thinking this is totally secure, though).

Once you've set the method of moving the information, you need also to tell a form where to send the information entered into it – we'll be sending ours to a file called `login.php`, which we'll create in a moment. As we said earlier, the name of the field is also the name of the variable in which the information is stored, so we'll be using the field name in `login.php` to access the information our user enters.

Making a form

Let's take a look at an example of a form in action. Before we start on our form, we have to do one thing, and that is to tell PHP to allow our variables to be passed using the GET method. PHP is by default set to not allow this with version 4.2.2 (earlier versions were different), because of the risk of someone using this rather less-than-secure method to pass secure information.

1. PC users: open up your php.ini file using the instructions from the last chapter, and find the line above. Change the register_globals value from off to on, as shown, and restart your Apache server.

   ```
   You should do your best to write your scripts so that they do not require
   ; register_globals to be on;  Using form variables as globals can easily
   ➥lead
   ; to possible security problems, if the code is not very well thought of.
   register_globals = on
   ```

   Mac users: unlike PC users, you won't have altered your php.ini file in the last chapter. This is because you don't actually have a `php.ini` file. If you are running PHP 4.2.2 (run your `phpinfo.php` file again if you don't know), then you'll have to create one. To do this, return to your terminal, sign in as super user with –su, and navigate to the `usr/local` folder. Type `sudo mkdir -p /usr/local/lib` to create the directory, and then `sudo touch /usr/local/lib/php.ini` to create the `php.ini` file. Type `vi php.ini` to edit the file, and add the line: `register_globals = on` before exiting and saving.

2. Change the `register_globals` value from `off` to `on`, as shown above, and restart your Apache server.

3. Create a new PHP file in Dreamweaver.

4. Add the following after the `<body>` tag

   ```
   <form method="GET" action="login.php">
   ```

   This line tells the form to use the GET method we discussed earlier. It also tells the form what to do with the information once it is submitted - `action="login.php"` tells the browser to send the variable to `login.php`.

5. Now add this directly underneath the previous line:

   ```
   <font size="3">Username:</font size>
   <input type="text" name="name" size="10">

   <input type="submit">


   </form>
   ```

   This sets up the graphics that you'll see in the Design window – the text "Username", and a "Submit" button next to it.

6. Save this file as form.php, and test it in your browser. You should see something like the screenshot.

   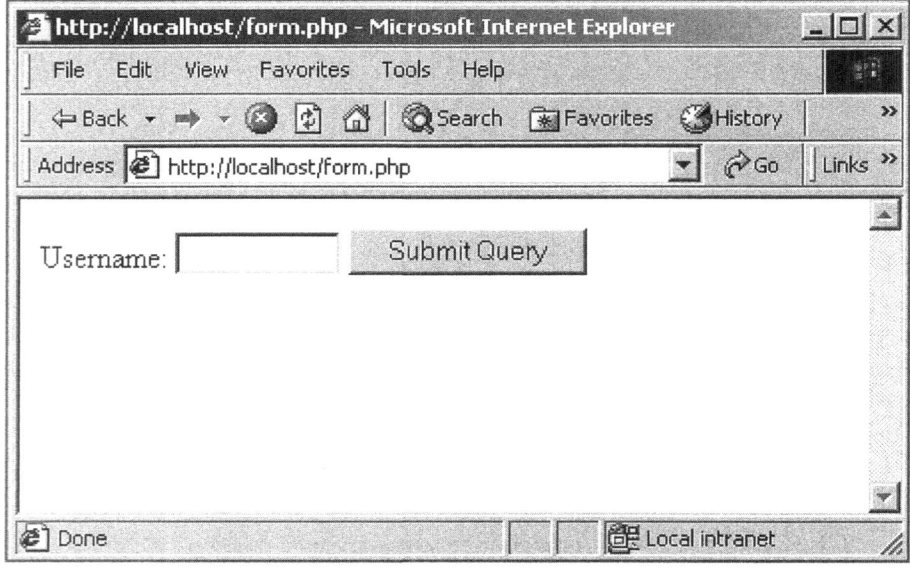

   Try to submit your name, and you'll get an error. Why? Because we haven't made login.php yet, so that the data we enter has nowhere to go when we hit the submit button.

7. Create another new PHP file in Dreamweaver.

8. Type the following after the <body> tag:

   ```
   <?
   echo "Username: $name";
   ?>
   ```

In `form.php`, we set the name of the field to `$name` (`<input type="text" name="name" size="10">`). As the name of the field is also the name of the variable, we get the variable `$name` from the form, and we're simply telling this file to display the value of our variable.

9. Save the file as `login.php`. Return to `form.php` again, test it in your browser, and type your name in the box. Hit Submit, and you should see something like the following in your browser (note the variable in the Address line):

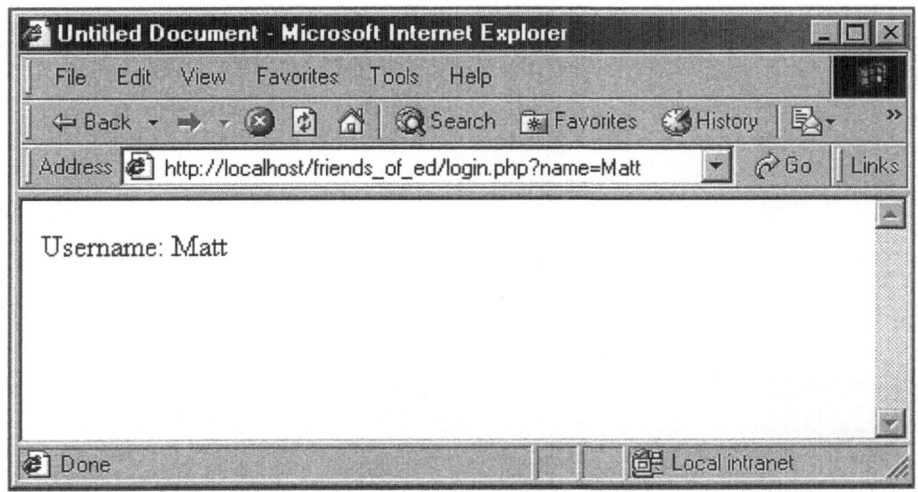

This way of using forms can be used to gather information about users, add products to shopping carts, send text to a chat room, or anything else that requires information from the user.

Conditional Statements

Comparing variables and numbers is a really helpful way of customizing how your site reacts to a user. For example, a form where the user enters their age could make sure that children under the age of 13 aren't allowed to join the site.

To do this, we'd have to tell the script to block the user from entering if the variable `$age` is less than 13:

```
if ($age < 13) {
  echo "You are too young to join.";
}
```

When opening an `if` statement, you start with the `if` statement, then an open parenthesis, then the variable you are comparing. Next comes the actual operator. This tells the script how to compare the two values.

Foundation Dreamweaver MX

There are several kinds of operators, listed in the table below. For the table, assume that $variable1 has a value of 10 and $variable2 a value of 5.

Operator	Definition	How It's Used	Result
==	is equal to	$variable1 == $variable2	False
!=	is not equal to	$variable1 != $variable2	True
>	is greater than	$variable1 > $variable2	True
<	is less than	$variable1 < $variable2	False
>=	is greater than or equal to	$variable1 >= $variable2	True
<=	is less than or equal to	$variable1 <= $variable2	False
===	string and type is equal to	$variable1 === $variable2	True

It's important to remember that = is very different from ==. The first assigns values to things while the other compares one value to another.

"Toto, I have a feeling we're not in Kansas anymore"

Let's try out some slightly more complex 'if' statements. Let's say we can't let in people from Oklahoma that are under the age of 13.

1. Create a new PHP file in Dreamweaver.

2. After the `<body>` tag, type:

   ```
   <form method="GET" action="enter.php">
   
   <font size="-1">Age: </font>
   <input type="text" name="age" size="10"><BR>
   
   <font size="-1">State: </font>
   <input type="text" name="state" size="10">
   
   
   <input type="submit">
   
   
   </form>
   ```

3. You can see that this is very similar to what we've done before – we're setting a form up, this time with two fields (Age and State), and a submit button that's the same as last time. Save this file as `form2.php` in your root directory.

4. Create another new PHP file, and add the following after the `<body>` tag:

```
<?

if ($age < 13) {
    if ($state == "Oklahoma")
        {
echo "We don't allow people under 13 from Oklahoma";
    }
   }
else {
    echo "You are able to enter.";
      }
?>
```

You can see that it's possible to use more than one 'if' statement together. In fact, it's possible to use as many as you want as long as you don't confuse yourself with all the brackets (this is why we line things up so we can see where one bracket begins and ends). We've also added an `else` statement at the end. This simply says that if the first conditional statement is false, or the age is above 13, then PHP should proceed to whatever the `else` action specifies.

5. Save this file as `enter.php` in your root directory.

6. Test `form2.php` in your browser, and you'll see that you get a variety of different options. If you enter an age of less than 13, but a state other than Oklahoma, you'll just get a blank screen. We've got some improvements to make, and this is what we'll be looking at next.

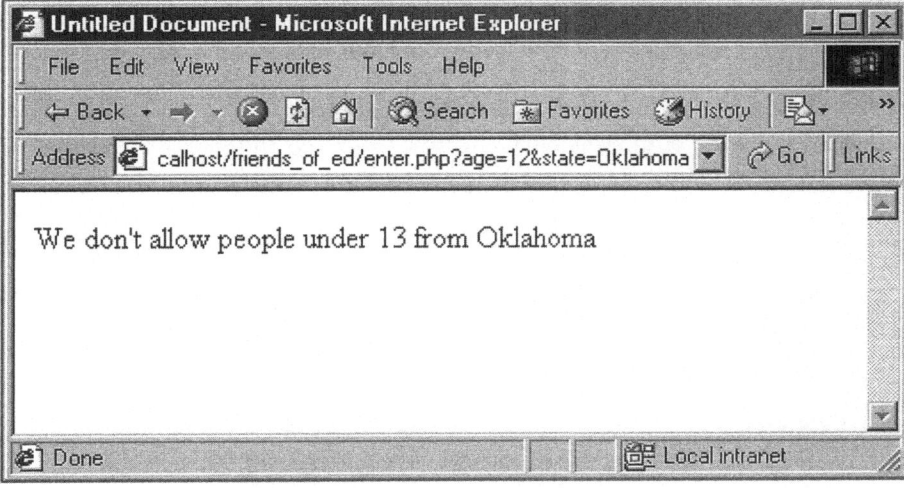

Dreamweaver MX's PHP bar also has `if` and `else` buttons, as shown.

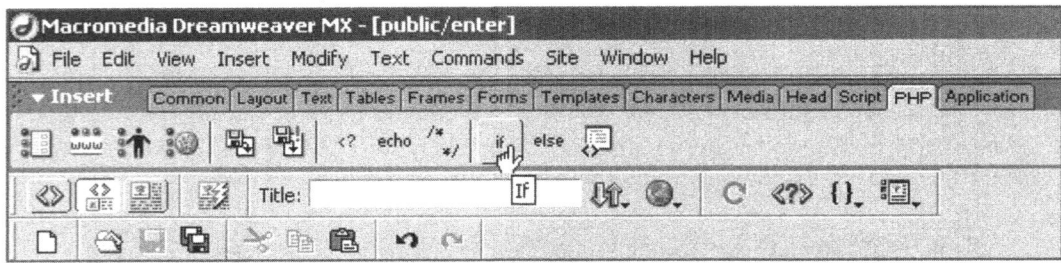

Logical operators

What if you want to exclude both Oklahoma and Texas? One way of doing this would be to combine elements in the 'if' statement using OR and AND. Basically, we could say:

> if the state equals Texas **or** Oklahoma, then don't let them in

OR and AND are **logical operators**. That sounds scary, but you can see from the table that they're quite simple. In the table $variable1="Texas" $variable2="Oklahoma" and $variable3="Kansas" for the sake of an example:

Operator	Definition	How It's Used	Result
&&	AND	if (($variable1=="") && ($variable2==""))	False
||	OR	if (($variable1=="Texas") II ($variable2=="Texas"))	True
!	NOT	if (!$variable1)	False
<=	is less than or equal to	if (($variable1=="") <= ($variable2==""))	True

To use AND or OR, you need two comparisons – say:

```
if ($state == "Oklahoma")
if ($state == "Texas")
```

You then put && or || between these, like so:

```
if ($state == "Oklahoma") || ($state == "Texas")
```

Finally, you have to put parentheses around any comparison you make, like this:

```
if (($state == "Oklahoma") || ($state == "Texas"))
```

(That's Right) You're not from Texas

Let's put what we've just learnt about the logical operators into practice.

1. Open enter.php from the last exercise, and change the second line of your PHP code from

   ```
   if ($state == "Oklahoma")
   ```

   to (not forgetting those parentheses):

   ```
   if (($state == "Oklahoma") || ($state == "Texas"))
      {
   ```

2. Save the file again, and open form2.php in a browser to test the script. This time, someone from Texas aged less than 13 also gets a message.

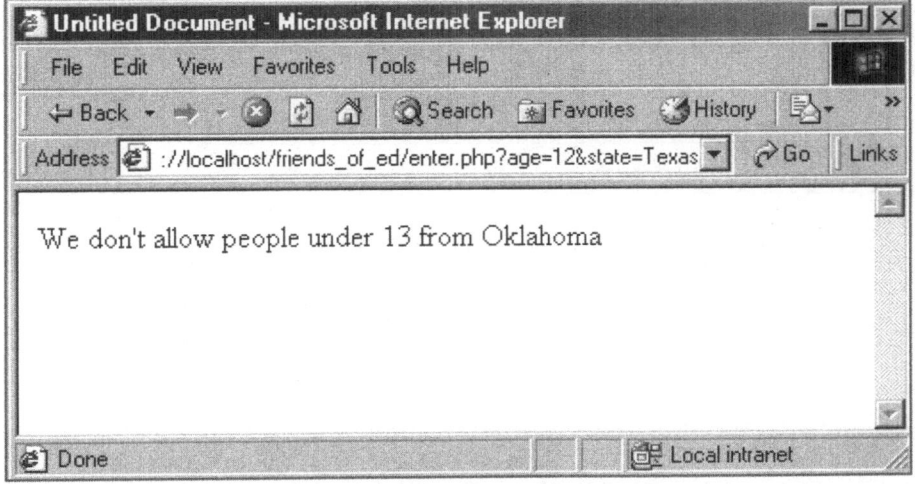

It's a bit of an incorrect message, though, as you can see from the screenshot. Suppose we have more than one situation that we want to check before our `else` takes over. We need to check if the user is from Oklahoma, and if they're not, carry on to check to see if they're from Texas. If both are false, we can grant them access.

3. Change your `enter.php` file so that it reads like this, adding the lines in bold, and removing our OR statement from the second line (not forgetting to remove the second parenthesis from the beginning of the line):

```
<?

if ($age < 13) {
    if ($state == "Oklahoma")
        {
echo "We don't allow people under 13 from Oklahoma";
}
    elseif ($state == "Texas")
    {
echo "We don't allow people under 13 from Texas";
}

}
else {
    echo "You are able to enter.";
    }
?>
```

4. Save this, and test `form2.php` in your browser. If you enter an age of less than 13 and Texas, then you now get an appropriate message returned.

Using PHP and Apache

5. As an extra step, we can make sure that people don't make a mistake. Add these two lines at the bottom of your `enter.php` file, just before the `?>` tag at the end.

   ```
   if ($state === $age) {
   echo "State and Age must be different types and not equal.";
   }
   ```

6. Save the file, and open `form2.php` in a browser to test the script. Enter the same number or state in both entry boxes. The `===` operator checks to see if the variable is the same type first, then also checks to see if the value is the same. If it is, then you get the error text.

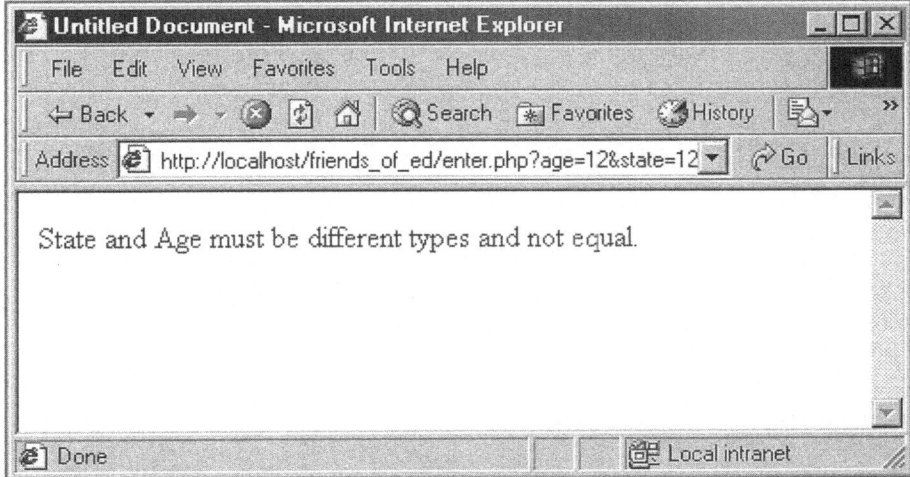

Integrating the form and entry screen

So far, we've been using separate form and enter PHP files. It's actually quite easy to do everything in one file, cutting down on the amount of PHP files you have running your site.

1. Create a new PHP file in Dreamweaver and add the following:

   ```
   <?
   if ($name=="")
    {
   // this says that if the name is empty, to display the form.
   ?>
   <font face="Verdana" size="2">
   Enter Your Name:
   ```

```
        </font>
        <form method="GET" action=greeting.php>

        <input type="text" name="name">
        <input type="submit" value="Submit">

        </form>
        </body>

        </html>

        <?
         }
        else
         {

         ?>

        <html>
        <font face="Verdana" size="2">
        <body>
        Hello, <? echo $name; ?>. How are you?
        </font>
        </body>
        </html>


        <? } ?>
```

We start out with an `if` statement to see if the form is being submitted or displayed. If it is being submitted then the variable $name will already have a value. If it's just being displayed, it will be empty. This also prevents people from entering nothing into the name field and hitting submit, as this would just mean that they see an empty form again.

What happens if the name isn't empty? We proceed to the `else` statement, which prints a greeting to the name that was initially entered.

2. Notice that we put the action as going to greeting.php. Save this file as greeting.php, and our code will submit to itself.

3. Test it in your browser to check that everything's ok, and you should be met by a friendly greeting...

Guest books

So, we've had some fun in this chapter, and learned a lot about PHP. We're going to finish off by putting this knowledge together to build something that can be really useful on any site – a guest book. You may remember that, back in chapter 6, we promised you that you'd be able to create this later in the book. Well, we're finally fulfilling our promise.

First, we're going to make the form for our guests to enter their details in, then we'll see how we process the information that we get.

Making the form for our guest book

Our guest book will use another of those forms that we've seen so much of in this chapter. It will mail you as webmaster with the details of the form and the person who filled out the form with a confirmation message.

1. Create a new PHP file in Dreamweaver. Give it the title Survey in the box in the bar just above the code window.

2. As usual, add this after the `<body>` tag:

```
<form name="guestbook" method="post" action="guestbook_post.php">
  <table width="400" border="0" cellspacing="1" cellpadding="2">
    <tr>
      <td><div align="right">Name:</div></td>
      <td><input type="text" name="name"></td>
    </tr>
    <tr>
```

```
                <td><div align="right">E-mail:</div></td>
                <td><input type="text" name="email"></td>
            </tr>
            <tr>
                <td><div align="right">Phone Number: </div></td>
                <td><input type="text" name="phone"></td>
            </tr>
            <tr>
                <td> </td>
                <td><input type="submit" name="Submit" value="Submit"></td>
            </tr>
        </table>
    </form>
```

3. Save this file as `guestbook.php`. Test it in your browser, or just look in Design view, and you should be able to see that we've created a form with three fields and a Submit button.

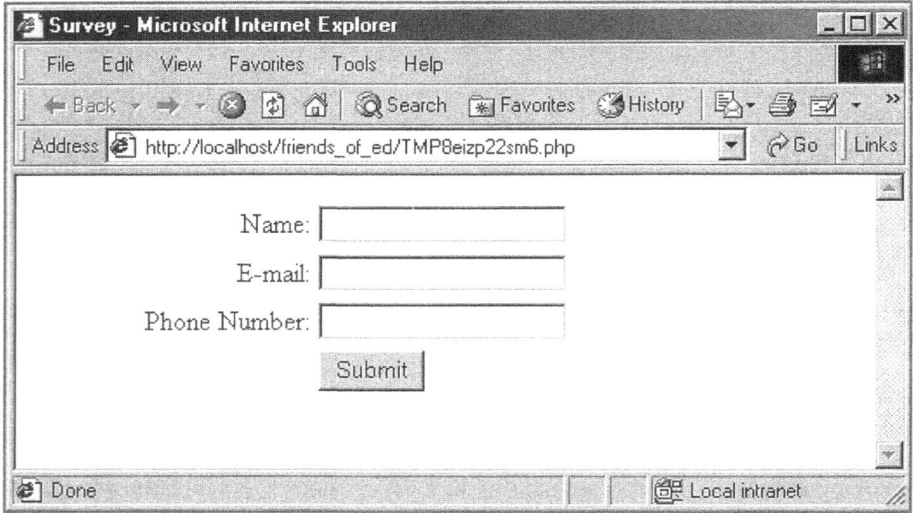

Processing the form

To process this form, we want to first make sure that all the fields are filled in, so that we don't lose any data. To do this, we can use OR in the same way that we did earlier to check if any of the three fields are empty:

```
<?
if (($email=="")||($name=="")||($phone==""))
```

And then display an error message if any of the fields do turn out to be empty:

```
{
        echo "Please fill out the guestbook completely before submitting.";
}
```

Don't worry about writing this into Dreamweaver just yet – we're going to make sure we understand the theory behind what we're doing before we enter the code.

That's got a little error-handling out of the way, but the big job here is that we want to send the data that the user fills in to a text file so that we can retrieve it later. We can continue our code by saying that if there isn't an error in any of the three fields, we want to open a file called guestbook.html. If it isn't there, it creates it.

```
else
{
        $fp = fopen("guestbook.html", "w") ;
//will append or create a new file
```

You may well have not come across this before, but you can hit real problems in server-run files if more than one person tries to save information to a file at the same time. Just imagine two people trying to save text files to the same drive with the same name at the same time, and you'll get an idea of how nasty this could be.

The way to avoid this is to **lock** the file so only one person can access it at the same time:

```
flock($fp, LOCK_EX); // lock the file
```

We've created the file, made sure that everyone isn't using at the same time, so what's left? Ah, yes, we actually want to transfer the information from the form to our file:

```
fwrite($fp, "$name signed the guestbook. \nHis e-mail address was $email
➥\nHis phone number was $phone\n\n");
```

Once we've transferred the data, we can unlock the file again, and close it:

```
flock($fp, LOCK_UN); // unlock the file
fclose($fp);
```

Great, we've stored our information. The next step is to sort out what we want to do with this information. We want the variables e-mailed to ourselves, and a gracious thank you sent to the person signing the guestbook. We're going to use the mail(); function to do this.

> *Unless you're using an actual server with e-mail set up on it, the* `mail();` *function won't work, because your machine isn't given the method of processing and sending e-mail that servers have. We're including this so that you can use it when you upload files to a server – you'll want to remove the mail code when you test locally, as it will cause errors.*

The format of `mail();` is:

```
mail(recipient, subject, message, return-path);
```

This means that :

```
mail("matteo@deviantart.com", "Guestbook Entry Added", wordwrap
("$name signed the guestbook. \nHis e-mail address was $email \nHis phone
number was $phone", 72, "\n", 1), "Return-Path:
<matteo@deviantart.com>\nFrom: Matthew Stephens");
```

sends me (matteo@deviantart.com) the variables of the form that has been filled in so that I can see who is signing my guest book. The `wordwrap` function is useful - if you don't use it, then the details will be sent as one long line of text.

The e-mail I get when someone fills in the form looks like this:

```
Matt signed the guestbook.
His e-mail address was matteo@deviantart.com
His phone number was 333-333-3333
```

We use the same format to mail the user a thank you note for signing the guest book:

```
mail("$email", "Thanks for Signing the Guestbook", wordwrap("Thanks,
$name, for signing the guestbook.", 72, "\n", 1), "Return-Path:
<matteo@deviantart.com>\nFrom: Matthew Stephens");
```

The message the user receives will read:

```
Thanks, Matt, for signing the guestbook.
```

We also send a Thanks for signing the guestbook **message** to the browser:

```
        echo "<font face=verdana size=1>Thanks, " . $name . ", for signing
    the guestbook.";
    }
```

And that's the end of our code:

```
    ?>
```

Mailing the information

You've seen the theory; all that remains is for us to do is enter the code.

1. Create a new PHP file in Dreamweaver.

2. Add the following after the `<body>` tag:

```
<?
if (($email=="")||($name=="")||($phone==""))
{
    echo "Please fill out the guestbook completely before submitting.";
}
else
{
    $fp = fopen("guestbook.txt", "w") ; //w will append or create a new file
    flock($fp, LOCK_EX); // lock the file

fwrite($fp, "$name signed the guestbook. \nHis e-mail address was $email \nHis phone number was $phone\n\n");

flock($fp, LOCK_UN); // unlock the file
    fclose($fp);

mail("matteo@deviantart.com", "Guestbook Entry Added", wordwrap("$name signed the guestbook. \nHis e-mail address was $email \nHis phone number was $phone", 72, "\n", 1), "Return-Path: <matteo@deviantart.com>\nFrom: Matthew Stephens");

mail("$email", "Thanks for Signing the Guestbook", wordwrap("Thanks, $name, for signing the guestbook.", 72, "\n", 1), "Return-Path: <matteo@deviantart.com>\nFrom: Matthew Stephens");

        echo "<font face=verdana size=1>Thanks, " . $name . ", for signing the guestbook.";
}
?>
```

3. Save this file as guestbook_post.php.

Remember what we said earlier – that `mail` will not work on our local server setup, but will work when you upload it to a hosting service. If you do have a hosting account with PHP, then upload guestbook.php guestbook_post.php, and test away – just please make sure that you've not used my e-mail address in your code (as above) and are mailing me with your details...

Using Snippets

Before we leave you, we're going to show you a nice little Dreamweaver feature added in by Macromedia to make things as easy as possible for you when coding. Hopefully, you've probably seen a few bits of code in this chapter that you wouldn't mind using again. Dreamweaver allows you to save them as **snippets** to use them whenever you want.

1. Open the Code panel, and expand it. Then click the Snippets tab.

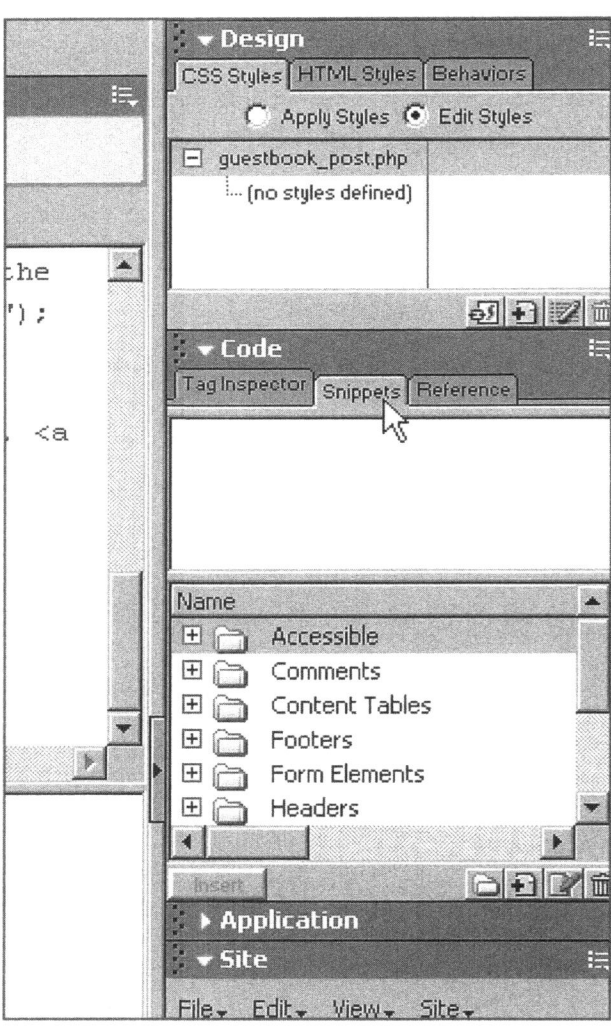

Using PHP and Apache

2. Create a new folder by clicking the folder icon at the bottom. Call the new folder PHP.

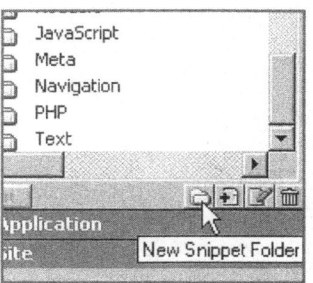

3. With your new folder highlighted, click the New Snippet icon.

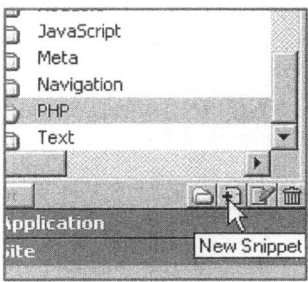

4. In the new dialog, you can enter your code. I'm entering that form that we're using for our guest book, because I think it might be useful in the future. (NB: the only problem with the Snippet window is that it won't allow you to select code from your code window when it's open, so you might want to close this, go find your code, and come back...)

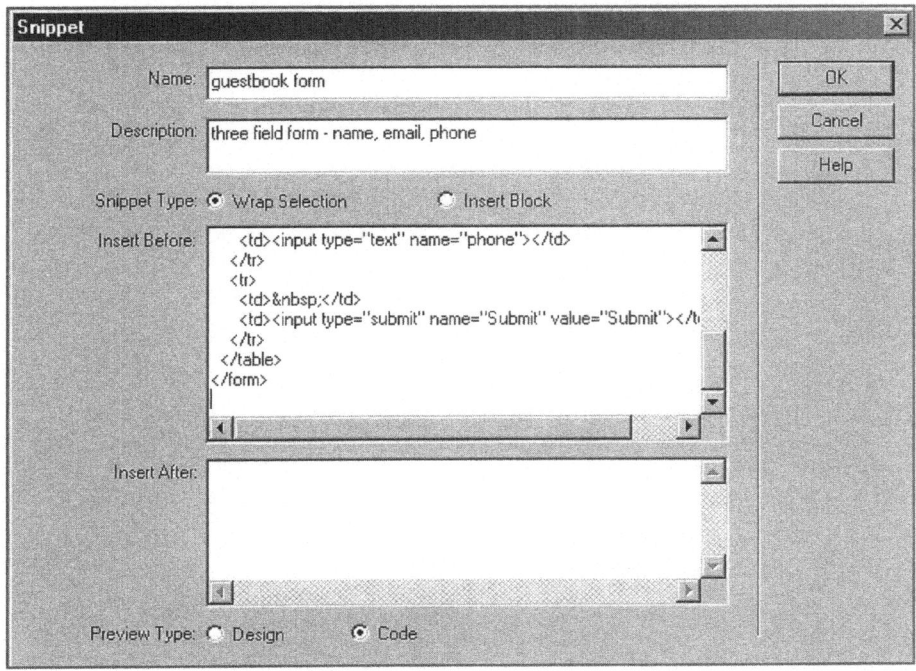

9   Foundation Dreamweaver MX

5. Hit OK, and your Code panel will update to show your new snippet:

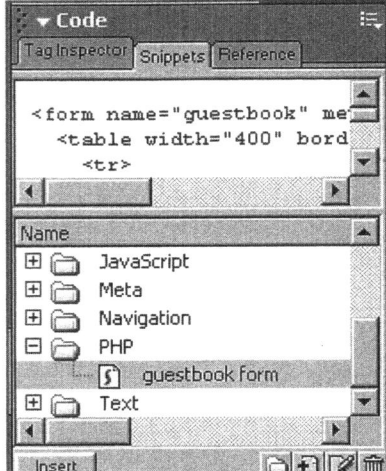

I can now enter the guest book form into any code I write at any time, just by double-clicking it in the code window.

Summary

This chapter has been hard, and we've covered topics that merit entire books on themselves. Don't be afraid to go back and look over this chapter again, but the important point is that you've created your first PHP applications in Dreamweaver. If you feel like you haven't got an absolute grip on all the concepts that we've been talking about, don't worry. The best way to understand them is by running through several examples, and the following chapters offer plenty of these.

Using PHP and Apache

Further PHP

What we'll cover in this chapter

- *Learning about using loops in our PHP*
- *Introducing Arrays*
- *Creating a login system using Cookies*

Foundation Dreamweaver MX

You should have had a good dose of PHP in the last chapter, and this chapter aims to complete your PHP education before we go on to look at adding databases into the mix. After covering variables, operators, and if statements in **Chapter 9**, we're going to take a look at looping, Arrays, and cookies here. You'll need to use the site we defined and the other relevant settings from the last chapter to run these examples.

Looping

Loops are a very common technique, used to shorten the length of a script and to make the page more dynamic. Let me explain how it works before we get started. A loop enables you to carry out specific tasks repeatedly until a condition or limit is met. The easiest way that PHP is able to do this is called the 'while' loop. Here's a quick example:

```
while (condition)
{
    execute something
}
```

Here's an example that actually works with PHP:

```
<?php
$x=1;
while ($x < 5)

{
    echo $x;
    $x++;
}
?>
```

What this does is set the variable $x to 1. Then we start the loop, saying while $x is less than 5, we want to do something. What we want to do is between the two brackets and, in this case, what we want to do is `echo $x;` and `$x++;`.

You should know what `echo $x;` does by now, but what about `$x++;`? Well, this is called an **auto-increment**. It's a shorter version of saying $x=$x+1;. You can also use `$x--;` to decrease the variable by 1. So this loop outputs the value of $x as it enters the loop, then adds 1 to it.

If you create a new PHP page in Dreamweaver, add the code after the <body> tag, and test in your browser, then the result is just: 1234. It starts at 1, goes through and outputs 1 to the browser, then adds 1 to the variable. Then it goes through again as 2, then as 3, and so on until it arrives at a variable value that exceeds the less than (<) 5 instruction, and stops.

Do... while loops

The 'do-while' loop is a little bit more advanced, but is useful when you're dealing with input from a user. Let's say, for instance, that a user was able to input the variable $x into the loop in the example above. If the user entered 5 or above, the loop wouldn't display anything.

To fix this problem, PHP has the 'do-while' loop that goes through the loop once before it ever gets to the condition. Let's take a look:

```
do
{
    execute this!
}   while (condition)
```

Let's alter our first script to ensure that at least one line of output is created. Add the while line at the end to your script (the rest should already be there):

```
<?php
$x=1;
do
{
    echo $x;
    $x++;
}
    while($x<5);
?>
```

This creates the same output as the first script. Now try changing the $x=1; to $x=10; and test again. You should get the number 10 displayed in your browser, whereas in the first script you would have seen a blank window.

This is because the first script checks the value, and then outputs a value to the browser – so if 10 is input, the script checks, and doesn't output anything. This second script outputs a number before checking anything, so it outputs 10, then checks it, and then stops.

A user who had input 10 into the loop would therefore see 10 displayed, and the PHP stop. That's a lot better than inputting something, and seeing nothing – when the user would probably conclude that our PHP didn't work.

For statements

Another way of doing this is with a for loop. The way this works is you set the initial number, the number to stop at, and how to increment it and the loop runs until this is satisfied. Sound confusing? Here's a better explanation:

```
for(initial value; final value; increment)
{
    execute this!
}
```

Let's take a look at how this might work in PHP. Enter this into a new PHP document:

```php
<?php
for($x=1; $x<=10; $x++)
{
    echo $x;
}
?>
```

Test in your browser, and you'll see 12345678910 displayed. The initial value is 1, so that's where we start. Until we get to 10, this loop will repeat. The action to loop is a simple echo of the variable $x. So we echo 1, then 2, then 3, then 4, etc. until 10 is reached.

Arrays

So far, we've only used variables with one value:

```
$username=deviantART;
```

for example. But what if you want to store more than one value in a variable? We can do this using an **array**. Think of an array as a filing cabinet – it might look like one thing from the outside, but in reality it holds lots of different values within it at any one time.

So, an array is a container for variables. Here's an example of how we define an array:

```
$colors = array("red", "orange", "yellow", "green");
```

To specify that we want information from an array, we need two things:

- The name of the array ($colors in this case).

- The index of the element (or "drawer") you want to use. This is a number, so $colors[2] would be "yellow".

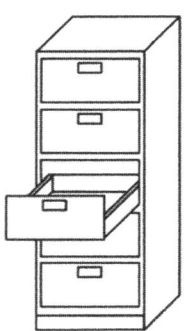

It's important to remember that the first entry is always 0, not 1. This is confusing to even the most experienced programmer. So red, since it is first, is 0 and orange would be 1. To echo red, we'd use `echo $colors[0];` to echo green, we'd use `echo $color[3];`.

To add to an array, we define the index key like this:

`$colors[2]="blue";`

The array `$colors` will now be: "red", "orange", "blue", "yellow", "green"

To delete something from an array, we use the `array_splice()` function. It's kind of confusing, but let me try and explain it. The syntax is:

array_splice(array_name, where to start, how many to delete).

So if we type:

`array_splice ($colors, 1, 1);`

then it will start at 1, which is "orange" and delete one - which is "orange" - leaving us with:

`$colors = array("red", "blue", "yellow", "green");`

If we change the `array_splice()` line to (`$colors, 1, 2`), then it will start at "orange" and delete two, leaving our array looking like this:

`$colors = array("red", "yellow", "green");`

To display an array, we can use the `foreach` loop. The syntax is like this:

```
foreach($colors as $display_color)
{
    echo $display_color , ", ";
}
```

The new variable, `$display_color`, will take the array, `$colors`, and display each entry. Assuming we're using the array we first saw a few paragraphs back, the output should be:

red, orange, yellow, green

Arrays might not seem very useful on their own like this, but once you start using them to sort through data, they can be extraordinarily powerful. Think about it – you've got a lot of data that you want to search through. How do you do it? You put the data in an array, and loop through the array until you find it, that's how. We'll be using arrays in our next exercise.

Processing forms with multiple options

Now that we know how arrays work, we can process forms with multiple options - like checklists and multiple selection menus. If you spend a lot of time surfing the web, you'll have seen forms where you are able to choose one or more options in a list - perhaps in surveys when they want to find out what you're interested in.

1. Create a new PHP file in Dreamweaver.

2. Type the following after the first `<body>` tag:

   ```
   <form action="form3.php" method="POST">
   <select name="book[]" size="6" multiple>
       <option value="Crime and Punishment">Fyodor Dostoevsky</option>
       <option value="Wuthering Heights">Emily Bronte</option>
       <option value="Moby Dick">Herman Melville</option>
   </select>
   <br>
   <input type="submit" name="submit" value="Submit">
   </form>
   ```

3. Save this file as `array.php` in the apache folder as we did with our PHP docs in **Chapter 9**.

4. Now that we have this setup, we can make `form3.php`. Since we told the form to select the `book[]` array, we'll be displaying it back to the user.

5. Create a new PHP file in Dreamweaver, and add the following:

   ```
   for($count = 0; $count < sizeof($book); $count++)
     {
        echo "$book[$count]<br>";
     }
   ```

   This takes the array from `array.php` and goes from 0 to the size of the array, which in this case is 2. While it's counting, it displays the contents of that part of the array. So when `$count=0`, it displays 'Crime and Punishment' and when `$count=1`, it displays 'Wuthering Heights'.

6. Save this file as `form3.php` in the same place as the last one.

7. Test `array.php` in a browser. Select any or all of the three authors by highlighting them with the mouse before clicking Submit, and watch the related works appear on the next screen.

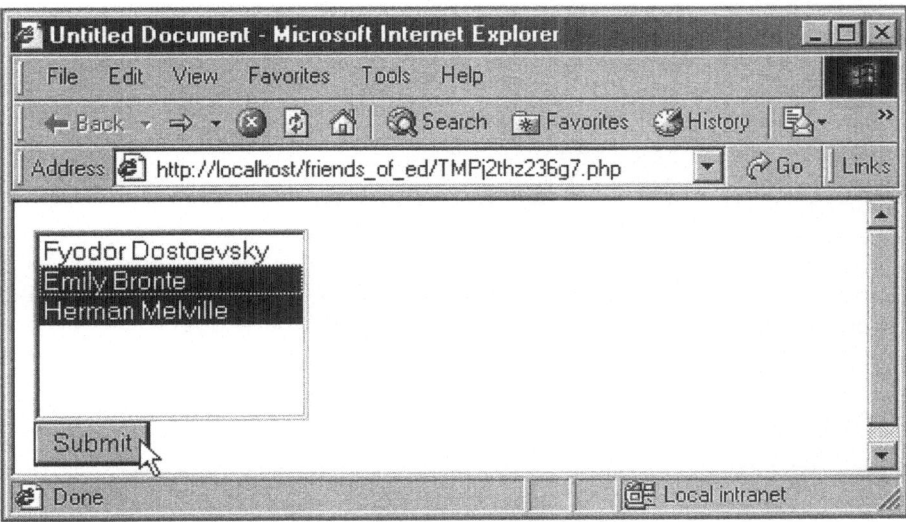

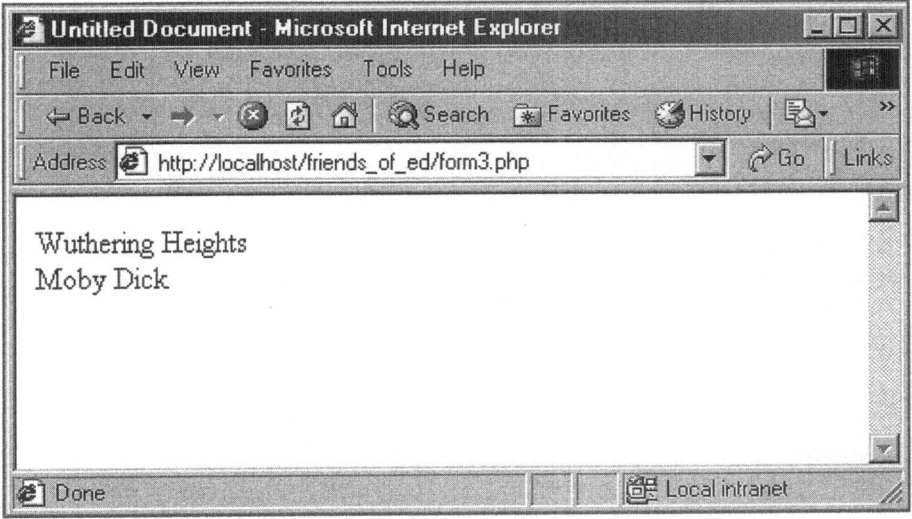

Cookies

When you access a web page, image, or file from the web, you get a HTTP header, which looks something like this:

```
HTTP/1.0 200 Found
Date: Thursday, 31 Jan 2002 12:23:12 CST
Server: Apache/1.1.1 deviantART/1.0
Location: http://www.deviantart.com
Content: text/deviantart/html
```

This may look completely new to you, but I assure you that it comes with every piece of data you download. Why don't you see it? Because your browser is smart enough to know that you don't need it. It hides it from you in a cookie, which is made to be invisible. A cookie is a small file that is stored on your computer to save information from websites. What the cookie does is simply put information in this header so that your browser can talk to the server and pass on information about you.

It's very common for large sites to use cookies in this way, so there's no need to be afraid of them. The settings are usually all those things you've come to depend on, like your favorite choice of color to browse a site in, or the layout of another. The hyper-security conscious can choose to refuse cookies in their browser options, but most of us just live with them. You can view any of the cookies on your computer by searching for them - they're usually stored in temporary folders or user settings (if you can't find them, go surfing for a few minutes, and then search for files created in the last 30 minutes).

In terms of PHP, a cookie is a value set by PHP that tells the browser to store variables on the user's machine. The most common use of cookies is to store login and password variables so that your computer remembers when you join a site. You may have noticed that when you create an account at a site like amazon.com and go back a week later, you're automatically logged in. Sites also store information like time, browsing habits, and other user information in cookies.

Setting up a cookie

Let's look at an example of how to set up a cookie to be written to a user's machine:

```
setcookie("username", $username, time()+500);
```

The syntax of a cookie is:

```
setcookie(name, variable, expires);
```

name=*VALUE*
> This names the cookie and is a sequence of characters excluding semi-colons, commas and white spaces. This is the only attribute that you **must** set on the `setcookie` header.

variable=*VALUE*
> This is the variable that you are setting into the cookie. If you want to store their username, then we set the variable as `$username`, as we have in our example above.

`expires=DATE`

The **expires** attribute is most commonly used with the `time()` function. Basically, we take `time()`, which is the present time, and add the amount of seconds we want. In our case, we've used 500 seconds, meaning that in 500 seconds from now, the cookie will expire. Here's a quick reference for you:

- 3600 seconds = 1 hour
- 86,400 = 1 day
- 604,800 = 1 week
- 2,419,200 = 1 month
- 29,030,400 = 1 year

expires is optional. If it isn't set, the cookie will be deleted when the session is closed. Why would we want a cookie to expire? The most common use is so that users log out automatically if they don't visit your site for a long time. There are more options in this syntax, but for now, this is all we need to know.

Removing cookies

Removing cookies is important if your users want to log out of your site manually. The method of deleting cookies is just as simple as setting them. The only difference is that you set the expiration date to negative. One example of this would be:

```
setcookie ("username", $username, time() - 3600);
```

This sets the cookie to expire an hour ago, which effectively removes it.

Setting up cookies for logins

We want to create a login system for our users that remembers them each time they come back to our site. We're going to give you screenshots as you go through so that you can see what you're creating is doing, but you'll have to wait until the end of the exercise before you can test everything - it works, so be patient.

> *Cookies are slightly funny things in that they form part of the HTTP header. In plain English, that means that they must come before any standard output in the code – even including whitespace before the opening <? tag. If you get an error like the one pictured on the next page, then go and check that there's absolutely nothing before your code starts - when we say delete everything in the Code window and start at the top, we really do mean it!*

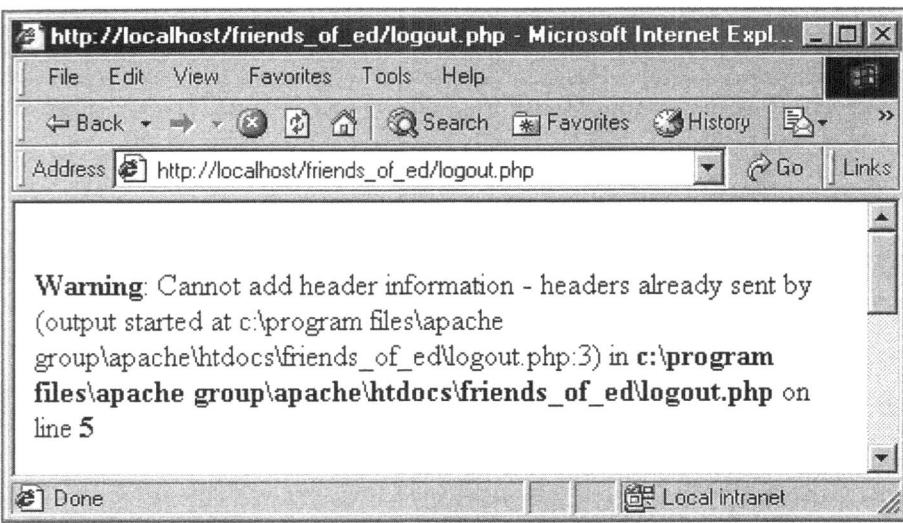

1. Create a new PHP file in Dreamweaver. This is our form, and it will check to see if the cookie is set. If it isn't, it will ask for a username. After this, we'll create our processing script to set the cookie after the form is entered.

2. Delete everything in the Code view and type the following:

```php
<?
if ($_COOKIE ['username'] !="")
{
echo "Logged in as " , $_COOKIE['username'];
} else {
?>
<form action="set.php" method="post" name="cookieset">
<input name="username" type="text" value="username" size="15" maxlength="30">
<input name="Submit" type="submit" value="Submit">
</form>
<? } ?>
```

The first part of this script checks to see if the cookie 'username' exists. If it does, it outputs the variable to the browser. If it doesn't exist, it outputs the form. The variable _COOKIE is a temporary array of the cookies in use. The first time a visitor sees this page, it will show the form (as the cookie hasn't been set yet), but once the user inputs a username and hits submit, it goes to set.php, which sets the cookie.

3. Save this file as `form.php` (this will probably mean that you'll have to overwrite a similarly named file from **Chapter 9**, so you might like to rename your old file before saving this one).

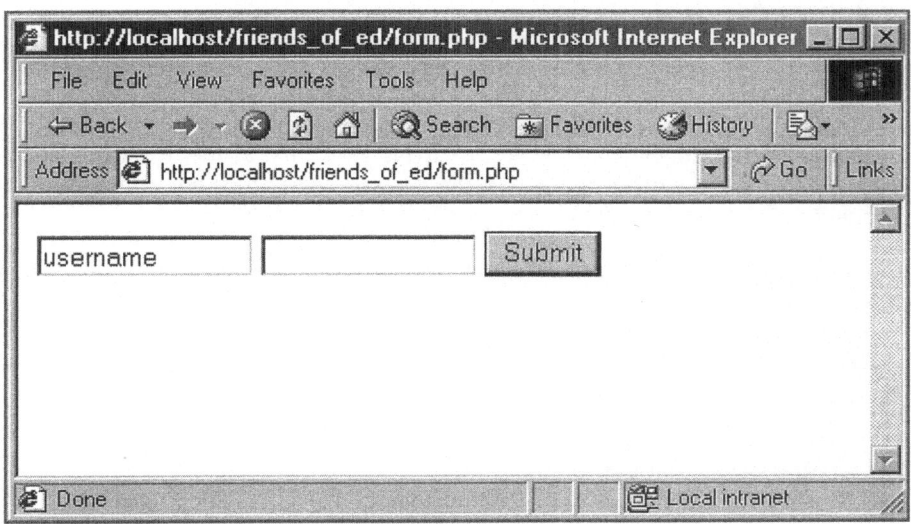

4. Create another new PHP file in Dreamweaver, delete everything in the code view and type the following:

```
<?
setcookie("username", $username, time()+2600);
echo "Cookie has been set. <a href=\" form.php\">Click Here to Go Back</a>";
?>
```

The only real line in this is what we learned earlier. It sets the cookie named `"username"` with the variable $username. When the person fills out the form and loads `form.php` again, it should echo back their username.

5. Save this file as `set.php`.

6. This works great for just echoing back the username. What if we want to keep people logged in, but only if they enter the correct username and password? This works great for admin or members-only sections. In `form.php`, modify the code so that it looks like this, by adding the code in bold:

```
<?
if (($_COOKIE['username'] == "admin") && ($_COOKIE['password'] == "root"))
{
echo "Logged in as ";
echo $_COOKIE['username'];
echo "<BR>This is where you put the valuable information.";
} else {
?>
<form action="set.php" method="post" name="cookieset">
```

```
        <input name="username" type="text" value="username" size="15"
➥maxlength="30">
        <input name="password" type="password" size="15" maxlength="30">
        <input name="Submit" type="submit" value="Submit">
        </form>
        <? } ?>
```

This checks to see if the cookies for $username and $password are admin and root respectively. Further down, you can see that we've set admin as the username, and root as the password. Feel free to customize these. If the cookie isn't set to these values (in other words, if someone inputs the wrong details), then it displays the form.

7. Now let's change set.php to work with this new form. Open set.php, delete the code we entered earlier, and add this:

```
<?
if (($username == "admin") && ($password == "root"))
{
setcookie("username", $username, time()+604800);
setcookie("password", $password, time()+604800);
echo "Cookie has been set. <a href= form.php>Click Here to Visit the Admin Section</a>";

}
else
{
    echo "You entered the wrong username and/or password.";
}
?>
```

This checks to see if the username and password are correct, and then sets the cookie if they are. If one is incorrect, it displays You entered the wrong username and/or password.

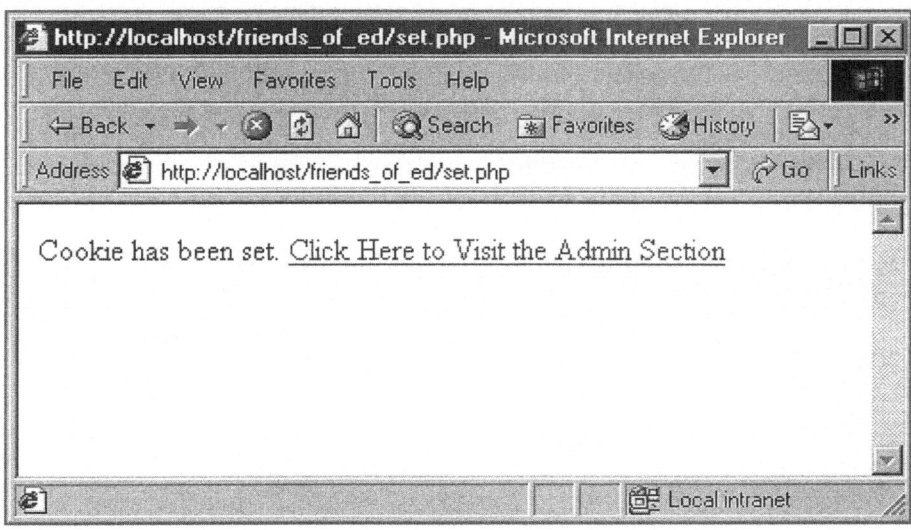

8. Now we need to add a logout button. This will mean that other people who use our admin machine won't be automatically logged in by the cookie. Basically, the logout button will link to PHP file that will delete the cookie. In form.php, add:

   echo "
<a href=logout.php>Logout</a>";

   just below:

   echo "
This is where you put the valuable information.";

9. Create a new PHP file in Dreamweaver, delete everything in the code view and type the following:

   ```
   <?

   setcookie("username", $username, time()-604800);
   setcookie("password", $password, time()-604800);
   header("Location: form.php");

   ?>
   ```

Foundation Dreamweaver MX

As discussed earlier, to delete a cookie, we just set the time to negative. So the first two lines delete `username` and `password`. The third line is a header function. As we discussed earlier in the chapter, the HTTP header sends a lot of information to the browser. In the example of a HTTP header that I showed you, there is a spot called `Location: http://www.deviantart.com`. What this third line of the script does is change the location of the header, making it load that URL. So after the cookies are deleted, it automatically forwards back to `form.php`.

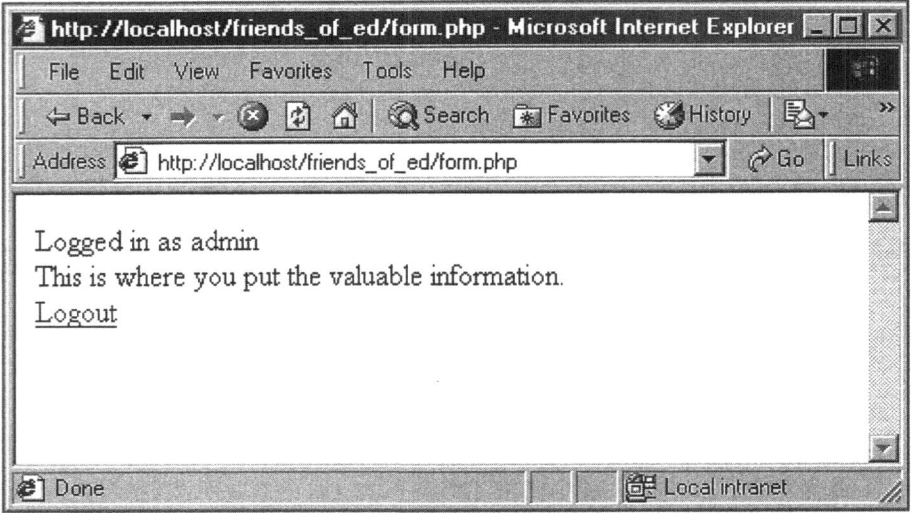

10. Save this file as `logout.php` in the usual folder.

11. Make sure that you've saved all three files, and have paid heed to our earlier note about not leaving any white space or other information before the beginning of the files, and test away. Remember that we've set our `username` and `password` to `admin` and `root` respectively, and that PHP is a case-sensitive language (so `Admin` won't work, while `admin` will).

> *Cookies are great for allowing users to customize sites, and for storing harmless data, but they're a huge security risk. Don't store any information that you don't want others to access in them – if you want to do this, then read on to the section on databases.*

Summary

PHP is a fun language, and extremely powerful. Some of the best sites started off with a small MySQL database and a few PHP scripts. You should be able to take what you've learned in the last couple of chapters, come up with some great ideas, and apply it to make some wonderful new sites.

In the past couple of chapters, we've discovered how to store information in PHP using variables and arrays. In our guest book in the last chapter, for example, we sent some of the data in these variables to e-mail addresses. Moving all this information about is a little bit difficult unless we've got somewhere decent to store it, though – it'd be much nicer if, instead of mailing us the details, PHP just went and created a database of everyone on our mailing list for us, wouldn't it? Our next chapter is all about databases, where we'll find out how to store and retrieve all this data.

11

PHP/MySQL: The Real Dynamic Duo

What we'll cover in this chapter

- Learning how a PHP/MySQL web application works
- Installing MySQL and phpMyAdmin
- Configuring Dreamweaver MX and PHP/MySQL to interact together
- Building a PHP application that will store and retrieve information in our database

Before Dreamweaver MX, the PHP/MySQL combination was available in Dreamweaver Ultradev 4, but only if you installed a third party server model called Phakt. One of the most exciting things about the release of Dreamweaver MX is its native support for the dynamic duo, which makes creating interactive web sites easy *PHPeasy*.

Let's look at what happens when a user requests a page with the PHP file extension. Below is a *simplified* explanation of what happens:

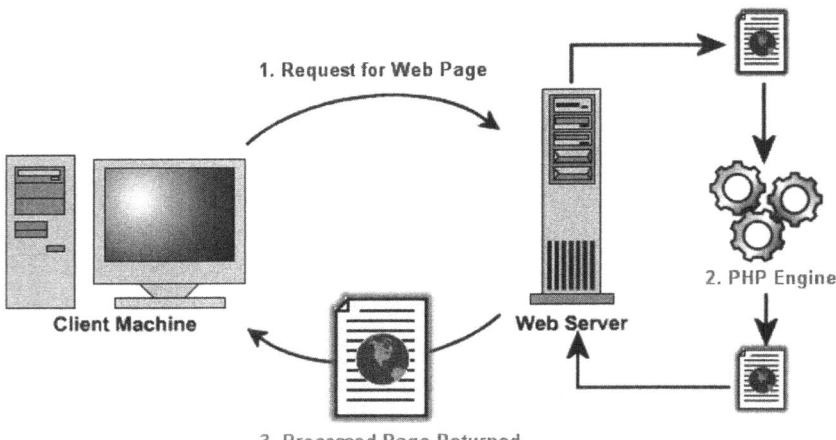

1. A user will request a page via their browser. This request is sent to the web server; in this case it's Apache.

2. Because the file has a PHP extension, Apache will know that it must be handled by the PHP pre-processor. This executes our PHP script.

3. In this case, our script opens a connection to the database and retrieves the requested information.

4. Once retrieved the remainder of the PHP script will deal with formatting the data (typically into HTML).

5. The final step is to send the resulting output back to Apache, which in turn returns this information to the user's browser.

This gives you a basic understanding of what will happen when we execute the PHP/MySQL application that we'll build in this chapter.

Installing, configuring and running MySQL on Win32

Before we can start using MySQL, we first need to install and configure it on our system. The instructions given here assume that you're using the pre-compiled Win32 binary version of MySQL. The latest stable version at the time of writing is 3.23.xx, and you can download the necessary files direct from the MySQL website at www.mysql.com/downloads/.

Installation

The installation files for MySQL come packaged in a self-extracting ZIP file, so the first thing we'll need to do is unzip them to a temporary directory. For this you can use a tool like **WinZip** (a trial version is available from www.winzip.com)

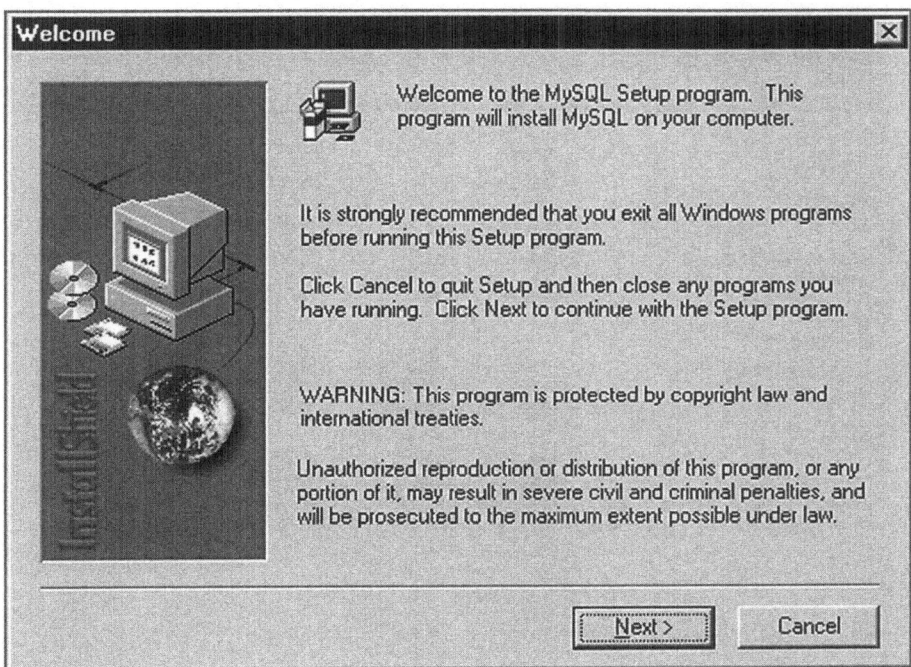

During the installation process, you will be asked where on your system you would like MySQL installed. It's a good idea to install it to the default `c:\mysql\` directory suggested, for the sake of compatibility with other software and ease of configuration for MySQL itself.

Once the wizard has completed its task and MySQL has been installed, it's time to find out how to control the MySQL daemon from within Windows.

The MySQL daemon

The MySQL daemon (we'll call it mysqld) can be thought of as a listening device. It's a program whose job is to sit around and listen for client requests for our MySQL server. When such a request is received, mysqld will fetch the required information and return a response to the calling client.

The first thing we need to do is to start mysqld. You will need to navigate to your chosen installation directory for MySQL. That's the one we just suggested as being `c:\mysql\`. You should see a directory structure such as the one shown below:

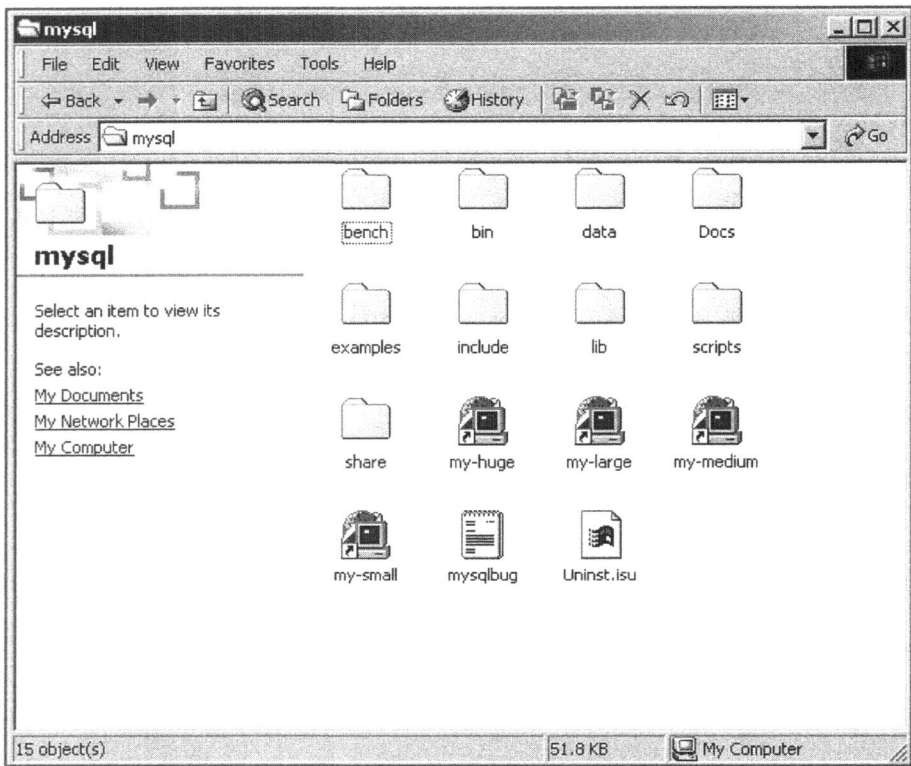

Open the bin directory and locate the mysqld.exe file and double-click to start the myslqd. Note that mysqld runs as a background process and there will be no outwardly visible sign that it's running. The easiest way to ensure that it *is* doing what it's told is to check the Windows Task Manager by pressing CTRL-ALT-DEL on your keyboard – you should see an entry labelled mysqld. Alternatively, you can use the **MySQL monitor** program, which will be covered in the next section.

To stop mysqld gracefully, you will need to open up an **MS-DOS Command Prompt**.

> *If you don't use the command line all that often, you might not know how to access it. Don't worry, it's easy. Just select* Start Menu > Programs > Accessories > Command Prompt. *You can also select* Start Menu > Run, *type* cmd *and click* OK.

Navigate to your MySQL directory (so type cd \mysql if you've been following these instructions to the letter). Next, type the following text, followed by the ENTER key:

PHP/MySQL The Real Dynamic Duo

```
bin\mysqladmin shutdown
```

Use the **Windows Task Manager** again to confirm that mysqld has indeed been shut down.

Note that you could have used the Windows Task Manager to kill the process, but this can have some unpredictable results. At best, mysqld will be shut down and you will keep all of your data intact – at worst, you could scramble your databases and your data would be toast!

On Windows NT and 2000 machines you should install mysqld as a service as follows:

```
mysqld -nt --install
```

You can now start and stop mysqld as follows:

```
NET START mysql
NET STOP mysql
```

Note that in this case, you can't use any other options for mysqld. You can remove the service as follows:

```
mysqld -nt -remove
```

MySQL monitor

Although it has a fairly grand name, the MySQL monitor is little more than a console interface to MySQL. It does, however, allow you to perform almost all MySQL-related tasks, including the creation and manipulation of databases, tables and data.

To start the MySQL monitor, you will again need to open an MS-DOS Command Prompt and navigate to the MySQL directory (again, `cd \mysql`). Then type the following text, followed by the ENTER key:

```
bin\mysql
```

If the MySQL monitor can connect to the MySQL daemon then you will see something like the following output:

```
Command Prompt -'bin\mysql
Microsoft Windows 2000 [Version 5.00.2195]
(C) Copyright 1985-2000 Microsoft Corp.

C:\>cd \mysql

C:\mysql>bin\mysql
Welcome to the MySQL monitor.  Commands end with ; or \g.
Your MySQL connection id is 5 to server version: 3.23.52-nt

Type 'help;' or '\h' for help. Type '\c' to clear the buffer.

mysql>
```

If the mysqld program isn't running when you attempt to start the MySQL monitor, then you will see something like the following output:

C:\mysql>bin\mysql
ERROR 2003: Can't connect to MySQL server on 'localhost' (10061)

If you get this output, then mysqld is not running on the local machine. Please return to the previous section on starting the MySQL daemon and try again.

To escape from the MySQL Monitor, simply type exit followed by the ENTER key. You will be returned to the command prompt.

Testing, testing

There's one final test that we can carry out at this stage to see if MySQL is working. Follow these simple steps:

1. Open up a text editor (like Notepad) and save the following as mysql_test.php in your web server's root directory (remember this is C:\Program Files\Apache Group\apache\htdocs). Don't worry about what it all means at this stage – you'll be learning more about the PHP language very soon:

```
<html>
<head>
<title>Test MySQL</title>
<body>
<!-- mysql_test.php -->
<?php
$host="hostname";

mysql_connect($host,"root","");
$sql="show status";
$result = mysql_query($sql);
if ($result == 0)
   echo("<b>Error " . mysql_errno() . ": " . mysql_error() . "</b>");
elseif (mysql_num_rows($result) == 0)
   echo("<b>Query executed successfully!</b>");
else
{
?>
<!-- Table that displays the results -->
<table border="1">
  <tr><td><b>Variable_name</b></td><td><b>Value</b></td></tr>
  <?php
    for ($i = 0; $i < mysql_num_rows($result); $i++) {
      echo("<TR>");
      $row_array = mysql_fetch_row($result);
      for ($j = 0; $j < mysql_num_fields($result); $j++) {
        echo("<TD>" . $row_array[$j] . "</td>");
        }
```

```
            echo("</tr>");
        }
    ?>
</table>
<?php } ?>
</body>
</html>
```

2. We need to change the following line:

    `$host="localhost";`

    Change the value (i.e. that which is between the "") of $host to the name of the computer where MySQL is installed. Because we're working locally this should be localhost.

3. Make sure you've saved the file after you've made the change and point your browser to http://localhost/mysql_test.php.

    You should see a table with a long list of variables like the one shown here. Don't worry about what they all mean at this stage – it's just telling us that PHP is 'talking' to MySQL and everything with our installation is fine and dandy.

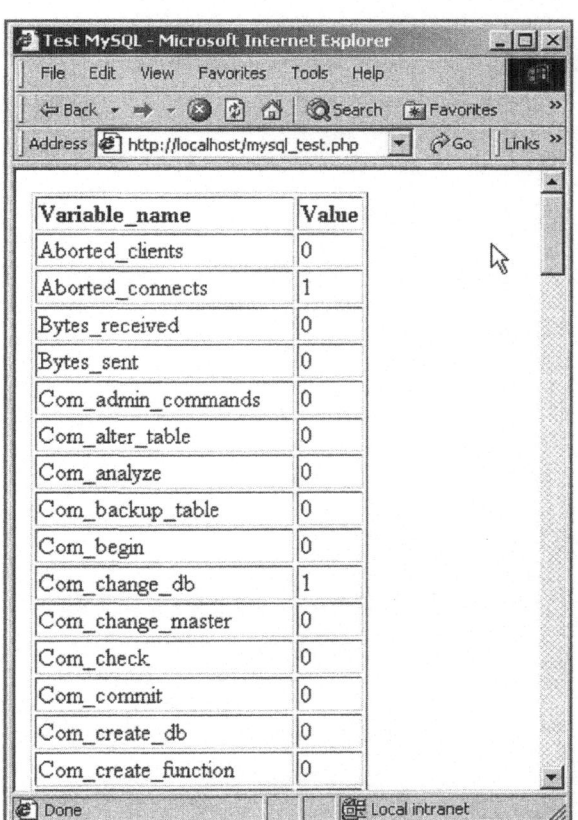

Installing and setting up MySQL for Mac OS X

If you just ran through all the Mac installation stuff for PHP in **chapter 8**, then you've done the hard work. Installing MySQL is relatively easy compared to that.

Firstly, you'll need to download a copy of MySQL. If you're familiar with UNIX and compiling code, then you might want to compile your own version from the source code, but for the benefit of most users, I'm going to recommend a pre-compiled (binary) version of it.

You can download a binary version of MySQL from: http://www.entropy.ch/software/macosx/mysql/ (it's just under a 4MB download).

> You'll need to have administrator rights to install MySQL on Mac OS X.

Once you've downloaded this file, don't install it just yet. Mac OS 10.1.x users will need to follow some additional instructions as below, while users of the newer version of the OS 10.2.x can skip the next part.

Initial instructions for Mac OS 10.1.x

Firstly, we need to set up a MySQL user profile. Open the Users control panel from the System Preferences.

Then click New User, entering MySQL User for the username and mysql as the short name.

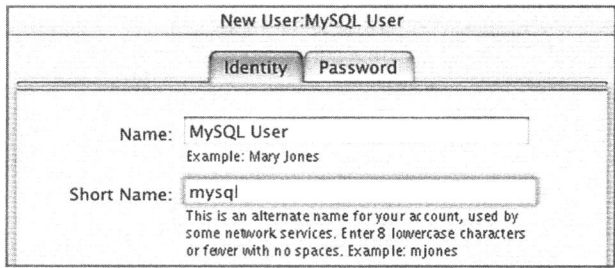

Now click the Password tab, and give the user a password. Make a note of this because we'll use it in a moment. When you're done here, click Save to store the new user information.

> You don't have to log in as the MySQL user to use or install MySQL. You can stay logged in as the current user.

Now proceed to the next set of instructions for both 10.1.x and 10.1.2.

PHP/MySQL The Real Dynamic Duo

Instructions for Mac OS 10.1.x and 10.2.x

Users of 10.1.x should have now already set up their own MySQL User profile. If you haven't, go back to the last section and follow the instructions. If you've already done this, carry on as below.

Users of 10.2.x can start from the instructions below.

Double-click and install MySQL from the .pkg file that should be on your desktop. This will open the Mac OS X installer. Go through the installer as normal.

Once the installation has finished, open the Terminal application. Now we need to configure and startup the MySQL database. On the command-line, type the following:

    cd /usr/local/mysql

And then:

    sudo ./scripts/mysql_install_db

Enter an administrator password when prompted for it. Then type:

    sudo chown -R mysql /usr/local/mysql

Entering a password when prompted. This allows the MySQL user to have access to the folder containing the MySQL installed files. (chown means change owner here.)

Now enter:

    sudo ./bin/safe_mysqld --user=mysql &

This starts up the MySQL daemon and lets the MySQL user access the database. The MySQL daemon simply listens for MySQL commands or queries on the system.

MySQL is now running and you can access the MySQL monitor by typing the following into the command-line:

    mysql

From here you can run and create databases, tables and so forth. You can also now run PHP scripts with MySQL queries. When you restart your Mac, you'll need to start up the MySQL daemon again with the following command:

    sudo safe_mysqld --user=mysql &

You can however download a MySQL start-up package which kicks it off automatically when you start up your Mac. You can download it from www2.entropy.ch/download/mysql-startupitem.pkg.tar.gz. Once this is installed, you never have to return to the Terminal to start it up, and can run queries through PHP automatically.

> *A word of warning – the way that MySQL has been configured here is not secure and is not recommended for live server use. It is intended for testing purposes only. If you would like to take steps to make it more secure, look on the Apple Knowledge Base for more info.*

MySQL security

MySQL has a strict set of security features. You can restrict who can access your databases, where they can access from, which databases they can access, what they can do with the databases and much more. This is an extremely important feature to get to grips with if you're going to be letting the general public loose on your servers.

However, such configuration has been known to fill whole books even bigger than this one. For this reason we won't be discussing the security features of MySQL in this section.

> *If you're interested in the security aspects of MySQL then you'll find more information in the friends of ED book* Advanced PHP for Flash, *which contains an appendix on MySQL security.*

Remember that the installation process for the simplest of applications can seem a little daunting. But if you installed PHP and MySQL on your machine, then you really should know no fear! Don't forget that as with the other technologies we've installed, there is a comprehensive set of documentation supplied online.

Preparing MySQL

If you've installed MySQL on Windows, then it will come with a program called **winmysqladmin**. This provides a GUI (Graphical User Interface) to help manage your MySQL Databases. There's also an application called **phpmyadmin**, which you can use to manage MySQL (we'll be using it later in the chapter). However, to start with we're going to bypass these and work straight from the command line.

Why do this? Quite simply, if you use the PHP/MySQL combination, at some point you'll have to connect via Telnet or SSH to a remote server to manage your MySQL databases. To do this you'll need to be familiar with using the command line, so I'll introduce you to it now. Let's look at how to connect to MySQL from the command line.

The information you enter from the command line varies between Windows and Mac so we will look at these separately.

Preparing on Windows

1. To allow us to connect to MySQL, we must browse to the MySQL bin directory by typing:

   `cd c:\mysql\bin`

   ```
   Microsoft Windows 2000 [Version 5.00.2195]
   (C) Copyright 1985-2000 Microsoft Corp.

   C:\>cd c:\mysql\bin

   C:\mysql\bin>
   ```

2. The first thing we'll do is create a database called `book_db`. It's the database we'll connect to from Dreamweaver. We do this using the following command and hitting ENTER:

   `mysqladmin create book_db`

   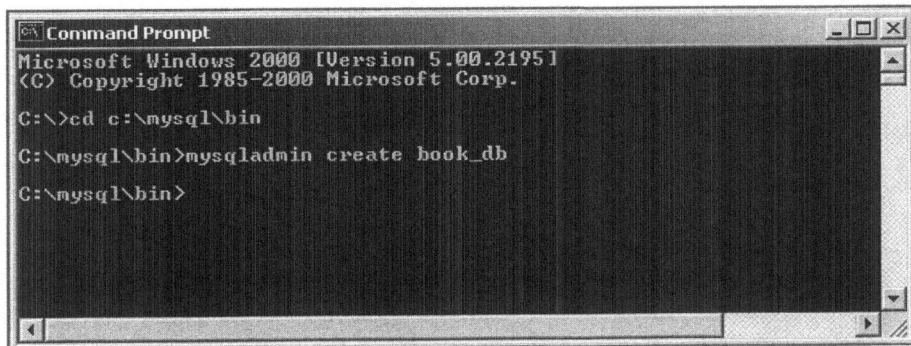

3. Now that we've created the `book_db` database, we'll add a user and give them universal rights over the database we created. MySQL user rights are stored in tables that are automatically created when MySQL is installed. These tables are kept in a database called `mysql`. While still in the `mysql\bin` folder, type the following command and hit ENTER:

   `mysql`

4. Once the MySQL monitor is running you will need to tell it which database you want to use. In this case we wish to connect to MySQL, so we type in this command followed by ENTER:

   `use mysql;`

5. You will get a message that the database has been changed. We are now connected to the MySQL database.

6. We're now going to use an SQL statement to add a user to the MySQL database and grant them the correct permissions to read/write to this database. It's simply done using this code:

```
GRANT ALL ON book_db.* TO your_username@localhost IDENTIFIED BY
"mypassword";
```

I'll be using the username pault and the password sesame.

7. To exit the MySQL monitor, type:

```
exit;
```

...and hit ENTER.

PHP/MySQL The Real Dynamic Duo

Preparing on Mac

1. As with Windows, to connect to MySQL we must browse to the MySQL `bin` directory by typing:

   `cd /path/to/mysql/bin`

   ```
   $ cd /path/to/mysql
   ```

2. We must create a database called `book_db`. It's the database we'll connect to from Dreamweaver. We do this using the following command:

   `./mysqladmin -uroot create book_db`

   ```
   $ ./mysqladmin -uroot create book_db
   ```

3. Now that we've created the `book_db` database, we'll add a user and give them universal rights over the database we created. MySQL user rights are stored in tables that are automatically created when MySQL is installed. These tables are kept in a database called MySQL. While still in the `mysql/bin` folder, type the following command:

   `./mysql -uroot`

   ```
   $ ./mysql -uroot
   ```

4. This will start the MySQL monitor. You will need to tell MySQL that you wish to use the MySQL database. You do this by entering the following command:

   `use mysql;`

   ```
   Welcome to the MySQL monitor.  Commands end with ; or \g.
   Your MySQL connection id is 1 to server version: 4.0.3-beta-max

   Type 'help;' or '\h' for help. Type '\c' to clear the buffer.

   mysql> use mysql
   Reading table information for completion of table and column names
   You can turn off this feature to get a quicker startup with -A

   Database changed
   mysql>
   ```

   You will get a message that the database has been changed. We are now connected to the MySQL database.

5. We're now going to use an SQL statement to add a user to the MySQL database and grant them the correct permissions to read and write to this database. It's simply done using this code:

   `GRANT ALL ON book_db.* TO your_username@localhost IDENTIFIED BY`
   ➥`"mypassword";`

   I'll be using the username `pault` and the password `sesame`.

325

```
mysql> use mysql;
Reading table information for completion of table and column names
You can turn off this feature to get a quicker startup with -A

Database changed
mysql> GRANT ALL ON book_db.* TO pault@localhost IDENTIFIED BY "sesame";
```

Once you have done this you will see a message like this:

```
mysql> GRANT ALL ON book_db.* TO pault@localhost IDENTIFIED BY "sesame";
Query OK, 0 rows affected (0.00 sec)
```

6. Next you will need to reload the permissions table, you do this by using the following command.

   FLUSH PRIVILEGES

```
mysql> GRANT ALL ON book_db.* TO pault@localhost IDENTIFIED BY "sesame";
Query OK, 0 rows affected (0.00 sec)

mysql> FLUSH PRIVILEGES;
```

7. Type exit; to leave the MySQL monitor.

```
mysql> exit
```

8. You can now close the terminal window.

Downloading phpMyAdmin

phpMyAdmin is a collection of ready-made PHP scripts that you can use to create and edit MySQL databases from your browser window. It's free to download and comes with plenty of online documentation and help forums. We'll be downloading the latest stable version at time of writing which is 2.3.0 from www.phpmyadmin.net.

Although the files we will download are the same for both the Mac and PC, the way we download and unpack them are slightly different.

On Windows

As Windows is the easier of the two options we will begin with this.

1. Download the ZIP file phpMyAdmin-2.x.x-php.zip (where 2.x.x is the version number.)

2. Unzip this file to a folder on your hard drive.

3. Browse to the folder to which you unzipped the files. Check that the folder phpMyAdmin-2.x.x-php contains the PHP files. Sometimes, depending on the method you used to unzip the file, this folder will contain another folder of the same name. We must select the folder which contains the PHP files, not the folder which contains the sub-folder. Copy and paste the whole folder into your web server's root directory (C:\Program Files\Apache Group\apache\htdocs).

PHP/MySQL The Real Dynamic Duo

4. Rename the folder that you have unpacked from `phpMyAdmin-2.x.x` to `phpMyAdmin`.

On Mac

1. Open up the Terminal window.

2. We will use the following command to change directory so that you are in the web server's root folder (normally `htdocs`):

   `cd /path/to/webservers/rootfolder`

3. Enter the following command:

   `curl 0 http://umn.dl.sourceforge.net/sourceforge/phpmyadmin/phpMyAdmin-2.x.x-php.tar.gz`

Note: The above command will only work in 10.1 or greater. If you have version 10, then you will need to replace it with the command below:

   `wget http://umn.dl.sourceforge.net/sourceforge/phpmyadmin/phpMyAdmin-2.x.x-`
   `➥php.tar.gz`

   ...where `2.x.x` is the version number of phpMyAdmin. This will download the tarball to our web directory.

4. Next, we must unpack it by entering:

   `gunzip phpMyAdmin-2.x.x-php.tar.gz`

5. Now that we have created our `tar` file, we must unpack this by using the following command:

   `tar -xvf phpMyAdmin-2.x.x-php.tar`

6. Finally, rename the folder that you have unpacked from `phpMyAdmin-2.x.x` to `phpMyAdmin`.

Configuring phpMyAdmin

Now that we have the `phpMyAdmin` folder within our web server root folder, the last thing we have to do is enter some values into the `phpMyAdmin` configuration file which is called `config.inc.php`.

1. Open up the file in a text editor like Notepad or SimpleText.

2. First look for the following (you can use Edit > Find to do this):

   `$cfgPmaAbsoluteUri = ' ';`

   We need to set this variable to the complete URL of your copy of phpMyAdmin. This should be http://localhost/phpMyAdmin.

   `$cfgPmaAbsoluteUri = 'http://localhost/phpMyAdmin';`

Foundation Dreamweaver MX

3. Now look for the following block of code:

   ```
   $cfg['Servers'][$i]['auth_type']    = 'config';   // Authentication
       ➥method (config, http or cookie based)?
   $cfg['Servers'][$i]['user']         = 'root';     // MySQL user
   $cfg['Servers'][$i]['password']     = '';         // MySQL password
       ➥(only needed // with 'config' auth_type)
   $cfg['Servers'][$i]['only_db']      = '';         // If set to a db-
       ➥name, only
   ```

   We must change the above values to represent our environment:

   ```
   $cfg['Servers'][$i]['auth_type']    = 'config';   // Authentication
       ➥method (config, http or cookie based)?
   $cfg['Servers'][$i]['user']         = 'pault';    // MySQL user
   $cfg['Servers'][$i]['password']     = 'sesame';   // MySQL password
       ➥(only needed // with 'config' auth_type)
   $cfg['Servers'][$i]['only_db']      = 'book_db';  // If set to a db-
       ➥name, only
   ```

4. Once you've made all the changes to config.inc.php, save it.

5. Point your browser at http://localhost/phpMyAdmin and you should see the following:

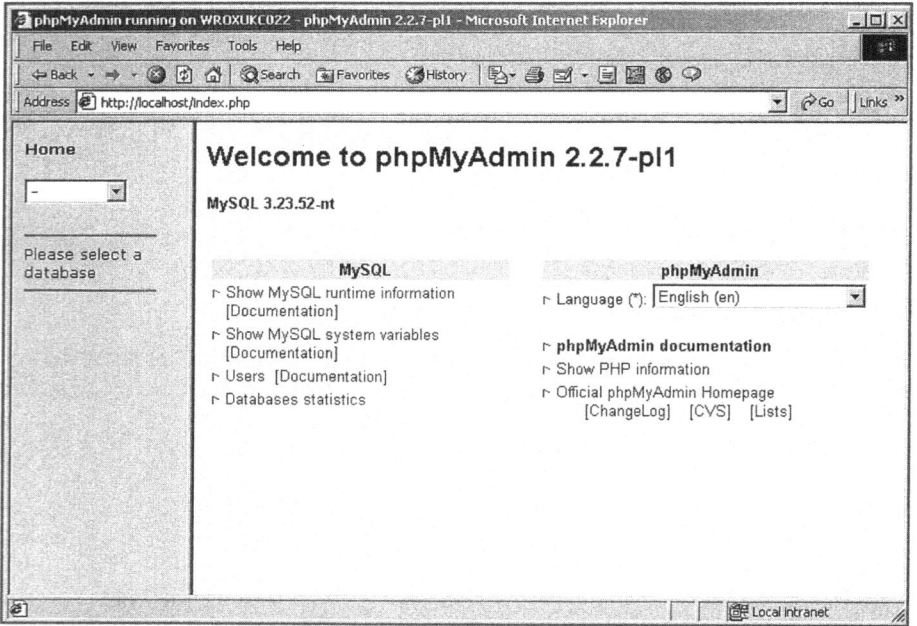

Congratulations! You've now installed all the software that you need for the rest of the book!

Configuring Dreamweaver to use MySQL

> *There is an issue with some versions of Dreamweaver MX and some older versions of PHP. Version 4.1.0 of PHP will not work correctly with MX because of an issue with the* `mysql_pconnect()` *function. If you're currently running this version of PHP, then I'm afraid you'll need to upgrade. You can download the latest release from www.php.net/downloads. This won't be a problem if you've followed our installation instructions.*

1. We now have to create a connection to our MySQL database. If it isn't already selected, click on the Application panel on the right-hand side of the Dreamweaver screen. Click on the [+] button on the Databases tab and select MySQL Connection.

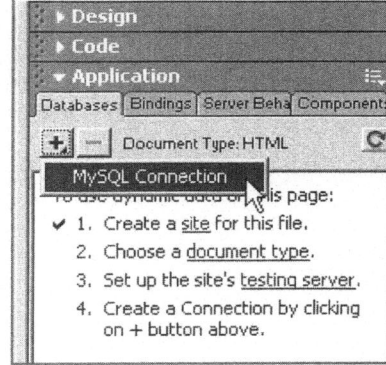

2. A box will open, into which you must enter your details. To begin with, you have to provide a name for the connection. I've called it:

   `myConn`

3. You will need to provide the host name of the MySQL server. As you're running MySQL locally, the hostname is:

   `localhost`

4. Next we provide a username. Use the username you created in the **Preparing MySQL** section earlier in this chapter; in my case the username is:

   `pault`

5. Next we supply a password. Use the password you created in the **Preparing MySQL** section.

Foundation Dreamweaver MX

6. Finally, we select the database to which we wish to connect. In this case, we use the database:

   book_db

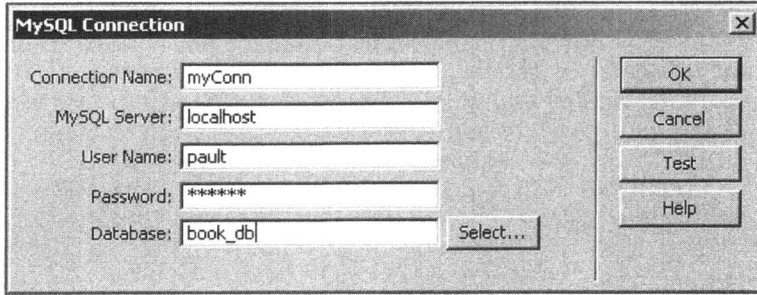

7. Click OK.

   The connection you have created will now be displayed in the Databases panel:

If you look at the database information, you'll see that there are currently no tables in our database. We shall create the tables required for our PHP application next.

If, when you try to connect to your database, you get Unidentified Error, and all the information you have entered is correct, check your php.ini file. If the include_path has been set and the default "." has been removed, this may be the cause

To fix this change the MMHTTPDB.php file, line 15:

from:

require("mysql.php");

to:

require('./mysql.php");

PHP/MySQL The Real Dynamic Duo

Building a PHP application

Now that we've successfully set up our Dreamweaver connection, it's time to build our first PHP application. We're going to look at how to build a contact form for our web site. This form will contain three fields: a field for the user to enter their name, a field for their e-mail address, and a field to allow them to enter their comments.

Planning our database table

Now before we rush in, let's look at the information we wish to gather, and how that affects the structure of our database. We have three fields in our form. That means in this instance, our database table must contain at least three fields as well. However, we also want a way of indexing the entries in the database so we'll add another field, which will give each entry a unique number. We do this by using MySQL's **auto-increment** feature.

Now we're going to use phpMyAdmin to setup our database.

> If you're using Windows, then another option available to you is **mysqlfront**. This is a free program that provides a GUI front-end for MySQL, and it can be downloaded from:
> www.anse.de/mysqlfront/download.php.

Creating our table with phpMyAdmin

Because phpMyAdmin is a collection of PHP scripts, it must be accessed through your browser. Point your browser at http://localhost/index.php to start it.

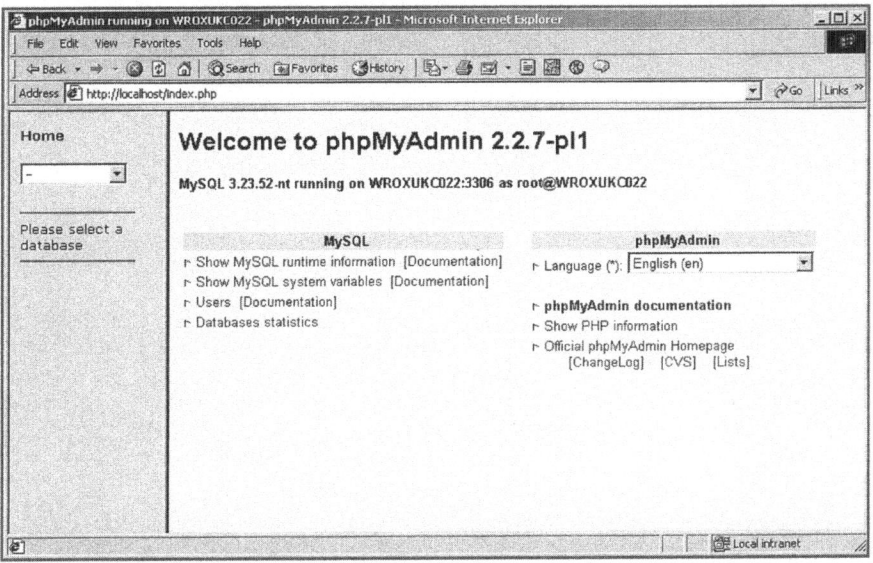

Foundation Dreamweaver MX

1. Let's start by selecting the correct database. From the drop-down menu on the left-hand side, select the database `book_db`.

2. Once we've done this, we need to create a table in our database. We shall call the table `contacts`. Our table will have four fields. These fields will be called `id`, `name`, `email` and `comments`. So, underneath the heading Create new table on database book_db: fill in the Name and Fields boxes as shown in the screenshot below and click Go.

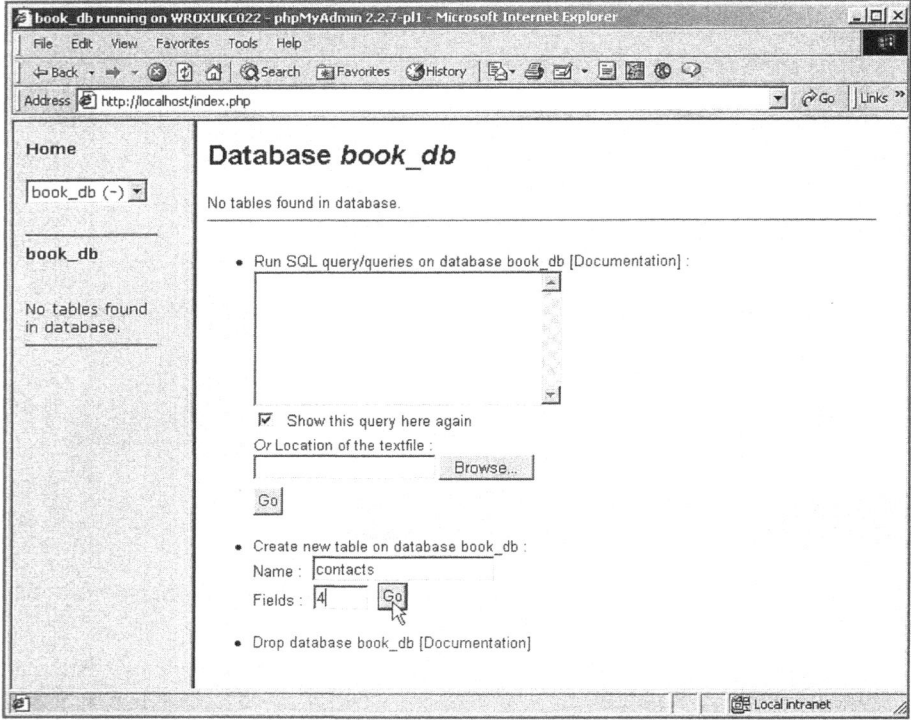

PHP/MySQL The Real Dynamic Duo

3. Next we have to give our fields values. We're going to use the first field to index our entries. We'll call it id, the column type will be INT, and its maximum length is going to be 10. But the most important part of this field is shown on the right-hand side. We have set it to auto_increment and also made it the **primary key**. This means every time an entry is made into the database, the value of this field will increase by 1. Fill in the boxes as shown in the screenshot below:

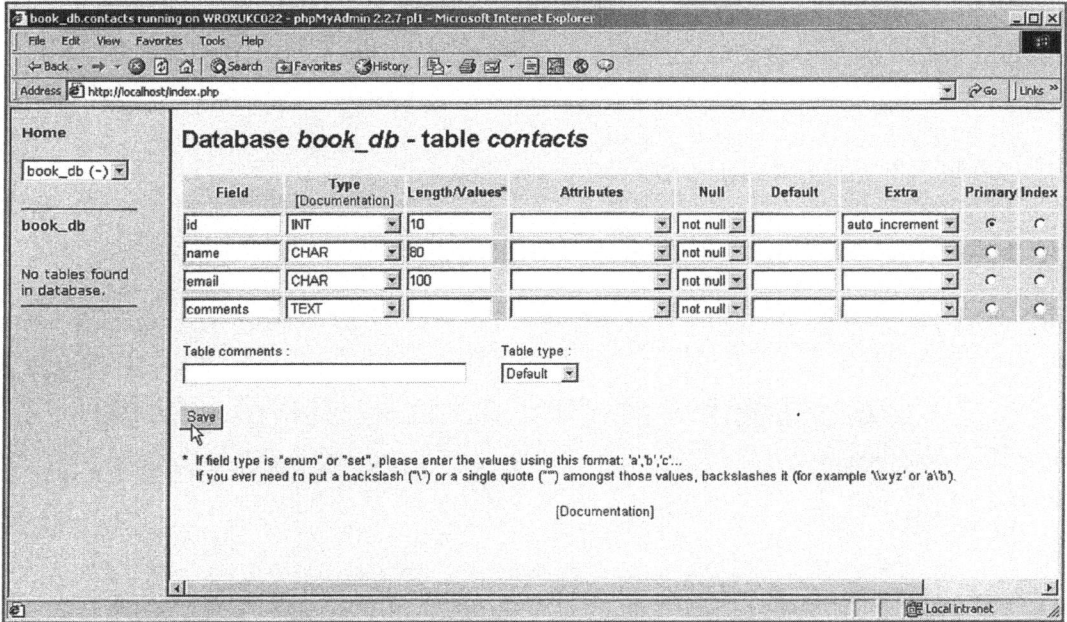

4. The second field is called name, set the column type to CHAR and set its length to 80.

5. The third field is called email and again you should set the column type to CHAR, but this time set its length to 100.

6. The last field is called comments. Set this column type to text, because the maximum length for CHAR and VARCHAR is 255, which may not be enough. Once you've entered the information above, click on the Save button.

Creating our form in Dreamweaver MX

Now that we've created the table in our database to store the form data, we need to make the form so that the data can be entered.

1. If we go back into Dreamweaver, the tables that we created should now be visible from the Databases panel:

    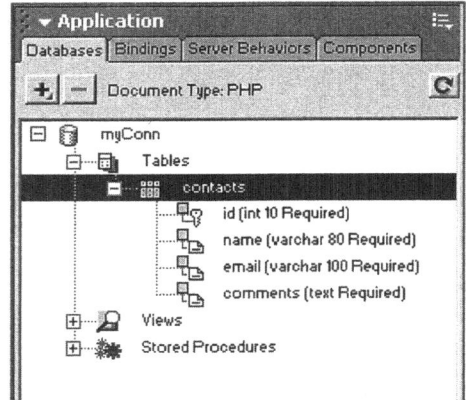

    If they're not visible, click on the Refresh button, which is the small circular arrow on the top right of the panel.

2. Create a new PHP page and save it as contact.php.

3. Now we can insert the form tags onto the page. Do this by placing your cursor between the <body> tags in the Code view and selecting Insert > Form.

    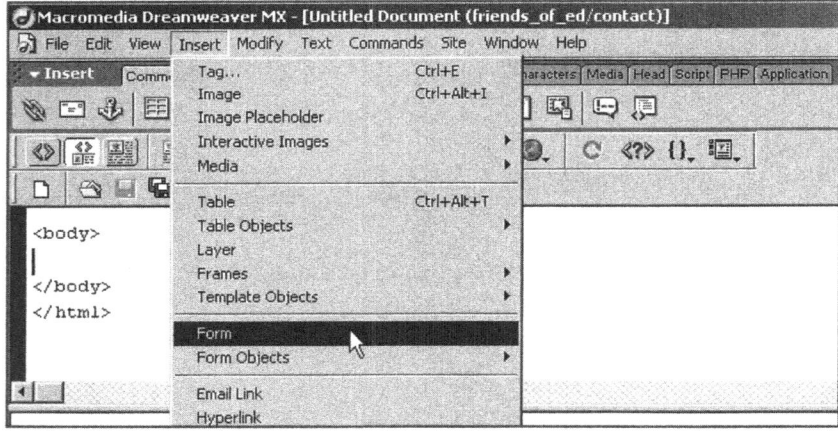

4. You should see the Form Wizard pop up on your screen. We can use it to name our form. To do this, type contact in the Name: box (leave all the other fields as they are):

    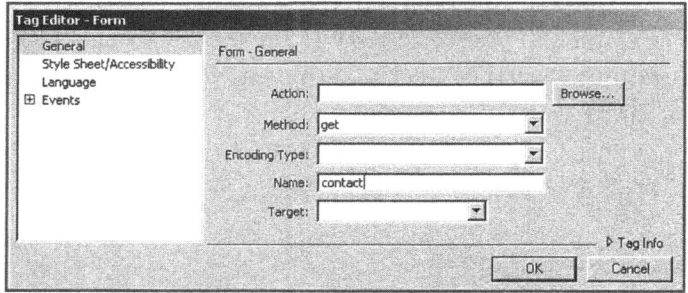

5. In order to keep our form layout tidy, we'll place a table within our form tags. Position your cursor just in front of the </form> tag and then select Insert > Table from the top menu. Our table will be 400px wide, it will have four rows and two columns, a Cell Spacing of 5, a Cell Padding of 0 and the Border will be set to 0. Input these values to the Insert Table dialog box, as shown here:

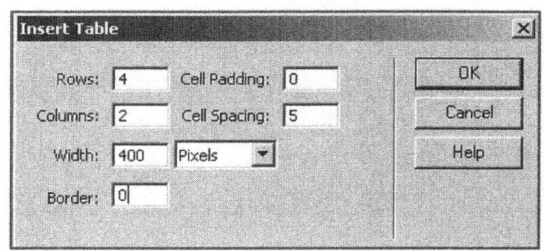

Your page should now look like this:

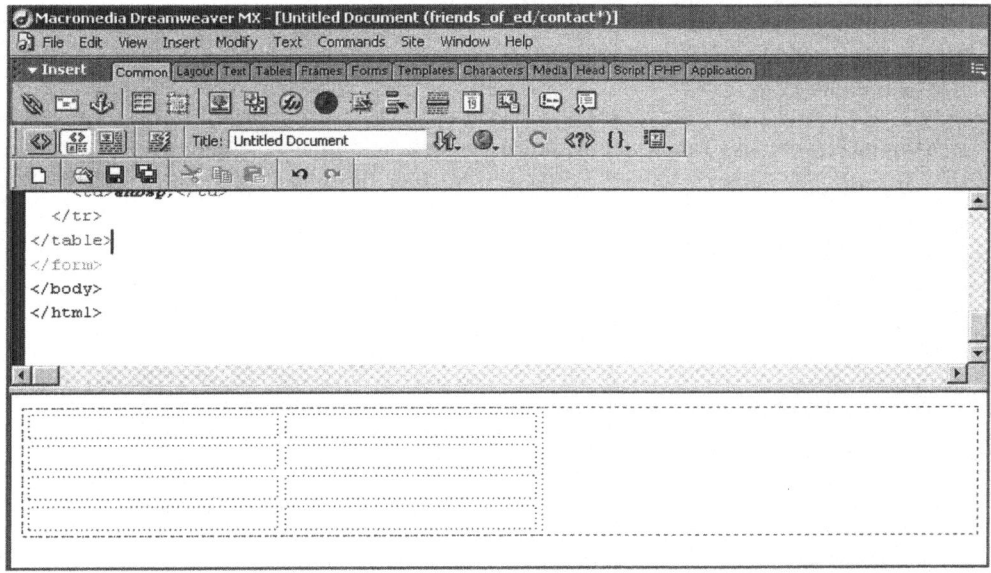

6. Next, we'll place text fields in the right-hand side of our table. Position the cursor in the top right table cell. From the top menu select Insert > Form Objects > Text Field.

7. Once you've inserted your text field, move down to the Properties panel and rename it from textfield to name, as shown below:

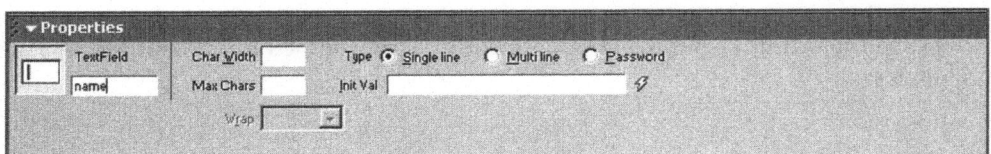

8. Place your cursor in the table cell directly below and insert another text field. We shall label this email:

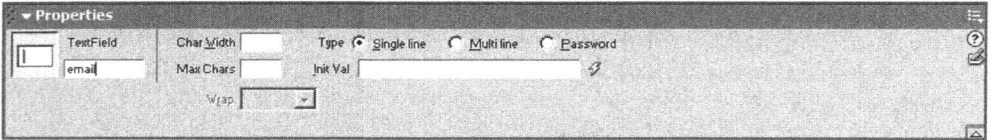

9. Now position the cursor in the table cell directly below the cell containing our **email** text field. This time, instead of selecting Text Field, select Textarea. Because of this, we need to enter more information into the Properties panel. We shall label the text area comments, set the Char Width to 20, Num Lines to 6, and the Wrap to Virtual.

10. Select the bottom right-hand table cell. This time, select Insert > Form Objects > Button from the top menu.

11. Finally, select the table cell directly opposite the text field that we labeled 'name' and type Name. Do the same for 'email' and 'comments' so that your form now looks like the example below:

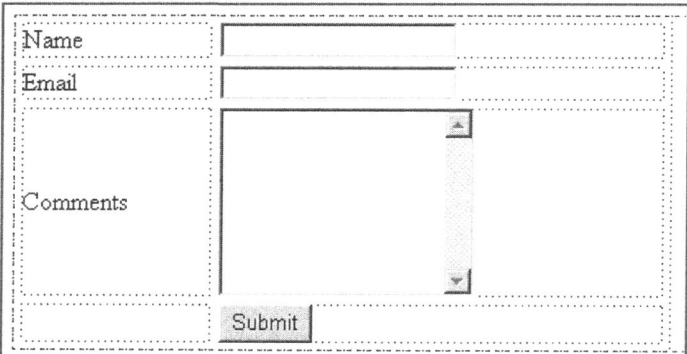

Validating our form

Now that our form is complete, we will need to add some validation to ensure that no empty values are sent in the form.

1. Highlight the form by positioning your cursor just outside the red dotted form boundary and clicking once:

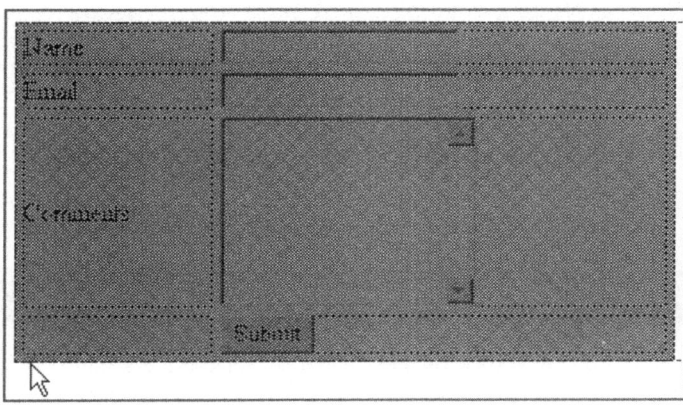

2. Dreamweaver comes with its own Form Validation Behavior, which can be accessed under the Behaviors tab in the Design panel. Select Validate Form from the drop-down menu that appears when you click the [+] button.

   When this is selected, a new box will open with a list of the form fields on the page:

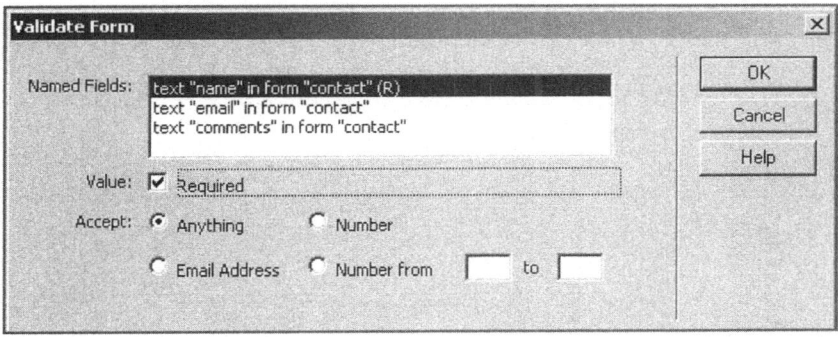

3. Select text "name" in form "contact", check the Required box and select Anything from the Accept menu.

4. Select text "email" in form "contact", check the Required box and select Email Address from the Accept menu.

5. Select text "comments" in form "contact", check the Required box and select Anything from the Accept menu.

   Once you've done this, click OK and save the page.

Now press F12 to preview your page and press the Submit button without entering any form text. You should get the following message:

Inserting the form information into the database

We have created the table in our database that will store our data. We have created the form to enter the data, and we have added validation to our form to ensure no empty values are entered. The last thing to do is to insert the information from the form into the database.

1. Go to the Server Behaviors tab in the Application panel, click on the [+] button and select Insert Record from the drop-down menu.

2. This will open the Insert Record dialog box; select the connection we created earlier (myConn):

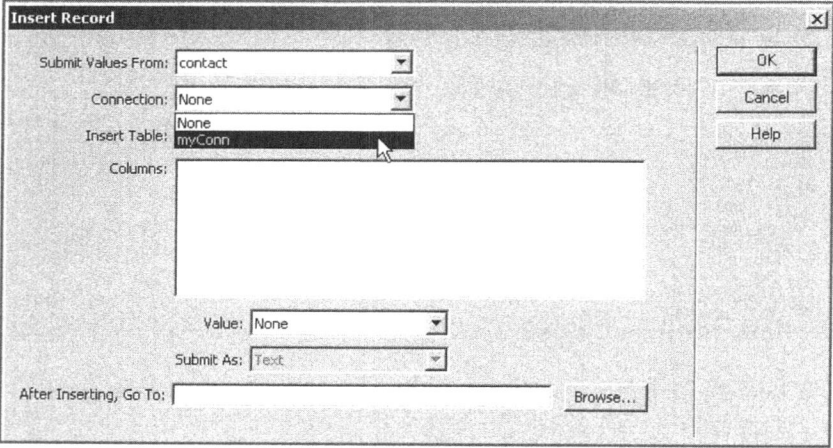

3. Once you've selected your connection, the columns field will become populated. Make sure the correct value is entered into the correct database field. In the screenshot on the next page all the values are correct. Enter thanks.php into the last field in the box and click OK:

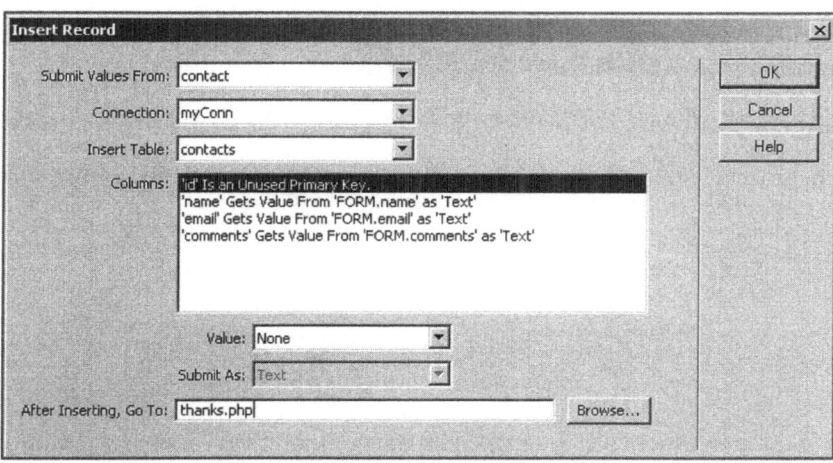

4. Now we need to create a 'thank you' message. Open up a new PHP page and type an appropriate message in the Design view. Format it as bold text in a large font, as shown in the screenshot below. Save it as `thanks.php` when you're done:

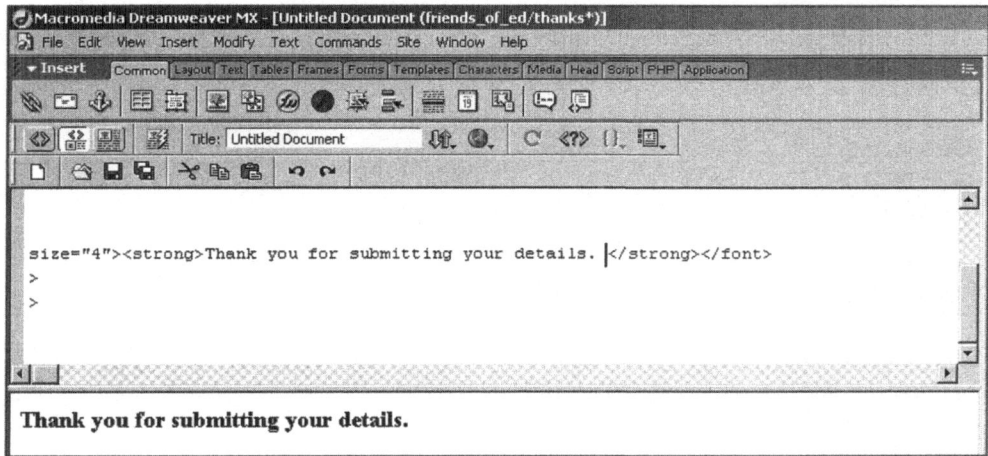

Testing our form by retrieving information

We're now ready to test the form. Open your browser and point it towards http://localhost/friends_of_ed/contact.php. You should see the form you just created in the browser window. When you fill out the form and hit Submit, you should be directed to the 'thank you' message. But where has the data gone and how can we retrieve it?

Now that we've built a way for someone to contact us, we need a way of viewing this information.

Creating a form to hold our data

1. Create a new PHP page in Dreamweaver MX and save it as `view_contacts.php`.

2. Into the page we'll insert a table with the following values:

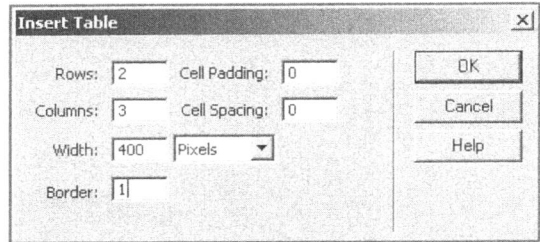

3. In the top row of the table, enter the text Name, Email and Comments into the cells:

4. Center the text in the table cells by placing the cursor in the cell and selecting Center from the Horz menu in the Properties panel.

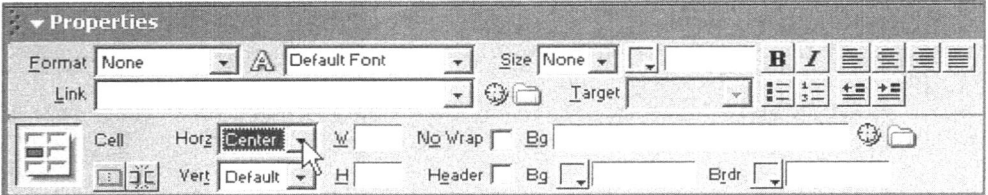

5. Finish by adding a background color to the cells. Do this by placing your cursor in the cell and clicking the Bg tool in the Properties panel. Select the color of your choice. Save the page.

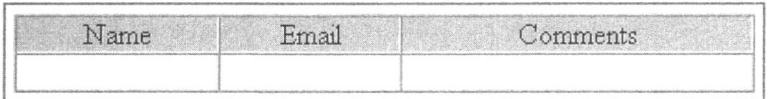

Building the Recordset

Before we can retrieve any data from our database, we must first create a **Recordset**.

1. Select the Server Behaviors tab from the Application panel. Click on the [+] button and select Recordset from the drop-down menu.

PHP/MySQL The Real Dynamic Duo

2. When you've done this, the Recordset window will open. Name your Recordset my_contacts and select our connection from the Connection menu.

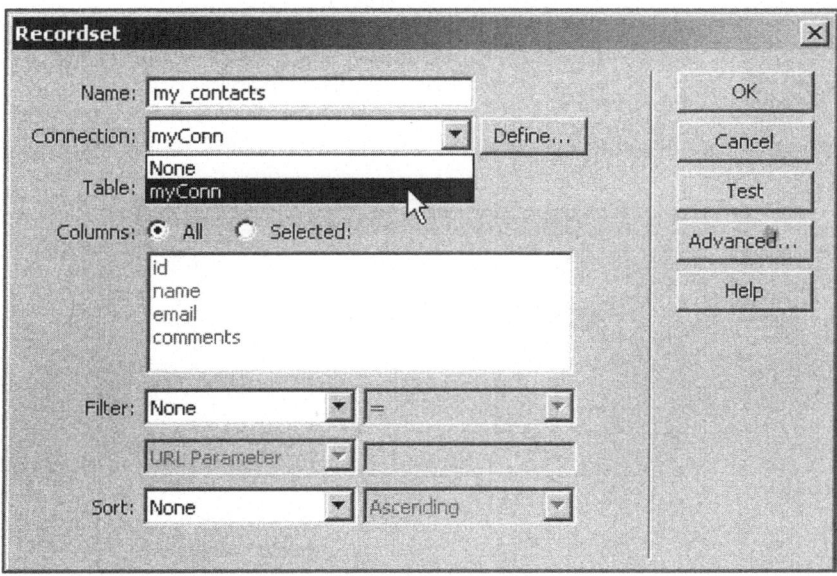

3. We can leave the Column and Filter options unchanged.

4. Lastly we need to change the Sort options to id and Ascending. Click OK.

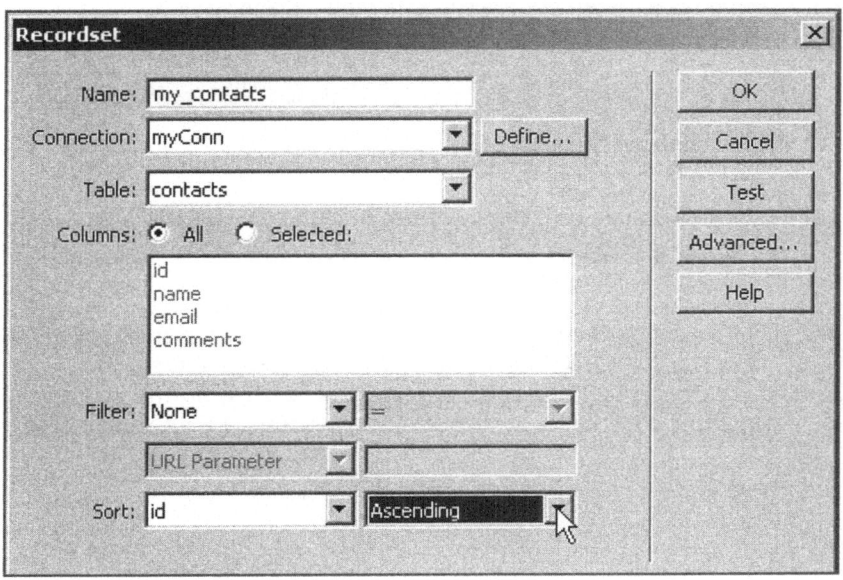

Displaying our information

Now that we've created our Recordset, we need to display the information.

1. Place the cursor in the table cell directly below Name. Click on the [+] button in the Server Behaviors tab and select Dynamic Text from the drop-down.

2. This will open the Dynamic Text dialog. From this box, highlight name and then click OK.

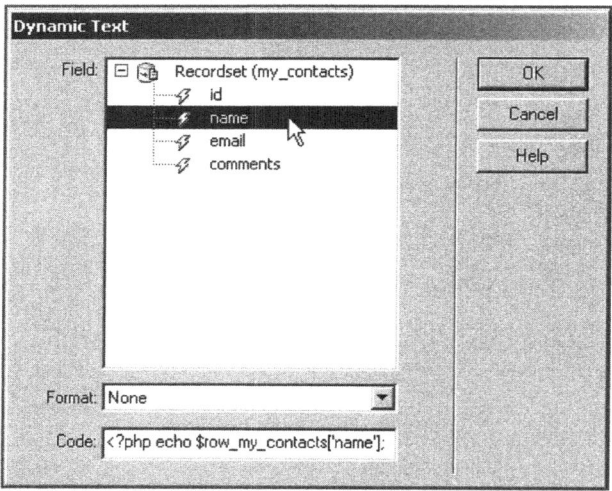

This will insert the code required to display the data into this cell:

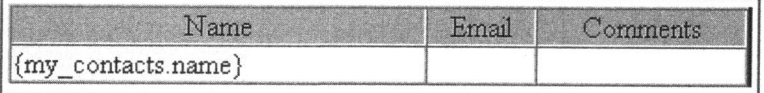

3. Place the cursor in the table cell directly below Email. Select Dynamic text from the drop-down menu in the Server Behaviors tab. This time select email from the Dynamic Text dialog and then click OK.

4. Place the cursor in the table cell below Comments and repeat the steps above. This time, select comments from the Dynamic Text window. Before we insert the code, we must make an alteration to the code that Dreamweaver generates. We'll wrap the code with the nl2br() function. Change the code in the Code field at the bottom of the Dynamic Text box from:

```
<?php echo $row_my_contacts['comments']; ?>
```

to:

```
<?php echo nl2br($row_my_contacts['comments']); ?>
```

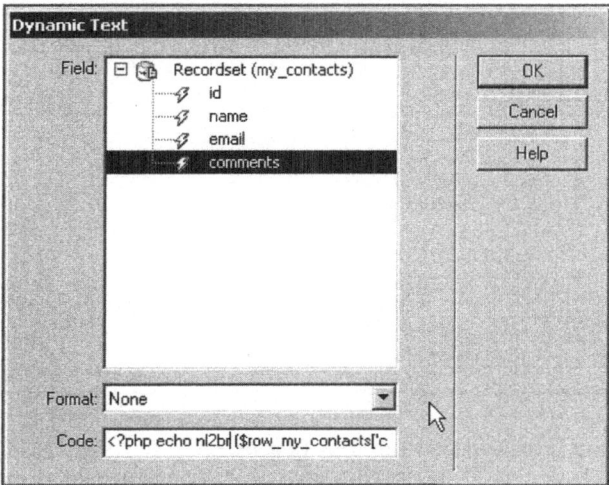

Why do we do this? Well, MySQL will pass out the data to the page as plain ASCII text, with normal line breaks. This is fine for bringing text out into a text file that will be opened by a text editor that understands ASCII, but with a web page you'll lose all the formatting that people have put in when they filled in the comments *box. To remedy this, we have to add a piece of PHP code that replaces the ASCII line breaks output by MySQL with the <br> tag so that a web browser knows to put in a new line. For more information visit www.php.net/nl2br.*

11   Foundation Dreamweaver MX

Your page should now look like this:

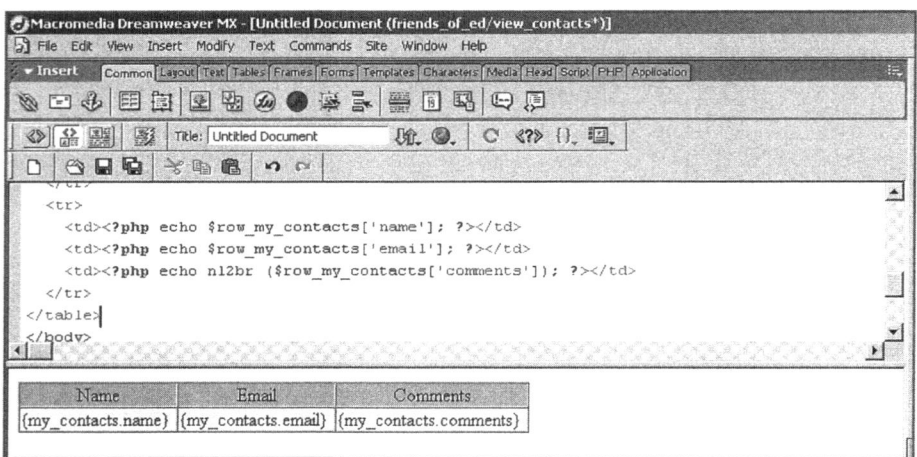

5. What we've done so far will only pull the first record from the database, so we must apply a **Repeat Region** to the table. Select the three dynamic text regions by holding down the CTRL key and clicking on each one. A black border will appear around them when selected:

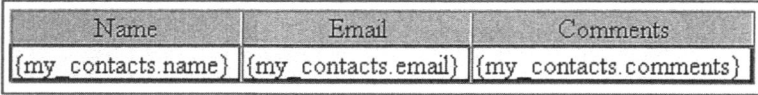

6. Click on the [+] button in the Server Behaviors tab. This time select Repeat Region.

7. This opens the Repeat Region dialog. Leave the settings as they are:

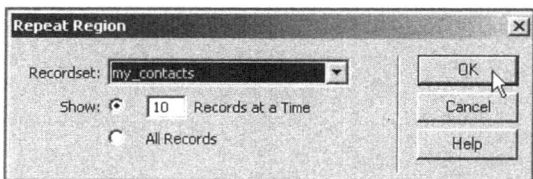

8. Click on OK. Your page should now include the Repeat tag:

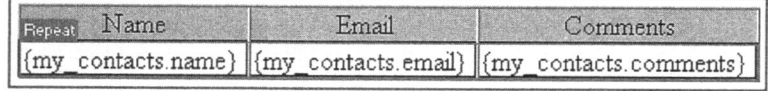

9. Save the changes you made to view_contacts.php.

   Congratulations! You've now completed your first dynamic database-driven web application with Dreamweaver MX.

Testing the Complete Application

Now for the moment of truth. Point your browser at http://localhost/friends_of_ed/contact.php. Enter some details into the form and hit Submit. You should get the 'thank you' message. If you open up http://localhost/friends_of_ed/view_contacts.php you should see a table containing the information you entered into the form:

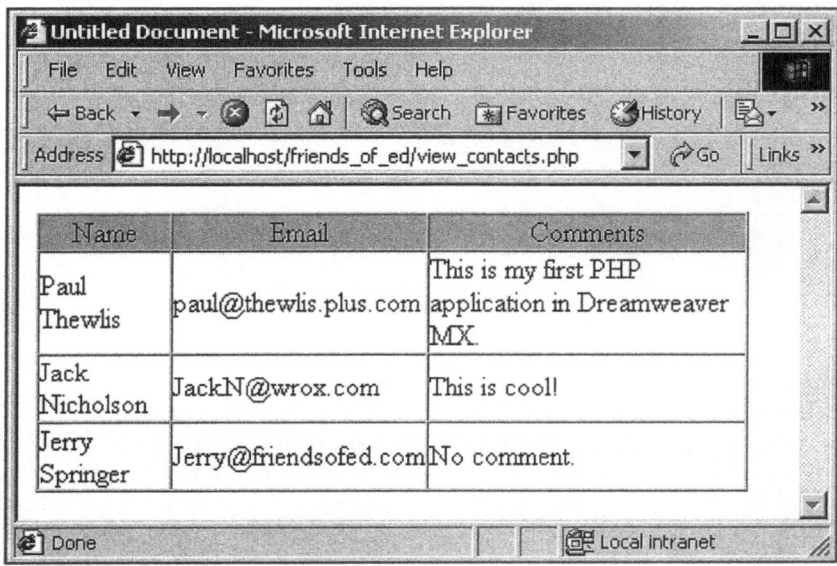

Summary

In this chapter, we looked at:

- How a PHP/MySQL web application works.

- How to connect to MySQL from the command line.

- How to create a database and how to grant a user the correct privileges.

- How to configure Dreamweaver MX to use PHP/MySQL and create a connection to MySQL from Dreamweaver.

- Creating MySQL tables using phpMyAdmin.

- Building a form that will enter information into our database, validating the information entered, and retrieving the information from the database.

After completing this chapter, you will now have a much better understanding of PHP and MySQL. We will carry this knowledge into the next chapter, where we will look at building a more complex PHP application. Now that we have installed and configured our dynamic duo, the sky's the limit...

Secure Login and Registration

What we'll cover in this chapter

- Security issues in PHP
- Building a simple application using sessions
- How to build a Registration and Login PHP application using Dreamweaver and hand coding
- Protecting our secret pages using sessions

You don't have to be a secret agent to have information you don't want to be available to the public. But what can you do if you want to put it online and share it with certain people - but not the entire English-speaking world? In this chapter we're going to build a Login / Registration application using a mixture of code generated by Dreamweaver MX and some PHP which we'll code by hand.

Again, don't worry if you're not experienced with code – as with previous chapters we'll go through it step by step, and you'll see once more that often, a little hand-woven magic can lead to some amazingly dynamic web pages!

Let's start with a little housekeeping.

PHP coding conventions used in this chapter

The developers of PHP made a major decision when they released PHP 4.2.0. They decided that `register_globals` would be set to `off` by default (I'll explain this in more detail in just a moment). While it is possible to write secure code with `register_globals` set to on, the PHP developers rightly felt that it made it too easy to write insecure code.

When `register_globals` is set to `on`, `form`, `server`, and `environment` variables become part of the global namespace automatically. For example, if we had a form with a single field called **test** we could access the value of test in the PHP script that processed the form by simply prefixing it with a variable sign **$**. Therefore, we could get its value by using `$test`.

With the previous worries in mind, the developers introduced several new variables in PHP 4.1.0. These will help developers when register_globals is set to `off`:

- `$_GET` – contains form variables sent through GET
- `$_POST` – contains form variables sent through POST
- `$_COOKIE` – contains HTTP cookie variables
- `$_SERVER` – contains server variables
- `$_ENV` – contains the environment variables
- `$_REQUEST` – a merge of the GET variables, POST variables and cookie variables
- `$_SESSION` – contains HTTP variables registered by the session module

With `register_globals` set to `off`, we could only access the value of the variable by using `$_POST["test"]` if we used the POST method for our form, or `$_GET["test"]` if we used the GET method. The same rule applies to cookies and sessions. Before, we could simply access the value of a cookie or session called `test` by using `$test`. Now we must use `$_COOKIE["test"]` or `$_SESSION["test"]` to access the value.

Security Issues

Why is having `register_globals` set to **on** a security risk? Let's look at an example. We have a form that allows the site administrator to log in when they enter the correct username and password. A session is set with the value admin:

```php
<?php
    if($admin) {
        // I have admin privileges for this page and could destroy this site
    }
?>
```

If a malicious user was to call any page like this www.mydomain.com/anypage.php?admin=1 they would have admin privileges for this page.

Now look at the secure alternative that having `register_globals` set to **off** forces you to use:

```php
<?php
    if($_SESSION["admin"]) {
        // I have admin privileges for this page and could destroy this site
    }
?>
```

The only way a malicious user could now gain admin privileges would be by hijacking the session. While this looks like a simple example, in reality quite a few PHP applications were exploitable in this way.

You can find further examples of different problems that can occur due to `register_globals` being on in a paper written by Shaun Clowes called 'A Study in Scarlet – Exploiting Common Vulnerabilities in PHP Applications' at the following URL: www.securereality.com.au/studyinscarlet.txt.

> *Because in this chapter, we're actually striving to create secure applications, we feel it's important to keep* `register_globals` *set to off, for the sake of good practice.*

Working with PHP sessions

Sessions are variables that are preserved after your PHP script has finished executing. The session can be destroyed by another page on the site. It can also expire after a set amount of time as defined in the `php.ini` file. PHP sessions are initiated by the `session_start()` function. This tells PHP to start a session and to look for the session ID (SID). If the SID is found, variables associated with the session are loaded from the server. You can register a session variable by using the `session_register()` function. If you wish to destroy the session, you can use `session_destroy()`. Destroying the session enhances the security of the site. To check that a session has been registered, you can use the `session_is_registered()` function.

There are many more session functions available. For more details on session support in PHP4, plus a complete list of PHP's session functions visit http://uk.php.net/manual/en/ref.session.php.

Since we're going to use sessions to protect our secret pages, it's a good idea to gain a basic understanding of how they work. PHP4 has native session support; you can view session settings in the `phpinfo.php` page we made in **Chapter 8**.

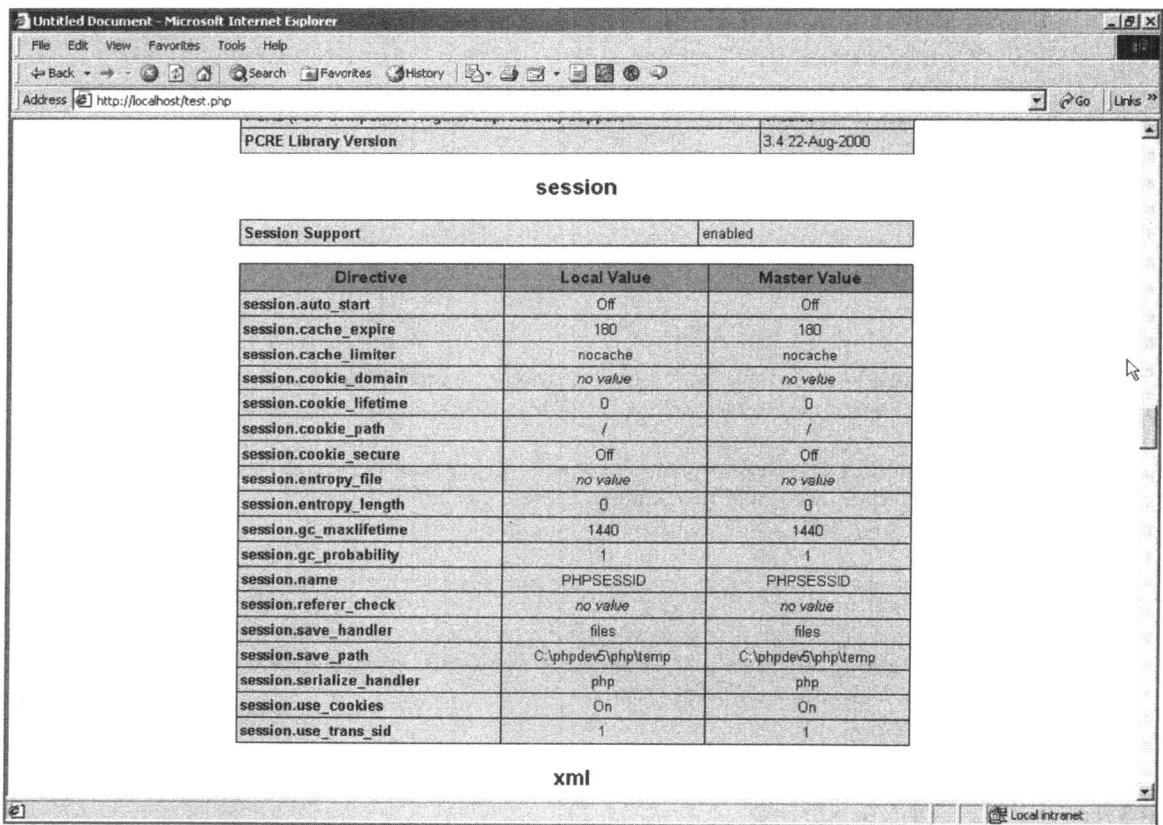

Additional Configuration

Sessions are files which are stored on the server. When PHP is installed, the default directory these sessions are stored in is `/tmp`. This directory does not exist in Windows. Because of this, some nasty error messages will appear when we try to use sessions. Luckily for us, we can change this in our `php.ini` file.

1. The first thing we have to do is create a folder to hold our sessions. In this example, I have created a folder in `c:\Program Files` called `sessions`.

2. Next, we have to open the `php.ini` file. This will be stored in `c:\windows` for Windows 95/98 and `c:\winnt` or `c:\winnt40` for NT/2000/XP.

3. Look for the following line:

    ```
    session.save_path = /tmp
    ```

4. Change it to:

    ```
    session.save_path = c:\Program Files\sessions
    ```

5. Save the changes to `php.ini`.

6. Restart the Apache web server.

7. View the `phpinfo.php` page again and you will see that it reflects the changes you made.

A Simple Session Example

Let's get our hands dirty (and possibly our feet too) by creating a simple script that uses sessions.

1. Open a new PHP page in Dreamweaver MX and save it in your root directory as `session.php`. Insert the `<form>` tags onto your page. You can do this easily by positioning the cursor between the `<body>` tags in the Code view and selecting Insert > Form from the menu.

2. Inserting our form in code view means you will see the **Tag Editor** dialog box open. Enter `my_first_session.php` in the **Action** box. Set the method as **post**. Click **OK**.

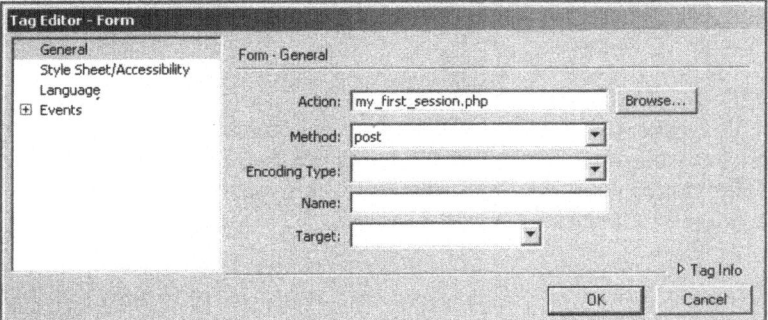

3. Just as we did in Chapter 10 (you did read Chapter 10, didn't you?), we'll insert a text field into our form. In the Properties panel, give it the label **name**. Finally, insert a Submit button next to the text field.

    Your form should now look like this:

4. Save the changes to `session.php` and close the file.

5. Next, open another new PHP page in Dreamweaver and save it in your root directory as `my_first_session.php`. Insert this code above the opening `<html>` tag:

```
<?php
session_start();
$name=$_POST["name"];
session_register("name");
?>
```

Let's break down the code within the PHP tags, line by line:

```
session_start();
```

Whenever you use sessions in PHP, you must begin with this line. This line of code looks for an existing session, and if none exists, it will create a new one. Without it, you will be unable to create or access any session variables.

```
$name=$_POST["name"];
```

This line of code simply assigns to the variable $name the value that is passed from our text field in `session.php` via the POST method.

```
    session_register("name");
```

This function registers the value of the variable. In our example, we will register the variable $name. However, when you register this value using the function `session_register()`, you need to use the name of the variable without the $ sign.

6. Then insert this code between the `<body>` tags:

```
<?php
echo("Hello ". $name);
?>
```

Although the session has been registered, we won't be able to access $_SESSION["name"] on this page. This is because you are unable to access the value of a session on the same page as it is set. The session will only be available to you on subsequent pages where you use the `session_start()` function.

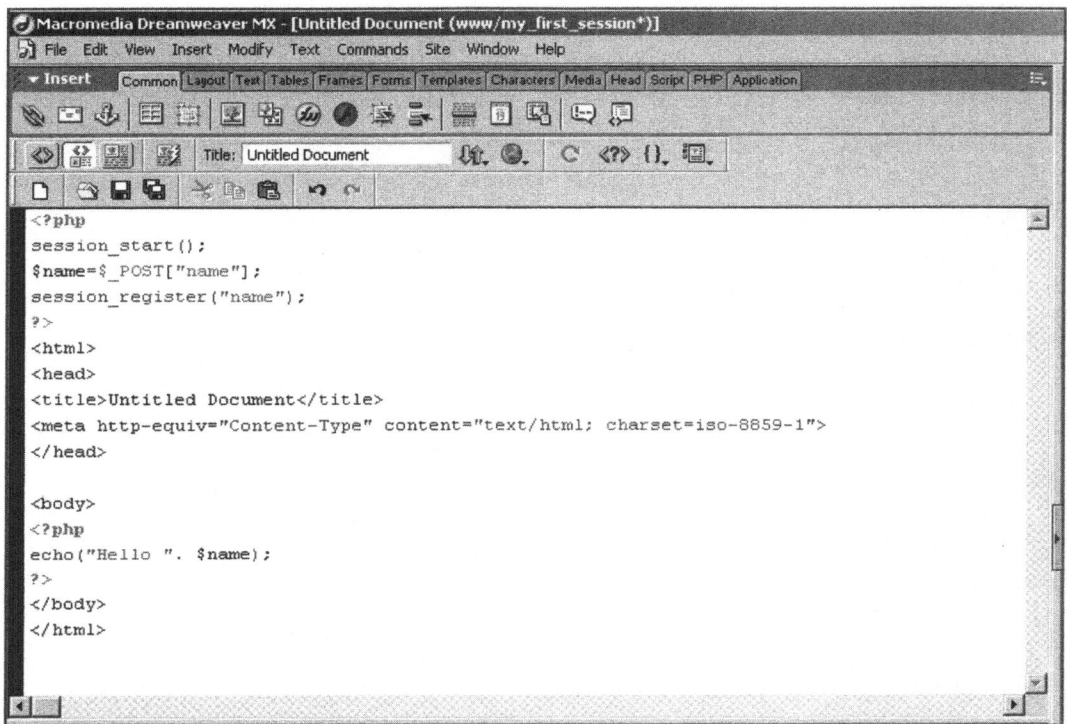

7. Save the changes to my_first_session.php and close the file.

8. Open a third PHP page in MX and save it in your root directory as hello.php. Insert this code above the opening <html> tag:

```
<?php
session_start();
?>
```

As we discussed earlier, to be able to access session values, you must use the session_start() function at the top of your page.

9. Then in between the <body> tags insert:

```
<?php
    echo("Hello ". $_SESSION["name"]);
?>
```

This code will print out the value of the session called name to the page.

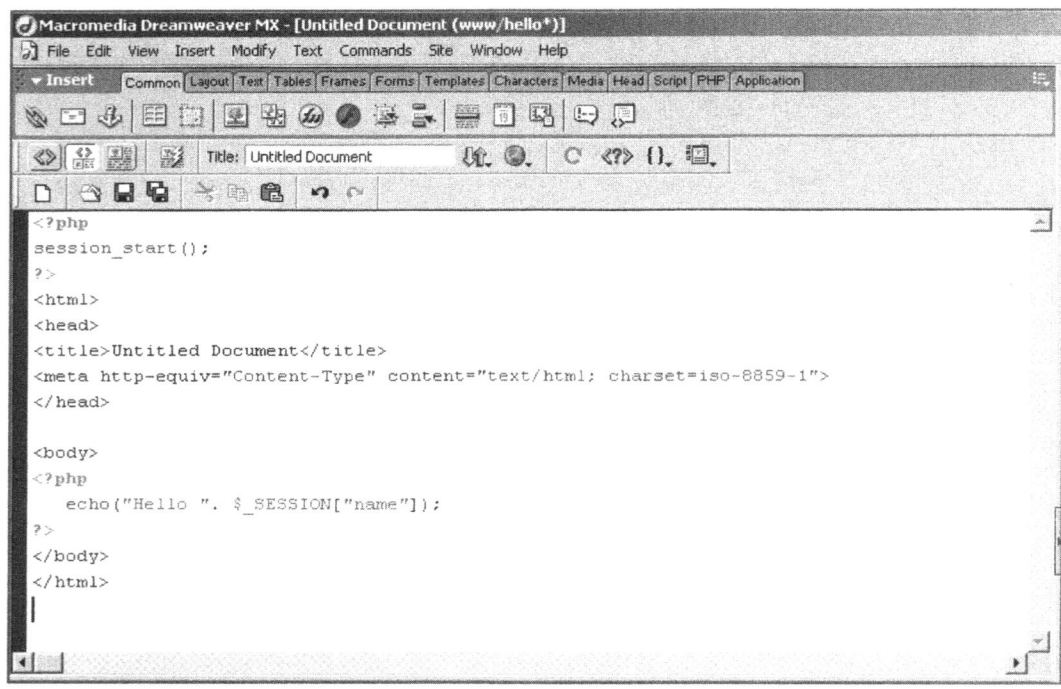

10. Save the changes you made to hello.php and close the file.

11. Finally, create a link from my_first_session.php to hello.php. To do this, just open up my_first_session.php and type hello.php at the top of the Design view window. Highlight the text and enter hello.php in the **Link** box of the Properties panel. Save your changes.

With this complete, point your browser to session.php. Enter your name in the text field then press Submit.

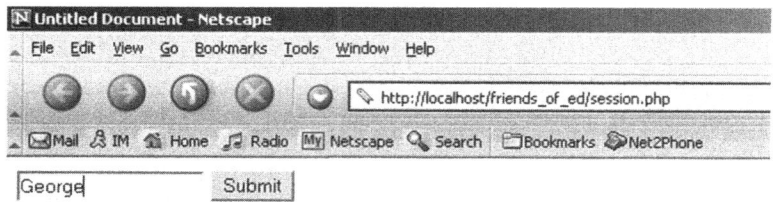

You should see the following page. Now click on the link to hello.php.

Secure Login and Registration

You can now access this variable using $_SESSION["name"] on any page as long as session_start() is used at the top of the page. So what does this teach us? Remember that the internet is a *stateless* environment; Apache has no idea who is requesting the web page, and without sessions or cookies has no way of keeping track of each user as he or she moves from page to page. By using sessions, you can store information on a single user between pages. This enables you to create more complex applications such as shopping carts; after all, what good would a shopping cart be if it lost track of each user (and their baskets) as they moved from page to page? You wouldn't be impressed if Amazon's checkout consisted of a page which said, "Remind me again, who are you and what did you order?"

Next, more affairs of *state* as we shall look at a more complex example when we build a registration/login application using sessions.

> NB When working with sessions or cookies, you must make sure that you send the cookie/session information before any headers are sent to the browser. For instance, placing text or even whitespace before your session_start() function will result in the error below.

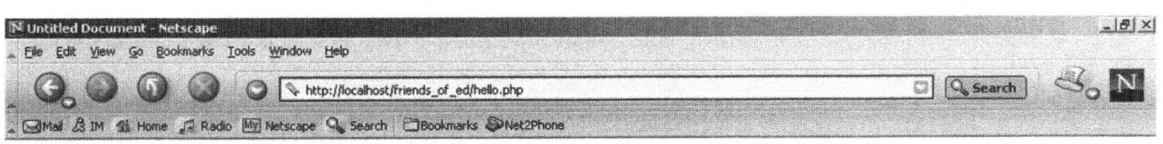

Putting text or whitespace here will cause this error
Warning: Cannot send session cookie - headers already sent by (output started at C:\Program Files\Apache Group\Apache\htdocs\session\hello.php:2) in C:**Program Files\Apache Group\Apache\htdocs\session\hello.php** on line **3**

Warning: Cannot send session cache limiter - headers already sent (output started at C:\Program Files\Apache Group\Apache\htdocs\session\hello.php:2) in C:**Program Files\Apache Group\Apache\htdocs\session\hello.php** on line **3**
Hello

Building our Registration / Login application

Before you start on any application, you must always take time to plan exactly what you want it to do. What will we require of our application?

1. We want to allow new users to register by themselves.

2. We have to decide what information we need to collect.

3. We must validate the information entered.

4. Once registered, a user must be able to log in.

After a little thought, we come up with some answers:

- We can allow a new user to register by themselves by using a web-based application form.

- In this case, we need to collect a first name, last name, e-mail address, username and password.

- We'll use a mixture of client-side and server-side validation.

- We'll create another form into which our user will enter their username and password once they've been registered.

Building our Database Tables

Now that we know what information we wish to collect, we can plan out our tables. We'll need six fields on our database table, which we shall call members. The fields will be called id, firstname, lastname, email, username and password. Our id field will be used to index the entries and will, therefore, be **auto-incremented**. As we did in the last chapter, we'll use phpMyAdmin to create our table.

1. Open your browser and point it to the phpMyAdmin installation directory.

2. Select the database (book_db) we created in the last chapter from the drop-down menu in the left hand frame.

3. We enter members into the Name field and 6 into the Fields field, and then press the Go button:

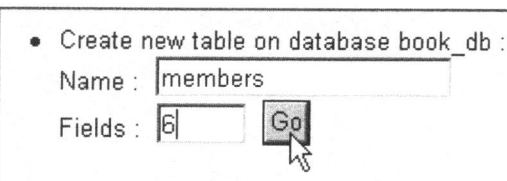

Secure Login and Registration   12

4. Once you've done this, phpMyAdmin will require you to enter more information about your table.

5. As we covered this in more detail in the previous chapter, we will not break down each individual row. Instead, enter the information into the fields as detailed below.

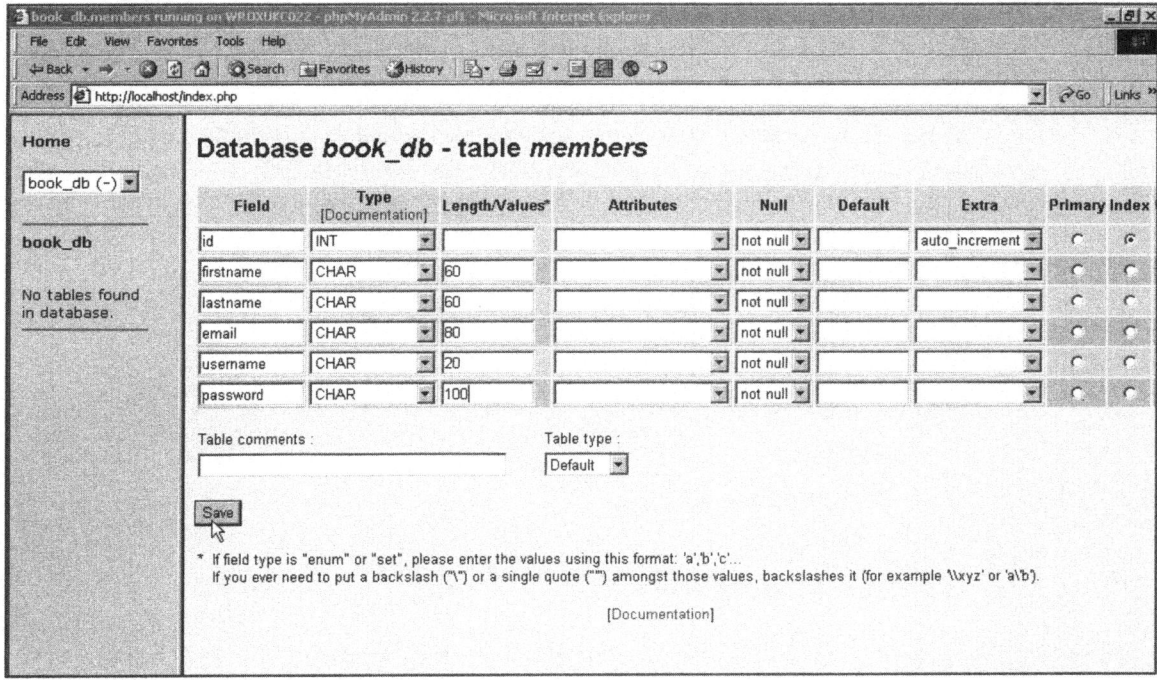

6. Once you have completed this, click the Save button. Our database table is now complete.

Now that our tables have been created in our database, it's time to make our registration form.

Building the form in Dreamweaver

1. Open Dreamweaver and create a new PHP page. Save it as `register.php`. Insert form tags onto your page by choosing Insert from the menu, then Form.

2. As we did in the previous chapter, insert a table within our form tags. Give the table the attributes shown:

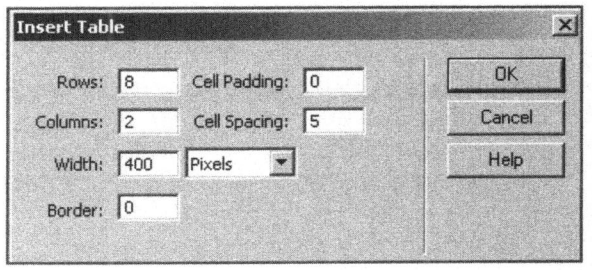

3. Once this is done, select the top two table cells by holding down the CTRL key and clicking on them. With both cells selected, right-click and select Table, then Merge Cells from the menu.

4. This will merge both cells into a single cell. We shall use this cell for our heading. So with your cursor in the top cell, type New User Registration. Center the text in the table cell by selecting Center from the Horz menu in the Properties panel.

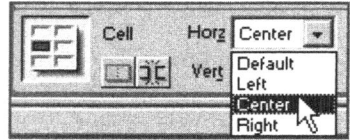

5. Place the cursor in the left hand table cell directly below the cell we just merged and type First Name. Select the cell directly below again and type Last Name. Do the same again, this time typing E-mail. Continue this down the left hand column typing Username, Password and Confirm Password as you move down.

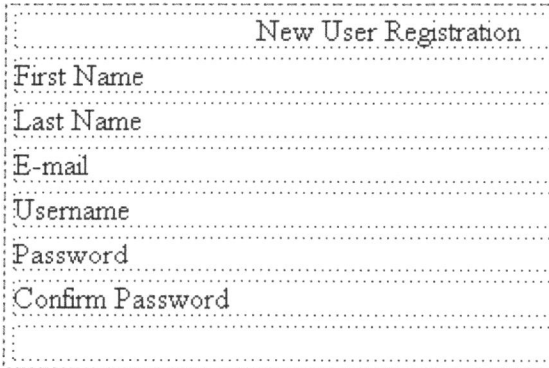

6. Next, we'll place a text field in the cell opposite First Name. Select Insert from the top menu, then Form Objects, and then Text Field.

7. With the newly inserted text field selected, go to the Properties panel.

8. Label this cell firstname by entering it in the box.

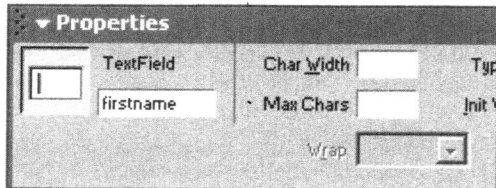

9. Insert another text field directly below and opposite Last Name, this time labeling the text field lastname. Do the same for the cells opposite E-mail, Username, Password and Confirm Password: labeling them email, username, password and con_password respectively. Finally in the bottom right-hand cell, insert a Submit button.

Make sure you select the password radio button in the Properties panel when you label the password *and* con_password *text fields.*

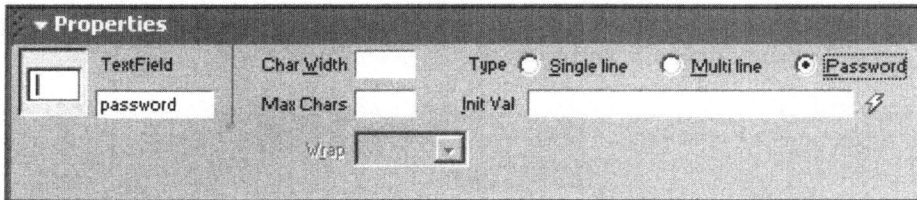

Your form should now look like this:

```
         New User Registration
First Name        [                    ]
Last Name         [                    ]
E-mail            [                    ]
Username          [                    ]
Password          [                    ]
Confirm Password  [                    ]
                        [Submit]
```

10. Save the changes you made to register.php.

Validation

In the previous chapter, we used the Validate Form Behavior that is built into MX. However, this doesn't offer enough options to allow us to validate this form correctly. So we will use a third party extension called Check Form MX. This can be downloaded from Yaro's site www.yaromat.com under the 'Extend Dreamweaver' section.

If you have never installed an extension before, don't worry – there is nothing to it. An extension will come as an MXP file. All you have to do is double-click on the file and let MX take care of the rest. For more details, see the appendix on extensions.

Validating our form

1. Once you've installed the extension, restarted Dreamweaver and re-opened `register.php`, the extension can be accessed from the Design panel. Select the Behaviors tab and click the [+] button, it's listed under yaromat.

2. Once selected, a box will open. At the top will be a field with a list of all the form objects on the page; firstname should be highlighted.

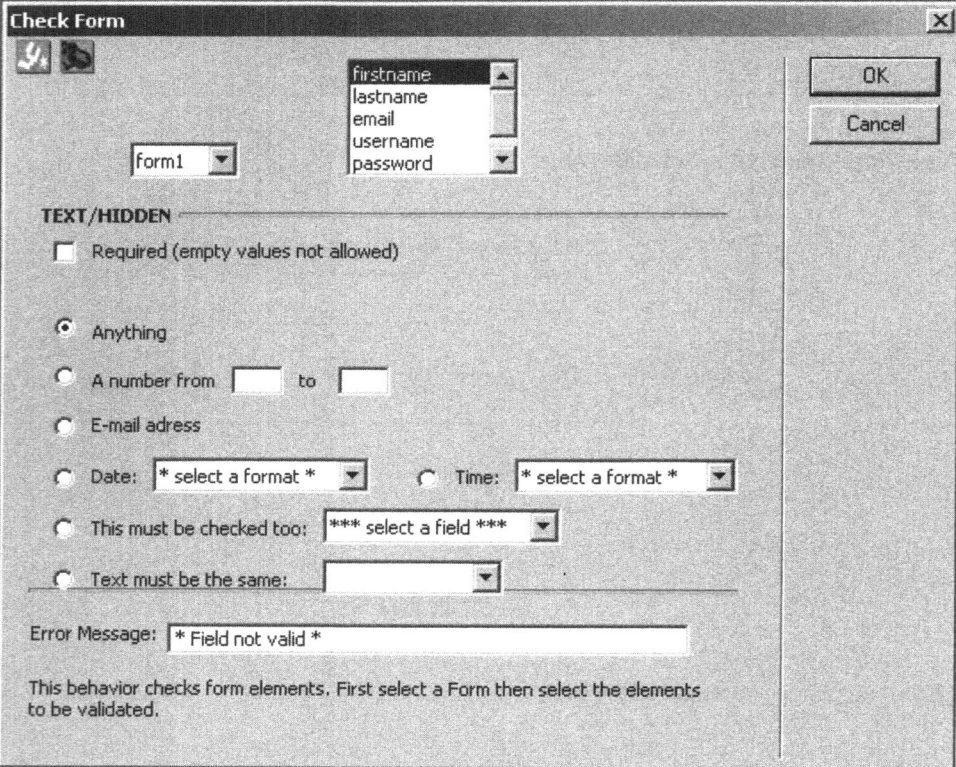

3. With firstname selected, check the Required box and then select Anything from the radio buttons below.

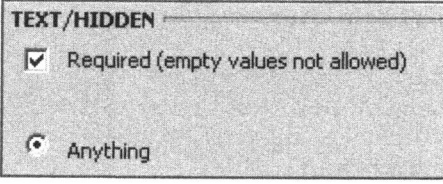

4. Select lastname from the list and check the Required box and then select Anything from the radio button below.

Secure Login and Registration 12

5. Select email from the list and check the Required box. This time, instead of selecting Anything, select the E-mail address radio button.

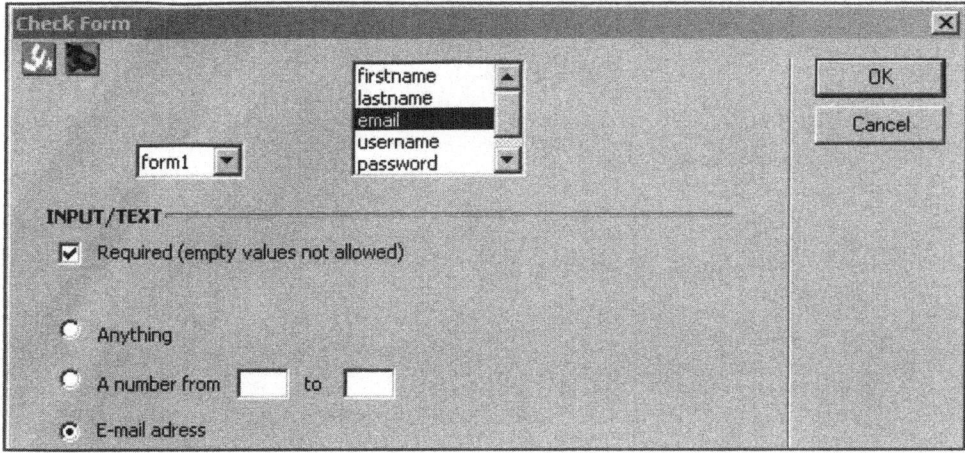

6. Select username from the menu, check the Required box and then select Anything from the radio button below.

7. Select password from the menu, check the Required box and then select Anything from the radio button below.

8. Select con_password from the menu, check the Required box and select the option Text must be the same: then select password from the drop-down menu.

Foundation Dreamweaver MX

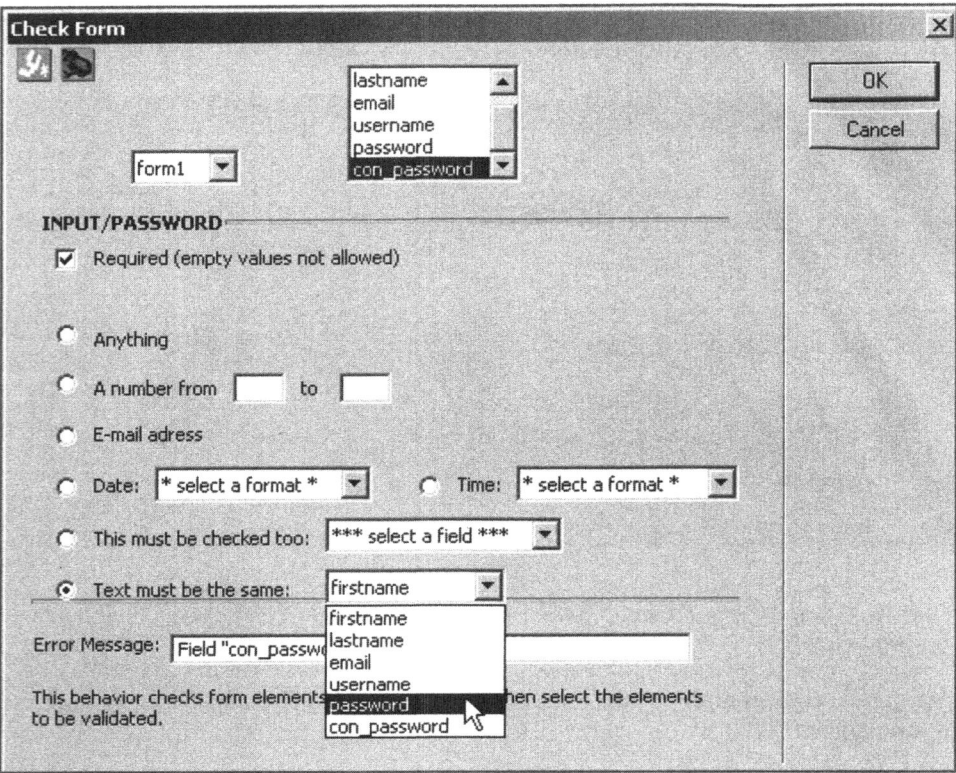

9. Click OK.

10. Now that we've added the necessary code to validate our form, let's try it. Save your work, press F12 to preview the page, and then press the Submit button without entering any values into the fields. You should get a pop-up message similar to the one below.

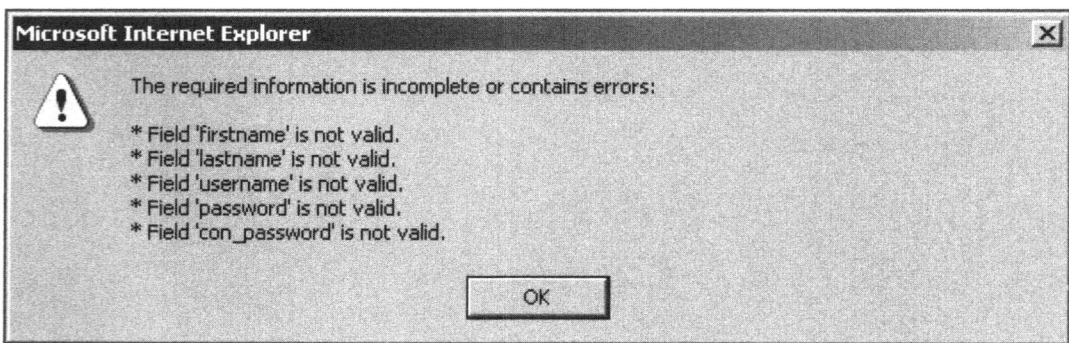

Inserting Information into the Database

We've created our form and validated the information placed in it. We now need to insert this information into our database.

1. If you select the Database tab from the Applications panel, you should now see the new table (members) that we created under myConn, the connection we made in the previous chapter. Click on the [+] sign and the members table will expand to show all the fields in our table. If you cannot see the table created, then click on the Refresh button (the small circular arrow on the top right-hand side).

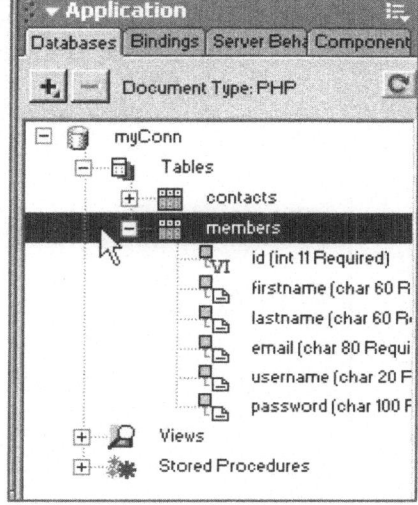

2. Go to the Server Behaviors tab, and click on the [+] button. Select Insert Record from the drop-down menu.

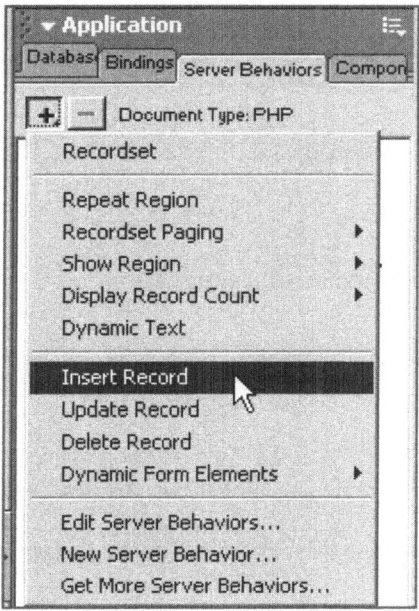

3. The Insert Record dialog will open. Select myConn from the Connection menu.

4. Select members from the Insert Table menu.

5. You should now see a list of fields in the database table members.

> As our form input fields have the same name as their respective database fields, Dreamweaver will automatically sort which value goes into which field.

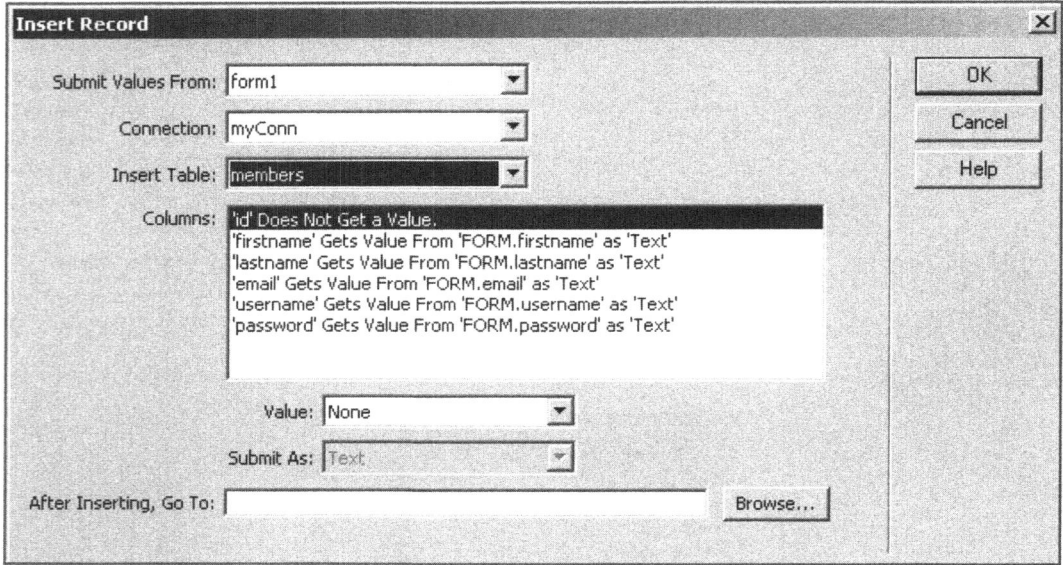

6. Click on OK.

7. Save the changes you've made to register.php.

Security issues

Well, we have two problems actually.

1. We don't want two or more users to have the same username.

2. It's considered bad practice to store plain text passwords in a database.

So how do we get round these problems?

Secure Login and Registration   12

- We'll query the database to find out if the username entered already exists.

- We have a few options for storing passwords in MySQL. In this case we're going to use PHP's `md5()` function.

This is where we roll up our sleeves and do some hand coding.

Solving multiple usernames

1. Look for the following line of code in the Code view. You can use Edit > Find and Replace to run a search of the code – it might not necessarily be on line 41 of your code:

   ```
   41    mysql_select_db($database_myConn, $myConn);
   ```

2. Directly underneath it, enter this code:

   ```
   $username_check=mysql_query("SELECT username FROM members WHERE
   ↳username='$_POST[username]'");
   ```

   So what does this code do? We're simply requesting information from our database using a simple SQL statement. In plain English, the code asks the database to select all the entries from:

   username field within the members table which match the value of the username entered in our form

3. Next, add this piece of code beneath the line you just added:

   ```
   if(mysql_num_rows($username_check)>=1) {
         print("Error: This Username is already Taken");
            } else {
   ```

4. Now look for this line below the code we just added:

   ```
   46    $Result1 = mysql_query($insertSQL, $myConn) or die(mysql_error());
   ```

5. Insert the following code *below* the line above:

   ```
   header("Location: thanks.php");
      exit;
      }
   ```

Once you have done this, your code should look like this:

```
41  mysql_select_db($database_myConn, $myConn);
42  $username_check=mysql_query("SELECT username FROM members WHERE username='$_POST[username]'");
43    if(mysql_num_rows($username_check)>=1) {
44       print("Error: This Username is already Taken");
45       } else {
46    $Result1 = mysql_query($insertSQL, $myConn) or die(mysql_error());
47    header("Location: thanks.php");
48    exit;
49    }
50  }
51  ?>
```

So what does the above code do? We've queried the database and asked it to return any rows that contain the same username that has been entered in the form. We then used the `mysql_num_rows()` function to check the number of rows returned. We inserted an if/else statement. This tells Dreamweaver that **if** the amount of rows returned is greater than or equal to 1, it should print the error message, **else** enter the information into the database. Finally, if the information is entered in the database, redirect the user to thanks.php (the page we created in **Chapter 11**).

Encrypting our passwords

1. Now we have to look for this line of code.

   ```
   39       GetSQLValueString($HTTP_POST_VARS['password'], "text"));
   ```

2. We have to change the code above to:

   ```
   39       GetSQLValueString (md5($HTTP_POST_VARS['password']), "text"));
   ```

The function `md5()` is a one-way encryption; *there is no way to un-encrypt it*. If you're interested in two-way encryption, you will need to use the `mcrypt` functions explained at: www.php.net/manual/en/ref.mcrypt.php.

Testing the form

Now that we've finished making the adjustments to the PHP code, let's test the form again.

1. Press F12 to preview the page and enter your information. Then press Submit.

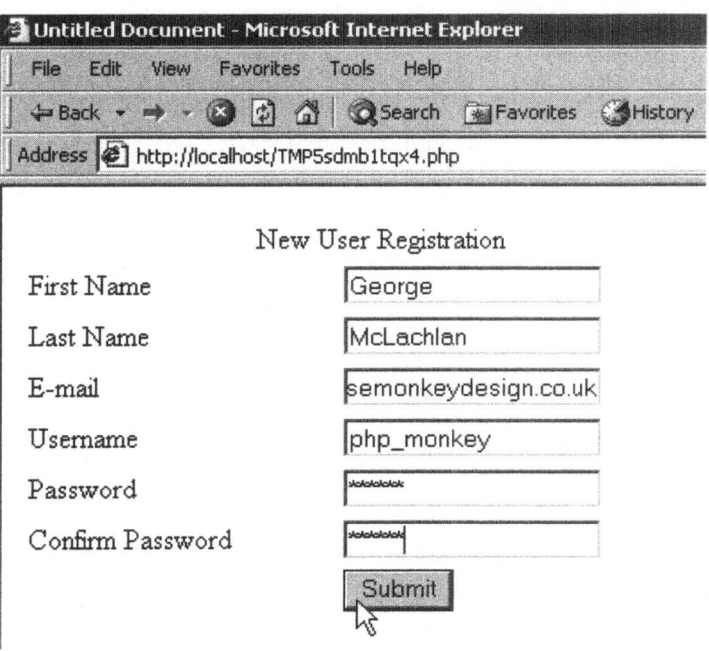

2. Let's look at the entry for this in our database. Look at the password field. You'll see that the information there has been encrypted.

3. We have one final test for our form. Let's try entering the same username again. This time, when you press Submit you'll get this error:

   Now the only problem is that when this happens, the user has to enter all their information again. Luckily, we can avoid this with a few lines of code.

12   Foundation Dreamweaver MX

Look for this line on your page:

`131`
```
<td><input name="firstname" type="text" id="firstname"></td>
```

4. We'll add the following PHP code into the <input> tag directly after id="firstname":

```
<?php if(isset($_POST["firstname"])) { print
➥"value=\"$_POST[firstname]\""; }?>
```

So it should now look like:

```
id="firstname"><?php if(isset($_POST["firstname"])) { print "value=\"$_POST[firstname]\""; }?></
```

5. Repeat the process for the lastname and email input tags, changing $_POST[firstname] to $_POST[lastname] and $_POST[email] respectively.

6. Now let's try entering the same username again.

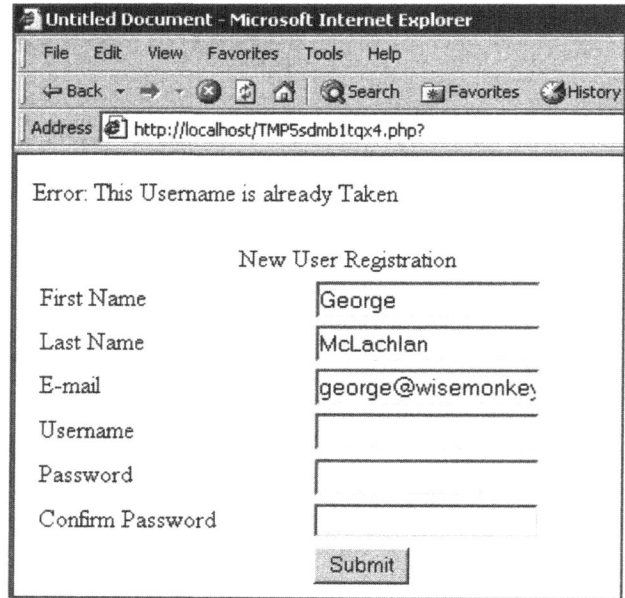

7. Save the changes we made to register.php and close the file.

Now that we've finished creating the registration form, we'll turn our attention to the login form.

Creating Our Login Form

1. Open a new PHP page in Dreamweaver and save it as `login.php`.

2. Create a form with two text fields called username and password. Add validation as we did earlier in the chapter.

   Your form should now look similar to the one below:

   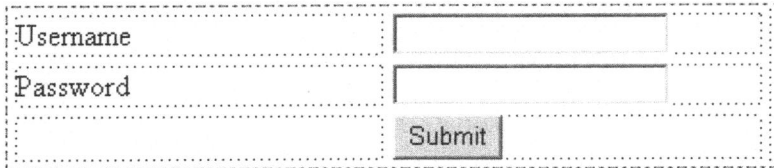

3. Give the form an action of `do_login.php` in the Properties panel.

   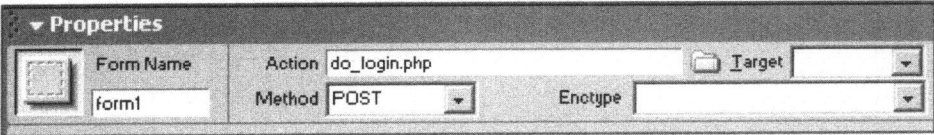

4. Save the changes you made to `login.php` and close the file.

5. Now create another new PHP page in Dreamweaver. Save this one as `do_login.php`.

6. Select the Recordset option from the Server Behaviors tab in the Application panel.

7. When the Recordset box opens, click on the Advanced button on the right-hand side of the box.

8. Type login into the Name field, and select myConn from the Connection menu.

9. Type the following SQL statement in the SQL field.

   ```
   SELECT username,password FROM members WHERE username='$username' and
   ↪password='$password'
   ```

Foundation Dreamweaver MX

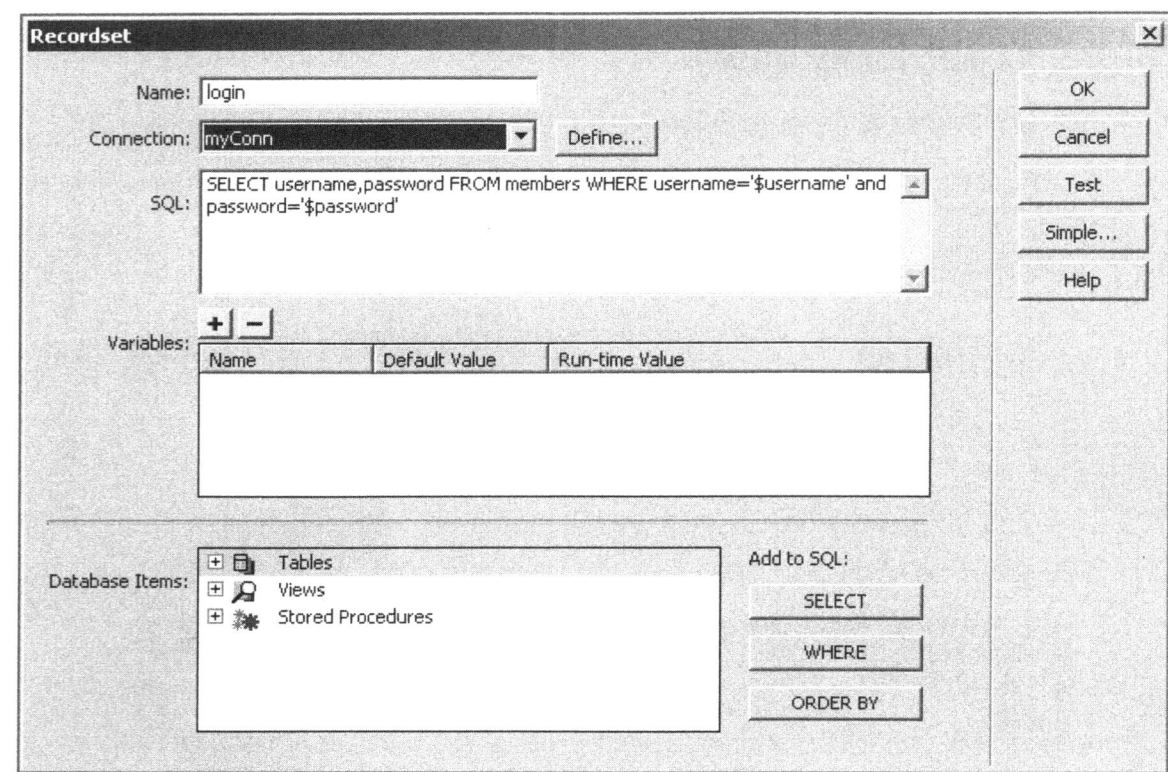

10. Click OK.

    Dreamweaver will automatically insert the code into the top of the page.

11. At this point, we'll have to add a few lines of code by hand. First of all, we must assign values to variables we used in the SQL statement: $username and $password. These will come from the values entered in our form which can be accessed by using `$_POST["username"]` and `$_POST["password"]`.

    The password stored in the database is encrypted using md5(). Therefore, the only way we can compare the two is by passing the information the user has entered into the password field of the form through the md5() function:

    ```
    $username=$_POST["username"];
    $password=md5($_POST["password"]);
    ```

    ```php
    1  <?php require_once('Connections/myConn.php'); ?>
    2  <?php
    3  $username=$_POST["username"];
    4  $password=md5($_POST["password"]);
    5  mysql_select_db($database_myConn, $myConn);
    ```

Secure Login and Registration

12. The final bit of code we add will check the number of rows returned from the database that contain that username and password. If a row is returned, then the user has logged in correctly. We can then register the session that will allow them access to our secret pages. Once the session has been registered, they are re-directed to `my_secret_index.php`. If no rows are returned that contain that username and password, they are redirected back to the `login.php` page.

```php
if($totalRows_login >=1) {
 session_start();
 session_register("auth");
 header("Location: my_secret_index.php");
 exit;
 } else {
 header("Location: login.php");
 exit;
 }
```

The complete code block should now look like this:

```php
<?php require_once('Connections/myConn.php'); ?>
<?php
$username=$_POST["username"];
$password=md5($_POST["password"]);
mysql_select_db($database_myConn, $myConn);
$query_login = "SELECT username,password FROM members WHERE username='$username' and password='$password'";
$login = mysql_query($query_login, $myConn) or die(mysql_error());
$row_login = mysql_fetch_assoc($login);
$totalRows_login = mysql_num_rows($login);
if($totalRows_login >=1) {
 session_start();
 session_register("auth");
 header("Location: my_secret_index.php");
 exit;
 } else {
 header("Location: login.php");
 exit;
 }
?>
```

13. Save the changes we made to `do_login.php` and close the file.

Protecting our secret pages

The final thing that we have to do is protect our secret pages. How is this done? At the top of each page we wish to protect, we'll check to see if the session `auth` has been registered. This is only registered when a user enters the correct username and password. If the session hasn't been registered (in other words the user hasn't signed in), they will be re-directed back to `login.php`.

1. Create a new PHP page in Dreamweaver and save it as `my_secret_index.php`.

2. At the very top of the page before the opening HTML tag, add this code:

```php
<?php
session_start();
if(!session_is_registered("auth")) {
header("Location: login.php");
exit;
}
?>
```

Let's look at this code in some more detail. We already know what `session_start()` does and it's importance when you need to use sessions. However, it's the lines below this that do all the work.

```php
if(!session_is_registered("auth")) {
header("Location: login.php");
exit;
```

We start by using a conditional statement. The important thing to notice here is the use of `!`. By using this, we are saying that if this statement does *not* evaluate as `true` (that is, there is no session registered with the name of `auth`), the user will be re-directed to `login.php` using the `header()` function. The next line of code contains the `exit` command. This is to make sure that the rest of our PHP code is not executed when the user is re-directed.

```php
1  <?php
2  session_start();
3  if(!session_is_registered("auth")) {
4  header("Location: login.php");
5  exit;
6  }
7  ?>
```

3. Now create two links from this page to `my_secret_page1.php` and `my_secret_page2.php`.

4. Save the changes to `my_secret_index.php` and close the file.

5. Create a new PHP page in MX and save it as `my_secret_page1.php`.

6. As we did in `my_secret_index.php`, add this code above the opening `<html>` tag:

```php
<?php
session_start();
if(!session_is_registered("auth")) {
header("Location: login.php");
exit;
}
?>
```

7. Save the changes to `my_secret_page1.php` and close the file.

Secure Login and Registration

8. Create a new PHP page in MX and save it as `my_secret_page2.php`.

9. Insert the same code above the opening `<html>` tag.

10. Save the changes to `my_secret_page2.php` and close the file.

Allowing a user to logout

Many sites you visit will have an option for a user to log out. This is done by using the `session_destroy()` function. Here's the details:

1. Create a new PHP page in Dreamweaver and save it as `logout.php`.

2. All we have to do is add the following code above the opening `<html>` tag:

   ```
   <?php
   session_start();
   session_destroy();
   header("Location: login.php");
   ?>
   ```

3. This code will destroy the session. It will then re-direct the user back to the login page.

4. Save your changes to `logout.php` and close the file.

5. Finally, open up `my_secret_index.php` and add a link to `logout.php`. Then save your changes and close the file.

Testing our application

Open up your browser and point it to the `login.php`. If you haven't registered already, then go to `register.php` first and enter your information.

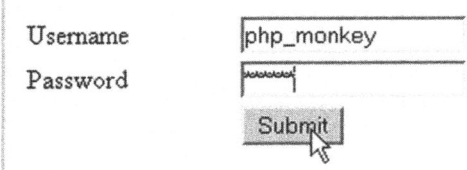

If you have entered your login details correctly, you should see `my_secret_index.php`.

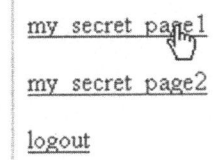

Click on the my_secret_page1 link and the my_secret_page2 link. You will be able to access both these pages.

Now click on the logout link. This will take you back to login.php.

Instead of logging in this time, type the URL of my_secret_index.php in the address bar in the browser.

You will be re-directed straight back to the login.php page!

That is our Registration / Login application finished! If you wish to protect any more pages, you can easily do so by adding this code to them. However, remember that no application is totally secure; if you have to store highly sensitive information online, then there are better ways of doing so.

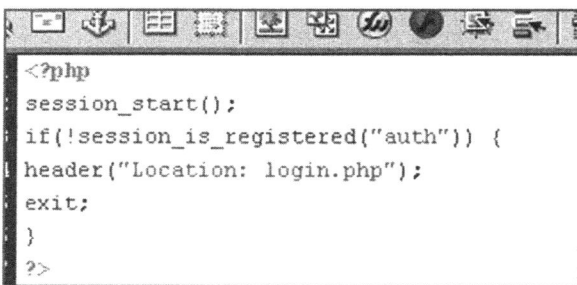

Summary

We've covered so much in this chapter. If it's still the same day as when you started the chapter, you've done extremely well. There have been lots of hands-on exercises, and a little sprinkling of theory in there too. We looked at:

- PHP's new way of accessing global variables.
- Some common PHP security issues.
- Session basics.
- A simple example to show how sessions work.
- Building a Registration / Login application to put it all into practice.

Well, it's not time for the index just yet. We've got some more powerhouse web designing to do in the next and final chapter. Take a break and come back refreshed and ready for your last dose of PHP, MySQL and Dreamweaver MX magic.

Case Study: Dynamic Image Viewer

What we'll cover in this chapter

- Defining a site for our image viewer
- Adding JavaScript functions to open browser windows
- Using iFrames to create a modular layout
- Displaying image data from our database
- Adding a connection to paypal so that people can purchase images

13 Foundation Dreamweaver MX

What is important about your Dreamweaver site is not only that it's easy to create, but that it's easy to keep updated. The dynamic technologies that we've been looking at in the second half of this book enable you to do just this, and – in this last chapter – we're going to take a look at a case study example.

You've probably already taken a look, and realized that this chapter is one of the longer ones in the book. You've reached a stage of Dreamweaver competency where you're now ready for a serious, real-world site with some serious functionality. Be patient, stay around, and you'll have a great, highly customizable, Dreamweaver MX application.

This chapter focuses on making a modular page layout with a dynamic image viewer that will allow you to easily add additional sections to your project, to store name, cost, description, paths to the downloadable files, and the dimensions of the images in a database, and allow users to download and pay for the images using PayPal. Remember creating our thumbnails gallery back in **Chapter 6**? Well, in the chapters since, we've reached a point where we can now automatically generate something like that, straight from our database.

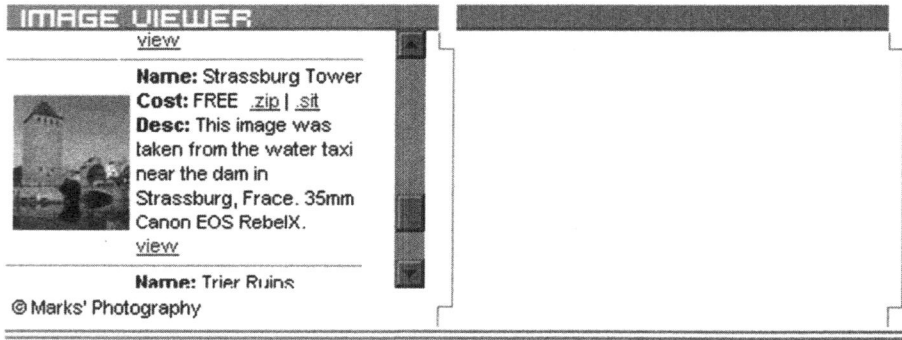

You'll see an overall flowchart of the files used to create the image viewer below. This might seem complex now, but we'll be taking you through every step of creating each file. The flowchart is here so that you can refer back to it as we go through the chapter, whenever you get lost and wonder where what you're creating fits into things.

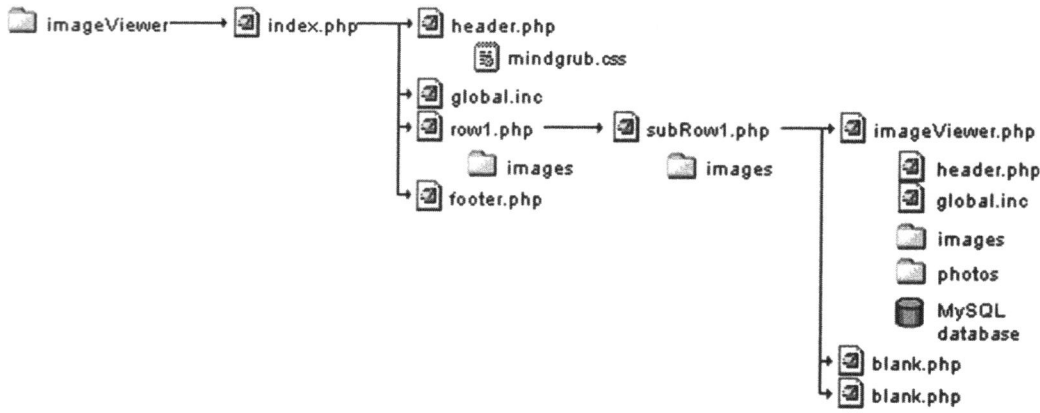

We're going to start by defining a site, then we'll create our main PHP files. After that, we'll sort out our database, before creating `imageViewer.php` to pull in data from our database and the PHP files.

Case Study: Dynamic Image Viewer

Site Definition

First things first: we want to define a new site.

1. Go to Site > New Site, and choose the Basic tab on the Site Definition dialog. Begin by naming the site imageViewer.

2. Click Next, and pick PHP MySQL as the sever technology for the image viewer, and then hit the Next button.

3. Use the Browse option to select the Apache folder where you created the friends_of_ed folder we used in **Chapters 9** and **10**, and create a new folder called imageViewer there. Choose this, and hit the Next button.

4. Unless you've got a server to connect to, choose the Edit and test locally option, and then define this as http://localhost/imageViewer on the next screen.

5. The next dialog asks if you want to connect to a remote server. Select No and click Next. Finally, click Done.

Making things modular

We're going to make the files for our image viewer modular, and make use of the include() statement to attach additional files. Our initial page, index.php, will contain three include statements. We are going to include:

- a header file
- a file to contain one row of our modular system
- a footer file

By doing this, we can very easily add additional content above or below the image viewer on this page by including additional pages in our index.php page. When the PHP file is parsed by the server, the HTML tags in the file index.php will replace the include() statements and will pass to the client's web browser.

There are two ways to 'include' additional code and files inside another PHP document. These two methods are to use an include() statement, or a require() statement. The difference between the two is that an include() statement will only insert the code when that particular statement is read, whereas a require() statement will always insert the additional code.

So, for example, if you had an include() statement inside an if(color = blue) statement, the include() statement won't run unless color = blue. Replace that include with require, though, and it'll run regardless of whether or not color = blue.

When using include() or require(), parsing shifts out of PHP mode and into HTML mode. Any file that uses include() or require() needs valid PHP start and end tags.

index.php

We're going to start off by creating `index.php`. As we'll see, this sets up things for the rest of the site. After this, we'll create the files that we've just listed, and which we include in `index.php`.

1. Create a PHP page in our newly defined site.

2. Choose the split Code / Design view. We'll be using Dreamweaver's built-in panels and windows, but we'll also keep an eye on the code created behind the scenes to check that we've entered the information correctly.

   As you begin creating projects and web sites, it's good practice to watch the formation of the code behind the scenes. As your comfort level increases, you'll be able to do more in Code view to shorten some of the steps necessary to create some aspects of your designs.

3. Select all of the code that's been generated in the source window, and delete it, as we don't need it. The HTML tags that Dreamweaver puts into the document by default will be found within the header file that we'll be including next.

4. Select the Code Block button from the PHP menu, as shown.

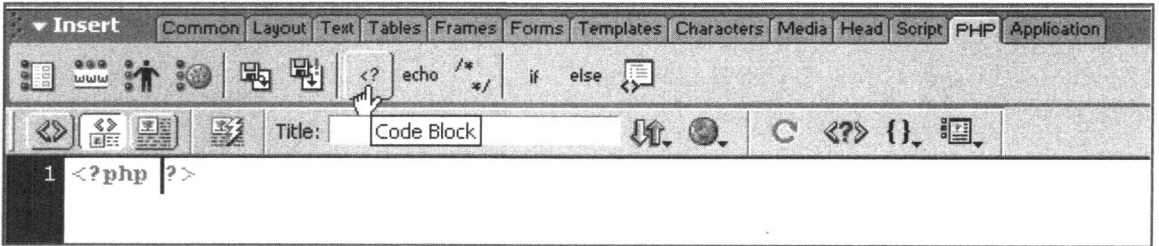

5. We're now ready to enter some code. The `header.php` file is going to be used for the main page of the site, as well as within the iframe that houses `imageViewer.php`. Start by adding this line in the code window between the php tags:

   ```
   include ("header.php");
   ```

   You can use the include() button on the PHP tab to add include statements to your file, but it always adds additional start and end tags. You need to add the file name anyway, so in this case, it's easier to type the entire statement in the document.

6. Now we need to include the file that will contain the bulk of our other files, as well as our image viewer. Add this line of code:

   ```
   include ("row1.php");
   ```

7. Next, add a comment to remind yourself that you can include any files to add additional content to your modular web page in this list.

8. Just as with `header.php`, it's a good idea to keep all of the footer information in one place. You can add contact information (such as telephone number, address, and e-mail) in the footer, and it's far easier to change this information in one place when need be, than to open and edit each individual file. You should be getting used to the `include()` statement by now, so add this to our PHP file:

   ```
   include ("footer.php");
   ```

9. Check that the code in your code window looks like this before we carry on to `header.php`:

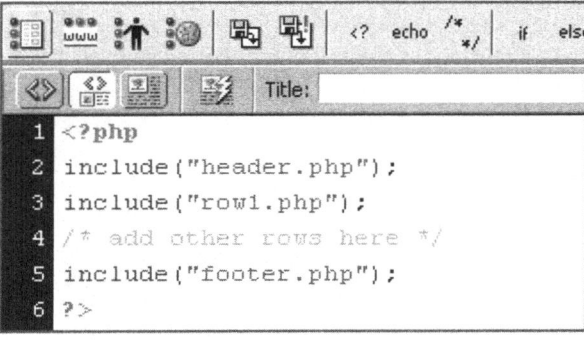

10. When you're happy with this, save your file as `index.php`.

Creating the three main PHP files

We're now going to create the four files we've just included in our `index.php` page:

- `header.php`
- `row1.php`
- `footer.php`

header.php

`header.php` will actually be devoid of any PHP code. It will, however, contain a style sheet, two JavaScript functions, and – as mentioned previously – the typical header information for a web page.

The CSS file will contain styles for the `<p>`, `<td>`, `<h2>`, and `<body>` tags. We'll also add our own class (`.rfelement`) to give padding to an **iFrame** (more about what this is later) that we'll later incorporate in the file `subRow1.php`.

1. Begin by selecting File > New, and choosing a Basic Page with HTML. Save this file as `header.php`. (Dreamweaver should automatically save this in our `imageViewer` folder, but check that it's in the right place in the Site panel before continuing.)

2. You can add useful information to the header file such as keywords that give spiders information about the contents of your web page. Dreamweaver doesn't automatically add keywords to your document, so it is always a good idea to add this **meta** information to your page. Do this by typing it directly in the code window, just after the `<head>` tag:

   ```
   <meta name="keywords" content="image, viewer">
   ```

3. Change the title of `header.php` to Image Viewer. There's two ways to do this: you can either change the Untitled Document text between the `<title></title>` tags to Image Viewer, or you can add it to the Title: box in the toolbar across the top of the Code view.

4. Add a Style Sheet and style by going to Text > CSS Styles > New CSS Style, and selecting New CSS Style from the drop-down menu.

Case Study: Dynamic Image Viewer

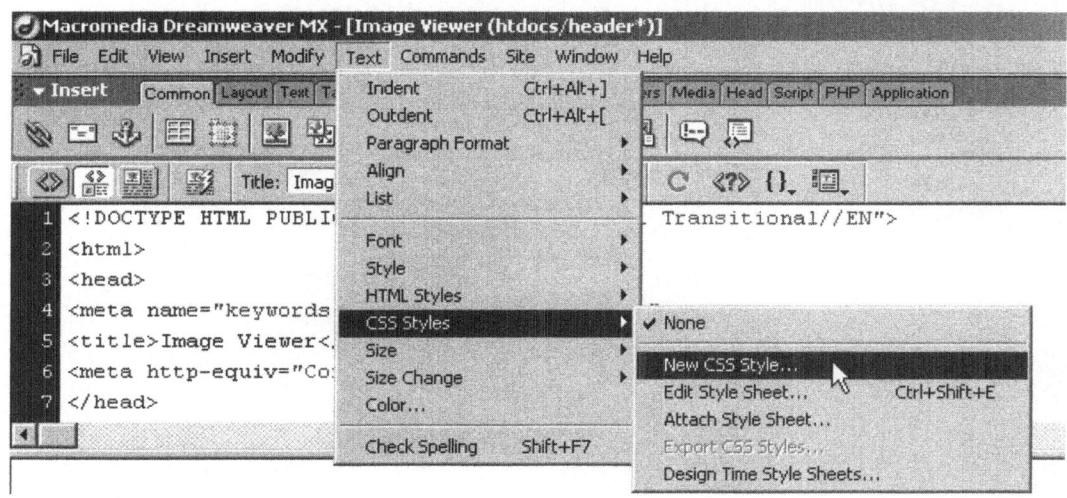

5. Select the Redefine HTML Tag radio button in the CSS Style dialog, and choose the paragraph tag `<p>` from the first drop-down menu. Leave the Define In attribute as (New Style Sheet File) and hit OK.

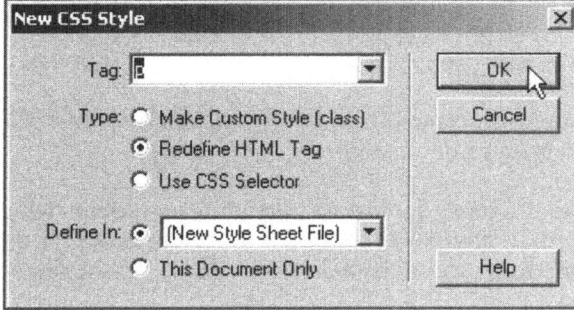

6. Give the style sheet a name – I labeled mine `mindgrub` – and save it in the `imageViewer` folder.

7. After saving the name of your new style sheet, the CSS Style Definition dialog will appear. Choose "Arial, Helvetica, sans-serif" for the Font, and type in 11 for the Size of the Type for our `<p>` tag.

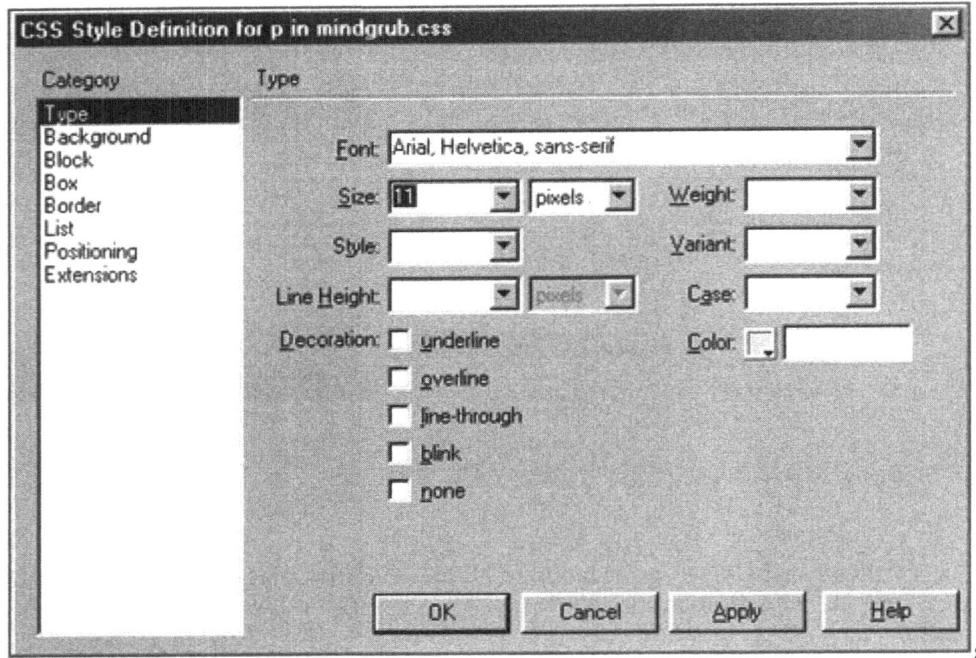

8. OK this, and you'll notice this line of code:

```
<link href="mindgrub.css" rel="stylesheet" type="text/css">
```

...has been added to the document. This tells the browser where to look for the particular visual attributes we're adding to our document.

9. Repeat steps **4** and **5** above to add two additional tag definitions, td and h2. Use the same settings for the td tag, and simply change the font size to 12 for the h2 tag. You should notice this time, however, that the Define-In drop-down is already pointing to our new file, mindgrub.css.

> *Dreamweaver MX gives you the ability to add many styles from their menus in the New CSS Style dialog. I have found it is easier, however, to keep a long list of potential styles in a text document and cut and paste the styles you need for each particular project.*

Case Study: Dynamic Image Viewer

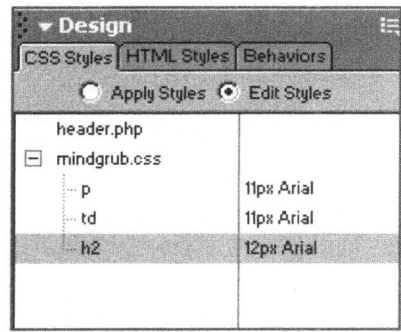

10. In addition, we want to add a style to the `<body>` attribute that will make the color of the scroll bars on the page match the color of our image viewer. This attribute, unfortunately, is not available in the Style Sheet window, so open `mingrub.css` (or whatever you called your CSS file) directly by double-clicking on it in your Site panel.

11. Once open, add the following attribute to change the color of the browser's scrollbar:

    body { scrollbar-base-color:#6B7BA5}

12. We also need to add some padding to the `.rfelement` to add some buffer around the content within our inline frames, which we'll create later in the chapter. Add the following custom style to the style sheet:

    .rfelement { clip: rect( ); padding-top: 5px; padding-right: 0px;
    ↪padding-bottom: 8px; padding-left: 8px }

```
 1  p {
 2      font-family: Arial, Helvetica, sans-serif;
 3      font-size: 11px;
 4  }
 5  td {
 6      font-family: Arial, Helvetica, sans-serif;
 7      font-size: 11px;
 8  }
 9  h2 {
10      font-family: Arial, Helvetica, sans-serif;
11      font-size: 12px;
12  }
13  body { scrollbar-base-color:#6B7BA5}
14  .rfelement { clip: rect( ); padding-top: 5px; padding-right: 0px; padding-bottom: 8px;
    padding-left: 8px }
15
16
```

13. Once you're happy your file matches the screenshot, save and close the CSS file.

Adding JavaScript functions

Now we need to add two JavaScript functions to the header in order to open the full-size images in a pop-up window. We'll explain these, but they're not the easiest things to understand first time around. If your eyes start glazing over, make sure you've got the code entered, and come back and have a look at the end – they're both very useful and re-usable bits of code. You won't ever have to re-create these, just re-use them.

The first function will determine whether the user is using Internet Explorer for Macs – some versions of Internet Explorer for Mac will add 16 pixels to the right side of the pop-up for a scrollbar. The second function will then subtract 16 pixels from the dimensions of the popUpWindow when the function detect() returns a true value, thus eliminating the unsightly dead space for Mac users.

1. Back in header.php, add a couple of blank lines in your code window, just after the link to the style sheet, and just before the end </head> tag.

> *You can let Dreamweaver 'run' with the insertion of code in your document. It is, however, a good idea to watch the formatting of the code, and add returns after each section of code. This way, when you come looking for something, you'll be able to find it...*

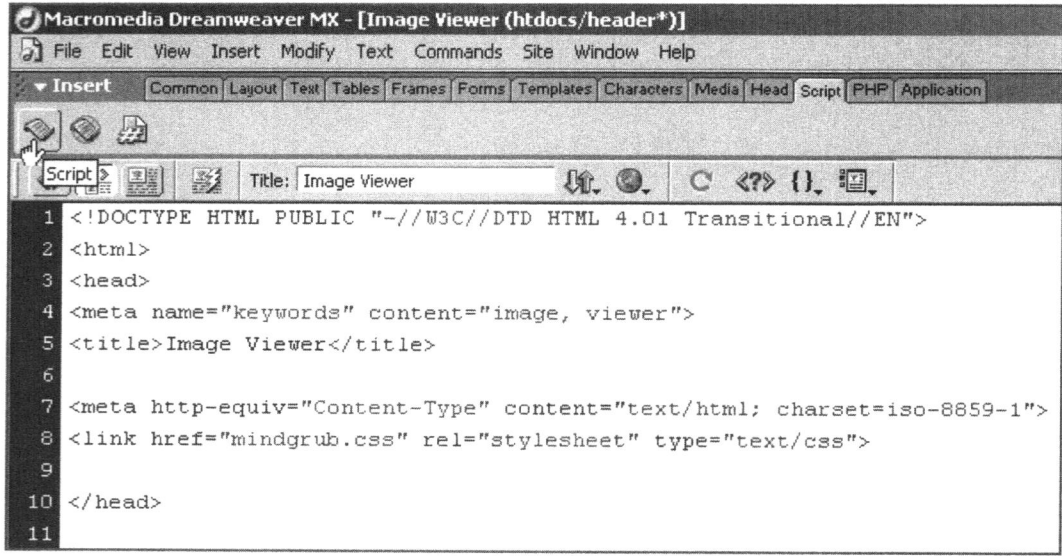

2. Select the Script tab at the top of the window, and press the Script button at the top left (as shown above). We're now going to add the two JavaScript functions to the header.

3. In the Content field, check that the Language is set to JavaScript, and add the detect function:

```
function detect() {
 if (navigator.appName == 'Microsoft Internet Explorer' && navigator.platform
== 'MacPPC') {
   return true;
 } else {
   return false;
 }
}
```

Next, we add the function `openNewWindow()` to the Content field, after the function `detect()`. We're going to take this one section at a time, as it's a little longer than the last function.

4. This function first sets the variable `Macit` equal to the value returned from the function `detect()` so that the function later knows whether or not it must make the pop-up window 16 pixels narrower:

```
function openNewWindow(URLtoOpen, popwidth, popheight) {
        var Macit = detect();
```

5. We then set the variables `screenWidth` and `screenHeight` equal to the width and height of your monitor:

```
var screenWidth = screen.availWidth;
var screenHeight = screen.availHeight;
```

6. Next, we find the x and y positions where we want to open the pop-up window by subtracting half of the width of the pop-up window from half of the width of the monitor:

```
var x = (screenWidth/2)-(popwidth/2);
var y = (screenHeight/2)-(popheight/2);
```

7. We then subtract half of the height of the pop-up window from half of the height of the monitor. The result for both calculations is where the top left corner of the pop-up window will sit so that the pop-up window appears perfectly centered on your monitor:

```
if (Macit == 1) {
        popwidth2 = popwidth - 16;
        popheight2 = popheight - 16;
} else {
        popwidth2 = popwidth;
        popheight2 = popheight;
}
```

8. Lets look at the math for the calculation of the x co-ordinate for the pop-up window. Let's use a monitor screen that is 800 pixels wide, with a pop-up window that is 250 pixels wide.

```
  var x = (screenWidth/2)-(popwidth/2);
        =  (800/2) - (250/2);
        =   400 - 125;
        =       275
```

13 Foundation Dreamweaver MX

This would mean that the pop-up window would open at an x co-ordinate for the top left corner of 275. If the monitor screen was 600 pixels tall, and the image was 300 pixels tall, the y co-ordinate would come to 150, meaning that the pop-up window would open at (275, 150).

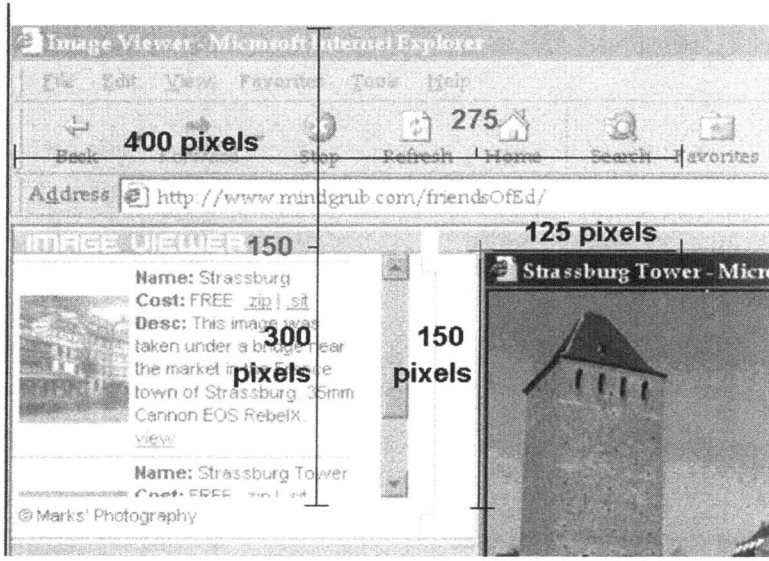

9. The function `openNewWindow()` uses the built-in JavaScript function `window.open()` to open the new window with the values specified. `Window.open()` has three parameters that it looks for when opening a new window: the URL to open, the name of the window to open the file in (in this case a new window labeled as `_blank`), and the properties of the new window (such as x position, y position, width and height).

```
    var winParams = "height=" + popheight2 + ",width=" + popwidth2 +
➥",resizable=0,directories=0,dependent=1,toolbar=0,scrollbar=0,tollbar=0,
➥screenX=" + x + ",screenY=" + y + ",left=" + x + ",top=" + y;
    newWindow = window.open(URLtoOpen,'_blank', winParams);
}
```

For readability, we save all of the parameters that we want (including height, width, x position, and y position) as the variable `winParams`, and simply pass that variable into the `window.open` function as the third parameter. The URL that should be opened (`URLtoOpen`), the width to open that file (`popwidth`), and the height to open that file (`popheight`) are passed into the JavaScript function `openNewWindow` when the function is called, and will later be stored in our MySQL database.

10. If you haven't been entering code as you've gone through this, enter it all now:

```
function openNewWindow(URLtoOpen, popwidth, popheight) {
var Macit = detect();
var screenWidth = screen.availWidth;
var screenHeight = screen.availHeight;
```

```
    var x = (screenWidth/2)-(popwidth/2);
    var y = (screenHeight/2)-(popheight/2);
    if (Macit == 1) {
    popwidth2 = popwidth - 16;
    popheight2 = popheight - 16;
    } else {
    popwidth2 = popwidth;
    popheight2 = popheight;
    }
    var winParams = "height=" + popheight2 + ",width=" + popwidth2 +
➥",resizable=0,directories=0,dependent=1,toolbar=0,scrollbar=0,tollbar=0,
➥screenX=" + x + ",screenY=" + y + ",left=" + x + ",top=" + y;
    newWindow = window.open(URLtoOpen,'_blank', winParams);

}
```

11. After adding both functions to the content field, hit the OK button, and Dreamweaver will insert the two functions in your document. You'll find it easier to check your code in the Code view than in the small Script panel, so do a quick check that your code looks similar to the listing above now. Pay particular attention to making sure that you've got no unnecessary carriage returns in the last few lines, as they're particularly long.

12. Finally, we need to change the background color and the margins for the page. Select Modify > Page Properties from the drop-down window and give the page a background color of #9C9CC6, and a value of 0 for each of the margins. You'll notice that Dreamweaver already knows the title of the document, which you typed into the code window in step **2**. Click OK and save the file.

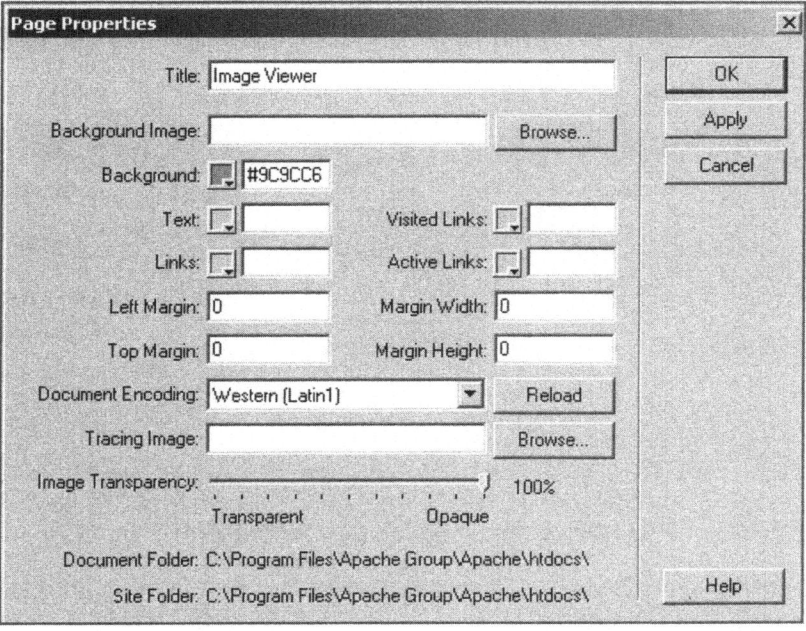

13 Foundation Dreamweaver MX

Good work! We've finally finished `header.php`, which is one of the longer files we're going to make. This file is useful for any project, as it has two very reusable pieces of information: a Cascading Style Sheet, and a JavaScript function to open a window with set dimensions.

footer.php

The footer file is a good place to put contact information for a web project. In this example, we only use the footer once, but it's still good practice to keep it as a separate file. That way, when you do make a project with multiple pages, you only need to edit one file to change the footer on every page.

1. Make a new HTML file, and clear out all of the HTML code in the Code view. Leave just the start `<HTML>` and end `</HTML>` tags.

   All included files are treated as HTML unless specified otherwise, but it's always a good idea to add tags to clearly specify this, if not just for readability.

2. Add some footer information to the Design view– you can see from the screenshot below that I've added my job description, qualifications, and telephone / e-mail contact details.

3. Turn your e-mail into a link by entering mailto:you@youraddress.com in the Link box. Add a link to your website if you have one.

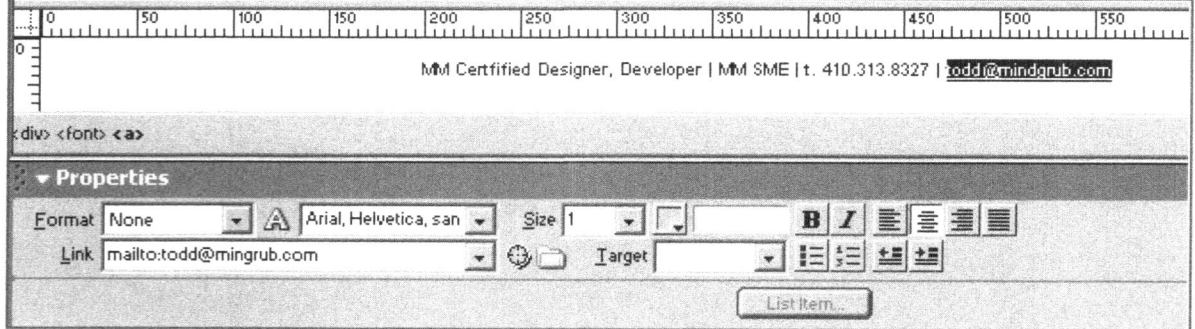

4. Save the file as `footer.php` in the `imageViewer` folder.

iFrames

The final file included in `index.php` is `row1.php`. This in turn contains `subRow1.php`, which in turn contains `imageViewer.php`. Confused? Take a look back at the diagram at the beginning of the chapter. These files each include other files by means of an inline frame, known as an **iFrame**.

An inline frame works in much the same fashion as a regular frame, letting you load additional HTML documents and refer to it by its NAME attribute, but differs in the fact that it can be positioned anywhere within a document, much like the OBJECT tag. Inline frames, in addition, can scroll along with text and objects within the body of another page.

As we mentioned back in **Chapter 3**, frames have been regarded as something to avoid since not all browsers accept them, and they're not searchable by search engine spiders. At least 95 percent of all current web users have browsers that support frames, however, and you can add informative tags as described in the beginning of the chapter for the spiders. Using frames can allow you to do some pretty neat things in your web sites, as we're about to see.

> *Inline frames are only supported on Windows in Internet Explorer 3.0 and above, Netscape 4.7 for Mac, Mozilla M12, and Netscape 6. That means the comparatively low numbers of folk with Netscape 4.7 on PC are going to be out of luck. As ever with site design, it's a matter of looking carefully at your audience - I've decided that people with an out-of-date browser aren't really going to be terribly interested in photographs.*

row1.php is a table with an iFrame to hold subRow1.php. If you can imagine it visually, row1 is an iFrame that extends across the entire width of the page. Within row1 is subRow1, which is broken up into three separate iFrames. The beauty of this system is that, if you need additional room to display content selected in the smaller iFrames of subRow1, you can open that content in the larger iFrame within row1.php.

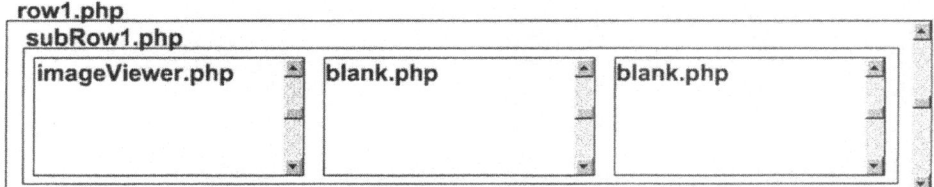

What we need to do is to target the iFrame NAME attribute as you would target a normal frame, and open the additional content. In addition, we'll add a 'close' button to the new page that will reload subRow1.php into row1.php when released, returning the row to the previous state.

The core piece of this file is the second row that holds the iFrame. The other rows are simply in place to add margins around that second row, and to add the white and blue lines that extend across the entire browser window. Without further ado, let's begin.

row1.php

We're going to create our table, and then we're going to go cell by cell, starting with the left column of the top row, adding attributes to each cell. These tables are going to get fairly intricate in order to produce the nice clean layout of the final imageViewer, and were first developed through a lot of trial and error.

> *WARNING: tables frustrate most people at some time or other. If at any point you're unable to select a cell in the design view, then you can highlight from the start tag to the end tag in the code window of that particular row or cell to change the properties of that row or cell in the Properties panel.*

Tables can sometimes display in different ways in different browsers (particularly when you're using cells with smaller dimensions than the font you're using, as we are here), so we're going to use an invisible graphic to lock tables into the correct dimensions. The graphic itself is a simple transparent graphic that, visually, we cannot see. It does, however, get treated just like any visible graphic when the browser reads the HTML. The graphic will span the size of the cell and therefore force the browser to display the table at the correct size.

1. Create a new HTML document, and cut out the HTML code that Dreamweaver inserts.

2. Insert a new table into the document (Insert > Table). Give the new table four rows, two columns, a width of 100 percent, and 0 values for border, cell padding, and cell spacing.

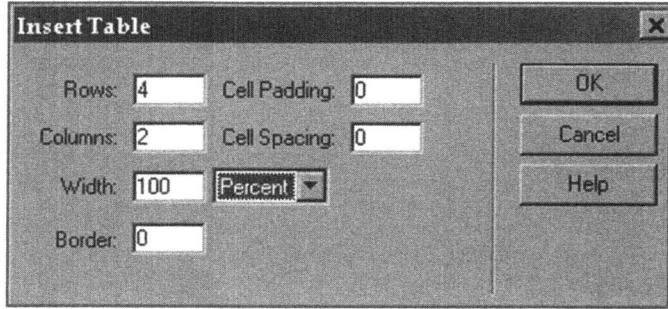

3. You can create an invisible graphic of your own if you want – just create a 1 pixel by 1 pixel invisible GIF – but it's just as easy to use `shim.gif` from the images folder provided with the source files. Create a new folder in the imageViewer site, call it images, and place `shim.gif` there now.

4. Select the entire table and give it a background color of white (#FFFFFF) in the Properties panel.

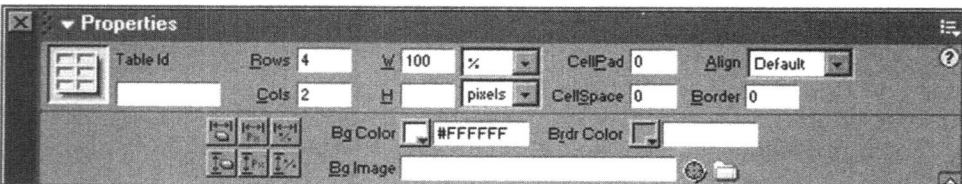

5. Select the top left cell. Give it a width of 753, a height of 2, and a vertical alignment of Top in the Properties panel.

6. Now is as good a time as any to remember to save your file as `row1.php`.

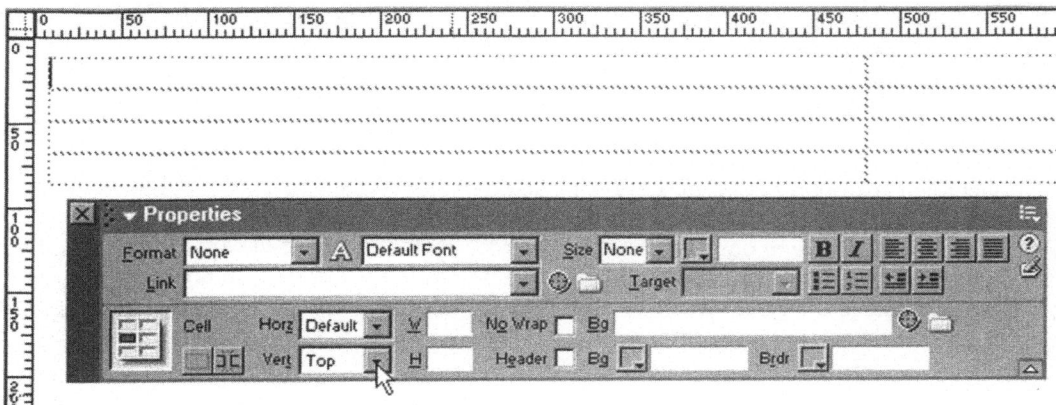

7. Then, add `shim.gif` to that cell and give it the dimensions of 753 by 2 as well. Because it's rather small, you're probably going to find `shim.gif` tricky to select, so you might have to highlight the image in the Code view, as pictured.

```html
<html>
<table width="100%" border="0" cellpadding="0" cellspacing="0" bordercolor="#FFFFFF">
  <tr>
    <td width="753" height="2" valign="top"><img src="images/shim.gif" width="1" height="1"></td>
    <td> </td>
  </tr>
  <tr>
    <td> </td>
```

> *You might think that `shim.gif` would have no impact, since you've also told the cell that it's in that it should be 753 by 2. Try removing it when you've finished the other files for the project, and you'll find that the table – including the iFrame – will completely disappear.*

8. Click on the right-hand cell in the first row, and give it a width of 100% (add a percentage sign after the 100 to tell Dreamweaver that you're dealing in percentages and not pixels), and a height of 2 pixels.

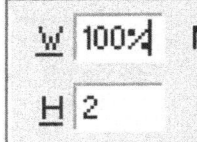

> *Since we made the top row two pixels tall, it can be difficult to select the cell in the Design view. Remember, you can always click on the start tag, or highlight the start tag (`<tr>`) to the end tag (`</tr>`) in the Code view to change the properties of that row in the Properties inspector. The same goes for any other table row that you have problems selecting.*

9. Select all of the second row (both cells) and set the horizontal alignment to Left, and the vertical alignment to Top in the Properties panel. Select the left-hand one and give it a width of 753.

10. Now, we need to type our iFrame manually, since there is no built-in window to do so. The left hand cell in the second row should still be selected from the last step, so take a look in the Code view, and place the cursor between start tag for the cell (`<td width="753">`) and the end tag (`</td>`). Add the following information:

```
<iFrame name="topRow" scrolling="no" marginwidth="0" marginheight="0"
➥src="subRow1.php" frameborder="0" height="186" width="100%"></iFrame>
```

11. Just before the final `</iFrame>` tag, add:

```
Please upgrade your browser.
```

If the user has a non-frames friendly browser, this comment will appear in place of the file `subRow1.php` to tell them that they need to upgrade.

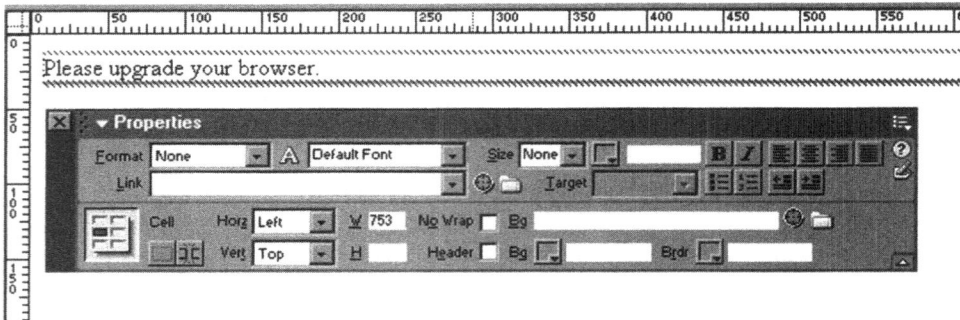

12. Click on the right hand cell in the second row, and give it a width of 100 percent (using the percentage sign as before) and a background color of white in the Properties panel.

13. Select the entire third row and set the horizontal alignment to Left and the vertical alignment to Top.

Case Study: Dynamic Image Viewer

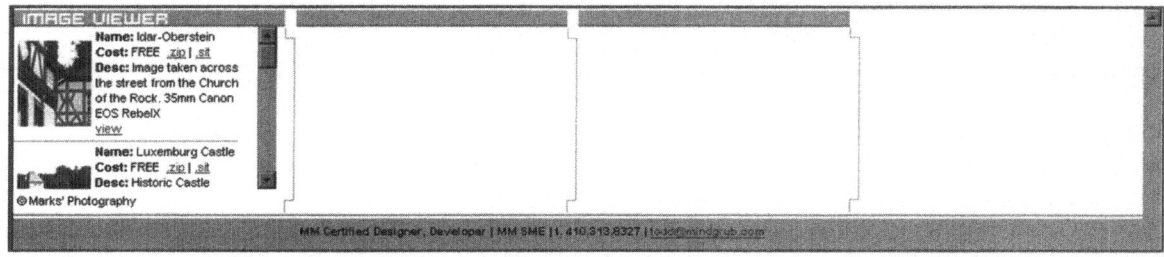

The last two rows are in place to add the white and blue lines that traverse the entire width of the page above the footer information. This isn't crucial to the functionality of our app, but it does make it look nicer...

14. Select the left cell of the third row and give it a width of 753, a height of 2, and a background color of #9C9CC6 in the Properties panel.

15. Select the right cell of the third row and give it a width of 100 percent, a height of 2, and a background color of #9C9CC6 in the Properties panel.

16. Select the left cell of the fourth row and give it a width of 753 and a height of 2.

17. Select the right cell of the fourth row and give it a width of 100 percent and a height of 2.

18. We've left this step until last, as it actually makes sure that your table doesn't shrink too much. What you now want to do is go through your table and remove all of the   tags that Dreamweaver helpfully inserts between the table <td> tags as placeholders for any text that you might want to include.

```
    <td width="753" height="2" valign="top"><img src="image
</td>
    <td width="100" height="2"> </td>
</tr>
<tr>
```

19. Save your file as row1.php in the imageViewer folder.

You should be able to see something like the screenshot pictured:

Please upgrade your browser.

20. If things don't quite work as they should, then here's a listing of the code that you should have generated with your table:

```
<table width="100%"  border="0" cellpadding="0" cellspacing="0" bgcolor="#FFFFFF">
  <tr>
    <td width="753" height="2" valign="top"><img src="images/shim.gif" width="753" height="2"></td>
    <td width="100%" height="2"></td>
  </tr>
  <tr align="left" valign="top">
    <td width="753"><iframe name="topRow" scrolling="no" marginwidth="0" marginheight="0"src="subRow1.php" frameborder="0" height="186" width="100%">Please upgrade your browser.</iframe></td>
    <td width="100%" bgcolor="#FFFFFF"></td>
  </tr>
  <tr align="left" valign="top">
    <td width="753" height="2" bgcolor="9c9cc6"></td>
    <td width="100%" height="2" bgcolor="9c9cc6"></td>
  </tr>
  <tr>
    <td width="753" height="2"></td>
    <td width="100%" height="2"></td>
  </tr>
</table>
```

Whew, that was quite a table, but a good warm-up for the next file - subRow1.php.

subRow1.php

subRow1.php, as described earlier, sits within the 753 pixel wide iFrame of row1.php, and contains three iFrames. This is a great way to keep content organized on the screen.

> You could customize this, and add as many boxes horizontally as you wanted, although you'd need to lengthen the table in row1.php to do this. To add further rows to the project, you just need to include row2, row3, ... row(n) in the index.php file. You can build entire web pages by adding cells to a table like this.

1. Create a new PHP document (File > New), and once again start with a blank page by clearing out the HTML script in the Code view. Save the file as subRow1.php in the image viewer folder.

```
<?php
include("header.php");
?>
```

2. Add start and end PHP tags, and then include header.php, as shown in the screenshot:

Case Study: Dynamic Image Viewer

3. Drop the cursor to the line *after* the end PHP tag – the table is HTML, and nothing to do with our PHP. Insert a new table (Insert > Table) with the values shown below:

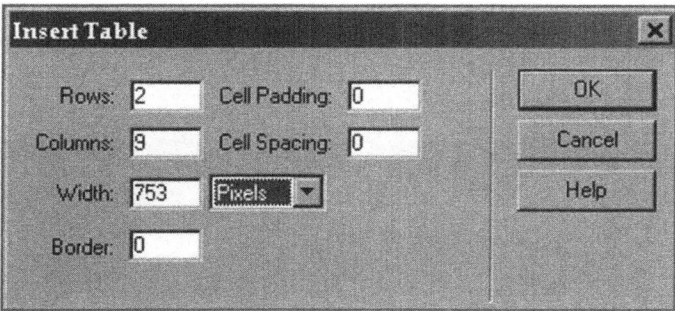

4. Select the entire table in the Design view by right-clicking/CTRL-clicking on the table and selecting Table > Select Table from the menu (as shown).

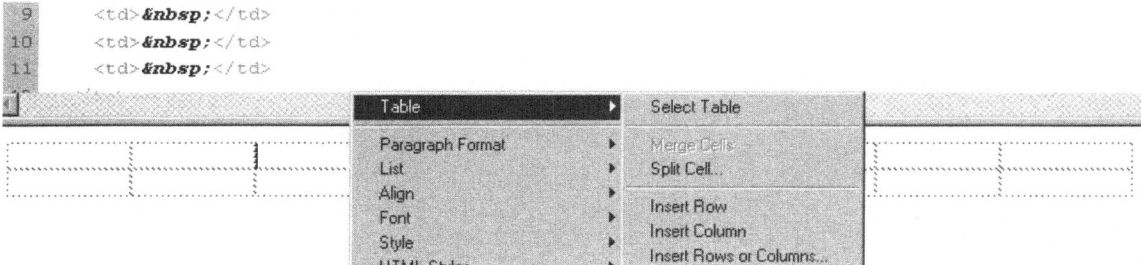

5. Add a height of 186 pixels, and a background color of white (#FFFFFF). This should leave your table looking like the screenshot below. (If your cells look taller, then you've selected all the cells together, and not the table – check your Code view to make sure that there's just one `height=186` setting at the top.)

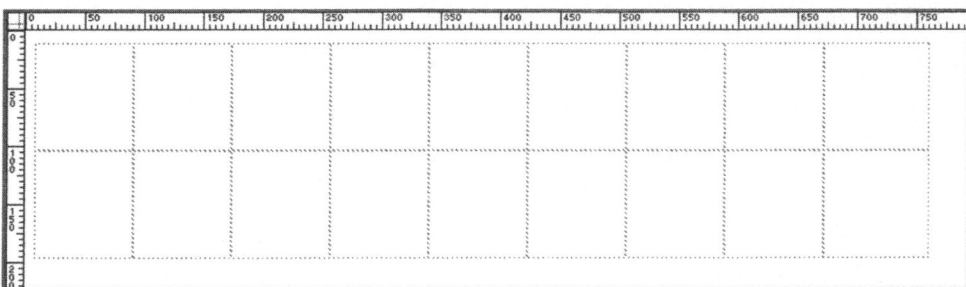

6. In the first row, select cells 1 and 2. You can do this by clicking on the first cell, holding down the shift key and selecting the second cell, by clicking in the first cell and dragging into the second, or just giving up and highlighting them in the Code view. Merge these by selecting the merge button in the Properties panel, as shown:

Foundation Dreamweaver MX

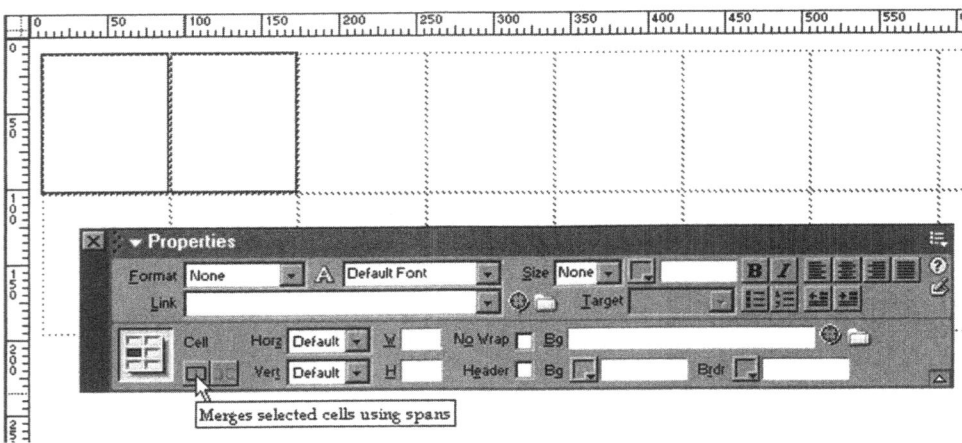

7. Now merge cells 4 and 5, and 7 and 8. The three merged cells are going to hold the title graphics for the content attached in the upcoming iFrames.

8. Select each of the three merged cells, and give them a height of 15.

9. Because we've set the table width previously, we're going to have to make our width alterations in the Code view this time. Select the merged cells again, and after the height setting (but still within the <td tag), add width="250".

```
<tr>
  <td height="15" width="250" colspan="2"> </td>
  <td> </td>
  <td height="15" width="250"colspan="2"> </td>
  <td> </td>
  <td height="15" width="250" colspan="2"> </td>
  <td> </td>
</tr>
```

10. Then make the cells in the first row that we didn't merge (hint: they're the ones without `colspan` settings in the Code view) 1 pixel wide and 15 pixels tall. They will act as a visual buffer between sections.

11. After all that hard work, save your file as `subrow1.php` before we go any further.

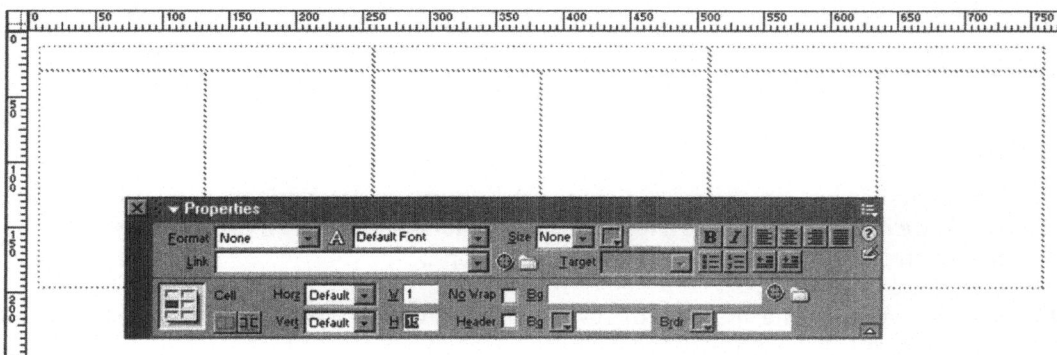

We're now going to add the graphics for the titles of the sections and `shim.gif` as a placeholder in the 1 pixel wide buffer cell. You can either create your own 250 x 15 graphics for the titles, or use `imageViewer.gif` and `blankTitle.gif` from the source files (put these in the `images` sub-directory as well, to keep things tidy).

12. Add `imageViewer.gif` to the first set of merged cells in row 1. Make sure to set the size of the graphic to 250 pixels wide and 15 pixels tall in the Properties panel.

13. Add `shim.gif` to the third cell in row 1 and make sure to give it a width of 1 pixel and a height of 15 pixels. (As this cell is only 1 pixel wide, you'll have to highlight the start and end tags in the Code view to add settings in the Properties panel.)

```
<table width="753" height="186" border="0" cellpadding="0" cellspacing="0" bgcolor="#FFFFFF">
  <tr>
    <td height="15" width="250" colspan="2"><img src="images/imageViewer.gif" width="250" height="15"></td>
    <td width="1" height="15"><img src="images/shim.gif" width="1" height="15"></td>
    <td height="15" width="250"colspan="2"> </td>
    <td width="1" height="15"> </td>
    <td height="15" width="250" colspan="2"> </td>
```

14. Continue this process for the next two sets of joined cells and the last two 1 pixel wide buffer cells. This time, however, add the `blankTitle.gif` graphic – we're not going to be filling these cells. After adding the first `blankTitle.gif` graphic, you may well find it easier to copy the `img src` tag, and place it between the `<td>` and `</td>` tags in the Code view. Whatever, you should have some code that looks like this:

Foundation Dreamweaver MX

```
<table width="753" height="186" border="0" cellpadding="0" cellspacing="0" bgcolor="#FFFFFF">
  <tr>
    <td height="15" width="250" colspan="2"><img src="images/imageViewer.gif" width="250" height="15"></td>
    <td width="1" height="15"><img src="images/shim.gif" width="1" height="15"></td>
    <td height="15" width="250"colspan="2"><img src="images/blankTitle.gif" width="250" height="15"></td>
    <td width="1" height="15"><img src="images/shim.gif" width="1" height="15"></td>
    <td height="15" width="250" colspan="2"><img src="images/blankTitle.gif" width="250" height="15"></td>
    <td width="1" height="15"><img src="images/shim.gif" width="1" height="15"></td>
  </tr>
```

We're finished with the first row. Time to take a quick breather and then move on to row 2. In row 2, we're going to add the iFrames that will hold `imageViewer.php` as well as a placeholder file for the remaining two pages called `blank.php`.

15. Start by selecting the first cell of row 2. In the Properties panel, give this cell a horizontal alignment of Left, a vertical assignment of Top, and a width of 234.

16. We're going to add a custom style attribute to these iFrames. If you remember, we added a `.rfelement` style to the Cascading Style Sheet that we created earlier, and we're finally going to implement that style. Add `class="rfelement"` to the tag information of the current cell. When you are finished, the tag should read something like this (it doesn't really matter what order the table settings come in after `<td>`):

`<td align="left" valign="top" class="rfelement" width="234"></td>`

17. After you have added the style attribute, place the cursor between the `>` and `</td>` in the tag above, so that we can add our inline frame.

18. Add this iFrame tag:

```
<iFrame name="inframe1" scrolling="auto" marginwidth="0"
    ➥marginheight="0" frameborder="0" width="100%" height="148"
    ➥src="imageViewer.php"></iFrame>
```

19. Add the shim graphic to this cell (Insert > Image) with a width of 10 and a height of 4. This will vertically space any information that you wish to include at the bottom of the table (copyright, for example).

20. Still in the same cell, hit RETURN, and add another shim graphic with a width of 4 and a height of 2 to move the text away from the left edge of the table.

21. Still in the same cell, now add the text you want – I've used ©Marks' Photography.

22. We're going to add the bracket graphic to the right side of the first table, which sits in the second cell of the bottom row. Add `right_side.gif` from the source files to the second cell, and check that it has a width of 16 and a height of 171.

Case Study: Dynamic Image Viewer

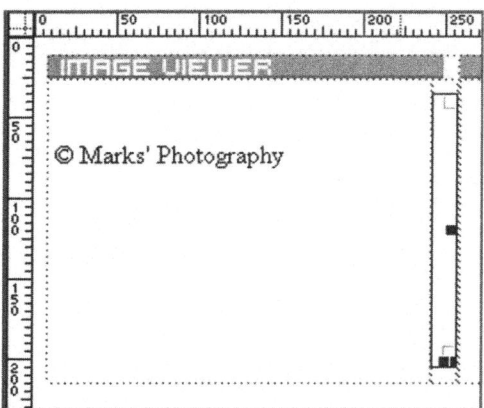

23. Still in the second row, give the third cell a width of 1 pixel. Add the shim graphic to this cell with a width of 1 and a height of 171. Make absolutely sure you're in the third cell, and not the fourth cell – it's very easy to get the wrong cell here.

24. Repeat steps **15 – 19**, and **22 - 23** for the next two groups of cells - 4, 5, 6 and 7, 8, 9.

25. Return to your two new groups of cells, and rename the iFrames `inframe2` and `inframe3` accordingly.

26. We need to create a placeholder file for the source tag of the iFrame. Create a new Dreamweaver file, strip out all code, and add a set of `<? ?>` php tags.

27. Save this file as `blank.php`. Now go to the iFrame tag in your fourth and seventh cells, and replace `imageviewer.php` with `blank.php`.

28. Finally, in the Code view, add a `</body>` and an `</html>` tag to the end of the file. Since we attached the header information, the start body tag and start HTML tags were added to the document. For most pages in the project, you could simply include the `footer.php` file instead, but we don't want to see the contact information to appear a second time in the bottom of the iFrame here.

Your completed code should now look like this:

```
<?php
include ("header.php");
?>

<table width="753" height="186" border="0" cellpadding="0" Xcellspacing="0" bgcolor="#FFFFFF">
  <tr>
    <td colspan="2" width="250" height="15"><img src="imageViewer.gif" width="250" height="15"></td>
    <td width="1" height="15"><img src="shim.gif" width="1" Xheight="15"></td>
    <td colspan="2" width="250" height="15"><img src="blankTitle.gif" width="250" height="15"></td>
```

```
            <td width="1" height="15"><img src="shim.gif" width="1" height="15"></td>
            <td colspan="2" width="250" height="15"><img src="blankTitle.gif"
        ➥width="250" height="15"></td>
            <td width="1" height="15"><img src="shim.gif" width="1"
        ➥height="15"></td>
      </tr>
      <tr>
            <td   width="234"   align="left"   valign="top"   class="rfelement"><iFrame
        ➥name="inframe1" scrolling="auto" marginwidth="0" marginheight="0"
        ➥frameborder="0" width="100%" height="148"
        ➥src="imageViewer.php"></iFrame>
              <p><img src="shim.gif" width="10" height="4"></p>
              <p><img src="shim.gif" width="4" height="2">&copy;Mark's
                 ➥Photography</p></td>
            <td><img src="right_side.gif" width="16" height="171"></td>
            <td width="1"><img src="shim.gif" width="1" height="171"></td>
             <td   align="left"   valign="top"   class="rfelement"   width="234"><iFrame
        ➥name="inframe2" scrolling="auto" marginwidth="0" marginheight="0"
        ➥frameborder="0" width="100%" height="148"
        ➥src="blank.php"></iFrame></td>
            <td><img src="right_side.gif" width="16" height="171"></td>
            <td width="1"><img src="shim.gif" width="1" height="171"></td>
             <td   align="left"   valign="top"   class="rfelement"   width="234">   <iFrame
        ➥name="inframe3" scrolling="auto" marginwidth="0" marginheight="0"
        ➥frameborder="0" height="148" width="100%"
        ➥src="blank.php"></iFrame></td>
            <td><img src="right_side.gif" width="16" height="171"></td>
            <td width="1"><img src="shim.gif" width="1" height="171"></td>
      </tr>
    </table>
    </body>
</html>
```

Databases

We're almost there. We only have one more file to create, even if it is the most important one – imageViewer.php. This file will make use of a MySQL database to store information about the images you'll be dynamically displaying. We're going to create a recordset to output all of the images in the database, and create a link to PayPal to sell the images through.

To start, we'll create the database and link to it through Dreamweaver. I'm not going to go into great detail about creating and managing MySQL databases here. If you've got some time, and want to come back when everything's working, then try doing what I did and create a database with the same structure as the screenshot showing the pics_europe table on page 404.

I then used PHPMyAdmin to "dump", or write all the information from the database (including the table data) to a text file (select the radio button for Structure and data, check off Complete inserts, and then hit the Go button). This text file will create the SQL statements to build the table we need and input the relevant data to it.

Case Study: Dynamic Image Viewer

You can download my text file from the friends of ED site in the usual way – it's called `sql.txt`. Once you've done that, open up PHPMyAdmin and select the `book_db` database from the drop-down menu. Open up `sql.txt` in a text editor and copy and paste the whole lot into the Run SQL query/queries on database field in PHPMyAdmin.

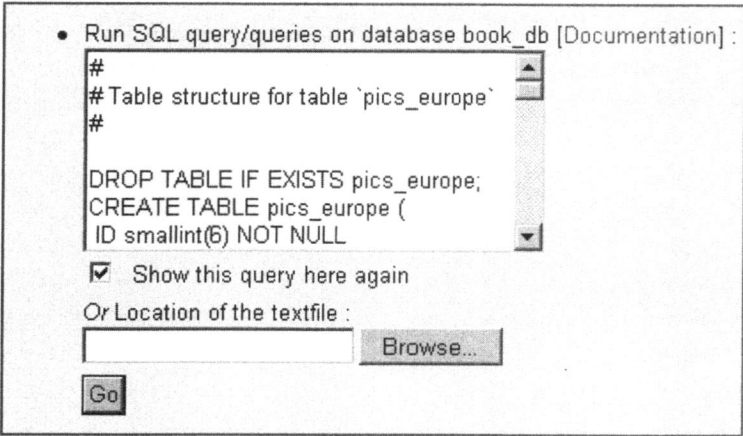

Click Go and you'll see the dialog box below. Click OK.

You should see a page telling you that your SQL query has been executed successfully and our new table `pics_europe` will have appeared under `books_db`. If you open up the table, you'll see the fields the SQL script has created.

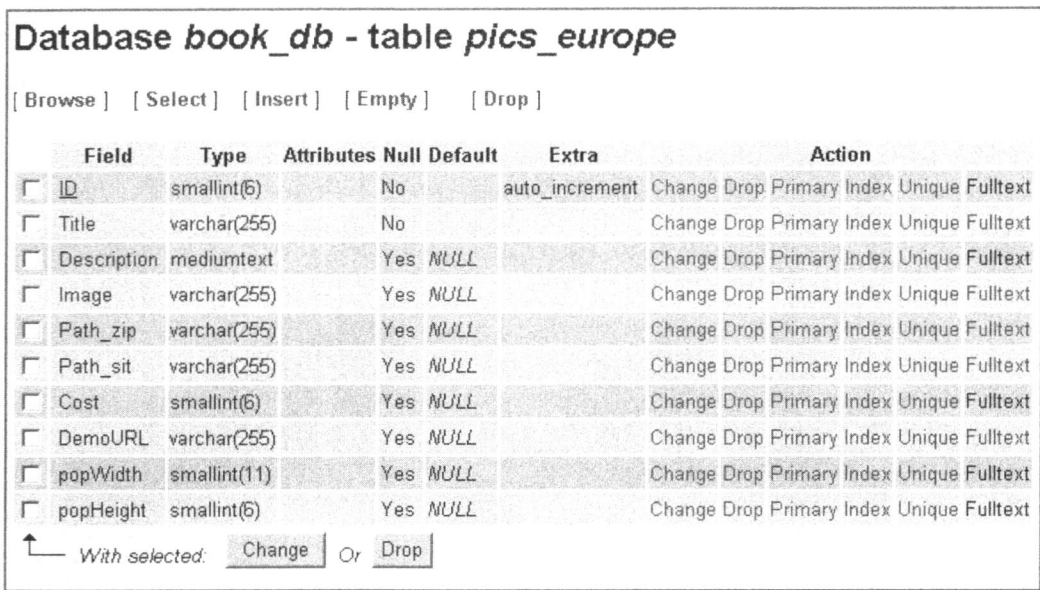

Now, back to Dreamweaver. The next step is to establish a connection to the database.

Establishing a connection to the database

If you don't already have a connection to your database with the newly uploaded pics_europe table and data, now is the time to create one.

1. In the Applications panel, select the MySQL Connection in the menu options of the Databases tab.

2. Enter the information necessary to connect to your MySQL database in the MySQL Connection dialog. You should have set up a book_db database for earlier chapters in the book, and you can simply reuse that database. We have already added a table to that database.

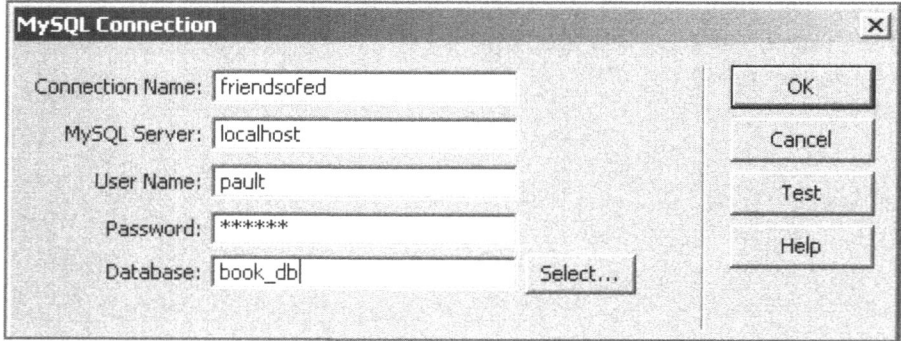

3. Hit the Test button to make sure that you have an active connection to the database

Once an active connection has been made to the database, we can view all of the fields within the pics_europe table, making it possible to create the recordset in the final file, imageViewer.php.

imageViewer.php

The beauty of imageViewer.php is that it can be used to display any number of different items. It is simply a way to organize and potentially sell data. This includes, but is not limited to pictures, sound loops, graphics, videos, SWFs, or even Flash MX components. All of the information found within the image viewer is dynamic, excluding the table that contains it.

When the view button is selected from the list of items, the function openNewWindow() created in the header.php file simply opens an HTML file with its dimensions retrieved from the database. This HTML file, in our case, holds the images to be displayed, but could contain any of the items we've just listed.

The HTML pages that house the images for display all have onBlur="parent.close() in the body tag. This makes sure that when the user starts interacting with something else on their computer (including viewing other images) the pop-up window closes. This prevents an abundance of pop-up windows being created.

The image viewer

1. Start with a new PHP document, and clear out the default HTML code.

2. Add a new table with two rows, two columns, a width of 210 pixels, and border, cell spacing, and cell padding all equal to 0.

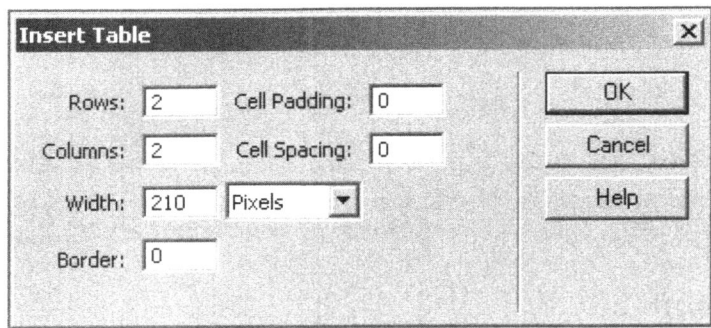

3. Select the entire table in the Design view and change its height to 49 pixels, and its background color to white (#FFFFFF) in the Properties panel.

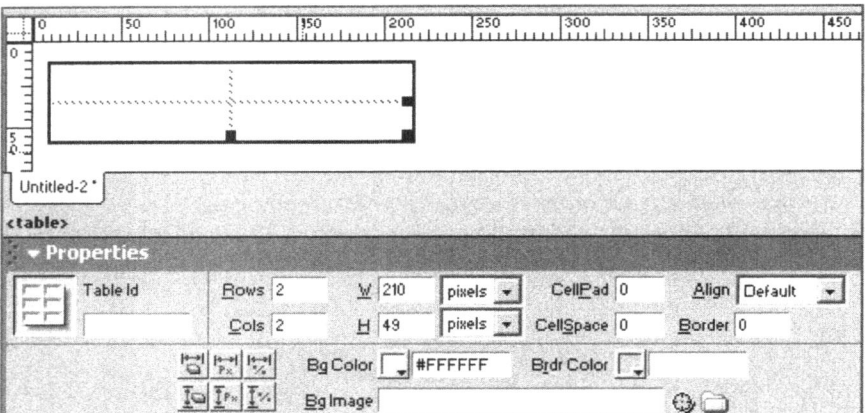

Case Study: Dynamic Image Viewer

4. We're going to add the dynamic text to our image viewer, but we have to create a recordset first, so select Recordset from the drop-down menu of the Server Behaviors tab in the Application panel.

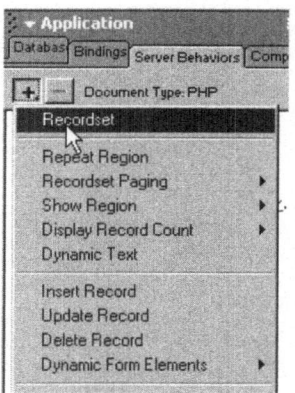

5. If the dialog that appears doesn't look like the screenshot below, click Simple. Select your connection name (friendsofed in this case) from the Connection field and make sure our pics_europe table is selected. Choose ID for the Sort field, and Ascending. Then hit OK.

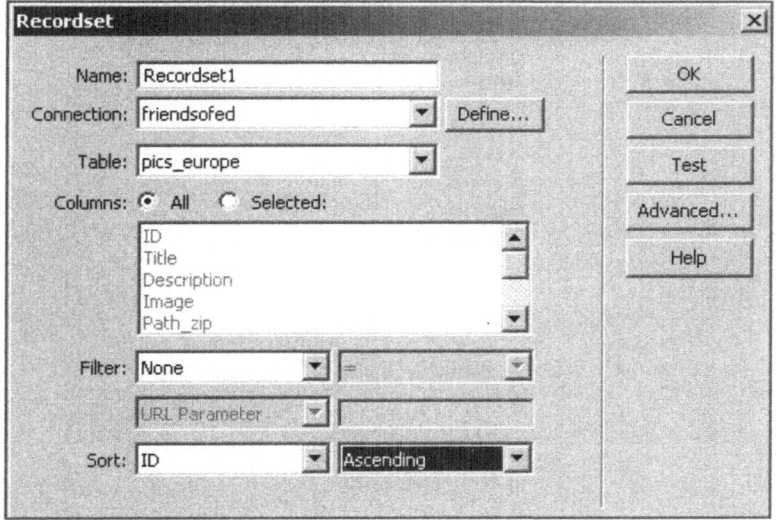

6. We're now going to begin adding the dynamic text to our table. Click in the top right cell of the table and type Name:. Make this bold, but be careful not to turn the dynamic text we're adding in the next step bold (the easiest way to do this is probably to make sure that you place the cursor to the right of the `</strong>` tag before continuing to the next step).

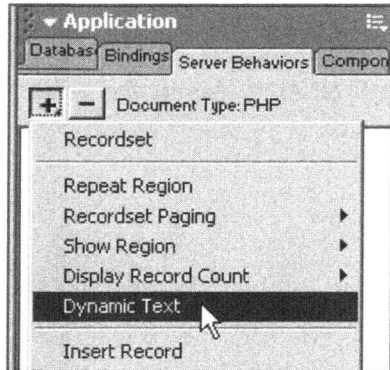

7. Select Dynamic Text from the drop-down menu of the Server Behaviors tab in the Application panel, and then Title from the Dynamic Text dialog. Click OK.

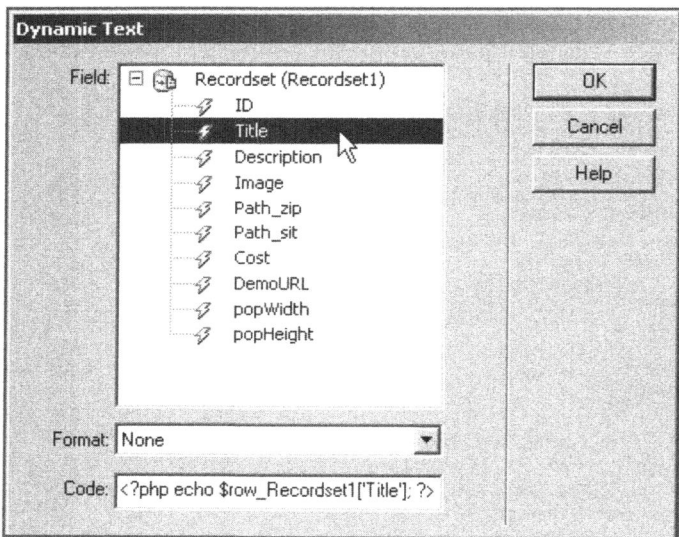

8. Hit a soft return (SHIFT + ENTER) after the {Recordset1.Title} placeholder, and type Cost:.

    You could simply display the cost of the image pulled from the database and add a description in the same way we've just used to add the title by following step **7**, but clicking on Cost instead of Title.

    However, with a slight addition in the Code view, we can write out the word FREE and links to the .zip and .sit files if the cost equals 0. If the image has a price, then we can write our price, and dynamically send that information along the URL string to PayPal.

9. If you're going down this path, insert this code into the Code view right after Cost:

```php
<?php
  if ($row_Recordset1["Cost"] == 0) {
        echo "FREE  <A HREF=\"photos/".$row_Recordset1
        ➥["Path_zip"]."\">.zip</A> | <A HREF
        ➥=\"photos/".$row_Recordset1["Path_sit"]."\">.sit</A> ";
  } else {
        echo "$".$row_Recordset1["Cost"]."  <a href=
        \"https://www.paypal.com/cgibin/webscr?amount=".
        ➥$row_Recordset1["Cost"]."&no_shipping1&item_name=".$row_
        ➥Recordset1["Title"]."&business=todd%40mindgrub.com&
        ➥item_number=".$row_Recordset1["ID"]."&invoice=".$row_
        ➥Recordset1["ID"]."&cmd=_xclick&no_note=1\"target=\"_blank\
        ➥">BUY</a>";
  }
?>
```

If you look at the code, you can see what's happening here: we're checking if the cost in our record equals 0. If it does, then we provide the links to the `.zip` and `.sit` files. If not, then we proceed to our else statement, which displays the cost, the link to PayPal, and the information PayPal will need (more on PayPal in a moment).

Your table should now look like this:

Selling items through PayPal

Any individual can be a web-based entrepreneur in no time at all by signing up for a business account with PayPal. All you need to do is to register your company address and your e-mail with PayPal at www.PayPal.com, and they are more then happy to start receiving money for you in return for a nominal fee.

In the `else` statement above, when the image's `Cost` field in the database is not 0, the code writes out the price of the image, and a link to PayPal's web site. All of the information for the sale of the item is passed on as variables. PayPal then charges the user the amount for the item, and sends the individual with the account (you) a check once a month.

The variables are passed on the end of the URL string so that you can see how the information is being passed. This isn't really a huge problem for us here, as the information is the cost, the title, and ID field. Strictly speaking, it's a better idea to pass variables via POST, so they are not visible to the end user.

Paypal's website has a link for developers which provides a wealth of different tools to add forms and links so that you can use their services to make e-commerce sites. There is a link, for instance, to download a toolkit to use with Dreamweaver to create a payment form. That link is www.webaddist.com/Products/ProductDetails.asp?PID=18.

Dynamic images

Here, we're going to add the URL to the view link, the dynamic thumbnail, and the horizontal line beneath the image. We're also going to make the recordset output the entire list of images in the database. After that, we're done.

1. In the same cell that we've just been dealing with, hit a soft return with SHIFT + ENTER after Cost:, and type Desc:.

2. Select Dynamic Text from the drop-down menu of the Server Behaviors tab in the Application panel, and then Description from the Dynamic Text dialog. Click OK.

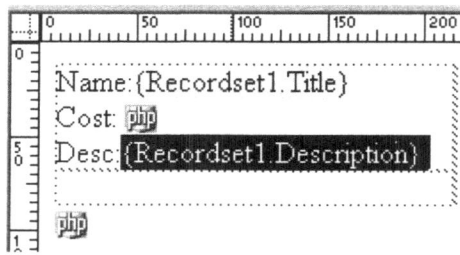

3. Next, we want to dynamically attach a URL to a view link, so that we can have the image files pop-up as per their specific dimensions and image. Unfortunately, we cannot add the link in the Properties panel, so add the following code in the Code view after {Recordset1.Description}:

```
<?php echo"<a href=\"javascript:openNewWindow
    ↪('photos/".$row_Recordset1["DemoURL"]."','".$row_Recordset1
    ↪["popWidth"]."," .$row_Recordset1["popHeight"].")\">view</a>"?>
```

This code grabs the values of `popWidth`, `popHeight`, and `URL` from the database for each photo, and sends those values to the JavaScript function `openNewWindow` that we created in the file `header.php`. Your table should now look like this:

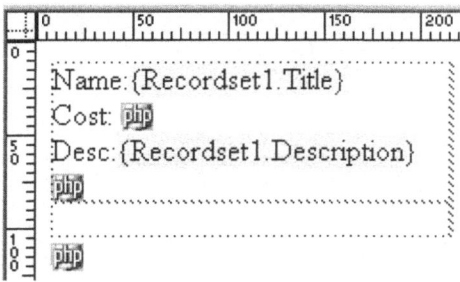

4. We have to add a placeholder for our dynamic image before we can include the dynamic image itself, so highlight the first non-breaking space ( ) in the table. This will put our cursor within the first cell of the top row, which is otherwise too small to select.

5. Add an image placeholder to the cell by selecting Insert > Image Placeholder.

6. Give the image a name of `dynamicImage`, with a width of 73 pixels, a height of 78 pixels, and a background color of white.

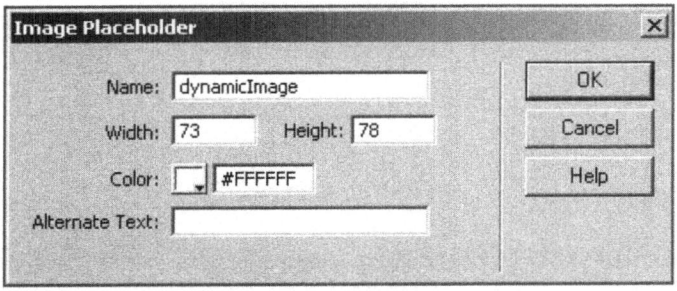

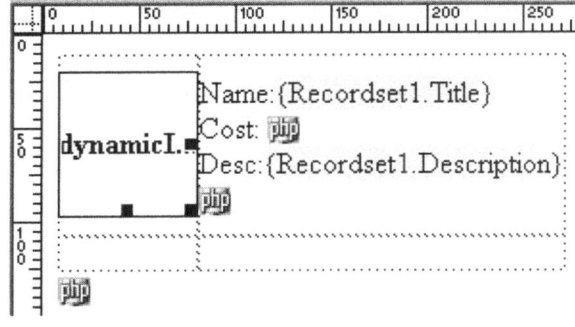

7. Select the placeholder. Select the Image field in the Bindings tab of the Application panel, and press the Bind button. You should notice that the image placeholder changes from some text to an icon.

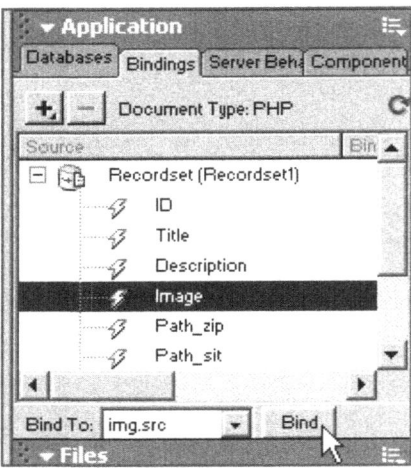

8. Click on the icon, and give it a horizontal space of 6 with the H Space setting at the bottom of the Properties panel, as shown. This makes sure that there is some separation between the image and the text.

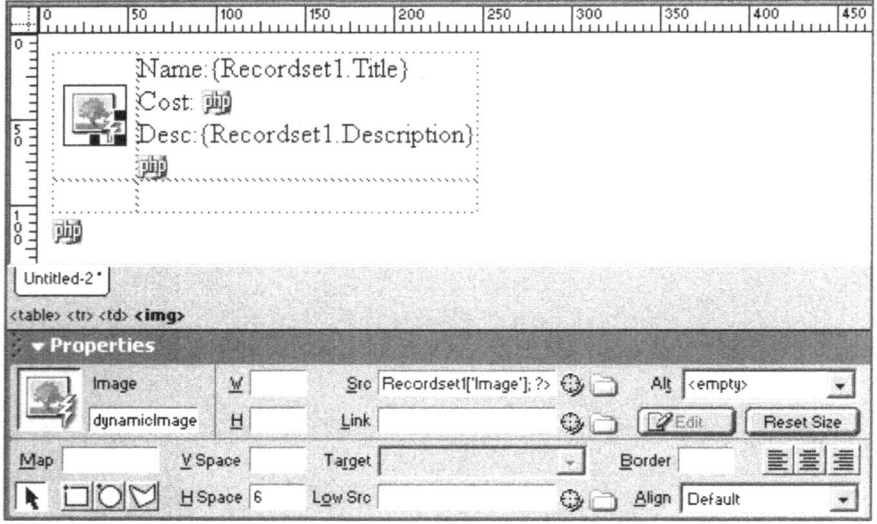

We need to add graphics to the bottom cells of the second row to create a line separation between images and text. Again, you can create these yourself, but you probably just want to use gray.gif from the source files.

9. Save your file as imageViewer.php.

10. Add the `gray.gif` graphic to both of the bottom cells. In the left cell, make it 100% wide and 1 pixel tall. In the right cell, make it 90% wide and 1 pixel high.

11. Lastly, we need this entire table to repeat for each of the images in the database. Select the entire table by Right/CTRL-clicking on it and going to Table > Select Table. Then select Repeat Region in the drop-down menu of the Server Behaviors tab in the Application panel.

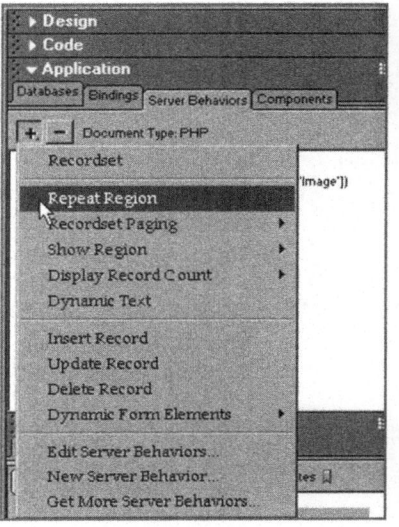

12. Select the radio button for All Records, and hit OK. Dreamweaver will add a nice repeat graphic (as shown in the screenshot) to the table after it has added the code necessary to continuously print out the tables until it runs out of values.

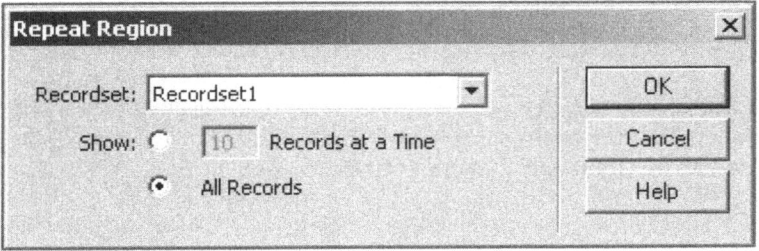

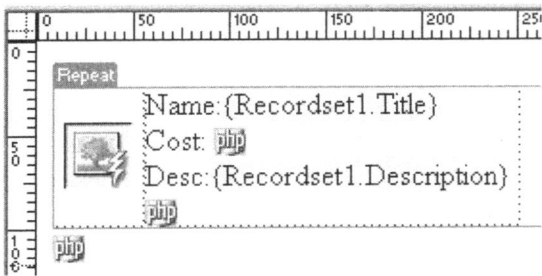

13. If you haven't already downloaded them, now is the time to add in the `photos` directory from the code downloads into your image viewer site. For things to work, they need to be in a `photos` directory in your site, so you can just drag the whole directory across. (You'll notice that each pic

has a thumbnail and full-size JPEG, a `.zip` and a `.sit` version, and a HTML file for them to sit in.)

14. At the very top of the Code view, add start and end PHP tags and include `header.php`:

```
<?php
    include("header.php");
?>
```

15. If you run the file `imageViewer.php` directly, you will see a column of the pictures and descriptions. Since this file resides in an iFrame, it is kept nicely contained, and you must scroll to see all of the images.

16. After creating all of the elements necessary to create this modular page system and image viewer, we are finally ready to test our files. Click on the index file in the Site tab of the Files panel. Click on the Preview / Debug in Browser button

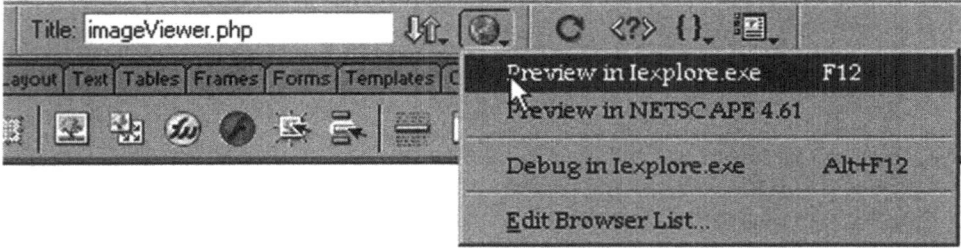

If for any reason your application does not work, then try the following things:

- Compare your source code for each file with the versions available for download. (The File > Print Code option in Dreamweaver is great for doing this.) If there is a large discrepancy anywhere, go back and follow the steps again for that section.

- Make sure that all of your files are sitting in the correct directories, and have the correct paths for each link.

- Make sure you have a current browser. Browsers before IE 5.0 and NS 4.7 will not work with iFrames.

- Make sure that PHP and the MySQL database are correctly installed.

- Use phpMyAdmin to check that your database contains the `pics_europe` table, and the data that Dreamweaver needs is in that table.

Summary

The system we've used here is a great way to make not just dynamic image viewers, but dynamic page layouts as well, and you now have an image viewer that you can use to showcase any amount of information or media types. Now that you've got it working, you can go and try customizing this to your needs – all you need is a server with PHP, a MySQL database, and something worth displaying.

This final chapter has seen you add everything that you've learned in the rest of the book to create a really useful, professional-standard web application. You've now got all the difficult bits out the way (yes, I'm thinking about that PHP installation!), and have all the skills you need to go forward with your Dreamweaver web design. This brings us to the end of the book, but leaves you with the potential to go and design some great web sites.

A

Dreamweaver Extensions

A Dreamweaver Extension can be added into Dreamweaver to add new and extra features. In the past, this has provided a way for Dreamweaver users to add some really useful functionality to Dreamweaver, and Macromedia have made it very easy to install and manage Extensions in Dreamweaver. This appendix takes a quick look at where to get Extensions from, how to install them, and how to manage them in Dreamweaver.

> Note that almost all Extensions written for previous versions of Dreamweaver will work with MX. Check the instructions and details for the individual Extension for further details.

Extensions come in a variety of formats, and are created both by Macromedia and members of the Dreamweaver community. We're going to set Dreamweaver up so that we can install some extensions, go through a sample installation, and then leave you with the best places to find Extensions on the web.

A   **Foundation Dreamweaver MX**

Using the Extension Manager

Extensions in Dreamweaver are managed by the Extension Manager, which runs side-by-side with Dreamweaver and lets you easily install new Extensions and manage the ones you already have.

1. Go to http://www.macromedia.com/exchange (you may have to scroll down, as it's at the bottom of the list), and download the Extension Manager v1.5 installer for Windows or Mac as appropriate.

2. Double-click on the installer to begin the installation process. You will need to close Dreamweaver if you have it running for this to work.

3. Now open Dreamweaver back up, and go to Help > Manage Extensions. You should see a window like the one pictured – although you're unlikely to have the Reset Image Size Extension installed already, as I do.

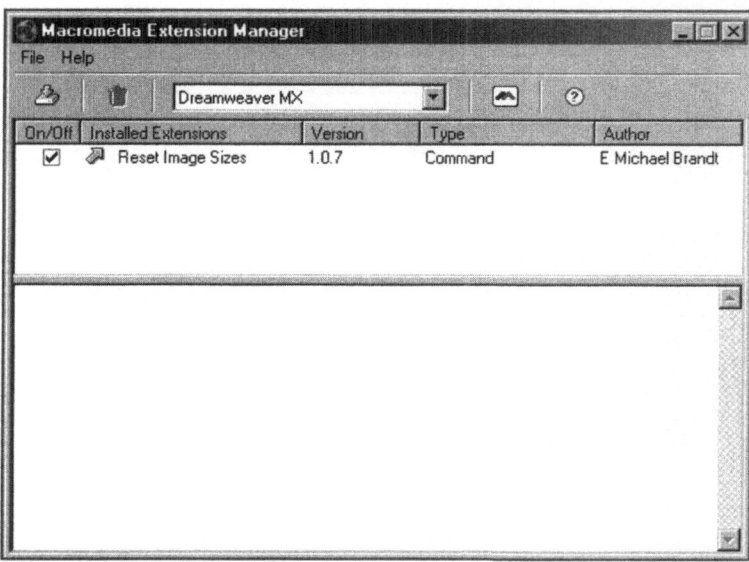

4. Still in Dreamweaver, choose Help > Dreamweaver Exchange to go directly to the Macromedia Exchange site.

5. Here, pick an Extension to download. I've picked one of the Featured Extensions, called Cube Stores Designers. This lets designers create and customize E-commerce web sites quickly and easily using visual composition tools.

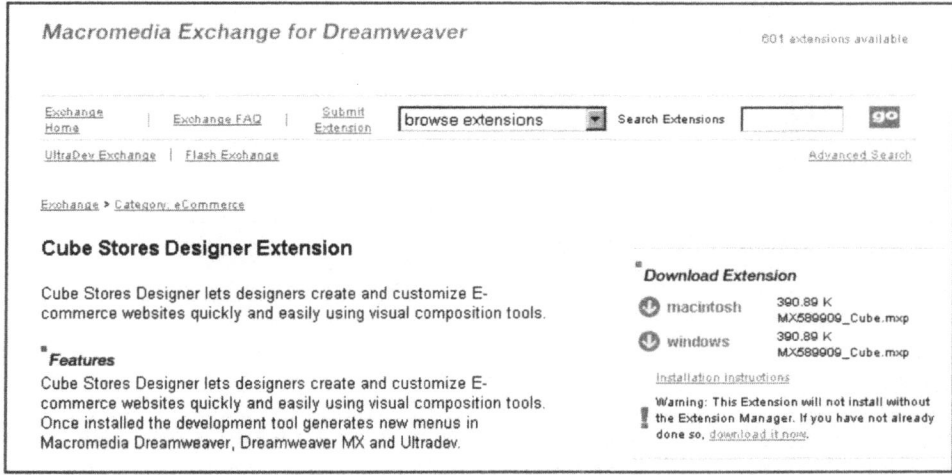

6. The extension package file will be in the .MXP format. Once you've chosen your Extension, save the MXP package to the Downloaded Extensions folder within the Dreamweaver folder on your machine.

A Foundation Dreamweaver MX

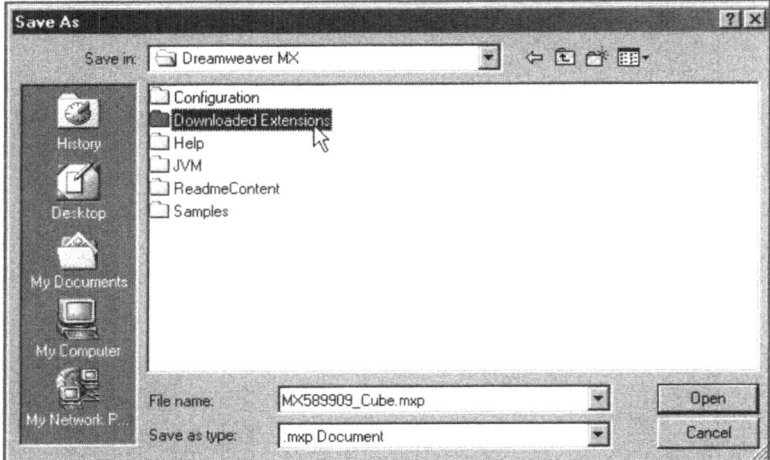

7. Once downloaded, open up the Extension Manager (confusingly, you can use the Manage Extensions option from the Help menu or from the Commands menu – both have the same effect).

8. Choose File > Install Extension, select your new Extension, and it will be installed in Dreamweaver.

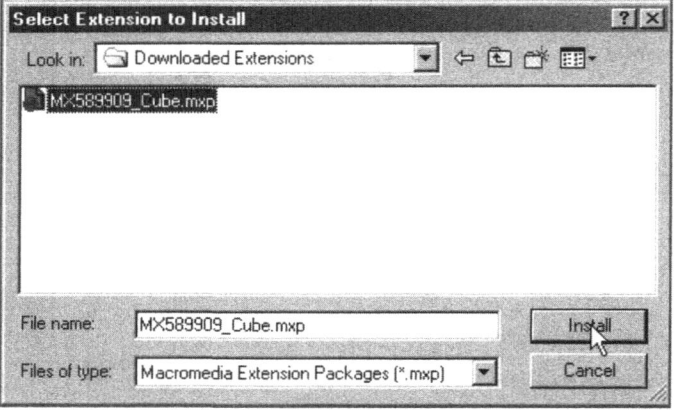

9. Some extensions need Dreamweaver to restart before they can be used, so you may be prompted to quit and restart Dreamweaver.

10. Once you're back in Dreamweaver, go to the Extension Manager again, and highlight the Extension. This will give you some basic information on where you can access the Extension in Dreamweaver, how to remove it, and usually a web site address for further details.

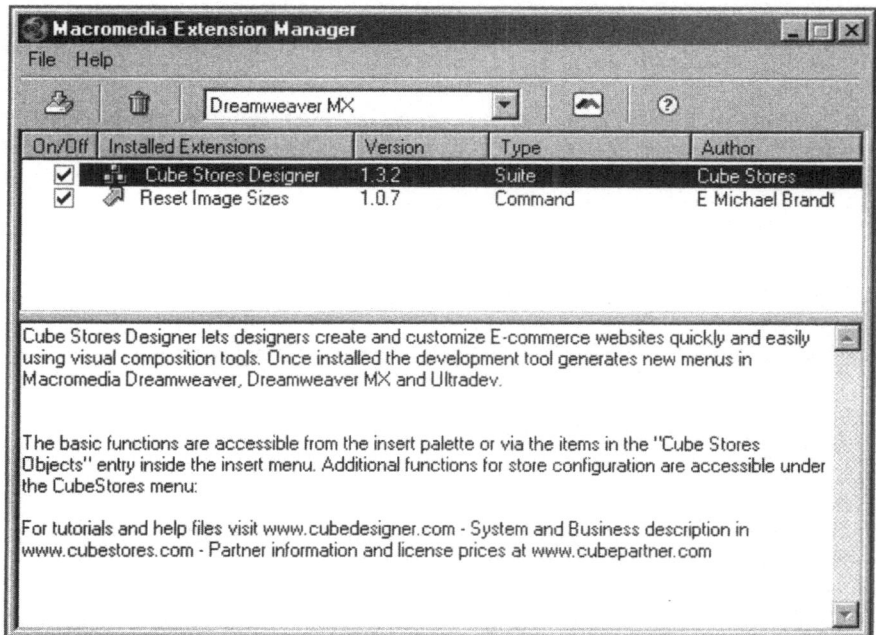

Where to find Extensions

As you probably saw when we visited earlier, Macromedia Dreamweaver Exchange is the number one source for downloading Dreamweaver Extensions. Here you can get over 700 Extensions, all approved by Macromedia. Go to

http://www.macromedia.com/exchange

and choose Dreamweaver from the list of software at the top, or just select Dreamweaver Exchange from the Help menu, in Dreamweaver, as we did earlier.

In addition, there are many other community sites that offer Extensions (and much more) for Dreamweaver MX. Be aware that no guarantees are offered on many of these, so don't go basing a huge commercial project on them without some careful testing first!

Some of the most popular are:

Dreamweaver Extensions Database
http://www.idest.com/cgi-bin/database.cgi

This is a simple search engine that allows you to search for Dreamweaver Extensions by keyword.

eButtonz
http://www.webdevindex.org/cgi-bin/links/jump.cgi?ID=1301

The eButtonz Extension is a free-to-use shopping cart plug-in for Macromedia Dreamweaver. eButtonz integrates itself within Dreamweaver so that it's always available when building or modifying a site.

Massimo's Corner
http://www.massimocorner.com/

Massimo Foti has won awards for being the best Dreamweaver Extension developer in the past couple of years. Besides the Cold Fusion XHTML Editor for MX that he recently developed, and won top honors for, he has an excellent list of Extensions that he has developed for past versions of Dreamweaver. He's sure to develop more for MX, so keep an eye on his site.

Late Night Software
http://www.latenightsw.com/freeware/OSADreamweaver/index.html

The OSA Extension allows Mac owners to use AppleScript with Dreamweaver.

Project Seven
http://www.projectseven.com/extensions/index.htm

The developers at Project Seven have two popular Dreamweaver extensions: Menu Magic and Geewizz. Menu Magic lets you create awesome DHTML menus with just a few mouse clicks, while Geewizz lets you create DHTML scrollers with ease. They have full demos of the extensions on their site, but these are commercial extensions that you'll have to buy.

Rabi's Dreamweaver Extensions
http://www.dreamweaver-extensions.com/

Another Macromedia winner for Best Extension, this site provides several useful Extensions, including a News Ticker.

UDZone
http://udzone.com/categories.asp?TypeId=3

UD Zone continuously updates their list of new Extensions, and also reviews them. The reviews and the subsequent ratings system can help give you a solid idea of how good the Extensions are.

Webmonkey's Editor Extensions Library
http://www.hotwired.com/webmonkey/javascript/code_library/ed_ext

A useful list of Extensions.

Yaromat
http://www.yaromat.com/dw/index.php

Dreamweaver Extensions A

Index

The index is arranged hierarchically, in alphabetical order, with symbols preceding the letter A. Many second-level entries also occur as first-level entries. This is to ensure that you will find the information you require however you choose to search for it.

Any comments or suggestions about the index would be welcome at fionamu@friendsofed.com.

$x++ variable 298
$_COOKIE 348
$_ENV 348
$_GET 348
$_POST 348
$_REQUEST 348
$_SERVER 348
$_SESSION 348, 355

A

about pages 153-160
accessibility 104
alt attribute 225
Amazon 236
Apache
   backing up configuration file 254
   installing 239
   installing PHP 244
   Server Information screen 241
   Setup Type options 242
   starting in Mac OS X 246
   testing in browser 242
   troubleshooting 243
Application panel 53, 55, 363
   Bindings tab 412
   Server Behaviors tab 407
arrays 300
array_splice function 301
ASP 238
ASP.NET 237
assets 41
auto-increments 298

B

Bindings tab 412
browser selection 58

C

Cascading Style Sheets (CSS) 107, 133
   attaching in Properties panel 110
   classes for altering defaults 112
   creating 108
   defaults 112
   font tags 112
   Style Definition 113
   typing into Style Sheets 120
cells 75
   adding text 80
   creating new cells 78
   merging 87
   resizing cells 77, 85
   resizing images 76
   testing in browser 86
   text colors 86
   text formatting 86
Check Form MX extension 359

classes 138
   altering style Sheet defaults 112
   applying to elements within site 114
   creating 113
   defining in global Style Sheet 113
   editing 117
   spans 116
Code view 53, 55, 189
   adding attributes 200
   adding behaviors 204
   adding tables 200
   adding tags 197
   code coloring preferences 190
   code format preferences 192
   code hint preferences 193
   code rewriting preferences 194
   internal preferences 195
   JavaScript 203
   .js files 215
   Snippets panel 210
   switching to Design view 201
   Tag Editor 202
ColdFusion 237
Commands menu 56
conditional statements
   $variable1 - $variable3 282
   === operator 285
   AND operator 282, 283
   echo function 284
   enter.php 281, 283, 284, 285
   form2.php 280, 281, 283, 284, 285
   GET method 280
   OR operator 282, 283
   testing 281
contact pages
   adding Submit/Send button 174
   adding text to table 171
   Form Element composition 173
   inserting table 170
   Multi-line text field 172
   onecolumn.dwt template 170
   resizing text box 172
   Text Field command 171
cookies
   removing 305
   security 310
   setting up 304
   setting up for logins 305
   username and password details 308
cropping images 66
CSS Styles panel 115, 383
   editing classes 117, 118
   options 119
CSS Validator 229

Index

D

Databases tab 404
Design view 53, 55, 64, 73
detect function 386
do while loops 298
Document window
  Code and Design view 50
  Code view 49
  Design view 48
  monitor sizes 49
Dreamweaver Exchange 421
Dreamweaver Extensions Database 421
Dreamweaver MX 1
  native support of PHP/MySQL 314
  settings 10
  web page creation 11
dynamic content 235, 239
Dynamic Image Viewer (case study) 377
   tag removal 395
  adding Style Sheets 382
  adding to header file 382
  adding to tables 397
  background color 389
  blank.php placeholder file 401
  blankTitle.gif 399
  <body> attribute 385
  browser upgrade information 394
  changing header.php title 382
  Code Block button 380
  comments 381
  cost if else statement 409
  creating php files 382
  databaseconnection 404
  debugging/troubleshooting 414
  dynamic image placeholder 411
  dynamic images 410
  dynamic text for table 407
  dynamically attaching URL to view link 410
  file flowchart 378
  footer information and links 390
  footer.php file 381, 390
  gray.gif 412
  header.php file 380
  iFrames 390
  image viewer table 406
  images folder 392
  imageViewer folder 379
  imageViewer.gif 399
  imageViewer.php file 390, 402
  include statement 379, 380
  index.php 380
  invisible graphic to lock tables 392
  JavaScript functions 386
  Macit variable 387
  merging cells 397
  modular files 379
  MySQL database 402
  NAME attribute 391
  onBlur="parent.close() 405
  openNewWindow function 387, 388
  photos directory 413
  pics_europe table 403
  popup window calculations 387
  recordsets 407
  repeating tables 413
  .rfelement padding 385
  rfelement style 400
  right_side.gif 400
  row1.php file 390
  row1.php table 391
  screenWidth and screenHeight variables 387
  scrollbar color 385
  shim.gif 392
  site definition 379
  Style Sheet definition 383
  subRow1.php file 390, 396
  table alignment 394
  table background color 392
  table dimensions 393
  table width alterations 398
  tag definitions 384
  testing files 414
  title graphics 399
  window.open function 388
  winParams variable 388
  x and y variables 387
dynamic sites 236, 237

E

eButtonz 421
Edit menu 56, 59
editable regions
Extension Manager 418
extensions (list) 421

F

File menu 56
files and folders 42, 46
Fireworks 66
Flash
  adding button text 182
  animated site content 175
  Beveled Rect-Blue style 182
  file use in Dreamweaver 179-181
  Flash 6 player 179
  Flash MX 179
  folder organization 182
  previewing buttons 183
  resizing button text 183
  setting button background color 182
  SWF preparation 176
  trial version 176

floating elements 143
font tags 112
for loops 299
foreach loops 301
form creation
   adding text background color 340
   Bg tool 340
   comments text area 336
   contact.php 334
   creating 'thank you' message 339
   creating form to hold data 340
   creating Recordset 340
   displaying information 342
   Dynamic Text dialog box 342
   email text field 336
   inserting form information into database 338
   inserting form tags 334
   inserting table 335, 340
   inserting text fields 335
   my_contacts Recordset 341
   name text field 336
   naming form 334
   nl2br function 342, 343
   Repeat Region dialog box 344
   testing complete application 345
   testing form 339
   thanks.php 338, 339
   validating form 336, 337
   view_contacts.php 340, 344
frames 97
   altering dimensions 100
   creating 98
   editing in Properties panel 99
   framesets 101
   iFrames 390
   naming 100
   <noframes> tag 101
Frames panel 99
Framesets options 99

G

GIFs 69

H

<head> tags 122
History panel 55
hotspots 91
HTML Template option 121
HTTP headers 304, 310

I

if statements 372
iFrames (inline frames) 390

image preparation 65
   cropping 66
   optimizing for web 67
   re-sizing 66
include statements 379
index.html page 64
   properties 72
Insert panel 51, 56
interface 39, 40
   assets 41
   diagram 47
   Document window 48
   Insert panel 51
   menus 55
   Panels 53
   Properties panel 52
   Site Definition window 43
Internet Explorer for Mac, detecting 386

J

JavaScript 203
   adding behaviors 204, 205
   detect function 386
   event trigger 207
   hand-coding versus built-in behaviors 209
   illegal characters 206
   js files 215
   Snippets panel 210
   syntax 204
   window.open function 388
Jerome Turner Photography (case study)
   a:active element 141
   a:hover element 141
   a:link element 140
   a:visited element 140
   about.html link 136, 156, 157
   Accessibility preferences 61
   adding graphic to about page 158, 159
   aligning pictures 87
   aligning text to top of 'content' area 156, 157
   alt attribute 225
   altering head content 123
   amending links 224
   Assets folder 71
   attaching Style Sheets 123
   audience 21
   background 146
   background color setting 129
   background transparent images 69
   <body> tag 125
   bordersetting 129
   brainstorming 21
   Browser options 58
   buy.html link 136
   camera.gif 158Cascading Style Sheets 122
   cell alignment 226
   cell colors 85

Index

cell manipulation 75, 82
center class 145
centering image in text column 160
classes 138
client needs 22
Code view improvements 218
columnOneContent region 155
column alterations 83
comments 125
connection speed 61
contact page improvements 218
contact.html link 136
content 29, 30
copyPadding class 145
corner.gif 84
creating main table 135
cross-platform compatibility 126
deadlines and timing 23
description 123
design 25
Design View 73
design, finalising 31, 32, 33, 35
div tags 130
Dogs in Cars pages improvements 222
download areas 85
drop-down menu 146
editable regions 147
file and folder organization 231
floating images 143
floatRight class 143
folio.html link 136
<form> tag 146
frames 99
GIFs 70
graphics folder 158
gray bars 144
halfPage style 219
<head> elements 122
History Steps 59
image preparation 65
images, moving into site folder 71
imgPhoto image 224
index.html properties 72
<input> tag 146
inserting images into splash page 74
JavaScript for swapping out main image 224
jtphotography.css 122
jtplogo.gif 142
keywords 123
Layout Cells 74
layout plans 127
layout upgrading to CSS 218
<li> tags 138
link order 142
linking template and CSS 130
links 136
logo 142
mainContent editable region
margin setting 129
merging cells 88
navigation area 136
navigation bulleted list 136
navigation bullets, changing to graphic 137
navigation system 27
navigation text formatting 138
navlistBullet class 139
navUnderline class 139
nav_bullets.gif 137
news.html link 136
padding 220
page defaults 124
photoSRC variable 224
preferences 56
purpose 21
removing tables 223
rowGray class 144
saving page defaults 131
<select> tag 146
Site window preferences 56
size of site 22
splash folder 72
splash page background color 73
splash page setup 71
splash page text 80
splash pages 65
Standard View 82
Status Bar 60
structure 27
swapPhoto function 225
template ID selector 127
templates 120
testing in browser 88
text 145
text formatting 86
text-align setting 129
threeColumn.dwt template 153, 156
thumbnail gallery 161-170
title attribute 225
<tr> tag 144
<ul> tag 142
updating pages 227
visual mock-up 134
visual plans 23
W3C validation 229
web links 88
Web research 24
width setting 129
wrapper 127
wrapper settings 128 JPEGs 69
.js files 215
linking to HTML documents 217
setting up 216

L

Late Night Software 422
layout 63, 134
 Cascading Style Sheets 107
 frames 97
 plain text 96
 splash pages 64
 tables 104
Layout View 83
links
 hotspots 91
 internal links 90
 web links 88
login cookies 305
loops
 arrays 300
 auto-increments 298
 do while loops 298
 for loops 299
 foreach loops 301
 while loops 298

M

Mac OS X
 backing up Apache configuration file 254
 enabling root user access 253
 NetInfo Manager 251
 starting Apache web server 246
 switching on PHP 246
 Terminal application 247
 vi text editor 249
Macromedia Dreamweaver See Dreamweaver
Macromedia Flash See Flash
mailto link 170
Massimo's Corner 422
menus 55
Modify menu 56
monitor sizes 49
MySQL 4, 237
 configuring Dreamweaver to use 329, 330
 configuring phpMyAdmin 327, 328
 connecting (Macs) 325, 326
 connecting (Windows) 323, 324
 downloading phpMyAdmin (Macs)327
 downloading phpMyAdmin (Windows) 326
 installing and configuring (Macs) 319, 320, 321
 installing and configuring (Windows) 314, 315
 MySQL monitor 317, 318, 321
 mysqld (MySQL daemon) 315, 316, 317, 321
 Phakt third party server model 314
 PHP/MySQL combination 314
 phpmyadmin 322
 security 322
 setting up user profile 320
 testing nstallation 318, 319
 Windows Task Manager 317
 winmysqladmin 322

N

navigation 136
NetInfo Manager
 authentication 252
 enabling root user access 253
 logging in as root 251
 password 252
<noframes> tag 101

O

optimizing images 67

P

Page Properties option 389
panels 53
 Arrange Panels option 55
 Hide/Show Panels option 55
 naming difficulties 54
 opening and closing 54
PayPal
 payment forms 410
 selling items 409
Photoshop 66
PHP 4, 237, 264, 348
 $name field 279
 arrays 300
 case-sensitivity 310
 coding conventions 348
 commenting 269
 conditional statements 279
 cookies 304
 creating files 382
 echoing 301
 forms 276-279
 GET and POST methods 276, 277
 guest book forms 287-291
 clude statement 276
 installing 239
 installing on Apache for Windows 244
 logging in as root 251
 logical operators 282
 loops 298
 modifying httpd.conf file 245
 OR operator 288
 Phakt third party server model 314
 PHP/MySQL combination 314
 phpmyadmin 322
 processing forms with multiple options 302
 register_globals 348
 security issues 348, 364
 sessions 349
 start tags 269
 support 261
 switching on in Mac OS X 246

Index

syntax 269
tables 331-333
testing 257, 259
troubleshooting 260
variable data types 271
variable names 270
vi text editor 249
plain text format 96
plug-ins 64
preferences 59
   Accessibility 105
   Code coloring 190
   Code format 192
Project Seven 422
Properties panel 52, 86, 99, 110
   applying classes 115
   attaching Style Sheets 110
   context-specific 52
   frame editing 99
   Link field 88
   text color 86

Q

QuickTime 184
   cameraopener.mov 184
   creating table 184
   inserting movie into table 185
   playing and stopping movie 185
   VCR type controls 186
   Video folder 184

R

Rabi's Dreamweaver Extensions 422
re-sizing images 66
recordsets 407
Reference panel 196
register_globals 348
registration and login application
   assigning values 370
   auth session 371
   checking number of rows returned 371
   Connection menu 364
   creating links 372
   database tables 356
   do_login.php action 369
   exit command 372
   form input fields 364
   form tags 357
   id field 356
   if statement 372
   Insert Record option 363
   inserting information into database 363
   login form 369
   logout.php 373
   md5 function 370
   members 356

   members table 363
   merging cells 358
   my_secret_index.php 371
   passwords 359, 370
   protecting secret pages 371
   redirecting users 372
   registration form 357
   security 364
   Server Behaviors tab 363
   session_destroy function 373
   table attributes 357
   testing application 373
   testing form for encryption 366
   text fields 358
   validation test 362
   validation using Check Form MX 359, 360, 361, 369
require statements 379

S

security 364
   cookies 310
   md5 function 365, 370
   multiple usernames 365
   password encryption 366
   PHP 348
Server Behaviors tab
   Dynamic Text option 408
   Recordset option 407
   Repeat Region option 413
server models
   Connections folder 265
   copying phpinfo.php file 268
   defining folder storage location 265
   entering path to root folder 267
   foe_book site 264, 268
   friends_of_ed folder 264, 265
   opening site wizard 264
   selecting PHP MySQL server 265
   testing URL 267
   _mmserverscripts folder 265
sessions 349
   accessing session values 353
   altering php.ini file 350
   creating 351
   creating links 354
   session_destroy function 349, 373
   session_is_registered function 349
   session_register function 349, 352
   session_start function 349, 352
   support 350
set.php 306
setcookie header 304
Show Design View button 12

Site Definition window 42, 379
   Access drop-down 44
   Advanced tab 43
   Local Info option 44
   Local Root Folder option 44
   Site Name option 44
   Site panel 45
   Testing Server option 44
Site Files option 227
Site panel 56
   Expand button 45
   file display 46
   Refresh button 47
   Remote Site list 47
   Site chooser 47
   Site Map option 47
   Testing Server Folder 47
Snippets panel 210, 292-294
   adding 212
   creating 211
   defining 212
   editing 211
splash pages 64, 65
sql.txt 403
Standard View 82
Style Sheets See Cascading Style Sheets
SWFs, preparing for Dreamweaver 176-178
   animation.fla 176
   default frame rate 177
   Document Properties dialog box 176
   Export Movie command 177
   exporting SWF as transparent GIF 177
   JPEG Quality setting 178
   setting background color 177
   Version setting 178

T

tables 104
   accessibility 104
   borders 106
   cell padding 105
   creating 104
   creating with phpMyAdmin 331-333
   editing cell contents 106
   editing row and column properties 106
   inserting/deleting rows and columns 107
   invisible graphic to lock 392
   merging cells 106
   width 106
Tag Editor 202, 203, 351
templates 120
   creating new pages
   editable regions 120
   updating
Terminal application 247
   backing up Apache configuration file 254

   cd command 249
   command-line interface 248
   cp command 254
   editing httpd.conf file 255
   logging in as root 253
   ls command 248
   vi text editor 249
Text menu 56
thumbnail galleries 161-170
   adding gallery page navigation 168
   applying CSS style to image captions 166
   creating text table 161
   creating thumbnail table 163
   creating thumbnails 162
   deleting placeholder text 164
   dog1.html – dog15.html 168, 169
   dog1.jpg - dog15.jpg 162
   dog1t.jpg - dog15t.jpg 162
   dogs folder 169
   dogsgallery.html 162
   dogsincars directory 162
   dogsincars.html 167
   folio.html 170
   photography.css 165
   setting thumbnail table properties 164
   testing thumbnail links 168
   thumbs directory 162
   twoColumn.dwt template 161
Tidy (CSS Validator) 230
time function 305
title attribute 225

U

Update Pages option 228
URL links 89
URLs
   http://free-php.cjb.net/ 261
   http://httpd.apache.org/dist/httpd/binaries/win32/ 239
   www.apache.org 261
   www.deviantART.com 276
   www.dotservant.com/ 261
   www.dreamweaver-extensions.com/ 422
   www.entropy.ch/software/macosx/mysql/ 320
   www.flashkit.com 176
   www.free-php-hosting.com/ 261
   www.idest.com/cgi-bin/database.cgi 421
   www.latenightsw.com/freeware/OSADreamweaver/index.html 422
   www.macromedia.com/exchange 421
   www.macromedia.com/software/flash 176
   www.massimocorner.com/ 422
   www.mysql.com/downloads 314
   www.newstoday.com 98
   www.oinko.net/freephp/link.php 261
   www.paypal.com 409
   www.php.net 261
   www.php.net/downloads 329
   www.php.net/downloads.php 239

Index

www.php.net/nl2br 343
www.phpforflash.com 239
www.phpwebhosting.com/ 261
www.webaddist.com/Products/ProductDetails.asp?PID=18 410
www.webdevindex.org/cgi-bin/links/jump.cgi?ID=1301 421
www.winzip.com 315
www.yaromat.com 359
www.zend.com 238
www2.entropy.ch/download/mysql-startupitem.pkg.tar.gz 321

V

variables
  $password variable 272
  $sum variable 273
  $username variable 272
  adding string variables 274
  applying mathematical operators 273
  echo function 272, 274
vi text editor 249
  editing httpd.conf file 255
  inserting/deleting text 250
  moving around screen 250
View menu 56

W

W3C (World Wide Web Consortium) CSS Validator 229
web page layout See layout
web pages 11
  creating 11
  customizing standard layouts 15
  directory setup 12
  Document window 12
  images 16
  journal layout 15
  navigating to home page 18
  New Site option 12
  remote server connection 14
  saving pages 20
  site definition 13
  site name 13
  testing pages in browser 20
while loops 298
Window menu 56
window.open function 388
wrappers 127

Notes

Notes

Notes

Notes